SECOND EDITION

Grammar and Vocabulary *for* Cambridge First

Luke Prodromou

For students preparing for the
Cambridge English First exam

Pearson Education Limited
Edinburgh Gate
Harlow
Essex CM20 2JE
England
and Associated Companies throughout the world.

www.pearsonelt.com

© Pearson Education Limited 1999, 2012

The right of Luke Prodromou to be identified as author of this Work has been asserted by him in accordance with the Copyright, Designs and Patents Act 1988.

All rights reserved; no part of this publication may be reproduced, stored in a retrieval system, or transmitted in any form or by any means, electronic, mechanical, photocopying, recording, or otherwise without the prior written permission of the Publishers.

First published 1999
Second edition 2012

ISBN: 9781408290590 (with key)
ISBN: 9781447903055 (without key)

Set in Whitney and Minion
Printed in Malaysia (CTP-VP)

Acknowledgements
The author and publishers would like to thank everyone who has helped to develop and revise the contents of this book, including the following for their invaluable reports on the text of the first edition:
Eftaxia Chatzoglou, Maria Chrematopoulou, Anna Chrysouergi, Jain Cook, Konstantinos Giagkoulovitos, Felicity Harwood, Philip Kerr, Maria Anne Leventeris, Anne Robinson, Rogerio Sanches, Vilma Sicas, Elsa Silivistra and Emma Tuhill.

Illustrated by Simon Smith

Contents

Introduction	7

Unit 1   12
Entry test   12
Grammar
1a	Present simple and present continuous	14
1b	Past simple, present perfect simple, present perfect continuous	18
1c	Past continuous, past perfect simple, past perfect continuous	21

Vocabulary
| 1d | *for*, *since*, *during*, *yet*, etc. | 23 |
| 1e | Suffixes (1) | 26 |

Unit 2   28
Entry test   28
Grammar
2a	Future forms (1): ways to talk about the future	30
2b	Future forms (2): *be going to*, present continuous, present simple	32
2c	Future forms (3): future continuous, future perfect, future in the past	34

Vocabulary
| 2d | Phrasal verbs: time and change | 36 |
| 2e | Prefixes (1) | 38 |

Exam practice 1   40

Unit 3   44
Entry test   44
Grammar
3a	Modal verbs (1)	46
3b	Modal verbs (2)	49
3c	Linking words and phrases: reason and purpose	52

Vocabulary
| 3d | *have*, *take*, *bring* | 55 |
| 3e | Suffixes (2) | 58 |

Unit 4   60
Entry test   60
Grammar
4a	Questions, question words	62
4b	Question tags	64
4c	Expressing agreement	66

Vocabulary
| 4d | *do* and *make* | 69 |
| 4e | Suffixes (3) | 73 |

Exam practice 2   76

CONTENTS

■ Unit 5 — 80
Entry test — 80

Grammar
- **5a** Zero, first and second conditionals — 82
- **5b** Third conditional, mixed conditionals — 84
- **5c** *wish*, *if only* — 86

Vocabulary
- **5d** *want*, *expect*, *love*, *can't bear*, etc. — 89
- **5e** Prefixes (2) — 92

■ Unit 6 — 94
Entry test — 94

Grammar
- **6a** Time and condition clauses with future reference — 96
- **6b** More future forms — 99
- **6c** Expressions of time and preference — 101

Vocabulary
- **6d** *afterwards*, *after*, *until*, *as far as*, etc. — 104
- **6e** Phrases with *time* — 106

Exam practice 3 — 108

■ Unit 7 — 112
Entry test — 112

Grammar
- **7a** The passive: form — 114
- **7b** The passive: use, agent — 117
- **7c** The causative — 120

Vocabulary
- **7d** *get* and *have* (*got*) — 122
- **7e** Compound nouns — 124

■ Unit 8 — 128
Entry test — 128

Grammar
- **8a** Reported speech (1) — 130
- **8b** Reported speech (2) — 134
- **8c** *-ing* forms and infinitives after verbs — 137

Vocabulary
- **8d** *say*, *tell*, *talk*, *speak*, etc. — 140
- **8e** *-ed* and *-ing* adjectives — 143

Exam practice 4 — 146

■ Unit 9 — 150
Entry test — 150

Grammar
- **9a** Comparative and superlative adjectives — 152
- **9b** Adjectives followed by prepositions — 155
- **9c** Order of adjectives — 157

Vocabulary
- **9d** Easily confused adjectives — 158
- **9e** Compound adjectives — 164

CONTENTS

Unit 10 — 166
Entry test — 166

Grammar
- **10a** Comparisons — 168
- **10b** *so* and *such*; *too*, *enough*, *very* — 170
- **10c** *quite*, *rather*, etc.; linking verbs — 173

Vocabulary
- **10d** Adjectives which are similar — 176
- **10e** Suffixes (4) — 179

Exam practice 5 — 182

Unit 11 — 186
Entry test — 186

Grammar
- **11a** Adverbs: use and form — 188
- **11b** Adverbs: word order — 191
- **11c** Adverbs: comparison — 194

Vocabulary
- **11d** Adverbs: different forms and meanings — 196
- **11e** Seeing and hearing — 198

Unit 12 — 202
Entry test — 202

Grammar
- **12a** Articles — 204
- **12b** Determiners — 208
- **12c** Countable and uncountable nouns — 212

Vocabulary
- **12d** Uncountable nouns ending in -s, plural nouns, collective nouns — 216
- **12e** Suffixes (5) — 219

Exam practice 6 — 224

Unit 13 — 228
Entry test — 228

Grammar
- **13a** Relative clauses — 230
- **13b** Participles — 234
- **13c** Linking words and phrases: contrast — 236

Vocabulary
- **13d** Phrasal verbs with *get* — 238
- **13e** Suffixes (6) — 240

Unit 14 — 244
Entry test — 244

Grammar
- **14a** Prepositions of time, place and movement — 246
- **14b** Prepositions after verbs and nouns — 250
- **14c** *it* and *there* — 252

Vocabulary
- **14d** Prepositional phrases — 254
- **14e** Phrasal verbs with *put* — 257

Exam practice 7 — 259

5

CONTENTS

Word store

Living conditions	263
Social relationships	265
Friendship	266
Occupations	267
Education	269
The arts	272
Sports	275
Hobbies	277
Travel and tourism	279
Shopping	281
Food and restaurants	283
Weather	286
Our environment and the natural world	289
The media	292
Science and technology	296
Health	298
Crime	302

Answer key 305

Introduction

About this book

Who is this book for?

This book is for people studying for the Cambridge First Certificate in English (FCE) examination. The aim is to practise the grammar and vocabulary needed for this examination. The book is useful as a supplement to any coursebook. It presents and practises key grammar and vocabulary points in an integrated way. I assume that anybody using this book has a reasonable knowledge of and ability to use English up to intermediate level. More advanced students should refer to *Grammar and Vocabulary for Cambridge Advanced and Proficiency*, by Richard Side and Guy Wellman.

What sort of grammar is in this book?

The book covers the main areas of English grammar at intermediate/upper-intermediate level and concentrates on areas you need to pass the FCE exam. Thus there is a thorough review of tenses together with verb, noun and adjective structures. Although grammar and vocabulary are obviously important in all the papers in the exam, special attention is given to those aspects of grammar which are frequently tested in Paper 3 – Use of English. For example, prepositions following nouns, verbs and adjectives are common in all parts of Paper 3. Problems of time and tense are also tested, for example, in conditional sentences and after *wish*, *if only* or *I'd rather*, and expressions with *time*. Such structures are reflected in the grammar presented and practised in this book.

What sort of vocabulary is in this book?

The book gives vocabulary special emphasis, including both individual words and common phrases. Words which are often confused are dealt with in the sections which make up the main body of the text, and common sources of error caused by words of related meaning are also considered. There is also a detailed focus on aspects of word-building in every unit. This reflects the importance of word-building in the Use of English paper. The Word Store section at the back of the book focuses on topic areas and lexical phrases, which the FCE exam gives particular importance to. A good knowledge of these phrases will help you perform better in the Use of English and Writing papers.

How can I use this book?

There are many ways to use this book. You can use the **Contents map** to look up particular aspects of grammar and vocabulary you want to study and practise. The **Agenda** at the beginning of each unit will show you the contents of each section. You can use the **Entry test** to identify which sections you need. Or you may wish to study complete units, perhaps in the order in which they appear. Several options are available to you, according to your needs.

How is this book organised?

The book comprises fourteen grammar and vocabulary **units**, followed by a topic-related **Word store** section. There is an **Exam practice** test after every two units. Throughout the book, there are cartoons which illustrate grammar points and also identify the language covered in each section. I hope this will make learning grammar and vocabulary more fun, as well as more memorable.

INTRODUCTION

The entry test
A typical sequence begins with an **Entry test** based on the target grammar and vocabulary of the unit. It consists of twenty-five diagnostic questions, which will direct you to areas you need to learn, revise or practise in the sections that follow. The test will give you an idea of your own strengths and weaknesses, in particular, areas of grammar or vocabulary. Each **Entry test** is divided into five parts (each with five questions) and these correspond to the five sections (a–e) of the unit. If you have difficulties with a part of the **Entry test**, there is a cross-reference to the relevant section where you will find all the information and practice you need. On the other hand, if you find that part easy, it may mean that you are sufficiently competent in that area and you may wish to skip that section. Since all **Entry tests** have the same number of questions (25), you can monitor your own progress using your total score for each test.

The grammar sections
Each unit contains three **Grammar sections**, which deal with aspects of a particular area of grammar, as listed in the **Agenda** on the first page of each unit. For a full list of the grammar covered in this book, see the **Contents** map (pages 3–6). The **Grammar sections** contain explanations and descriptions using numerous example sentences. Much of the information is presented in tables, which provide easy access to the essential details of meaning or use, together with examples illustrating common contexts.

The vocabulary sections
Each unit has two **Vocabulary** sections. There is a focus on word-building and lexical items related to particular areas of usage. Phrases and phrasal verbs are also given special attention and, again, the tables provide easy access to content.

The practice sections
All the presentations in the grammar and vocabulary sections are followed by **Practice** sections. These include a wide variety of exercises related to the content of each presentation. Many of these exercises are modelled on FCE exam questions but others are styled to achieve the best focus on the language being practised and provide for a more interesting set of activities.

The exam practice sections
After every two units, there is an **Exam practice** section, in the form of a complete Use of English paper, in the same format as in the actual FCE exam. Each **Exam practice** section tests your knowledge of the grammar and vocabulary of the previous two units. It allows you to revise what you have learnt, while getting valuable examination practice. Each paper has the same score, so you can monitor your progress as you work with different units.

Although grammar and vocabulary are presented separately in the units, in the **Exam practice** sections they are brought together within the same texts and activities. Thus, there is constant recycling of the target language.

The Word store section
At the end of the book is the **Word store** section, which includes a series of exercises presenting vocabulary in topic-related groups. These are extremely useful for all parts of the FCE exam. Emphasis is on the importance of common phrases and the way words combine together. The vocabulary items are presented in tables, which are followed by exercises that draw on items in these tables and allow you to work with them in different contexts. Special attention has been given to ensure that these exercises are lively and informative.

Will I pass the FCE exam if I do everything in this book?

One grammar and vocabulary practice book is not enough to make you fluent in English. I recommend that you read widely in English (simplified readers, magazines, newspapers, etc.) and take every opportunity to listen to English (satellite television, film, radio, songs, etc.). You should also try and speak the language so that you can use it naturally and easily.

About FCE

What level is FCE?

The First Certificate in English is an intermediate-level examination which follows on from the PET (Preliminary English Test) and precedes the CAE (Certificate in Advanced English) examinations. FCE is CEF level B2. The certificate is frequently used as proof that you will be competent to begin a career such as those related to tourism or banking, or that you can pursue an advanced course of study in English. Learners at this level should be able to handle the main structures with some confidence and communicate in English in a variety of social situations. You should be able to tell the difference between the main and secondary points of a text, as well as between the gist of a text and specific detail. You are expected to show an ability to describe and recount events. Grades A, B and C are passes. D is a narrow fail, and E is a fail. The exam is usually taken after approximately 500–600 hours of studying English. It consists of 5 papers. Papers 1–4 (Reading, Writing, Use of English and Listening) are usually taken on the same day and Paper 5 (Speaking) is usually taken on a different day.

Paper 1: Reading
This paper, lasting one hour, consists of three parts and is intended to encourage familiarity with different types of written material. The reading texts may be correspondence, informational material, newspaper or magazine articles, advertisements, etc. There are thirty questions and three different task types: multiple choice, gapped text and multiple matching. You will be tested on understanding the gist of a text, main grammar points, detail in the information and text structure or meaning.

Paper 2: Writing
For this paper, lasting one hour and twenty minutes, you must complete one compulsory task in Part 1 (a letter or email, using information given in the form of an advertisement, an extract from a letter, an email, a schedule, etc.) and one from a choice of five in Part 2. You will need to demonstrate your ability to write a range of texts such as letters (formal or informal), articles or reports, as well as stories and argumentative compositions. For Part 1, you will need to write a letter or email of 120–150 words. For Part 2, you will need to write a text of 120–180 words.

Paper 3: Use of English
This paper lasts forty-five minutes. There are four tasks with a total of forty-two questions focusing on grammar and vocabulary (see pages 10–11). The paper is divided according to the language focus and task type. The exercises are: multiple choice, open cloze, word formation and key word transformation.

Paper 4: Listening
This paper lasts approximately forty minutes. There is a total of four parts and thirty questions. The recordings may be phone messages, commentaries, announcements, speeches, reports, etc. The tasks are designed to test your understanding of the gist of the recording, as well as specific information. The task types are: multiple choice, sentence completion and multiple matching.

Paper 5: Speaking
This part of the examination, lasting approximately fifteen minutes, has four parts. During the examination, you will interact with another candidate, as well as an examiner/interlocutor. There will also be a second examiner present (an assessor), who will remain silent. The first part is a very short interview. After that, you will be asked to give information or express your opinion by comparing a pair of photographs. The next part is a conversation between you and another candidate, in which you may be asked to agree or disagree, make a decision about a drawing or photograph, etc. Finally, you take part in a discussion with the interlocutor and the other candidate. You will be marked according to your overall performance. You should be able to respond to questions, organise your ideas, express your opinions and exchange views.

INTRODUCTION

What types of questions can I expect in Paper 3?

This book concentrates on the grammar and vocabulary you will need to pass this paper. The exercises in the **Practice** and **Exam practice** sections reflect the types of questions you will be given in the FCE exam. There are four parts.

Part 1: Multiple choice cloze

This includes a text with twelve numbered gaps, followed by four-option multiple choice items (A, B, C and D). You must choose the best answer to fill each gap. Example:

> ### Part 1
>
> For questions **1–12**, read the text below and decide which answer (**A**, **B**, **C** or **D**) best fits each gap. There is an example at the beginning (**0**).
>
> #### TEEN FASHION
>
> It is widely believed that boys are less interested in fashion ⁽⁰⁾.......... girls. While it is true that fashion for guys is not as widely followed ⁽¹⁾.......... fashion for girls, it is becoming more and more important. Girls' fashion ⁽²⁾.......... to change more often, or at least it is ...
>
> **0 A** that **B** as (**C** than) **D** from
>
> **1 A** as **B** than **C** so **D** that
>
> **2 A** looks **B** comes **C** becomes **D** seems

Part 1 (questions 1–12) has an emphasis on vocabulary but often includes items that focus on grammar as well.

Part 2: Open cloze

This consists of a text with twelve numbered gaps. You must provide the correct word to fill each one. Example:

> ### Part 2
>
> For questions **13–24**, read the text below and think of the word which best fits each gap. Use only one word in each gap. There is an example at the beginning (**0**).
>
> #### THE MYSTERY OF STONEHENGE
>
> Stonehenge is one of England's ⁽⁰⁾ *most* famous landmarks. It is a group of large, tall stones that are arranged in circles on Salisbury Plain in the south of England. They are ⁽¹³⁾.......... big and heavy that their transportation over from Wales, 240 miles away, ⁽¹⁴⁾.......... to us today almost miraculous. Who could have carried them such ⁽¹⁵⁾.......... distance without the help of modern technology? The question is also ...

Part 2 (questions 13–24) tests both grammar and vocabulary. Learning common phrases and collocations is very useful for this task.

Part 3: Word formation

This word-building task includes a text with ten numbered gaps. It may test prefixes, suffixes, changes to the whole word (e.g. *wide → width*), forming compounds, etc. The base words are given, and you must use them to form words to fill the gaps in the text. Example:

> ### Part 3
>
> For questions **25-34**, read the text below. Use the word given in capitals at the end of some of the lines to form a word that fits in the gap **in the same line**. There is an example at the beginning (**0**).
>
> | | |
> |---|---|
> | We all know now what a ⁽⁰⁾ *powerful* tool | **POWER** |
> | information technology is. It is more or less ⁽²⁵⁾ .... to live a full | **POSSIBLE** |
> | life in the twenty-first century without being ⁽²⁶⁾ .... with computers and how to ... | **COMFORT** |

Part 3 (questions 25–34) tests mainly vocabulary, for example prefixes, suffixes and compounds.

Part 4: Key word transformations

There are eight items, each with a lead-in sentence and a gapped second sentence. You must complete the second sentence with two to five words, using a given word which cannot be changed. Example:

> ### Part 4
>
> For questions **35-42**, complete the second sentence so that it has a similar meaning to the first sentence, using the word given. **Do not change the word given.** You must use between **two** and **five** words, including the word given. Here is an example (0).
>
> **Example:**
>
> **0** So, do you regret what you did?
> **SORRY**
> So, *are you sorry for* what you did?
>
> **35** I think his wife is a journalist.
> **MARRIED**
> I think he's .... a journalist.
>
> **36** I don't like cooking very much.
> **FOND**
> I .... cooking.

Part 4 (questions 35–42) tests both grammar and vocabulary. Areas like tenses, reported speech, the passive, conditionals, etc. may be tested.

1

AGENDA

Grammar
- 1a Present simple and present continuous
- 1b Past simple, present perfect simple, present perfect continuous
- 1c Past continuous, past perfect simple, past perfect continuous

Vocabulary
- 1d *for*, *since*, *during*, *yet*, etc.
- 1e Suffixes (1)

Entry test

1 Choose the correct answer.

1 I *stay / am staying* at the Imperial Hotel until they get my flat ready.
2 The Amazon *flows / is flowing* into the Atlantic Ocean.
3 Buying a house *becomes / is becoming* more and more expensive nowadays.
4 We haven't decided yet but we *think / are thinking* of moving house.
5 Whether we play on Saturday *depends / is depending* on the weather.

Now look at **1a** on pages 14–17.

2 Complete the sentences. Use the past simple, present perfect simple or present perfect continuous of the verbs in the box.

already / win   discuss   not find   originate   try

6 Jazz .... in the US around 1900.
7 He's a brilliant actor. At the age of thirty, he .... several awards.
8 Even when we were children, our parents .... our family problems with us.
9 They .... to fix this pipe since this morning and it's still leaking.
10 Scientists still .... a cure for cancer.

Now look at **1b** on pages 18–20.

3 Choose the correct answer, A, B, C or D.

11 About 100 people .... outside the theatre for tickets when we got there.
   A queue   B queued   C were queuing   D have queued

12 This time last week I .... to London.
   A drove   B was driving   C have driven   D have been driving

13 By the time the teacher arrived, the classroom was empty. The students ....
   A left   B were leaving   C have left   D had left

14 The witness claimed he .... the man before.
   A didn't see   B wasn't seeing   C hasn't seen   D hadn't seen

15 I .... a shower when the phone rang.
   A had   B was having   C have had   D have been having

SCORE / 5

Now look at **1c** on pages 21–22.

4 Choose the correct answer, A, B, C or D.

16 She's changed a lot .... she left school.
   A for   B since   C during   D after

17 I've been waiting in the rain .... hours!
   A for   B since   C during   D from

18 .... I was coming home, I met my old English teacher.
   A While   B Since   C During   D Before

19 She was born in Yorkshire twenty-five years ....
   A over   B since   C ago   D before

20 I've .... seen the film – I don't want to see it again.
   A still   B already   C yet   D before

SCORE / 5

Now look at **1d** on pages 23–25.

5 Choose the correct answer, A, B, C or D.

21 How long have you been looking for ....?
   A employ   B employer   C employee   D employment

22 I need a tin .... to open this tin of peas.
   A open   B opening   C opener   D opened

23 You have to be a very good .... to get a job as a chef.
   A cook   B cooker   C cookery   D cooked

24 She's doing an evening course in ....
   A photograph   B photography   C photographic   D photographer

25 Passing the exam at such a young age was quite an ....
   A achieve   B achiever   C achievement   D achievable

SCORE / 5

Now look at **1e** on pages 26–27.

TOTAL SCORE / 25

Grammar

1a Present simple and present continuous

Present simple	Present continuous
Form	
Affirmative: They **live** in Cambridge. Question: **Does** he **live** in Brighton? Negative: I **don't live** in London.	Affirmative: She**'s waiting** for Keith. Question: **Are** they **having** a good time? Negative: I**'m not talking** to you!
Use	
We use the present simple: • for permanent situations. I **live** in a flat. She **works** for an insurance company. • for repeated actions or habits: I **use** my mobile phone every day. We usually **have** dinner at eight. • for general truths: The sun **rises** in the east. Water **boils** at 100°C. • when we tell stories or summarise the plot of a film or book: Our hero **goes** off to search for the treasure, which he eventually **finds** after many adventures.	We use the present continuous: • for temporary situations: I**'m staying** with a friend at the moment. • for situations that are changing: The weather**'s getting** hotter and hotter. • for actions in progress at the moment of speaking: I**'m using** John's mobile because I left mine at home. You**'re eating** too fast! • for annoying habits, often with *always*: You**'re always borrowing** money!

- When we use *always* with the present simple, it means 'all the time' or 'every time':
  I **always complain** if the service is bad in restaurants.
- When we use *always* with the present continuous, it means 'too often'. We use it to show that we find something annoying.
  You**'re always** complaining that waiters are rude!

State verbs

- We do not normally use certain verbs with the present continuous, or other continuous tenses. These verbs describe a state, not an activity. They are called state verbs and they include:
  - mental/thinking verbs: *agree, believe, disagree, doubt, expect, forget, imagine, know, notice, realise, remember, suppose, think, understand*

- attitude verbs: *dislike, hate, like, love, need, prefer, want, wish*
- sense/perception verbs: *hear, see, smell, taste*
- appearance, qualities: *appear, look, resemble, seem, sound*
- existence, being, possession: *be, belong to, come (from), exist, have, lack, own, possess*
- other verbs: *consist of, contain, cost, depend, fit, include, matter, mean, need, owe, suit, weigh*
- We can use some state verbs with continuous tenses but with a change in meaning. Here are some examples:

14

1 PRESENT SIMPLE AND PRESENT CONTINUOUS

Present simple	Present continuous
He **is** friendly. (= It's one of his qualities/characteristics.)	He **is being** friendly. (= behaving in a particular way)
She **has** (**got**) a car. (= owns)	She**'s having** dinner. (= eating)
They **think** it's too expensive. (= believe)	They**'re thinking** of buying a car. (= considering)
She **looks** sad. (= seems)	She**'s looking** at you. (= turned her eyes in a particular direction)
He **feels** what we did was wrong. (= thinks)	He**'s feeling** the baby's forehead. (= touching)
Do you **see** what I mean? (= understand)	I**'m seeing** Alex on Friday. (= meeting)
This juice **tastes** good. (= has a particular taste)	He**'s tasting** the milk to see if it's OK. (= putting it in his mouth to check its quality)
It **depends** on the weather. (= The weather may change the situation.)	I**'m depending** on you. (= relying on)
She **appears** to be very upset. (= seems)	The Blues Band **is appearing** at the Odeon on Saturday. (= performing)

- We can use the verbs *feel*, *look*, *ache* and *hurt* in the simple or the present continuous form, with no change in meaning:
  I **feel**/**'m feeling** sick.
  You **look**/**'re looking** tired.
  My feet **ache**/**are aching**.
  My leg **hurts**/**is hurting**.

PRACTICE

1 Choose the correct answer.

0 We *rarely see* / *'re rarely seeing* each other now.
1 I *sleep* / *'m sleeping* on Nick's sofa until I find a place of my own.
2 I *only work* / *'m only working* there for a couple of months – I'm going abroad in the summer.
3 If you *don't listen* / *aren't listening* to the radio, why don't you switch it off?
4 His only bad habit is that he *talks* / *is talking* too loudly.
5 So, in the first scene, we *see* / *are seeing* him getting up. Then he *goes out* / *is going out* and *meets* / *is meeting* a strange woman.
6 You *make* / *are making* goulash with meat, vegetables and paprika.
7 I never do anything I *feel* / *'m feeling* is against my principles.
8 He *appears* / *'s appearing* to be very friendly but I don't know him very well.
9 There's nobody at the door. You *just hear* / *'re just hearing* things.
10 So, what *do you think* / *are you thinking*? Is it a good idea?

15

1 PRESENT SIMPLE AND PRESENT CONTINUOUS

2 Complete the sentences. Use the present simple or present continuous of the verbs in brackets.

0 Diane's father **owns** (own) that restaurant over there.
1 My sister .... (wait) patiently for her exam results.
2 We .... (not travel) by train very often.
3 I .... (consider) accepting that job offer in Cambridge.
4 The film .... (end) with a dramatic car chase.
5 I'm sorry, I .... (feel) too tired to go out this evening.
6 We .... (have) a great time here in London.
7 .... (you / see) much of your brother these days?
8 We .... (rely on) you to bring the keys with you.
9 I'm really sorry; I .... (wish) I could help you.
10 Who .... (you / think) you are, speaking to me like that!

3 Complete the sentences. Use the present simple or present continuous of the verbs in brackets.

0 We **always visit** (visit / always) my grandparents at weekends but Aunt Roberta **never comes** (come / never) with us.
1 I .... (use / never) my mobile phone if I .... (drive).
2 I .... (get) lots of emails every day but I .... (seem / never) to have the time to reply!
3 The heroine .... (prefer) to be with Paul because James .... (argue / always).
4 Maria .... (forget / always) what time the soap .... (start).
5 You .... (moan / always) about the state of the flat but you .... (help / never) me tidy it up!
6 She .... (criticise / always) people! That's why she .... (not have) any friends!
7 Whether he .... (go out) or not .... (depend / always) on how busy he is.
8 I .... (shop / never) here – they .... (be / always) so rude!
9 We .... (smell / always) food cooking when we .... (pass) her house.
10 He .... (borrow / always) money! And he .... (pay / never) me back!

16

PRESENT SIMPLE AND PRESENT CONTINUOUS   1

4 Complete the email. Use the present simple or present continuous of the verbs in the box.

cost   depend   go   have   look   love   make   stay   still / study   taste   ~~write~~

Hi Rosa,

I ⁽⁰⁾ **'m writing** to you from an Internet café in the city centre. I ⁽¹⁾ .... in a cheap hotel near Plaza Catalunya. It ⁽²⁾ .... just forty euros a night – not bad!

Barcelona is a really exciting city and I ⁽³⁾ .... a wonderful time! This morning I visited the Sagrada Familia – a famous Catholic church in Barcelona. It's really weird – it ⁽⁴⁾ .... like a wedding cake! Later today I might go to the beach – it ⁽⁵⁾ .... on the weather.

The food's great. Crema Catalana is my favourite – I just ⁽⁶⁾ .... it! It's a dessert they ⁽⁷⁾ .... here with cold custard and sugar on top. It ⁽⁸⁾ .... absolutely delicious!

So, everything ⁽⁹⁾ .... well here. What about you? Is everything OK back in rainy Milan? ⁽¹⁰⁾ .... (you) for your exam next week?

See you soon!

Paola

5 Find and correct the mistakes in the sentences.

0   It's usually getting very cold here in the winter.
    It usually gets very cold here in the winter.

1   This week, the government holds a conference on nuclear energy.
    ....

2   Water is consisting of hydrogen and oxygen.
    ....

3   Things are get more and more expensive all the time. It really makes me angry!
    ....

4   I've got nowhere to live, so I stay with a friend for now.
    ....

5   Is this car belonging to you, sir?
    ....

6   You always moaning! Stop it!
    ....

7   In the novel, the story is taking place in Florence.
    ....

17

1b Past simple, present perfect simple, present perfect continuous

Past simple	Present perfect simple
Form	
Affirmative: *They **went out** on Saturday.* Question: ***Did** you **like** the film?* Negative: *We **didn't see** Terry last night.*	Affirmative: *I've **seen** this film.* Question: ***Have** you **heard** from Jim recently?* Negative: *She **hasn't phoned** yet.*
Use	
We use the past simple: • for past (finished) actions, often with time words like *a year ago, last Sunday, in 2010, yesterday*, etc.: *The first modern Olympics **took** place in Athens more than a hundred years ago.* *They **arrived** in Spain yesterday.* • for past habits or states: *He always **caught** the same train.* *Long ago, they **built** most houses out of wood.* • for past states, events or actions that lasted for a period of time in the past: *We **were** neighbours for twenty-five years.*	We use the present perfect: • for actions that happened at an unspecified time in the past: *They **have arrived** in Spain.* • for past actions that have a result which is obvious or important in the present: *They **have polluted** the river.* (= And now the fish are dead.) *You've **spilt** the coffee all over my trousers!* (= And now they're ruined.) • for recently completed actions, often with *just*: *The film's **just started**.* • to refer to a period of time that has not finished yet. *We've **built** twenty schools this year.* (= It is still this year.) • for general experiences, often with *before, ever* and *never*. *Have you **ever seen** an elephant?* *We've **never been** to Australia.* *She's **never flown before**.* • for actions, events or situations that began in the past and continue in the present, often with *for* and *since*: *They **have lived** here **for** six years.* (= They still live here.) *Mr Edwards **has worked** here **since** 2009.* (= He still works here.) • with the following words: *already, yet, recently, often, still*: *The rain **has already destroyed** the crops.* *We **still haven't discovered** life on other planets.* *They **haven't finished** the project yet.*

For *for* and *since*, see also: **1d**

18

PAST SIMPLE, PRESENT PERFECT SIMPLE, PRESENT PERFECT CONTINUOUS **1**

Past simple or present perfect simple?

- To talk about a period of time that has finished, we use the past simple. To talk about a period of time that has not yet finished, we use the present perfect simple. Compare:
*I **had** two sandwiches this morning.*
(= It is now afternoon or evening.)
*I'**ve had** two sandwiches this morning.*
(= It is still morning.)

- The choice between the past simple and the present perfect simple depends on whether the action links the past with the present. Compare:
*He **did** a lot in his short life.*
(= He is dead.)
*He **has done** a lot in his short life.*
(= He is alive and young.)

Present perfect continuous

Form
Affirmative: *It **has been raining** since Monday.*
Question: *How long **have** you **been waiting**?*
Negative: *I **haven't been sleeping** well lately.*

Use

- We use the present perfect continuous to talk about actions that started in the past and continue up to the moment of speaking. We use it especially when we are interested in the duration of the action:
*I'**ve been waiting** for a whole hour!*

- Notice the difference between the present perfect simple and the present perfect continuous:
*I'**ve read** this book.* (= I have finished it. The focus here is on the fact that the action is complete.)
*I'**ve been reading** a book about life on other planets.* (= I haven't finished it yet. The focus here is on the fact that the action is incomplete.)

PRACTICE

1 Complete the article. Use the past simple or present perfect simple of the verbs in brackets.

MACHU PICCHU

We (0) *have known* (know) about Machu Picchu for over a century now. Archaeologists (1) .... (discover) this ancient Inca site in 1911. They (2) .... (write) books and newspaper articles about their discovery, so people all over the world (3) .... (read) about the site and (4) .... (want) to see it for themselves. The first tourists (5) .... (start) to arrive in the 1960s. Now, more than half a century later, millions of visitors (6) .... (be) to Machu Picchu. Tourists from all over the world (7) .... (see) this marvellous Inca city with their own eyes.

In recent years, Machu Picchu (8) .... (become) one of the most popular tourist attractions in the world. Luxury hotels have been built not far from the site, while in the late 1990s, the Peruvian government (9) .... (allow) the construction of a cable car for visitors. However, all this (10) .... (do) a lot of harm to the site. It (11) .... (pollute) the atmosphere and caused noise pollution around the ancient city. In an effort to protect the site, UNESCO (12) .... (make) Machu Picchu a World Heritage site in 1983.

19

1 PAST SIMPLE, PRESENT PERFECT SIMPLE, PRESENT PERFECT CONTINUOUS

2 Read the sentences from a letter of application and choose the correct answer.

0 I am writing in connection with the advertisement which **appeared** / has appeared in *Career* online magazine on 3 December.
1 I *originally studied* / have originally studied Mechanical Engineering at university and I *graduated* / have been graduating with a first class degree.
2 I *now completed* / **have now completed** a postgraduate degree in Business and Administration.
3 I have tried / **have been trying** to find a permanent job for months.
4 I worked / **have worked** for several companies on a temporary basis till now.
5 In my first job, I **was** / have been responsible for marketing.
6 I applied / **have applied** for several posts this year.
7 However, I still did not manage / **have not managed** to find what I am looking for.
8 The last job I **applied** / have applied for required applicants to speak some Japanese.
9 I **started** / have started learning Spanish a few months ago but I did not obtain / **have not obtained** a qualification in it yet.
10 I did not apply / **have not applied** for a job with your company before.
11 I **hoped** / have hoped that you would consider my application favourably.
12 However, I have waited / **have been waiting** for a reply for several weeks and I still did not receive / **have not received** one from you.

3 Complete the text. Use the past simple, present perfect simple or present perfect continuous of the verbs in brackets.

The Internet (0) **has changed** (change) our lives in so many ways. Most people say it (1) **has made** (make) life better, and this is probably true. It (2) **has** (have) some bad influence, too but I think it (3) **has done** (do) more good than harm.

First of all, it has made communication much easier and it (4) **has brought** (bring) people around the world much closer. I have a friend in Mexico, who I (5) **have been writing** (write) to for years. First, I used to write her letters and I (6) **had to** (have to) wait for weeks before I (7) **got** (get) a reply. It (8) **took** (take) ages! Now we communicate by email. Already this week, I (9) **have sent** (sent) her five emails – and I (10) **received** (receive) a reply to all of them in just a few minutes!

What else? Well, for the last few days, my son (11) **has been teaching** (teach) me to make video calls so I can talk to friends and see them at the same time. It's amazing – and highly addictive, too! Already this morning, I (12) **have been sitting** (sit) in front of the screen for three hours, and I (13) **haven't finished** (not finish) half my emails yet!

> 'Flying? I've been to almost as many places as my luggage!' BOB HOPE

Past continuous, past perfect simple, past perfect continuous

Past continuous

Form
Affirmative: *He **was talking** to you.*
Question: ***Were** you **working** at six?*
Negative: *Sorry, I **wasn't listening**.*

Use
We use the past continuous:
- for actions in progress at a particular time in the past:
  *I **was watching** TV at nine o'clock last night.*
- for two or more actions happening at the same time in the past:
  *She **was studying** while I **was watching**.*
- to set the scene or give background information in a story:
  *It **was pouring** with rain and she **was wondering** what to do.*
- with the past simple, to say that something happened in the middle of something else:
  *I **was sleeping** when my friend **called**.*

Past perfect simple

Form
Affirmative: *They **had left** at four o'clock.*
Question: ***Had** the party **finished** at eleven?*
Negative: *I **hadn't seen** him before.*

Use
- We use the past perfect simple to talk about a past action that happened before another past action:
  *When I **had picked** some fruit, I went back to the beach.*
- We often use the past perfect simple with *when* and *after*:
  *After they **had eaten**, they cleared the table.*
- Compare:
  *When I arrived at the party, Mary **left**.*
  (= I arrived and then Mary left.)
  *When I arrived at the party, Mary **had left**.*
  (= Mary left and then I arrived.)

Past perfect continuous

Form
Affirmative: *She **had been working** for hours.*
Question: ***Had** they **been waiting** long?*
Negative: *I **hadn't been feeling** well.*

Use
- We use the past perfect continuous to talk about something that started in the past and continued up until another time in the past:
  *They **had been climbing** for five hours before they reached the top.*
- We often use the past perfect continuous to emphasise how long a past action, event or state lasted:
  *I **had been feeling sleepy** all day, so I went to bed.*

PRACTICE

1 Choose the correct answer.

0 Columbus *(discovered)* / *was discovering* America though at first he believed he *(had reached)* / *had been reaching* Asia.
1 Hillary and Tenzing *were climbing* / *had been climbing* for several days when they *reached* / *had reached* the summit.
2 Scott *reached* / *was reaching* the South Pole in 1912 but Amundsen *had beaten* / *was beating* him by a month.
3 Franklin *flew* / *was flying* a kite when he *made* / *was making* a very important discovery about electricity.
4 Before Columbus *discovered* / *was discovering* America, people *were believing* / *had believed* that the Earth was flat.
5 Newton *made* / *was making* his great discovery while he *was sitting* / *had been sitting* under an apple tree.

21

1 PAST CONTINUOUS, PAST PERFECT SIMPLE, PAST PERFECT CONTINUOUS

2 Complete the sentences. Use the past continuous, past perfect simple or past perfect continuous of the verbs in brackets.

0 They stayed in the tent because it **was raining** (rain).
1 The roads were wet because it .... (rain) all night.
2 He was broke. He .... (spend) all his money on clothes.
3 I .... (have) a nightmare when the alarm went off and woke me up.
4 His hands were covered in oil because he .... (try) to fix the car all morning.
5 When she opened the window, she was happy to see it .... (snow) lightly. If fact, it .... (snow) all night and snow .... (cover) all the rooftops.
6 When Mrs Morgan came into the classroom, the pupils .... (run) around and they .... (scream) at the top of their voices. They .... (knock) over chairs and desks and someone .... (draw) funny pictures on the board.
7 Although I .... (set off) early, I got there late and everyone .... (wait) for me to start the meeting. Mr Wilson told me they .... (wait) for a whole hour.
8 When we got back from our holiday, we discovered that someone .... (break into) our house. The burglars, however, ... (drop) a piece of paper with an address on it as they .... (climb) out of the window.

> *Before John Kennedy became President in 1960, he **had said** that the state of the country was bad. When he became President, he said things were just as bad as he **'d been saying** they were.*

3 Complete the article. Use the past simple, past continuous, past perfect simple or past perfect continuous of the verbs in brackets.

Mark Zuckerberg, creator of *Facebook*

The pre-Facebook years

By the time he (0) **began** (begin) classes at Harvard, Mark Zuckerberg (1) .... (achieve) a reputation as a programming genius. Before the end of his second year at university, he (2) .... (already / design) *CourseMatch*, a program that helped students choose classes based on the choices other students (3) .... (make). At the time, Mark (4) .... (study) psychology and computer science.

A short time later, he created *Facemash*, a program that let students select the best-looking person from different photos. Until then, students (5) .... (use) books called 'Face Books', which included the names and photos of everyone who lived in the student dorms. *Facemash* went up over the weekend but by Monday morning, the college (6) .... (take) it down because its popularity (7) .... (flood) Harvard's server. Before *Facemash*, students (8) .... (ask) the university to develop a similar website for months. Mark (9) .... (work) on a very similar idea when he heard about these requests, so he decided to do something about them – and promised to build a better site than what the university (10) .... (plan).

Vocabulary

 **1d** **for, since, during, yet, etc.**

for and *since*

- We use *for* to say how long something lasts:
  *I'm tired. We've been walking **for** four hours!*
  *I haven't seen Eva **for** ages.*
- We use *since* to indicate a starting point:
  *They haven't met **since** the wedding.*
  (since + noun)
  *A lot has happened **since** I last wrote to you.*
  (since + clause)
  ~~*I've been in London **since** four weeks.*~~ ✗
  *I've been in London **for** four weeks.* ✓

over and *during*

- We can use *over* and *during* in the same way, to indicate the period of time in which something happens or develops:
  ***Over/During** the last eighteen months, there have been three tax increases.*
- Compare the use of *since*:
  ***Since** the middle of last year, there have been three tax increases.* (the middle of last year = the starting point)

from ... to/until/till

- We use *from ... to/until/till* to indicate when something starts and ends:
  *Dinner is **from** eight o'clock **to** ten o'clock.*
  *I waited **from** ten **till** two.*
- We can use *from* on its own if we do not say when something ends:
  *I was training **from** ten o'clock.*

from and *since*

- Compare *from* and *since*:
  *They were here **from** ten o'clock.* (= They came at ten o'clock.)
  *They've been here **since** ten o'clock.* (= They're still here.)

for and *during*

- *For* answers the question *How long?* We use it with time expressions to talk about actions that last the whole of the period of time:
  *He was with the company **for** forty years.* (= His time with the company was forty years.)
- We use *during + that week/your stay/the match*/etc. to say that one action happened inside a period of time:
  ***During that year**, he rose from deputy manager to managing director.*
- Here are some common words and phrases we use with *for* and *during*:
  ***for** two hours/a whole week/a long time/a couple of days/a minute*
  ***during** office hours/the day/the full ninety minutes/the twentieth century/the interval*

during and *while*

- *During* is a preposition. We use it before a noun/noun phrase. We do not use *during* with a clause:
  *We didn't see anybody **during the holidays**.* (the holidays = noun)
- *While* is a conjunction. We use it with a clause:
  *We didn't see anybody **while we were on holiday**.* (we were on holiday = clause)
  ~~*During I was at home, a salesman called.*~~ ✗
  ***While** I was at home, a salesman called.* ✓

23

FOR, SINCE, DURING, YET, ETC.

ago, already, before, still and yet

- *Ago* shows how long before the moment of speaking something happened. We use it with the past simple, not the present perfect. *Ago* comes after a time word or phrase.
*I came to Rome exactly six months **ago**.*
*I'm writing in reply to your letter, which I received two days **ago**.*

- We often use *already* to show surprise that something has happened sooner than expected. We also use it to say that something has been done and does not need to be repeated. We normally use it in affirmative sentences and questions. We often use *already* with perfect tenses. It can come in the mid or end position.
*Is the taxi **already** here? Is the taxi here **already**?*
*I've **already** tried that.   I've tried that **already**.*

- We use *before* to mean 'earlier than a time in the past'.
I went to the airport last Monday to meet Sue.
*I hadn't been to the airport **before**.*
(i.e. before last Monday)

- *Still* tells us that something is continuing and has not finished. It can suggest surprise that it continues longer than expected. We use it in mid position, and in negative sentences it comes before the negative word.
*I've had fifty driving lessons and I **still** can't drive very well.*
*We've been waiting for over an hour but she **still** isn't here.*

- We use *yet* in negative sentences, to show that something that we expected to happen has not happened. We also use it in questions to ask if something has happened. *Yet* comes at the end of the sentence.
*I'm not ready **yet**.* (= I expected to be ready by now.)
*Aren't you ready **yet**?* (= I expected you to be ready by now.)

See also: **6d**

Practice

1 Choose the correct answer.

0 It must be a month *while /* (*since*) we last had a meal together.
1 We haven't had a meal together *for / since* about a month.
2 *Since / During* our meal, her phone rang six or seven times.
3 *During / While* her stay here, she made a lot of good friends.
4 *While / Since* she was staying here, she made a lot of good friends.
5 Keane was injured *during / while* the last minute of the match.
6 *For / Since* several seasons, Keane has not been seriously injured in a game.
7 *For / Since* 2009, Keane has only been badly injured once on the pitch.
8 You know, I had never been to Rome *from / before* our trip together.
9 I've *still / already* been to Rome twice this year.
10 If you visit Rome that often, do you *already / still* enjoy it?
11 I haven't been to Milan *already / yet*.
12 I went to Milan about a year *ago / before*.

24

FOR, SINCE, DURING, YET, ETC.   1

2 Complete the story. Use the words in the box.

> ~~ago~~ ago ~~already~~ already before
> ~~during~~ during for from since since
> since still ~~until~~ while yet

Flying home

A couple of months (0) ...**ago**..., Charles was in Athens on his way back to the States from a business trip. It had been ages (1) .... he had felt so angry. He had been at the airport (2) .... seven o'clock in the morning (3) .... the evening, waiting for a flight to New York. An announcement had (4) .... been made to say that the plane was delayed due to 'technical problems'. Half an hour (5) .... that, another announcement had said that there was going to be a delay because of air traffic congestion. Now the plane had been sitting on the runway (6) .... at least an hour and it was (7) .... not ready to board. (8) .... this delay, Charles tried to complete his report, which he hadn't finished (9) ...., even though his boss was expecting it on his return. There was a lot of noise going on around him (10) .... he was trying to put the finishing touches to his final paragraph, so in the end, he gave up.

It had been years (11) .... Charles had travelled by plane. He avoided flying if he could, (12) .... a particularly unpleasant flight some years (13) .... He (14) .... hated flying but (15) .... that flight, he was convinced that it was the worst way to get around.

3 Complete the sentences. Use one word in each gap.

0 ..**While**.. I was getting ready for bed, Sean called.
1 The accident happened ten years ....
2 Some animals hunt .... the day and sleep at night.
3 I know this place – I'm sure I've been here .... but I can't remember when.
4 I haven't heard from Jenny .... ages.
5 The museum is open .... 9.00 to 5.00.
6 I won't have a coffee, thanks. I've had one ....
7 I don't know the answer .... – I'll have to think about it. I'll let you know as soon as I can.
8 They .... haven't managed to find a solution to the problem.
9 Haven't you finished your shower .... ?
10 I started learning English two years ....

4 Rewrite the sentences. Use the words in brackets in the correct position. Sometimes more than one answer is possible.

0 I've asked her twice but she hasn't replied. (already, yet)
   I've already asked her twice but she hasn't replied yet.
1 The design of the building is similar to others that have been built. (already)
   ....
2 I'm sorry, your dry cleaning isn't ready. (yet)
   ....
3 Lucy asked me to email the office in Vienna but I've done it. (already)
   ....
4 Do you need my help? (still)
   ....
5 I haven't told Sam about the accident. (still)
   ....
6 It's raining, so there's no point in going to the beach. (still, yet)
   ....
7 Has your uncle arrived? (yet)
   ....
8 I've waited a whole hour and he hasn't come. (already, yet)
   ....

1e Suffixes (1)

- We normally use suffixes to change a word to a different part of speech:
  employ (verb) → *employment* (noun)
- Sometimes, the suffix does not change the part of speech but it changes the meaning:
  neighbour (noun) → *neighbourhood* (noun)
- We use the following suffixes to make nouns:

Form/Suffix	Use	Example
verb + -er	forms a noun that describes sb's occupation or what sb does	employ → employer, shop → shopper, teach → teacher, work → worker, write → writer
	forms a noun that describes what sth does	cook → cooker, grate → grater, dry hair → hair dryer, open tins → tin opener, sharpen pencils → pencil sharpener, wash dishes → dishwasher, wipe a windscreen → windscreen wiper
verb + -or	forms a noun that describes sb's occupation or what sb does	act → actor, invest → investor, operate → operator, sail → sailor, supervise → supervisor
verb/noun + -ee	forms a noun that describes what sb does or who sb is	employ → employee, pay → payee, interview → interviewee
verb/noun + -ing	forms a noun that describes an example of something or an action	draw → drawing, build → building, tube → tubing
noun + -eer	forms a noun that says what activity sb does	mountain → mountaineer
verb/noun + -ist	forms a noun that expresses sb's belief or occupation	type → typist, cycle → cyclist, art → artist, violin → violinist, anarchy → anarchist, Buddha → Buddhist
adjective + -ity	forms an abstract noun	equal → equality, flexible → flexibility
adjective + -ness	forms an abstract noun	good → goodness, great → greatness, happy → happiness, sad → sadness
noun/adjective + -hood	forms an abstract noun	brother → brotherhood, mother → motherhood, likely → likelihood
noun + -ship	forms an abstract noun	friend → friendship
verb/adjective + -ance/-ence	forms an abstract noun	admit → admittance, intelligent → intelligence
verb + -ment	forms an abstract noun	achieve → achievement, employ → employment, enjoy → enjoyment, excite → excitement
verb + -tion/-ation/-ition/-sion	forms an abstract noun	form → formation, alter → alteration, invent → invention, pollute → pollution, produce → production, complicate → complication, educate → education, occupy → occupation, qualify → qualification, oppose → opposition, omit → omission, profess → profession, revise → revision

See also: 3e, 4e, 10e, 12e, 13e

# SUFFIXES (1) — 1

Practice

1 Complete the table. The underlined words will help you.

Clue	Noun
0 the quality of being patient	patience
1 (s)he takes photographs	
2 (s)he plays the guitar	
3 it washes dishes	
4 the state of being able to do something	
5 the relationship you have with a friend	
6 the act of exploring a place	
7 something you arrange	
8 he acts in films or plays	
9 the thing we make when we build	
10 the quality of being important	
11 the period of time when you are a child	
12 the feeling of being excited	
13 the state of being happy	
14 (s)he is being trained for something	
15 the act of dividing something	
16 the act of performing a play, concert, etc.	
17 the thing we open tins with	
18 (s)he is forced to seek refuge in a new country	
19 the quality of being kind	
20 the state or fact of being great	

2 Complete the article. Use words formed from the words in CAPITALS at the end of some of the lines.

A challenge for Europe

Although recently there has been a small (0) **reduction** in the number of people out of work in Europe, finding (1)............ is still the biggest and most serious problem facing society today. The economic crisis that began in 2008 made the situation even worse, especially for women. (2)............ of opportunity between men and women is still a problem that (3)............ in many countries have still not solved. Thus, in a number of (4)............, women are still noticeable by their absence. Many (5)............ still pay women less than men, even when their work and (6)............ are the same as those of men. When women complain about unfair (7)............, they are usually ignored or even punished by, for example, not being offered (8)............. This is just not fair. It would be a great pity if the impressive (9)............ of the European Union did not include an (10)............ in the working conditions of women.

REDUCE
EMPLOY

EQUAL
POLITICS
OCCUPY
EMPLOY
QUALIFY
TREAT
PROMOTE
ACHIEVE
IMPROVE

'The roots of education are bitter but the fruit is sweet.'
ARISTOTLE

27

2

AGENDA

Grammar

- 2a Future forms (1): ways to talk about the future
- 2b Future forms (2): *be going to*, present continuous, present simple
- 2c Future forms (3): future continuous, future perfect, future in the past

Vocabulary

- 2d Phrasal verbs: time and change
- 2e Prefixes (1)

Entry test

1 Choose the correct answer.

1 Leave the dishes – I'*ll* / *'m going to* do them if you like.
2 It's already five to eight – you're going to *miss* / *missing* the train.
3 I think I *'ll* / *'m going to* have a break now – I'm exhausted.
4 *Am I going* / *Shall I go* and get a DVD for this evening?
5 Look out! You*'ll* / *'re going to* step on the cat!

SCORE ___ / 5

Now look at 2a on pages 30–31.

2 Choose the correct answer, A, B, C or D.

6 I can't come tonight – I .... my grandparents.
  A visit B visited
  C 'm going to visit D 'll visit

7 Next month, the National Theatre .... a new production of *Hamlet*.
  A put on B putting on
  C shall put on D is putting on

8 I .... a successful author one day.
  A be B 'm being
  C go to be D 'm going to be

9 According to the programme, the show .... at nine o'clock.
  A starts B is starting
  C start D shall start

10 I .... to John's party on Saturday. Do you want to come?
  A go B going
  C 'm going D will go

SCORE ___ / 5

Now look at 2b on pages 32–33.

28

ENTRY TEST 2

3 **Choose the correct answer, A, B, C or D.**

11 This time tomorrow, I'll .... on the beach sunbathing!
  A lie   B be lying   C have lain   D have been lying

12 By next August, I will .... my exams and I'll be ready for a holiday.
  A finishing   B be finishing   C have finished   D have been finishing

13 Shall I take your letters to the post office? I'll .... there anyway.
  A going   B be going   C have gone   D have been going

14 The work will .... by next week, so we'll be free to do what we want.
  A finishing   B be finishing   C have finished   D have been finishing

15 By August, I .... in this house for twenty years.
  A 'm living   B 'll live   C 'm going to live   D will have lived

SCORE / 5

Now look at **2c** on pages 34–35.

4 **Choose the correct answer, A, B, C or D.**

16 If the strike is still on, we'll have to .... our trip till another time.
  A put off   B bring back   C carry on   D go through

17 She .... till the early hours listening to pop music.
  A held me up   B caught me up   C kept me up   D took me up

18 As children, we were .... to respect our elders.
  A grown up   B kept up   C brought up   D held up

19 They said they were going to .... trams in the city centre.
  A get back   B carry on   C keep up   D bring back

20 I wish you'd stop chatting and .... with your work!
  A get down   B get on   C come on   D come back

SCORE / 5

Now look at **2d** on pages 36–37.

5 **Complete the words in the following sentences. Use prefixes.**

21 That was far too expensive! I think the waiter over..........charged us.

22 He was speaking so fast it was im..........possible to understand what he was saying.

23 I can't get my laces ....done. They're in a knot.

24 The music did not dis..........please her – she simply paid no attention to it.

25 The food is a bit under..........cooked. Ask them to put it back in the oven.

SCORE / 5

Now look at **2e** on pages 38–39.

TOTAL SCORE / 25

Grammar

2a Future forms (1): ways to talk about the future

We can use different forms to talk about the future in English.
Here are the main future forms and their uses:

Form	Meaning/Use	Example
Future simple: will + infinitive	decisions made at the moment of speaking	OK, **I'll stay** with you, then. ✓ OK, I'm going to stay with you, then. ✗
	predictions, often with *I think* / *believe* / *expect* / *hope* / etc.	I think it **will be** a difficult game.
	offers	**I'll give** you a lift if you like.
	requests	**Will** you **do** me a favour?
	promises	**I'll love** you forever.
	threats	Leave now or **I'll call** the police!
	facts about the future	Christmas Day **will fall** on Tuesday this year.
be going to + infinitive	intentions	**I'm going to phone** him tomorrow.
	predictions based on present evidence	Look! It**'s going to rain**. ✓ Look! It will rain. ✗
shall + infinitive (usually with *I* or *we*)	offers	**Shall** I **help** you with those bags?
	suggestions	**Shall** we **go** for a walk?
	asking for advice	What **shall** I **say** if he calls?
Future continuous: will be + -ing	actions in progress at a particular time in the future	**I'll be working** at six.
	events that are fixed or expected to happen	We**'ll be going** by bus, as usual.
	things that will happen in the normal course of events	**I'll be staying in** this evening.
Present continuous: be + -ing	arrangements, often with a time expression	**I'm having** my hair cut today.
be + to-infinitive	official arrangements, especially when announced	The President **is to visit** Brussels next week.
Present simple	events that are part of a timetable or schedule	The boat **leaves** the island on Friday.
	in future time clauses, after *when*, *as soon as*, *until*, etc.	I'll phone you when I **arrive**.

30

FUTURE FORMS (1): WAYS TO TALK ABOUT THE FUTURE 2

to faint

PRACTICE

1 Match 1–14 with a–o to make short exchanges.

0 'Look at all those dark clouds.' — n
1 'Our train leaves at six, doesn't it?' — f
2 'The meeting will be held at 3 p.m. on Tuesday.' — g
3 'What time did she say she's going to get here?' — h
4 'I told her to tidy her room but she won't.' — a
5 'How much longer are you going to be?' — b
6 'I feel awful. I think I'm going to faint.' — i
7 'I'll come and help you clear the attic.' — d
8 'Tessa seems to have gained a lot of weight.' — e
9 'Shall we go now? It's getting late.' — o
10 'Will you shut the door, please?' — l
11 'What shall I get for dinner?' — j
12 'When am I going to see you again?' — k
13 'What do you think you'll do when you finish?' — c
14 'I'm going shopping this afternoon.' — m

a 'Shall I have a word with her?'
b 'I'll be with you in just a minute.'
c 'I'm going to get a job, of course.'
d 'Thanks! I'll need all the help I can get!'
e 'That's because she's going to have a baby.'
f 'Yes, it does, so hurry up or we'll be late!'
g 'I'm not sure I'll be able to come.'
h '9.30. But I'm sure she'll be late, as usual!'
i 'I'll call the doctor right away!'
j 'Shall we have fish and chips?'
k 'Perhaps I'll see you tomorrow.'
l 'No, I won't! Do it yourself!'
m 'Are you? I'll come with you.'
n 'Yes, there's going to be a storm.'
o 'OK, I'll just get my coat.'

(are you? I'll come with you.)

2 Read the conversation and choose the correct answer.

KATE Hi! What (0) *are you doing* / shall you do this evening? (1) Will / Shall I come round?
BRIGIT No, not this evening. I (2) 'll be / 'm being busy till late.
KATE When do you think it (3) will / is going to be convenient for me to pop round?
BRIGIT Have you got your diary handy? (4) Are we going to / Shall we check the dates? I'm not busy tomorrow – Wednesday the twenty-first. What about you?
KATE I (5) 'm seeing / will see my dentist tomorrow. Is Thursday OK?
BRIGIT Yes, I think that (6) 's being / 'll be fine.
KATE Great! What time (7) am I going to / shall I come round?
BRIGIT I (8) 'm not / won't be leaving the house at all on Thursday, so I don't think it (9) will be / is being a problem whatever time you come. (10) Will / Shall you bring the manuscript with you, please?
KATE Yes, don't worry. I (11) 'm not forgetting / won't forget. Anything else?
BRIGIT No, we (12) aren't / won't be needing anything else – just the manuscript.
KATE OK. See you on Thursday, then.

> 'Things **will get** worse before they **get** better.' ENGLISH SAYING
> 'Things **will get** worse before they **get** worse.' PESSIMIST

Future forms (2): *be going to*, present continuous, present simple

Present continuous or *be going to*?

- We normally use the present continuous to talk about the near future rather than the distant future:
  I'**m taking** the kids to the cinema this evening.
  I'**m having lunch** with Pete tomorrow.
- We can use *be going to* or the present continuous for more distant events:
  We'**re going to sail**/'**re sailing** round the world next year.
- To talk about plans, we can use the present continuous or *be going to* in the same way, sometimes with a slight change of emphasis:
  I'**m going to see** my therapist tomorrow.
  (= I intend to see my therapist tomorrow.)
  I'**m seeing** my therapist tomorrow.
  (= I have already arranged to see my therapist tomorrow.)
- For predictions, we use *be going to*, not the present continuous.
  Those dark clouds mean we'**re going to have** a storm. ✓
  Those dark clouds mean we're having a storm. ✗

Present continuous or present simple?

- When it is used to talk about the future, the present simple suggests that the events are part of a timetable, a regular/fixed schedule or something similar.

We do not use the present continuous in these cases:
The sun **rises** at six tomorrow. ✓
The sun is rising at six tomorrow. ✗
Our boat **leaves** at noon. ✓
Our boat is leaving at noon. ✗

- We use the present continuous, not the present simple, for personal arrangements:
  I'**m seeing** Jenny this weekend. ✓
  I see Jenny this weekend. ✗

be going to or *will*?

- Compare *be going to* and *will* for predictions:
  - we use *be going to* to talk about something we know will happen because there is evidence in the present:
    The sky is grey – it'**s going to rain**.
    The meeting starts in five minutes – you'**re going to be** late again!
  - we use *will* to talk about something we believe will happen:
    Don't lift that box – you'**ll hurt** your back.
    I'm sure he'**ll fail** the exam.
- Compare *be going to* and *will* for decisions:
  - we use *be going to* to talk about something we have already decided to do:
    I'**m going to buy** the car – we've already agreed on the price.
  - we use *will* for sudden decisions:
    'I'll give it to you for £5,000.' 'OK, I'**ll buy** it.'

32

FUTURE FORMS (2): *BE GOING TO*, PRESENT CONTINUOUS, PRESENT SIMPLE **2**

PRACTICE

1 Complete the sentences. Use *be going to, will,* the present simple or the present continuous and the verbs in brackets. Sometimes more than one answer is possible.

0 So, what time *are you leaving* (you / leave) tomorrow?
1 Look! That car over there **is going to** (crash)!
2 I **'m not coming** (not come) with you tonight. I have to stay in and finish my project.
3 You look tired. Sit down and I **'ll make** (make) you a cup of tea.
4 The film **starts** (start) at half past eight.
5 Do you think Jim **will mind** (mind) if I use his computer?
6 What's wrong? You look as if you **are going to cry** (cry).
7 The library **closes** (close) at half past seven this evening.
8 Look – is that Harry over there? **I'll go** (go) and say hello.
9 Hurry up! Our train **leaves** (leave) in half an hour!
10 Laura and Ben **are going to have** (have) a party next week.

2 Complete the sentences. Use one word in each gap.

0 What *are* you doing this evening?
1 **Shall** we go to that new pizzeria tonight?
2 We'll **be** studying in the library all evening.
3 This lesson's really boring! When is it **going** to finish?
4 Don't worry. I'm sure he **'ll** forgive you if you apologise.
5 **Is** your brother coming with us on Saturday?
6 I **will** be waiting for you when you finish.

3 Read the text and choose the correct answer.

Aquarius

All Aquarians ⁽⁰⁾ get off / **are getting off** to a good start this month, with some good news on the home front. The news ⁽¹⁾ **will help** / is helping to relax recent tensions and give you the chance to make a fresh start. There ⁽²⁾ **will be** / are being lots of new things on other fronts this month. It really ⁽³⁾ **is going to be** / is being a time of great opportunity. Soon, a special person ⁽⁴⁾ **will come** / comes into your life – and this ⁽⁵⁾ **isn't going to be** / isn't being just another friendship. At work, you ⁽⁶⁾ **will need** / are needing to rise to new challenges that ⁽⁷⁾ **will test** / are testing your character. If you make a wrong move, you ⁽⁸⁾ **will definitely regret** / definitely regret it. In short, this is a month which ⁽⁹⁾ **will bring** / is bringing many opportunities but there ⁽¹⁰⁾ **will be** / will being risks, too, so be careful!

Woman:	I'm getting married on Saturday. We're having a traditional wedding.
Man:	Are you having a white wedding?
Woman:	Yes, and I'm going to wear my grandmother's dress.
Man:	And what's your grandmother going to wear?

33

2c Future forms (3): future continuous, future perfect, future in the past

Future continuous

The future continuous can refer to actions in progress at a particular time in the future:

- The future continuous often refers to events or actions that are part of a routine, or things that will happen in the normal course of events. It emphasises that no new arrangements are necessary:
  I can give you a lift to the station. I'll be going that way anyway.
- We can also use the future continuous to ask about someone's plans:
  Will you be using the library this afternoon?
  When will the President be arriving?

Future continuous or future simple?

- We use the future simple for a decision made at the moment of speaking:
  OK, I'll see you this evening.
- With the future continuous, the activity has already been decided. Compare:
  We'll be staying here until next weekend.
  (= We've already decided to stay.)
  OK, we will stay here until next weekend.
  (= We've just decided to stay.)

Future perfect

Form
Affirmative: *They **will have finished** the assignment by Saturday.*
Question: ***Will** they **have finished** the assignment by Saturday?*
Negative: *They **won't have finished** the assignment by Saturday.*

Use
We use the future perfect to talk about something that will be completed before a particular time in the future:

*Today is Tuesday. Rob says, 'I **will have finished** this assignment by Saturday.'* (= He will finish at any time up to Saturday but not later.)
*I **will have found** a better job by the time I'm forty.* ✓
I will find a better job by the time I'm forty. ✗

Future in the past

When we talk about the past, we often need to refer to things that were in the future at that time. To do this, we use the forms that we normally use to talk about the future but we make the verb forms past:
*I thought it **would be** a difficult game.*
*I **was meeting** a friend later that afternoon.*
*We **were going to stay** a bit longer but my brother got sick.*

34

FUTURE FORMS (3): FUTURE CONTINUOUS, FUTURE PERFECT, FUTURE IN THE PAST **2**

PRACTICE

1 Complete each pair of sentences. Use the phrases in brackets.

0 (Will you take, Will you be taking)
  a **Will you take** us to the airport, please?
  b **Will you be taking** Ben to the airport tomorrow?
1 (will be, will have been)
  a I .... in London next year, still doing the same job.
  b I .... in London for ten years by next June.
2 (will finish, was going to finish)
  a I .... my book, but I had to work late.
  b If I don't have too much work this year, I .... all of Marquez's books.
3 (will sunbathe, will be sunbathing)
  a This time tomorrow, Maria .... on a beach in Majorca.
  b I expect she .... until she gets badly burnt!
4 (will be sleeping, will have slept)
  a At midnight, I .... soundly – I hope!
  b Wake me up at nine – I .... long enough by then.
5 (will be flying, were flying)
  a We went to bed early as we .... to London the next day.
  b We .... to Australia later this summer.
6 (will drive, will be driving)
  a I'll give you a lift to the station. I .... that way anyway.
  b You'll be late – I .... you to the station if you like.

2 Complete the conversation. Use the future simple, future continuous or future perfect of the verbs in brackets.

ROSA   So, when shall I come round? Is Thursday still OK?
MARIA Yes, but don't come at six – I (0) **'ll be working** (work) then.
ROSA   What time do you think you (1) .... (be) free?
MARIA Let's see. As I said, I (2) .... (work) on the manuscript all day, and I expect I (3) .... (complete) the second chapter by about seven.
ROSA   Good, because I (4) .... (be) quite busy at about six tomorrow as well. I've got an appointment with my dentist and I don't think she (5) .... (finish) much before seven.
MARIA Well, we really must be getting on with the book, you know. By the end of this month, we (6) .... (spend) a whole year on this project! It's taking too long.
ROSA   Yes. I (7) .... (jump) for joy when it's finished!
MARIA Me too! By the way, (8) .... (you / go) near the post office?
ROSA   Probably. It's not far from the dentist.
MARIA I've been expecting an important parcel and I think it (9) .... (arrive) by Thursday. Could you collect it for me?
ROSA   Sure, no problem. So, I (10) .... (see) you later. Bye for now.

Vocabulary

Phrasal verbs: time and change

Phrasal verb	Meaning/Use	Example
bring back sth; bring sth back	reintroduce	They're going to **bring back** the old system.
bring up sb; bring sb up	raise (a child)	Mrs Evans **brought up** five children.
call off sth; call sth off	cancel	They **called off** the trip when Granny died.
carry on (doing sth)	continue	Are you going to **carry on** making that noise?
come back (from somewhere)	return	When did you **come back** from your holidays?
fall behind (with sth)	fail to produce sth at the right time	He's **falling behind** with the payments.
get back (to a place)	return somewhere	What time do you have to **get back** to college?
get down (to sth)	finally start doing sth	Isn't it time you **got down** to marking those exam papers?
get on (in life)	advance, make progress	He's new here but he'll **get on** fine, I'm sure.
give up (doing) sth; give sth up	stop doing sth	Why did you **give up** football?
go ahead (with sth)	begin to do sth planned or promised	He decided to **go ahead** with his plans in spite of her objections.
go through (sth)	experience (a difficult time)	After all they've **gone through**, they can still smile!
grow up	develop from a child to an adult	I **grew up** on a farm.
hold on	wait	**Hold on** a minute – I won't be long.
hold up sb/sth; hold sb/sth up	delay sb/sth	The building work has been **held up** by very bad weather.
keep sb up	prevent sb from going to bed	I won't **keep** you **up** long.
put sth off; put off sth	postpone	If it rains, they'll have to **put off** the match.
set off	start a journey	We **set off** at half past seven.
stay up	go to bed later than usual	We **stayed up** to watch the film on TV.
take up sth; take sth up	become interested in a new activity and spend time doing it	She's **taken up** tennis.

36

PHRASAL VERBS: TIME AND CHANGE 2

PRACTICE

1 Complete the sentences. Use the correct form of a phrasal verb from page 00.

0 Dad used to let us ..*stay up*.. late on Fridays.
1 If you want to .... in life, you'll have to work harder.
2 We'll have to .... before lunchtime if we want to get there in time.
3 You'll .... with your work if you don't get on with it.
4 I wanted to go to bed but she .... me .... till one o'clock.
5 What time do you have to .... home? I can give you a lift if you like.
6 Why don't you .... a sport now that you have more free time?
7 You really should .... smoking!
8 Can you .... a minute? I need to check my diary.
9 If he .... breaking the law like that, he'll end up in prison.
10 What do you want to be when you ....?

2 Complete the second sentence so that it has a similar meaning to the first sentence, using the word given. Use between two and five words. Do not change the word given.

0 They're going to revive some of the old customs in our village.
   BRING
   They have decided ..*to bring back*.. some of the old customs in our village.

1 Her grandparents raised her as her parents died when she was four.
   BROUGHT
   She .... by her grandparents as her parents died when she was four.

2 If you don't stop misbehaving, I'll have to ask you to leave the room.
   CARRY
   If you .... misbehaving, I'll have to ask you to leave the room.

3 This month's rent hasn't been paid yet.
   BEHIND
   You've .... the rent.

4 I'm planning to do some serious job-hunting after the holiday.
   GOING
   I'm .... down to some serious job-hunting after the holiday.

5 We didn't go to bed early because we were chatting.
   STAYED
   We .... late, chatting.

6 The meeting has been rearranged until later in the week.
   PUT
   They .... the meeting until later in the week.

7 I was late because of the heavy traffic.
   HELD
   I .... by the heavy traffic.

8 The performance has been cancelled.
   CALLED
   They've .... the performance.

> **A:** Why are policemen strong?
> **B:** Because they **hold up** the traffic.

37

2e Prefixes (1)

- We use prefixes to change the meaning of a word. Prefixes do not change the part of speech (but most suffixes do).
- Many prefixes give a word a meaning which is the opposite or negative of the original word. For example, we can use the prefixes *dis-* or *un-*:
  dis + appear → **dis**appear
  un + tie → **un**tie
- Here are some common prefixes:

Prefix	Meaning/Use	Example
anti- + adjective/noun	opposite or against	anti-clockwise, anti-climax, anti-European
co- + noun/verb	together	coworker, cohabit
dis- + verb	opposite/negative	dislike, disembark
il- + adjective	opposite	illegal
im- + adjective	opposite	impossible
in- + adjective	opposite	indirect
inter- + adjective	between	intercontinental
ir- + adjective	opposite	irregular
mis- + verb	wrongly/badly	mistook, mishandle
over- + verb	too much	overdo, overwork
out- + verb	more	outnumber
post- + noun/verb	after	postgraduate
pre- + noun/verb	before	pre-arrangement
pro- + noun/adjective	in favour of	pro-Unions, pro-European
sub- + adjective	below	substandard
super- + noun/adjective	greater than	superhuman
trans- + noun/verb/adjective	across	transatlantic
un- + verb/adjective	opposite/negative	unlock, unhappy
under- + verb	not enough, too little	undercook, undercharge

There are a few rules:
- We use *il-* instead of *in-* with words that begin with *-l*:
  il + legal → **il**legal
- We use *im-* instead of *in-* with words that begin with *-m* or *-p*:
  im + polite → **im**polite
- We use *ir-* instead of *in-* with words that begin with *-r*:
  ir + responsible → **ir**responsible
- Some common mistakes are:
  ~~You must **unconnect** the cables first.~~ ✗
  You must **disconnect** the cables first. ✓
  ~~They expelled him for **disbehaving**.~~ ✗
  They expelled him for **misbehaving**. ✓
- Note that many words with a prefix have a base part that never exists on its own. Here are some examples:
  immediate, incontrovertible, uncalled-for

For prefixes, see also: 5e

PRACTICE

1 Complete the words. Use prefixes.

0 ..*dis*...like
1 ....dependent
2 ....polite
3 ....do
4 ....driver
5 ....approve
6 ....behave
7 ....logical
8 ....zip
9 ....inform
10 ....agree
11 ....eat
12 ....historic
13 ....atlantic
14 ....graduate
15 ....moral
16 ....hear
17 ....interpret
18 ....national
19 ....sleep
20 ....relevant
21 ....believe
22 ....crowded
23 ....understand

PREFIXES (1) 2

2 Complete the crossword. Use prefixes.

Across

1. This prefix, followed by words that begin with -l, means 'not'.
2. The ....-Siberian railway goes from Moscow to Vladivostok.
5. Never ....estimate the time you need to study for an exam or test.
7. We use this prefix to mean 'in favour of'.
8. The opposite of *humane* is ....*humane*.
10. They told me I am ....qualified for the job.
11. ....-American protesters gathered round the embassy.
13. This prefix means 'wrongly' or 'badly'.

Down

1. Take the ....continental express train from Paris to Warsaw.
3. Do you believe in the ....natural?
4. ....*exist* means 'to exist at the same time'.
5. The opposite of *familiar* is ....*familiar*.
6. The boys ....appeared as soon as they saw the farmer.
8. The opposite of *responsible* is ....*responsible*.
9. If you ....-date a cheque, you write a later date on it.
12. We use this prefix meaning 'not' in front of words that begin with -m.

3 Complete the article. Use words formed from the words in CAPITALS at the end of some of the lines.

My attempts to communicate in a foreign language often (0) ..**misfire**.. I tried to speak Greek while I was on holiday in Mykonos a few years ago but the attempt was completely (1).............! — FIRE / SUCCESSFUL

So, there I was in a traditional Greek restaurant, where I tried to order in Greek. At first, the waiter (2)............. me for a German and started speaking to me in German. I find it (3)............. to communicate in German, so I carried on with Greek. The waiter (4)............. and instead of mushrooms, he brought me beetroots, which I (5)............. intensely. I must have looked very unhappy because he started apologising and then (6)............. into the kitchen. This time he came back with a plate of aubergines, which, (7)............., is not one of my favourite dishes either. I ate them anyway and asked for the bill. — TAKE / POSSIBLE / UNDERSTAND / LIKE / APPEAR / FORTUNATELY

When the waiter came back with the bill, I told him that he had (8)............. me – I must have sounded quite angry. But it was my mistake again. I had (9)............. the bill, as the waiter explained later, in excellent English! — CHARGE / READ

Luckily for me, English is still a(n) (10)............. language! — NATIONAL

39

Exam practice 1

Part 1

For questions **1–12**, read the text below and decide which answer (**A**, **B**, **C** or **D**) best fits each gap. There is an example at the beginning (**0**).

Teen sails around the world

A nineteen-year-old Australian who spent seven months at sea in her pink yacht **(0)** *crossed* the finishing line of her round-the-world journey on Saturday. She **(1)**.......... the youngest sailor to sail round the globe solo, non-stop and unassisted. Thousands of spectators **(2)**.......... into applause as Emily Watson sailed into Sydney Harbour, the finale to an epic journey from which critics said she'd never **(3)**.......... alive.

Watson's parents **(4)**.......... for her when she arrived, and the teenager burst into tears; she **(5)**.......... her mum and dad for seven months.

Emily Watson, from Buderim in Queensland, had **(6)**.......... from Sydney on October 18th, ignoring comments by critics who said she was too immature and inexperienced for the journey. Her parents said that they had **(7)**.......... her up to be independent and that she was well-prepared because she **(8)**.......... since she was eight.

How did Emily feel to be back home? 'Well, I haven't had a good meal **(9)**.......... seven months; I've been at sea, alone, **(10)**.......... October; I've missed my friends,' she told reporters. Is she planning another voyage? 'First, I think **(11)**.......... a nice long rest – chill out, you know. And then I'm **(12)**.......... my studies.' Emily is planning to study physical education at Sydney University.

0	**A**	crossed	**B**	has crossed	**C**	has been crossing	**D**	had crossed
1	**A**	becomes	**B**	is becoming	**C**	became	**D**	was becoming
2	**A**	burst	**B**	were bursting	**C**	had burst	**D**	had been bursting
3	**A**	get on	**B**	get back	**C**	get down	**D**	get up
4	**A**	were waiting	**B**	have waited	**C**	had waited	**D**	had been waiting
5	**A**	didn't see	**B**	wasn't seeing	**C**	hasn't seen	**D**	hadn't seen
6	**A**	put off	**B**	set off	**C**	called off	**D**	gone off
7	**A**	brought	**B**	given	**C**	held	**D**	grown
8	**A**	sailed	**B**	was sailing	**C**	had sailed	**D**	had been sailing
9	**A**	for	**B**	since	**C**	during	**D**	while
10	**A**	until	**B**	over	**C**	since	**D**	in
11	**A**	I have	**B**	I'll have	**C**	I'm having	**D**	I will have had
12	**A**	finishing	**B**	going to finish	**C**	about to finish	**D**	to finish

SCORE / 12

40

Part 2

For questions **13–24**, read the text below and think of the word which best fits each gap. Use only **one** word in each gap. There is an example at the beginning **(0)**.

3-D films have been around **(0)** ....*for*.... more than sixty years. They have existed **(13)**.................. the 1950s. However, they **(14)**.................. not very popular back then as they were too expensive to produce and display.

Today, 3-D **(15)**.................. becoming more and more popular and common in all kinds of film. 3-D films **(16)**.................. also become much more profitable for producers and although they have not **(17)**.................. become the 'norm', it looks like they soon **(18)**.................. . We're definitely **(19)**.................. to see more 3-D releases in the coming years.

3-D technology **(20)**.................. also getting better. There **(21)**.................. now viewing systems which **(22)**.................. not require the use of special viewing glasses, while 3-D TV **(23)**.................. also increasing in popularity. Soon, we will all **(24)**.................. getting rid of our old TV sets and replacing them with new, high-end 3-D ones. It looks like 3-D is here to stay!

SCORE ____ / 12

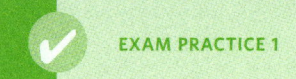

Part 3

For questions **25–34**, read the text below. Use the word given in capitals at the end of some of the lines to form a word that fits in the gap **in the same line**. There is an example at the beginning **(0)**.

Social networking: risks

Social networking sites have increased enormously in (0) *popularity* in recent years. They have millions of (25) .... from around the globe and they've done a lot to bring people closer together. They are a marvellous (26) .... and they are a unique way of encouraging (27) .... between people from many different parts of the world.

Sadly, social networking sites are becoming a target for Internet (28) ...., ruthless people who take advantage of the (29) .... of these sites and gather personal (30) .... about the people who use them – personal details that the (31) .... themselves have made publicly available.

Luckily, there are things we can do to reduce the risks without spoiling the fun and (32) .... Schools are a good place to start. (33) .... can inform children of the dos and don'ts of social networking. Internet safety should become a part of technology (34) ....

POPULAR
VISIT

INVENT
FRIEND

HACK
WEAK
INFORM
USE

EXCITE
TEACH

EDUCATE

Part 4

For questions **35–42**, complete the second sentence so that it has a similar meaning to the first sentence, using the word given. **Do not change the word given.** You must use between **two** and **five** words, including the word given. Here is an example **(0)**.

Example:

0 She started working at noon and she hasn't finished yet.
   BEEN
   She ......*has been working since*...... noon.

35 I last saw Helen before she left for Australia.
   SINCE
   I .... she left for Australia.

36 They're going to cancel the meeting.
   CALL
   They've decided .... the meeting.

37 My mobile rang during the nine o'clock news.
   WATCHING
   My mobile rang .... the nine o'clock news.

38 It was the best film I had ever seen.
   NEVER
   I .... such a good film before.

39 He learnt to use a computer when he was six years old.
   WAS
   He's known how to use a computer .... six years old.

40 At the moment, he is a reporter for the local newspaper.
   AS
   He .... a reporter for the local newspaper right now.

41 I started cooking about two hours ago.
   HAVE
   I .... two hours.

42 When did you meet Eric?
   KNOWN
   How long .... Eric?

SCORE / 16

TOTAL SCORE / 50

3

AGENDA

Grammar

- 3a Modal verbs (1)
- 3b Modal verbs (2)
- 3c Linking words and phrases: reason and purpose

Vocabulary

- 3d have, take, bring
- 3e Suffixes (2)

Entry test

1 Choose the correct answer.

1 Helen *must / had to* leave the meeting early because she had a train to catch.
2 What you *must / should* have done is call the police, not get involved yourself.
3 I *will / could* be able to speak better if I practise more.
4 Terry has done so little work – he *mustn't / needn't* have bothered to come to class today.
5 I *didn't need to / couldn't* get tickets after all – they were sold out.

Now look at 3a on pages 46–48.

SCORE / 5

2 Choose the correct answer, A, B, C or D.

6 It .... be weeks before the building is actually finished.
  A must   **B** would   **C** ought to   **D** could
7 You .... even have lost your job by then, who knows?
  A should   **B** may   **C** can   **D** will
8 It .... be a good film – the reviews were very good.
  A can't   **B** could have   **C** must   **D** must have
9 That .... be Tim – go and open the door for him, will you?
  A will   **B** can   **C** ought   **D** shall
10 Things .... have been worse – everything seemed to be going wrong!
  A shouldn't   **B** couldn't   **C** mustn't   **D** may

Now look at 3b on pages 49–51.

SCORE / 5

44

ENTRY TEST 3

3 **Choose the correct answer, A, B, C or D.**

11 She got the job .... she was the best candidate.
   A owing to   B due to   C on account of   D because
12 Flight 502 has been delayed .... to bad weather.
   A as   B for   C due   D on account
13 .... you are unable to accept the job, we offered it to someone else.
   A Because of   B As a result C Thanks to   D Since
14 I locked the door .... we could continue our discussion undisturbed.
   A in order to B in order   C so that   D for that
15 The pilots suddenly went on strike. .... result, our flight was cancelled.
   A As   B With   C As a   D With the

Now look at 3c on pages 52–54.   SCORE / 5

4 **Choose the correct answer, A, B, C or D.**

16 There's no need to rush back – just .... your time.
   A have   B get   C be on   D take
17 I .... the exam last week but I didn't do too well.
   A wrote   B passed   C took   D obtained
18 Could you .... me a hammer from the shed?
   A take   B carry   C bring   D deliver
19 The children were .... so much fun – I hated to call them inside.
   A making   B doing   C being   D having
20 Ronald took .... Julia from the first moment they met.
   A up   B to   C over   D out

Now look at 3d on pages 55–57.   SCORE / 5

5 **Choose the correct answer, A, B, C or D.**

21 Isobel has all the right .... to become a successful manager.
   A educations   B qualifications C experiences   D applications
22 Sometimes there's a lot of competition between children for their mother's ....
   A attraction   B protection C attention   D recognition
23 Several serious .... have been made against him by the police.
   A investigations B demonstrations C suggestions D accusations
24 Their team was knocked out of the .... in the first round.
   A demonstration B competition C production   D situation
25 They announced the .... of the flight this morning.
   A cancellation B abolition   C communication   D resignation

Now look at 3e on pages 58–59.   SCORE / 5

TOTAL SCORE / 25

45

Grammar

3a Modal verbs (1)

- There are ten modal verbs: *can, could, may, might, must, ought to, shall, should, will* and *would*.
- Modal verbs do not take *-s* in the third person singular.
- We use a bare infinitive (= infinitive without *to*) after modal verbs:
  You **should** go home early.
- We form questions by inverting the modal verb and subject:
  He **can** swim. **Can** he swim?
- We form negatives by adding *not* after the modal verb. We do not use *do*:
  I **cannot** swim. You **shouldn't** play with matches!
- In tag questions and short answers, we repeat the modal verb. We do not use *be* or *do*.
  You **can** drive, **can't** you? Yes, I **can**. / No, I **can't**.
- Modal verbs do not normally have past forms. (But in some cases, *would, could, should* and *might* may be used as past tenses of *will, can, shall* and *may*.)
- The same modal verb can sometimes be used to talk about the present, future or past.
  The train **might** be in the station. (present)
  The train **might** arrive late. (future)
  When I called, they said that their train **might** be late. (past)
- Modal verbs have perfect forms (modal verb + *have* + past participle):
  You **could have done** better.
- When a modal verb cannot be used to talk about the past, we often use another verb instead:
  I **must** help my father. (present)
  I **had to** help my father. (past)
- We cannot use one modal verb after another:
  ~~She **must can** do it.~~ ✗
  She **must be able to** do it. ✓
  ~~You **will can** go.~~ ✗
  You **will be able to** go. ✓
- The verbs *have to* and *need (to)* are often used in similar ways to modal verbs.
  You **have to** leave now.
  You **need to** leave now.

Obligation, necessity, advice, criticism

Verb	Meaning/Use	Example 1 (present or future)	Example 2 (past)
must	obligation, necessity	He **must** stay. They **must** have clean water.	He **had to** stay. They **had to** have clean water.
mustn't	prohibition	You **mustn't** smoke.	–
have to	necessity	We **have to** get some sleep.	We **had to** get some sleep.
have (got) to		I've **got to** find a job.	I **had to** find a job.
don't have to	no necessity	We **don't have to** wear a tie.	We **didn't have to** wear a tie.
need to	necessity	We **need to** book in advance.	We **needed to** book in advance.
needn't	no necessity	We **needn't** book in advance.	We **needn't have** booked in advance.
don't need to		We **don't need to** book in advance.	We **didn't need to** book in advance.
should	advice, criticism	You **should** work harder.	You **should have** worked harder.
ought to	advice, criticism	You **ought to** apologise.	You **ought to have** apologised.

must and have to

- *Must* often expresses the speaker's opinion. We use it to talk about what the speaker feels is necessary. *Have to* refers to something that is necessary because someone else says so, or because of laws, rules or regulations. Compare:
You **must** get your hair cut. (I think it's necessary.)
You **have to** wear a uniform. (= It's a regulation.)

- *Mustn't* and *don't have to* are different: *mustn't* expresses prohibition; *don't have to* expresses lack of necessity. Compare:
You **mustn't** stay here. (= You aren't allowed to stay here.)
You **don't have to** stay here. (It's not necessary but you can if you want to.)

- Unlike *must*, *have to* can be used in different tenses and forms. We use it whenever *must* is not possible.
I hate **having to stay** in on Saturdays!

need and need to

- *Need to* and *don't need to* have the same meaning as *have to/don't have to*:
We **need to** get some sleep.
You **don't need to** go.

- In negative sentences, we can also use *needn't*. *Needn't* is used like a modal verb:
You **needn't** go.

- Compare *didn't need to* and *needn't have*:
I **didn't need to** get up early. (= I didn't get up early because it wasn't necessary.)
I **needn't have** got up early. (= I got up early but it wasn't necessary.)

Ability and permission

For giving, refusing and asking for permission, see also: 3b

Verb	Meaning/Use	Example 1 (present or future)	Example 2 (past)
can	ability	She **can** play the piano. We **can** buy a new house now.	She **could** play the piano when she was five. We **were able to** buy a new house.
can't	no ability	She **can't** play the piano today.	She **couldn't** play the piano when she was four.
be able to	ability	She**'s able to** play the piano whenever she wants to.	She **was able to** play the piano whenever she wanted to.
not be able to	no ability	She **isn't able to** play the piano because her hand hurts.	She **wasn't able to** play the piano because her hand hurt.
can	permission	You **can** park here.	We **could** park there.
may		Visitors **may** use the car park.	Visitors **could** use the car park.
be allowed to		Visitors **are allowed to** use the car park.	Visitors **were allowed to** use the car park.
cannot/can't	prohibition	You **can't** park here.	We **couldn't** park there.
may not		Visitors **may not** use the car park.	Visitors **could not** use the car park.
not be allowed to		Visitors **are not allowed to** use the car park.	Visitors **were not allowed to** use the car park.

3 MODAL VERBS (1)

be able to

- When talking about the past, we normally use *was/were able to* to talk about particular instances, often suggesting that something was achieved with difficulty:
  She **was able to** swim across the river although it was very wide.
- We also use *will be able to* to talk about things a person will be capable of doing in the future:
  If she practises, she **will be able to** play Chopin.

can and could

- Note that *can* may refer to the present or future:
  You can visit the science museum. (now or in the future)
- We also use *can* and *could* to talk about typical behaviour or events, or things that are (or were) generally true:
  It **can** be very cold at night.
  It **could** be very cold at night.

PRACTICE

1 Choose the correct answer.

0 Unfortunately, we *didn't* / *weren't* allowed to enter the room.
1 When we were at school, we *had to* / *ought to* wear a uniform.
2 You *mustn't* / *don't have to* wear your seatbelt during the whole of the flight.
3 You *should* / *have got* to tell her the truth.
4 You *need* / *have to* be a member of the library before you can borrow books.
5 I *don't need to* / *shouldn't* wear glasses because my eyesight is still quite good.
6 We *wouldn't* / *weren't allowed to* talk to our partner during the exam.
7 We *needn't* / *couldn't* have ordered so much food as nobody was hungry.
8 She *didn't need* / *needn't have* to take any money because her friend was going to pay.
9 When I first came to Madrid, I *could* / *couldn't* speak only a few words of Spanish.
10 *Did you have to* / *Must you* have your hair cut before the interview last week?

2 Complete the second sentence so that it has a similar meaning to the first sentence, using the word given. Use between two and five words. Do not change the word given.

0 The teacher gave me permission to leave the room.
  COULD
  The teacher said *I could leave* the room.
1 In the end, I couldn't make it to the party because I was busy.
  ABLE
  In the end, I …………… go to the party, because I was busy.
2 At school, she was the fastest runner in her class.
  COULD
  At school, …………… faster than anyone else in her class.
3 He managed to get in through the window.
  ABLE
  He …………… in through the window.
4 It wasn't necessary for us to attend all the classes.
  HAVE
  We …………… attend all the classes.
5 Our parents didn't let us stay up late on weekdays when we were kids.
  ALLOWED
  When we were kids, we …………… up late on weekdays.
6 I took a lot of suntan oil with me, which I didn't use.
  TAKEN
  I …………… so much suntan oil with me.
7 Oxygen masks were essential at the top of the mountain.
  WEAR
  They …………… oxygen masks at the top of the mountain.
8 If I don't find a job soon, I'll be broke.
  HAVE
  I …………… a job soon, otherwise I'll be broke.

*'Those who **can**, do; those who **can't**, teach.'* GEORGE BERNARD SHAW

3b Modal verbs (2)

Certainty, probability and possibility

We use certain modal verbs to express certainty, probability and possibility. Here are some examples:

For *will* and *be going to*, see 2b

Certainty: negative	Possibility	Probability	Certainty: positive
Present			
She **can't be** in France. She **couldn't be** in France. (It's impossible; e.g. I saw her a moment ago.)	She **may/might** be in France. She **could** be in France. (I'm not sure.)	She**'ll be** in France now. She **should/ought to** be in France. (It's probable; e.g. she set off hours ago.)	She **must** be in France. (I'm sure.)
Past			
She **can't have been** in France. (e.g. She called me from Italy.)	She **might have been** in France. (I'm not sure.)		She **must have been** in France. (I'm almost sure.)

- We use *will* to express a strong probability that something is true, especially when we don't have actual evidence at that moment:
  That**'ll** be Maria on the phone – she said she'd call me today.
- We use *must* to express certainty:
  That **must** be Maria on the phone – she's the only person with my new number.
- We can also use *have to/had to* to express certainty:
  She **had to** be the person I saw on the train.
- We often use *can/could* or *will/would* in questions:
  Who **can** that **be** on the phone?
  Who **would** have phoned so late?

- We can use modal verbs to express different degrees of certainty to refer to the past, present or future:
  Don't drink it – it **could/may/might** be poisonous! (present)
  It **could/may/might/must/can't** have been poisonous. (past)
  We **may/ought to/might/should** get a reply tomorrow. (future)
  It **could/may/might** rain, so take an umbrella. (future)
- The modal verb often changes the meaning of the sentence:
  It **may/might have** rained. (I'm not sure.)
  It **could have** rained. (but luckily, it didn't)

3 MODAL VERBS (2)

Other uses of modal verbs

We also use modal verbs in the following situations:

Meaning/Use	Example
making requests	*Can I have a glass of water, please?* *Could you do me a favour?* *May I use your phone?* *Would you help me carry these bags?* *Will you please be quiet?*
giving and refusing permission	*'You can have the day off,' said the manager.* *You can't borrow my car tonight – I need it.* *Could I leave early today?* *You may wait inside. (formal)*
asking for advice	*Shall I take the exam now or wait till May?* *Should I go by car or by train?*
giving advice	*You should get your hair cut.* *You ought to be more careful.*
making offers	*Shall I help you clear the table?* *Can I give you a hand with your luggage?* *Would you like a lift to the airport?*
making suggestions	*Shall we open a window in here?* *We can stay in and watch a DVD.* *We could stay in and watch a DVD.*
complaining, criticising	*You could at least have asked me before taking the money!* *You shouldn't have taken the car without asking me.* *You ought to have revised a bit more.* *You might at least have helped me with the washing-up!*

50

MODAL VERBS (2) 3

PRACTICE

1 Choose the correct answer.

0 **Will** / Might you help me with my project?
1 She *can / can't* be Italian! Her name is Smith!
2 I *may / can't* be able to come.
3 'Someone's at the door.' 'That *can / will* be my uncle.'
4 You *could / must* have been crazy to do something as dangerous as that!
5 He *can't / may* have taken the money – he was with me all the time.
6 I *might / can* not be able to come, so don't wait for me.
7 It *may / must* be cold tomorrow.
8 Who *could / should* have done such a terrible thing?
9 Hurry up, we're late! We *might / should* have been ready hours ago!
10 He *can / could* have been the one who started the fire but we're not really sure.

2 Match the sentences with the functions. Write a letter in each box. You can use some letters more than once.

a = asking for advice	b = giving advice	c = making a request
d = making a suggestion	e = making an offer	f = asking for permission
g = refusing permission	h = criticising	

0 May I borrow your calculator for a moment? **f**
1 Shall we go to a Chinese restaurant this evening? ☐
2 Would you help me get the dinner ready? ☐
3 You shouldn't get upset so easily. ☐
4 You ought to have gone to the doctor. ☐
5 Do you think I should go and complain to the manager? ☐
6 I'm sorry, you can't hand in the assignment a month late. ☐
7 Could I close the door? ☐
8 Can I get you anything from the shops? ☐
9 You shouldn't have spoken to your mother like that! ☐
10 You ought to talk to Peter about this. ☐

3 Choose the correct answer.

0 She **must** / can't be married. She's wearing a wedding ring.
1 *That'll / That can't* be John on the phone – I was expecting him to call.
2 You look really tired. It *must / could* have been an exhausting journey.
3 I can't find my glasses – where *must / could* they be?
4 I failed the test. I *must / should* have studied harder.
5 You *shouldn't / can't* have washed the dishes! The sink is full!
6 It *must / can't* have been raining all night. The roads are wet.
7 I wonder if you *may / could* do me a favour: can I use your phone?
8 *Would / Should* you like me to do the shopping for you?

> JUDGE: You've been found guilty of not stopping at a red traffic light when you **should have**. What do you have to say for yourself?
> ACCUSED: But I often stop at green traffic lights when I **don't have to**!

51

3c Linking words and phrases: reason and purpose

because, as, since

- *Because*, *as* and *since* have similar meanings; they show the reason or cause of something. They come before a clause:

Clause +	Linking word +	Clause
We stayed at home	because as since	it was raining.

- There is almost no difference in meaning between *because*, *as* and *since* but sometimes *because* emphasises a reason more strongly. *As* and *since* assume that the reason is obvious:
  I'll do it **because** I want to, not **because** I have to.
  As/Since everyone's here, we can begin.
- When we answer with a clause of reason alone, we can only use *because*:
  'Why are you late?' '**Because** I missed the bus.'

because of, owing to, etc.

- *Because of*, *owing to*, *on account of*, *due to*, *as a result of* and *thanks to* also show the reason or cause of something. They come before a noun or noun phrase, not a clause:

Clause +	Linking word +	Noun (phrase)
We stayed at home	because of on account of owing to due to as a result of thanks to	the rain.

- ~~They came here looking for work owing to the wages are higher.~~ ✗
  They came here looking for work because the wages are higher. ✓ (*because* + clause)
- We use *because of* more often than the rest of the phrases, especially in spoken English.

- *Owing to* is more formal:
  Owing to lack of money, the project will not continue next year.
- *Due to* often comes after the verb *to be*:
  The crash **was due to** bad weather.
- We cannot use *owing to* after *to be*. We only use *due to*:
  ~~The accident was owing to human error.~~ ✗
  The accident was **due to** human error. ✓
- *On account of* often means 'because of a problem or difficulty':
  He can't run very fast **on account of** his asthma.
- *As a result of* often means 'because of something that has already happened':
  As a result of the pilots' strike, all flights have been cancelled.
- *Thanks to* usually explains why something good has happened:
  Thanks to Ron and his car, we managed to get all the deliveries done on time.

in order to, so as to

- *In order to* and *so as to* express the purpose of an action. We use them before a verb.
- *In order to* and *so as to* can be more emphatic than *to* alone:
  She went on a diet **to** lose weight.
  She went on a diet **in order to** lose weight.
  She went on a diet **so as to** lose weight.
- We can use the negative forms *in order not to* and *so as not to* but we do not use *not to* on its own:
  ~~They set off early not to miss their flight.~~ ✗
  They set off early **in order not to** miss their flight. ✓
  They set off early **so as not to** miss their flight. ✓

52

LINKING WORDS AND PHRASES: REASON AND PURPOSE   3

in order that, so (that), etc.

We use *in order that* and *so (that)* to express the purpose of an action. We use them before a clause that contains a modal verb.

Clause +	Linking word +	Clause with modal verb
We're leaving now	so so that in order that	we can catch the first bus.

consequently, as a result, etc.

- We can use *consequently*, *as a result* and *because of that* to express the result of an action mentioned earlier.

- When we use them at the beginning of the sentence, they are followed by a comma.
  We talked until the early hours of the morning.
  ***Consequently/As a result/Because of that,** I overslept.*
- We can also use *so* to express the result of an action. We use it before a clause:
  *She couldn't eat meat, **so** she just had vegetables.*

so or since?

Compare *so* and *since*:
~~Since it's his birthday on Monday, so he's having a party.~~ ✗
***Since** it's his birthday on Monday, he's having a party.* ✓
*It's his birthday on Monday, **so** he's having a party.* ✓

PRACTICE

1 **Choose the correct answer.**

0 *Because / **Due*** to bad weather, the train will arrive an hour late.
1 I phoned *because / since* I need to speak to you about Susan.
2 *Since / Due to* the rain has stopped, we can go back in the garden.
3 *Because / Because of* the bus was late, I missed the meeting.
4 We took a taxi *in order not to / not to* be late.
5 The traffic jam is *due to / owing to* major roadworks.
6 Emma came first *on account / as a result of* her hard work.
7 I'm going by bus *in order to / owing to* save time.
8 I'll give him the money *so that / consequently* he'll buy the ticket today.
9 She didn't water the plants, *since / so* they died.
10 I left them a note *so that / in order to* they'd know where I was.

2 **Complete the sentences. Use the words and phrases in the box.**

as a result	~~because~~	because of
in order to	owing	since	so
so	so as	so as not	thanks

0 I arrived late for work *because*. I didn't hear the alarm.
1 I am writing .... apologise for my behaviour.
2 I thought the party was going to be informal, ... I wore jeans.
3 The couple had a terrible row. .... they called the wedding off.
4 .... to his illness, he could not take part in the race.
5 .... I don't have a mobile phone, you can't send me text messages.
6 We're late .... you!
7 We went to the show early .... to get good seats.
8 They were whispering .... to wake her up.
9 I lent her some money .... that she could pay him back.
10 The party was a great success, ... to Jo and Eve – they did all the work!

53

3 LINKING WORDS AND PHRASES: REASON AND PURPOSE

3 **Complete the sentences. Use one word in each gap. Sometimes more than one answer is possible.**

0 We were tired, ...**so**... we decided not to go to the party after all.
1 Sandra is upset and it's all due .... your behaviour.
2 Prices have risen .... of an increase in demand.
3 The 5.30 train to Sheffield has been cancelled .... to circumstances beyond our control.
4 .... understand how the human body works, you need some knowledge of chemistry.
5 .... there was no food in the house, we rang for a pizza.
6 She put the vase on top of the cupboard .... that it wouldn't get broken.
7 In .... to get a clear idea of what is needed, we will need more information.
8 Milk is good for you, ... you should drink more of it.
9 I didn't go .... I didn't want to leave you alone.
10 They spoke quietly so .... not to disturb anyone.
11 The bank refused to give the company another loan. As a ...., it went bankrupt.
12 He stayed in on Saturday so as .... revise for his exam.

'Why are false teeth like stars?'
'**Because** they come out at night and go in in the morning.'

Vocabulary

3d have, take, bring

Common phrases/expressions with *have*, *take* and *bring*

We often use *have*, *take* and *bring* with nouns in phrases or fixed expressions. In these cases, the verbs have little meaning of their own – the meaning of the phrase depends on the noun that follows. Here are some examples:

Phrase	Example
have	
have a bath/shower	She's probably upstairs **having a bath**.
have dinner/lunch/etc.	We **had dinner** and then went for a walk.
have a drink	I'll collapse if I don't **have a drink** soon.
have sth to eat	I haven't **had anything to eat** since this morning.
have (an) experience	He **has no experience** of running a large company.
have fun	Bye! **Have fun!**
have a holiday	It's almost a year since we **had a** real **holiday**.
have an operation	Before I **had the operation**, I could hardly walk.
have a party	We're **having a party** on Saturday. Can you come?
have a picnic	If it's sunny, we can **have a picnic**.
have a rest	I'm just going to lie down and **have a rest**.
have time	I don't **have time** now. Can we talk later?
take	
take the bus/a taxi/etc.	**Take a taxi** – it's quicker.
take care of sb	Who **takes care of their children** when they're at work?
take control of sth	She **took control of** the situation.
take a decision	Who **took the decision** to cancel the project?
take a deep breath	She **took a deep breath** and dived off the cliff.
take an exam	Why do we have to **take** so many **exams**?
take my/her/their/etc. medicine	Don't forget to **take your medicine**.
take part (in) sth	Did you **take part in the play** last year?
take place	The concert **took place** at Wembley.
take a seat	**Take a seat**. The manager will see you in a minute.
take time	Learning to play the piano isn't easy – it **takes time**.
take your time	Don't rush – **take your time**.
bring	
bring sth to sb's attention	Thank you for **bringing the mistake to my attention**.
bring charges (against sb)	The police **brought charges against him**.
bring sth to a close	The evening was **brought to a close** with a song.
bring sth to an end	It's time we **brought the whole business to an end**.
bring a lump to sb's throat	It was so moving it **brought a lump to my throat**.
bring tears to sb's eyes	The film **brought tears to my eyes**.

3 HAVE, TAKE, BRING

take, bring, get or fetch?

- *Take something* (from a place), generally means 'remove something'.
  He **took** a key out of his pocket.
- *Take something* (with you) means 'carry something from one place to another'.
  Don't forget to **take** your briefcase (**with you**).
- *Bring* generally means 'take something or someone to the place where you are now'.
  Did you **bring** anything to drink?
- *Get* often means 'receive'.
  I **got** an email from Mark.
- *Fetch* means 'go to another place to get something and bring it back'.
  I'll go and **fetch** the others so we can eat.

take place or occur?

- If something *takes place*, it happens after a plan of some sort:
  The contest **takes place** every four years.
- If something *occurs*, it happens without someone planning it:
  Where did the accident **occur**?

Phrasal verbs with *take*

Phrasal verb	Meaning	Example
take after sb	look or behave like sb	Jenny **takes after** her mother.
take back sth; take sth back	return sth	If the shirt doesn't fit, **take** it **back**.
	say you regret saying sth	I'm sorry, I was wrong. I **take back** what I said.
take down sth; take sth down	make a note of sth	Let me **take down** your name and number.
take in sb; take sb in	deceive sb	Don't be **taken in** by products claiming to help you lose weight in a week.
take in sth; take sth in	include sth	The price **takes in** the cost of accommodation and meals.
	reduce the width (of clothing)	This dress is too big – I'll have to **take** it **in** a bit.
take in sb/sth; take sb/sth in	give a home to sb/sth	She often **takes in** stray animals.
take off	leave the ground	Our plane **took off** at 10.30.
take off sth; take sth off	remove (sth you are wearing)	**Take** your coat **off**.
		I forgot to **take off** my make-up.
take on sb; take sb on	employ sb	We're **taking on** fifty new employees this year.
take on sth; take sth on	agree to do sth	He's **taken on** too much work.
take out sb; take sb out	go somewhere with sb after inviting them	He was looking forward to **taking** his daughter **out** to a nice restaurant.
take over sth	take control of sth	Who's going to **take over** the shop when Mr Jones retires?
take to sb/sth	begin to like sb/sth	I **took to** Paul as soon as I met him.
take up sth; take sth up	start an activity	Glen has **taken up** painting.
	discuss sth	I'm going to **take** the matter **up** with my lawyer.
	start a job	She **took up** her first teaching post in 2008.
	accept	Are you going to **take up** their offer?
	take a period of time	Writing the report **took up** most of the weekend.

HAVE, TAKE, BRING

3

Practice

1 Complete the sentences. Use the phrases in the box.

> bring charges   bring to an end   have a shower   ~~have an operation~~   have any experience
> have fun   have lunch   have time   take a seat   take part   take place

0 Don't give him any supper – he's going to **have an operation**.
1 Do you .... of this type of work?
2 There will be a discussion afterwards – you can all .... in it.
3 If there is nothing else to discuss, I'd like to .... this meeting ....
4 .... and someone will be with you shortly.
5 I'm just going to .... – I'll be ready soon.
6 When will the tennis tournament ....?
7 Goodbye, enjoy the trip and ....!
8 We could .... in town while we're shopping if you like.
9 I think we .... for one more question before the Minister leaves.
10 They're going to .... of theft against him.

2 Complete the article. Use one verb in each gap.

There are many ways of making sure you do well in the FCE exam. If you're planning to (0) **take** the exam yourself and if you don't (1) .... previous experience of exams, read the following carefully:

- Make sure you (2) .... a good rest the night before the exam.
- Check that you know exactly where the exam is going to (3) .... place.
- You should not sit the exam on an empty stomach – make sure you (4) .... a good breakfast (but don't overdo it!).
- Don't forget to (5) .... a pen, a pencil and an eraser with you.
- Try to get to the examination centre in good time so you will (6) .... enough time to find the right room.
- As soon as you (7) .... your seat, (8) .... a deep breath, check your name and number on your answer sheet and (9) .... any errors to the attention of the supervisor immediately.
- Read the instructions carefully and (10) .... your time answering before the invigilator (11) .... the exam to a close.

3 Complete the sentences. Use after, back, in, off, on, out or up.

0 No, you won't be able to use your mobile after the plane takes **off**.
1 We ought to get rid of this table – it takes .... too much space.
2 If you're hot, take .... your jacket.
3 This meat smells awful! I'm taking it .... to the butcher!
4 John's always been difficult – he takes .... his dad.
5 You shouldn't take .... more responsibilities than you can handle.
6 It must be difficult to give .... teaching in order to travel.
7 We'll need to take .... more teachers for next year.
8 She took .... her glasses when she had her photograph taken.
9 Of course I believed him. He took me .... completely with his story.
10 Rachel took me .... to lunch the other day.

> CUSTOMER: Waiter, this steak tastes awful. **Take** it **back** to the chef!
> WAITER: I'm sorry, sir. The chef won't eat it either.

57

3e Suffixes (2)

Verb + -(a)tion, -(i)tion or -sion

- We normally use suffixes to change a word to a different part of speech. We can use the suffixes -(a)tion, -(i)tion and -sion to make nouns from verbs. Many of these nouns are abstract. Sometimes we use abstract nouns to make a sentence sound more formal:
  *It is important to **preserve** the rain forests.*
  *The **preservation** of the rain forests is important.*

- Abstract nouns are uncountable:
  *The **omission** of the victim's name was deliberate.*

- Some abstract nouns also have a concrete meaning. In these cases, they can be countable:
  *Your essay is full of errors and **omissions**.*

- Here is a list of nouns ending in -tion and -sion. You can check the meaning of any words you do not know in a dictionary:

Verb	Noun
abolish	abolition
accuse	accusation
apply	application
attend	attention
civilise	civilisation
compete	competition
conserve	conservation
demonstrate	demonstration
imagine	imagination
inflate	inflation
inspire	inspiration
oppose	opposition
revise	revision

For suffixes, see also: 1e, 4e, 10e, 12e, 13e

Practice

1 Complete the table. You can use a dictionary to help you.

Verb	Noun
divide	division
intend	
investigate	
omit	
organise	
preserve	
prevent	
produce	
repeat	
satisfy	
solve	
react	
tempt	

2 Complete the sentences. Use nouns formed from the verbs in the box.

attract cancel demonstrate explain hesitate
inform promote recognise suggest

0 For further ..information.. about the course, please contact Professor Richards.
1 The .... between Tom and Mary was immediate.
2 The award was in .... of her great acting ability.
3 I can say without .... that she's the best student I've ever had.
4 He couldn't give the court any .... for his strange behaviour.
5 I'd like a job with good .... prospects.
6 We're fully booked but sometimes there are last-minute ....

58

SUFFIXES (2) 3

3 Complete the second sentence so that it has a similar meaning to the first sentence, using the word given. Use between two and five words. Do not change the word given.

0 They use local labour when they construct roads.
   CARRY
   They *carry road construction* out with local labour.

1 I calculate the bill as being much less.
   COMES
   According to my .... to much less.

2 They were determined to educate their daughter the way they wanted.
   GIVE
   They were determined to .... they wanted.

3 Will he be fit enough to compete on Saturday?
   PART
   Will he be fit enough to .... on Saturday?

4 The authorities are planning to investigate the incident thoroughly.
   THOROUGH
   The authorities are planning to carry out .... of the incident.

5 Shortly afterwards, Dawson was invited to speak at the conference.
   GIVEN
   Shortly afterwards, Dawson was .... to speak at the conference.

6 They celebrate New Year's Day in the main square of the city.
   ARE
   The New Year's Day .... held in the main square of the city.

4 Complete the article. Use words formed from the words in CAPITALS at the end of some of the lines.

Globalisation

It is no (0) *exaggeration* to say that the world we live in has become a global village. Modern methods of (1) .... have made the world seem much smaller. The problems we face, such as (2) .... are not restricted to any one country alone. For example, the (3) .... of the rain forests in Brazil is everybody's problem; (4) ...., which is still a problem in many African countries, is a challenge for Europe, too. The extinction of rare species is a tragedy for the planet, while the (5) .... of oil supplies will shake the (6) .... of the world's economy.
The (7) .... of the environment is something that concerns all nations – rich or poor. However, uncontrolled economic (8) .... between strong and weak nations leads to the (9) .... of greater inequality between the rich and poor nations of the world. If we are to save the planet, we need to stop competing and start working together. (10) .... is the key to saving our 'global village'!

EXAGGERATE
COMMUNICATE
POLLUTE
DESTROY
STARVE

EXHAUST
FOUND
PROTECT
COMPETE
CREATE

COOPERATE

'I can resist everything except **temptation**.' OSCAR WILDE
'**Imagination** is more important than knowledge.' ALBERT EINSTEIN

4

AGENDA

Grammar
- **4a** Questions, question words
- **4b** Question tags
- **4c** Expressing agreement

Vocabulary
- **4d** *do* and *make*
- **4e** Suffixes (3)

Entry test

1 Choose the correct answer.

1 Who *paid you / did you pay* the money to?
2 What *did / have* you been doing all day?
3 Why *didn't / didn't you* give me a ring?
4 *What time / How long* does the lesson last?
5 *Who / Whose* painting won first prize – Picasso's or Van Gogh's?

Now look at **4a** on pages 62–63.

SCORE __ / 5

2 Choose the correct answer, A, B, C or D.

6 They'd rather go somewhere else, ... they?
   A hadn't   B didn't   C wouldn't   D would
7 You've got three sisters, ...?
   A have you got   B don't you   C isn't it   D haven't you
8 She needs to be more careful, ... she?
   A don't   B doesn't   C isn't   D needn't
9 You're having an operation next week, ...?
   A isn't it   B don't you have   C don't you   D aren't you
10 Let's go to the theatre tonight, ... we?
   A will   B do   C won't   D shall

Now look at **4b** on pages 64–65.

SCORE __ / 5

ENTRY TEST 4

3 Choose the correct answer, A, B, C or D.

11 Mary loves going to the cinema and ....
   A so I do   B so do I   C I do so   D I love, too
12 They haven't got a computer and ....
   A neither have I   B neither I have   C I haven't got   D I don't neither
13 'Did my son pass the test?' '..........'
   A I afraid no   B I afraid not   C I'm afraid to   D I'm afraid not
14 'I'd rather stay at home.' '.......... you?'
   A Would   B Wouldn't   C Had   D Hadn't
15 They never go skiing and I ....
   A haven't, too   B don't either   C do neither   D haven't either

Now look at **4c** on pages 66–68.   SCORE ...... / 5

4 Choose the correct answer, A, B, C or D.

16 We got in the car and made .... Chicago as fast as we could.
   A to   B at   C towards   D for
17 They grabbed the money and made ....
   A to   B from   C off   D on
18 We'd like to make the spare room .... a child's bedroom.
   A to   B up   C into   D for
19 You ought to .... more of an effort at school.
   A do   B take   C try   D make
20 They made a(n) .... on the radio – that's how I know about the accident.
   A announcement   B advertisement   C disturbance   D appearance

Now look at **4d** on pages 69–72.   SCORE 5 / 5

5 Choose the correct answer, A, B, C or D.

21 Under no .... will I allow such a thing.
   A situation   B situations   C circumstance   D circumstances
22 The economy needs more .... if it is to grow.
   A investigation   B insurance   C encouragement   D investment
23 They put the accident down to his ....
   A careless   B carelessly   C carelessness   D carefulness
24 What is the legal age of .... in your country?
   A retirement   B retiring   C retired   D retire
25 Her encouragement and support gave me the .... to carry on.
   A force   B warmth   C strength   D purpose

Now look at **4e** on pages 73–75.   SCORE 4 / 5

TOTAL SCORE ...... / 25

61

Grammar

4a Questions, question words

Questions about the subject

- When we ask questions about the subject of a sentence, the word order in the question is the same as in a statement:
  ~~Who did build this house?~~ ✗
  Who **built** this house? ✓
- We often use *what, who, which, whose* and *how many* in questions about the subject.

Questions about the object

- Questions about the object need an auxiliary verb (*do, have, be*, etc.) before the subject:
  Wren designed **this cathedral**.
  ~~Which cathedral Wren design?~~ ✗
  Which cathedral **did** Wren **design**? ✓
- We can use all question words in questions about the object.

Here is a summary of question words with examples:

Question word	Example: subject question	Example: object question
who	**Who** is teaching you?	**Who** do you know here? (**Whom** is very formal.)
what	**What** caused the problem?	**What** did you buy?
which	**Which** book sold most?	**Which** picture do you like?
whose	**Whose** book won the prize?	**Whose** book did you borrow?
how many	**How many** pupils came to the lesson?	**How many** people did you see?
how much	**How much** money remained in the account?	**How much** sugar do you need?
how		**How** do I get to your house?
why		**Why** did you get up so late?
when		**When** did you go to England?
how far		**How far** did you walk?
how long		**How long** does it take to get there?
how often		**How often** do you go swimming?

Prepositions in questions

Note the change in the position of a preposition in questions about the object:
I gave the book **to** John.
Who did you give the book **to**?
To whom did you give the book? (very formal)

what or *which*?

We use *what* when the choice is open. We use *which* when there is a limited choice:
What colour do you like? (open choice)
Which colour do you prefer – red or blue? (limited choice)
What countries have you visited? (open choice)
Which countries in South America have you visited? (limited choice)

QUESTIONS, QUESTION WORDS 4

PRACTICE

1 Put the words in the correct order.

0 where / you / born / were?
   Where were you born?

1 where / you / did / grow up?
   ....

2 what / like / did / you / doing / at school?
   ....

3 what / like / were / you / as / a child?
   ....

4 when / decide / you / did / an actor / become / to?
   ....

5 how / parents / your / did / react?
   ....

6 what / say / when / told / did / you / they / them?
   ....

7 how / you / when / old / left / were / you / home?
   ....

8 what / job / first / your / in the theatre / was?
   ....

9 what / of / directors / working / kind / with / you / do / like?
   ....

10 how / you / have / many / made / films?
    ....

2 Write a question about the underlined information in each sentence. Use question words.

0 Joe left the door open.
   Who left the door open?

1 We live in the old town.
   ....

2 I gave the book to Valerie.
   ....

3 Michael lent me the money.
   ....

4 I got married twenty years ago.
   ....

5 I like the red dress.
   ....

6 I'd like the green pullover, please.
   ....

7 I like big woolly pullovers.
   ....

8 Heather phoned Harry.
   ....

9 Heather phoned Harry.
   ....

10 She said nothing.
    ....

11 I go to the cinema at least once a week.
    ....

12 The journey takes about six hours.
    ....

13 I usually get to work by bus.
    ....

14 He keeps the key in that box.
    ....

15 There's a litre of milk left.
    ....

63

4b Question tags

Form

- We use question tags at the end of a statement:
  *It's Monday today, **isn't it**?*
- The general pattern for using question tags is:
  - positive sentence + negative question tag
    *She likes Beethoven, **doesn't she**?*
  - negative sentence + positive question tag
    *She doesn't like Beethoven, **does she**?*
- We form question tags with an auxiliary verb (*be, have, do,* etc.) + a personal pronoun (*you, she, they,* etc.). If there is an auxiliary verb in the statement, we repeat it in the question tag:
  *You're from Greece, **aren't you**?*
  *They don't speak English, **do they**?*
- The tense of the auxiliary verb agrees with the tense of the main verb:
  *She came home late, **didn't she**?* (past simple)
- If there is a modal verb in the statement, we repeat it in the question tag:
  *It shouldn't cost that much, **should it**?*
- After main verbs without an auxiliary verb or a modal, we use *do* or *did* in the question tag:
  *She plays the piano, **doesn't she**?*
  *You told him the truth, **didn't you**?*

Special cases

- The question tag for *I am* is *aren't I?* For *I'm not,* we use *am I?*
  *I'm your best friend, **aren't I**?*
- The question tag for *let's* is *shall we?*
  *Let's surprise them, **shall we**?*
- After imperatives, we use *will you?*
  *Turn the sound down, **will you**?*
- After *there is/was/*etc., we use *there*:
  *There isn't any cake left, **is there**?*
- After *somebody, someone, everybody, everyone, no one,* etc., we use *they*:
  *Everybody's sleeping, **aren't they**?*
- After *nothing, something* and *everything*, we use *it*:
  *Nothing happened, **did it**?*

Here is a summary of verbs used in question tags:

Verb in statement	Verb in tag	Example
statement without auxiliary or modal	do/did	You like him, **don't you**?
be	be	This is yours, **isn't it**?
have (= possess)	do	You don't have a watch, **do you**?
have got	have	You haven't got a brother, **have you**?
have (auxiliary)	have	You haven't seen Joe, **have you**?
do	do	You do aerobics, **don't you**?
can	can	She can swim, **can't she**?
could	could	We could do better, **couldn't we**?
may	might	It may rain, **mightn't it**?
will	will	You won't tell them, **will you**?
would	would	He'd like that, **wouldn't he**?
needn't	need	We needn't come, **need we**?
must	must	We mustn't make a noise, **must we**?
have to	do	We have to work harder, **don't we**?
need to	do	She needs to be there, **doesn't she**?

4 QUESTION TAGS

Use

We use question tags:

- when we expect the person we are speaking to to agree with us:
  *She's amazing, **isn't she**?* (The speaker expects the answer 'yes'. The speaker's voice falls on the tag.)
- like real questions, when we are not sure about something and want to check:
  *You come from Italy, **don't you**?* (The speaker's voice rises on the tag when it's a 'real' question.)

PRACTICE

1 Complete the sentences. Use question tags.

0 You're coming with us tomorrow, *aren't you*?
1 Your dad does the cooking, ……………?
2 There isn't much we can do about it, ……………?
3 'It's a beautiful day, ……………?' 'Yes. Let's go for a walk, ……………?'
4 'You've got a bike, ……………?' 'Yes. You no longer have yours, ……………?'
5 'You weren't cheating in the test, ……………?' 'No! I would never cheat, ……………?'
6 You don't know his secret, ……………?
7 You could swim when you were three, ……………?
8 You'd rather stay in, ……………?
9 'She lost her temper, ……………?' 'Yes, but she shouldn't have, ……………?'
10 Everybody thinks it's my fault, ……………?
11 I'm fat, ……………?
12 Stop asking so many questions, ……………?
13 Nothing happened after I left, ……………?
14 Keith hasn't been doing well at school lately, ……………?
15 They haven't announced the results yet, ……………?

2 Complete the sentences. Use question tags and any other words necessary.

0 You enjoyed the film. You say:
   'The film *was great, wasn't it*?'
1 Your friend has just read a book which you like, too. You say:
   'It's a(n) ……………?'
2 You look at your watch. It's early. You say:
   'We've got ……………?'
3 You're thirsty. You like tea. You say:
   'Let's have ……………?'
4 You want to make sure your name is on the list. You say:
   'I'm ……………?'
5 You want to go out for a walk. You say:
   'Let's ……………?'
6 You want to check if the train leaves from Platform 2. You say:
   'The train ……………?'
7 You can't reach the salt. Ask someone to pass it to you:
   'Pass ……………?'
8 Your little sister has got cake crumbs on her sweater. You say:
   'You've ……………?'
9 You are washing the dishes when the door bell rings. You say:
   'Answer the door, ……………?'
10 You want to check that you are leaving tomorrow morning, as agreed. You ask:
   'We're ……………?'

65

4c Expressing agreement

Short answers

- We often answer *yes/no* questions with short answers, using an auxiliary verb:
  '*Can* you come?' 'Yes, I *can*.'
- In short answers, we repeat the auxiliary or modal verb that we use in the question:
  '*Have* you got a pet?' 'Yes, I *have*.'
  '*Are* they good friends?' 'Yes, they *are*.'
  '*Does* she like acting?' 'No, she *doesn't*.'
  '*Will* you be there?' 'No, I *won't*.'
  '*Would* you ever lie to your best friend?' 'No, I *wouldn't*.'
  '*Did* you have a good time?' 'Yes, we *did*.'
  '*Was* Pete working when you got up?' 'No, he *wasn't*.'
- The short answer for *Shall we …?* is *Yes, let's./No, let's not.*
  '*Shall we* have a party?' 'Yes, *let's*.'

Short answers with *so* and *not*

- We can also answer *yes/no* questions with *think/be afraid/hope/suppose*/etc. + *so*.
  '*Is he coming with us?*' 'I *think so*.'
- To give a negative answer, we use the negative form of the verb:
  '*Is he coming with us?*' 'I *don't think so*.'
- But: after *be afraid*, *hope* and *suppose*, we use the affirmative form of the verb and *not* instead of *so* at the end:

Question	Answer
Are they good friends?	I think so./I don't think so.
Do they get on?	I think so./I don't think so.
Do you think they'll come to the party?	I hope so./I hope not.
Do we have to pay?	I'm afraid so.
Can I come with you?	I'm afraid not.
Are you going to lend them the money?	I suppose so.
You're not going to help them, are you?	I suppose not.

Expressing agreement with *so* and *neither*

- We can use *so* and *neither* to express agreement with something.
- We use *so* + auxiliary/modal verb to express agreement with affirmative sentences:
  '*Bill likes it.*' '*So do I.*'
  Bill likes it and *so do I.* ✓
  ~~Bill likes it and *I also*.~~ ✗
- We use *neither* + auxiliary/modal verb to express agreement with negative sentences:
  '*She hasn't got any money.*' '*Neither have I.*'
  She hasn't got any money and *neither have I.* ✓
  ~~She hasn't got any money and *I haven't*.~~ ✗

Statement	Reply (agreement)
I've got hundreds of CDs.	So have I.
We usually go camping in the summer.	So do we.
I don't have a photo of her.	Neither do I.
They didn't pass the test.	Neither did I.
John hasn't arrived yet.	Neither has Mary.
Steve isn't coming to the rehearsal.	Neither is Michael.
She hasn't finished her homework.	Neither have I.

4 EXPRESSING AGREEMENT

Echo questions

- We often use short questions to confirm that we have heard what the other person has said, or to show interest in what they are saying. These questions are called echo questions and they do not need an answer.
- The pattern for echo questions is:
  - positive statement → positive echo question:
    '*I have been* to the States.' '*Have you*?'
  - negative statement → negative echo question:
    'But *I haven't been* to Australia.' '*Haven't you*?'
- The pronoun we use in the echo question agrees with the subject of the statement. For example, when the subject of the statement is an object, animal, etc., we use *it* in the echo question. When the subject is a group of people, things, etc., we use *they*:
  'This bike is very expensive.' '*Is it*?'
  'United will win on Saturday.' '*Will they*?'
- As with all questions, the auxiliary/modal verb that we use in echo questions agrees with the verb/tense in the statement:

Statement	Echo question
I can come by taxi.	Can you?
I can't swim.	Can't you?
Lisa doesn't play the piano.	Doesn't she?
The Smiths haven't arrived yet.	Haven't they?
I've got two dogs.	Have you?
Mark isn't coming.	Isn't he?
Jo could walk when she was one.	Could she?
You should be more careful.	Should I?
You ought to be more careful.	Should I?
We shouldn't work so hard.	Shouldn't we?
I'll do the washing-up.	Will you?
I won't be able to join you.	Won't you?
I'd rather stay at home.	Would you?
I'd never lie to you.	Wouldn't you?

PRACTICE

1 Complete the short answers.

0 A: Would you tell him the truth if he asked?
  B: Yes, *I would*.
1 A: Have you done the washing-up?
  B: Yes, ...
2 A: Does he need help?
  B: No, ...
3 A: Would you like to come with me?'
  B: Yes, I think ....
4 A: Are you going to visit Owen?
  B: No, ...
5 A: Do I look all right?
  B: Yes, ...
6 A: Could you climb that wall if you had to?
  B: Yes, ... so.
7 A: Had you been waiting long before they arrived?
  B: No, ...
8 A: Can Bob come to the cinema, too?
  B: No, I'm afraid ....

2 Reply to the statements. Use echo questions.

0 A: She didn't get the job.
  B: *Didn't she?*
1 A: I can't use this computer.
  B: ....
2 A: Some parrots live longer than humans.
  B: ....
3 A: I'd wait a bit longer if I were you.
  B: ....
4 A: I won't invite him to my party.
  B: ....
5 A: She's got a very rich uncle.
  B: ....
6 A: It won't work without petrol!
  B: ....
7 A: He always makes me laugh.
  B: ....
8 A: She never says she's sorry.
  B: ....

4 EXPRESSING AGREEMENT

3 Complete the conversations. Use an auxiliary or modal verb.

0 A: She hasn't finished painting her house yet.
   B: Hasn't she?
1 A: I haven't got a computer yet.
   B: ………… you?
2 A: I ………… lend you my bike if you want.
   B: Can you? Thanks!
3 A: You shouldn't take more than three of those pills a day.
   B: ………… I?
4 A: We have to leave now.
   B: ………… we?
5 A: I'd rather stay at home tonight.
   B: ………… you?
6 A: We ………… have done more to help him.
   B: Could we?
7 A: You don't have to invite them.
   B: ………… I?
8 A: They ………… be able to visit this year.
   B: Won't they?
9 A: She should apologise.
   B: ………… she?
10 A: I'm afraid he ………… got a clue.
   B: Hasn't he?

4 Match 1–10 with a–k to make short exchanges.

0 I'm not going to take part in the play. — f
1 They've got a lovely house in the country.
2 I like going to the theatre.
3 I don't really enjoy thrillers.
4 I've never seen such a huge car before!
5 Mike didn't do his homework.
6 I arrived before Ken and Brigit.
7 They can't speak French.
8 You shouldn't lose your temper.
9 I'd love to be in Hawaii right now!
10 You should save some money if you want to go to India with them.

a So did I.
b Neither should you.
c Neither can she.
d So should you.
e So do I.
f Neither am I.
g So have we.
h Neither do I.
i Neither have I.
j So would I.
k Neither did Tony.

HUSBAND: I think our son got his intelligence from me, don't you?
WIFE: Yes, **I think so**. I've still got mine!

68

Vocabulary

4d do and make

do or make?

Here are some common phrases with *do* and *make*:

Phrase	Example
do	
do your best	I **did my best** – what else could I do?
do damage	Luckily, the storm didn't **do** much **damage**.
do (an) exercise	I try and **do** a bit of **exercise** every day.
do harm	A mistake like that will **do** his business a lot of **harm**.
do homework	I **did my homework**.
do (the) housework	She **does the housework**.
do research	They will have to **do** more **research** into the subject.
do shopping	I had some **shopping to do** before I came home.
do science (a subject at school)	We **do science** every day at school.
do well/badly	She's **doing** very **well** at school, isn't she?
do work	Let's **do** some **work** and then we can go out to dinner.
make	
make an attempt	She **made an attempt** to break the world record.
make a/some cake/pizza/coffee/etc.	I'm just **making some coffee** – would you like some?
make an effort	You'll have to **make** more of **an effort** if you want to succeed.
make an excuse	The pupil **made an excuse** after being late for class.
make a fortune	He **made a fortune** out of importing expensive cars.
make fun of sb/sth	You shouldn't **make fun of** the way people talk.
make a living	It's hard to **make** a decent **living** as an artist.
make a mess (of sth)	I tried to fix the car myself but **made a** complete **mess of** it.
make a mistake	Hopefully, she won't **make** the same **mistake** again.
make money	She **made** a lot of **money** as a model.
make the most (of sth)	**Make the most of** this opportunity.
make (a) noise	Who **made** that **noise**?
make notes	They **made notes** during the professor's speech.
make an offer	I'll **make** you **an offer** you can't refuse.
make progress	Have you **made** any **progress** with your project?
make sense (of sth)	I can't **make sense of** what you're saying.
make your way	We slowly **made our way** back to the campsite.

4 DO AND MAKE

Phrasal verbs with *do* and *make*

Here are some common phrasal verbs with *do* and *make*:

Phrasal verb	Meaning/Use	Example
do		
do away with sb/sth	abolish, get rid of sb/sth	It's time we **did away with** these rules and regulations.
do sb out of sth	dishonestly stop sb from having or keeping sth	She was trying to **do me out of** my promotion.
do without sth	live or do sth without a particular thing	I'll just have to **do without** a car – I can't afford one.
do up sth; do sth up	fasten sth	I can't **do** my laces **up**.
	repair and decorate sth	They **did up** the house and then sold it.
(could) do with sth	need or want sth	I **could do with** something to eat.
(have/be to) do with sb/sth	have a connection with sb/sth	The problem **has** nothing **to do with** me.
make		
make away with sth	steal sth and take it away with you	The robbers **made away with** her jewellery.
make for sth	go in the direction of a particular place	The two robbers **made for** the window.
make sth of sb/sth	have a particular opinion or understanding about sb/sth	What do you **make of** their proposal?
make off (with sth)	(steal sth and) leave quickly	They attacked him and **made off with** his watch.
make out sth; make sth out	be just able to see or hear sth	I can't **make out** her handwriting.
make up sth	form sth	Tourism **makes up** seventy percent of their income.
make up sth; make sth up	invent a story, an excuse, etc.	She **made up** a silly excuse for being late.

PRACTICE

1 Write the words and phrases in the box in the correct column. Some of them are not in the table on page 69 – you can use a dictionary to help you.

> ~~a bad impression~~   a cup of coffee
> a decision   a difference   a job   a living
> a mistake   a phone call   a profit
> a suggestion   an appointment   an offer
> badly   French   fun of somebody
> good   harm   housework   maths
> money   noise   research   some work
> something for a living   the bed   the dishes
> the washing-up   well   your hair
> your homework

do	make
	a bad impression

DO AND MAKE 4

2 Match the phrases (1-10) with their definitions (a-k).

0 make the most of sth — i
1 make notes
2 do badly
3 make an attempt
4 make fun of sth
5 do harm
6 do exercise
7 make sense of sth
8 make a fortune
9 do research
10 do your best

a try
b understand sth because it's clear
c investigate or study a subject very carefully
d write down information
e try as hard as possible
f laugh at sth
g earn a lot of money
h damage
i gain the greatest possible advantage from sth
j do sports or physical activities to stay healthy
k be unsuccessful

*Both players **made for** the ball at the same time.*

3 Complete the sentences. Use the correct form of *do* or *make*.

0 They're going to buy that old country house and ...*do*... it up.
1 Her job has something to .... with marketing.
2 Girls .... up half of the students in our school.
3 We'll just have to .... without the report if they can't get it to us in time.
4 The baby's asleep, so please try not to .... a noise when you go upstairs.
5 The government are going to .... away with the old tax law.
6 When the bell rang, the students .... for the door.
7 He's currently .... research into the causes of cancer.
8 Speak louder – I can't .... out what you're saying.
9 .... up your coat – it's cold.
10 Her cousins were trying to .... her out of her inheritance.
11 The two men .... off with the old lady's handbag.
12 Just .... your best to explain the problem – I'm sure he'll understand.
13 I think you should forgive him – we all .... mistakes.
14 It's about time you .... some exercise!
15 I don't know what to .... of Christine's behaviour.
16 I could have .... with a bit more help.
17 I don't believe him. He's .... it all up!
18 We usually .... our shopping on Saturdays.

71

4 DO AND MAKE

4 Complete the questionnaire. Use the correct form of *do* or *make*. Then answer the questions about you.

Question	Answer
Work	
0 What would you like to ...*do*... for a living?	....
1 Is .... a lot of money important to you?	....
2 Are you willing to .... your best in order to succeed?	....
3 Would you accept a well-paid job if you knew it might .... serious harm to your health?	....
4 Would you .... a job which involved responsibility for other people's lives?	....
School	
5 Do you always .... your homework?	....
6 Which subject do you .... well in at school?	....
7 How do you feel when you .... mistakes in English?	....
8 What do you do if you .... badly in an exam?	....
9 What kind of exercises do you like .... in class?	....
10 Do you often .... notes in class?	....

5 Complete the story. Use one word in each gap.

'OK, you may (0) ...*do*... your shirt up now,' said Doctor Jones. He had just given me a thorough examination and was (1) .... detailed notes on a big sheet of paper. 'What do you (2) .... of it all, Doctor?' I asked anxiously. 'Why am I so stressed out?'

'Well, for a start, I think you could (3) .... with a good rest. What do you (4) .... for a living?' he asked. 'Well,' I replied, 'I (5) .... a living by designing computer programs. Recently, I have worked late a few nights to (6) .... some work for an important client and I think I (7) .... a bit of a mess of it all.' The doctor agreed overwork had a lot to (8) .... with the stress I was feeling. I had also (9) .... the mistake of not eating healthily. In fact, my diet was mostly made (10) .... of coffee, hamburgers and chips. He said I should try and do (11) .... coffee for a few days and (12) .... a serious effort to cut down on junk food.

'There's no need to **do housework**. After four years, the dirt doesn't get worse.' QUENTIN CRISP

4e Suffixes (3)

We normally use suffixes to change a word to a different part of speech.

See also: 1e, 3e, 10e, 12e, 13e

Abstract nouns

- Abstract nouns express an idea, feeling, experience or state rather than an object, person or particular instance. Abstract nouns are uncountable:
  *There **is** no reliable **evidence**.* ✓
  *There **are** no reliable **evidences**.* ✗
  *They were satisfied with the new **equipment**.* ✓
  *They were satisfied with the new **equipments**.* ✗

- Some abstract nouns also have a concrete meaning. In these cases, they can be countable:
  ***Appearances** can be deceptive.*
  *We should consider all her **strengths** and **weaknesses**.*

-ance, -ence

- We add *-ance* or *-ence* to many verbs to form abstract nouns.
  accept + -ance → acceptance
  exist + -ence → existence

For abstract nouns ending in -(a)tion, -(i)tion or -sion, see 3e

- We can form abstract nouns from many adjectives that end in *-ant* or *-ent* by changing the final *-t* to *-ce*:
  fragrant → fragrance   dependent → dependence

-ment

- We also add *-ment* to many verbs to form abstract nouns:
  agree + -ment → agreement

- Note that many nouns ending in *-ment* are not abstract:
  document, monument, ointment

-ness

- We add *-ness* to many adjectives to form abstract nouns:
  good + -ness → goodness

- Some of these nouns can be countable:
  Their suggested plan has both strengths and weaknesses.

-th

- We use *-th* with numbers (except 1, 2 and 3), to form ordinal numbers:
  fourth   fifteenth   eightieth

- We also use *-th* to form abstract nouns, often connected with size or qualities:
  growth   warmth

Here are some examples of abstract nouns with the suffixes *-ance*, *-ence*, *-ment*, *-ness* and *-th*:

-ance	-ence	-ment	-ness	-th
acceptance	absence	achievement	brightness	breadth
annoyance	confidence	advertisement	carelessness	depth
appearance	correspondence	announcement	emptiness	fortieth
arrogance	defence	commitment	greatness	growth
avoidance	emergence	disappointment	happiness	health
distance	existence	embarrassment	kindness	hundredth
disturbance	intelligence	employment	loneliness	length
entrance	occurrence	encouragement	sleepiness	strength
importance	offence	enjoyment	tenderness	twentieth
insurance	patience	entertainment	tightness	warmth
reluctance	presence	fulfilment	ugliness	wealth
resistance	violence	movement	weakness	width

4 SUFFIXES (3)

PRACTICE

1 Complete the table. You can use a dictionary to help you.

Verb/Adjective	Noun	Verb/Adjective	Noun
inherit	*inheritance*	improve	....
convenient	....	willing	....
clumsy	....	retire	....
obey	....	silent	....
invest	....	disappoint	....
develop	....	excite	....
kind	....	polite	....
effective	....	argue	....
fair	....	punish	....
prefer	....	selfish	....
innocent	....	grow	....

2 Complete the expressions and quotes. Use the correct form of a noun formed from the word in brackets.

0 *Appearances* (appear) are deceptive.
1 .... (absent) makes the heart grow fonder.
2 Money can't buy you .... (happy).
3 Experience tells you what to do; .... (confident) allows you to do it.
4 .... (ignorant) is bliss.
5 .... (kind): a language the deaf can hear and the blind can see.
6 .... (patient) is a virtue.
7 .... (silent) is golden.

3 Are the underlined nouns countable (C) or uncountable (U)? Choose the correct answer.

0 His determination is his greatest strength. **(C)** U
1 It will take time for you to regain your strength. C U
2 There has been a significant movement towards organic food. C U
3 There's been no significant movement in the peace talks, I'm afraid. C U
4 Unfortunately, he showed no signs of improvement. C U
5 Well done! This is a great improvement on your previous work. C U
6 You'll get a great sense of achievement when you pass. C U
7 That medal was his greatest achievement. C U
8 Her inability to control her temper is her main weakness. C U
9 He didn't want to show any sign of weakness. C U
10 This program is an exciting new development. C U
11 You also need to think about opportunities for career development. C U

SUFFIXES (3) 4

4 Make adjectives from the following nouns.

0 strength — *strong*
1 intelligence — ....
2 carelessness — ....
3 patience — ....
4 depth — ....
5 arrogance — ....
6 ugliness — ....
7 width — ....
8 emptiness — ....
9 confidence — ....
10 million — ....

5 Complete the table.

Verb /Adjective	Noun	Verb/Adjective	Noun
great	*greatness*	insure	....
....	disturbance	....	annoyance
correspond	....	empty	....
emerge	....	....	defence
....	sleepiness	commit	....
resist	....	....	fulfilment

6 Complete the article. Use words formed from the words in CAPITALS at the end of some of the lines.

The SWOT analysis

These are hard times: **(0)** *unemployment* is growing and it is particularly high amongst young people. Economic **(1)** .... is slowing down, so it's getting more and more difficult to find a job. People often reach their **(2)** .... birthday without ever having had a regular job and this can lead to depression or lack of **(3)** .... But there are strategies which can help you cope.

I have found the SWOT test really useful. It's a planning method that is often used in **(4)** .... training but I've found it helpful in problem-solving generally. All you need is a piece of paper, a pencil and a little **(5)** ....! First of all, the 'S': make a list of your **(6)** .... – you've probably got more of these than you realise. They may include, for example, your qualifications, creativity or **(7)** .... Then make a second list with your **(8)** ....: for example, lack of experience or **(9)** .... to accept new ideas. Then, the 'O': think of all the opportunities for finding work, for example job **(10)** .... and social networking sites. Finally, the 'T' in SWOT: threats; for example, competition. Good luck!

EMPLOY
GROW

THIRTY
SELF-CONFIDENT

MANAGE

PATIENT
STRONG
OPEN-MINDED
WEAK
RELUCTANT
ADVERTISE

'There is nothing which we receive with so much **reluctance** as advice.' JOSEPH ADDISON

Exam practice 2

Part 1

For questions **1–12**, read the text below and decide which answer (**A**, **B**, **C** or **D**) best fits each gap. There is an example at the beginning (**0**).

The mystery of the *Marie Celeste*

We caught sight of the *Marie Celeste* drifting in the mid-Atlantic on December 5th, 1872. The ship looked damaged, (0).......... the captain said that the three of us would (1).......... to board her at once in order to investigate and (2).......... back any information we (3).......... get hold of. We were (4).......... to climb on board without too much difficulty but we couldn't see any sign of life anywhere. (5).......... the ship's small lifeboat was missing, we all thought the crew had abandoned ship. Some navigational instruments which a ship of that kind should (6).......... had on board were also missing. The crew (7).......... have had much time to abandon ship (8).......... they hadn't taken any of their personal belongings with them. We found the ship's log and (9).........., we were able to find a lot of useful information – it really helped us in our (10).......... . The last time the captain of the *Marie Celeste* had written something in the ship's log was November 21st. Something must have taken (11).......... between this date and December 5th. The captain, Benjamin Briggs, had a lot of experience of the high seas, so what had forced him to (12).......... the decision to abandon ship in the middle of nowhere?

0	A	because	B	as	C	since	**D**	**so**
1	A	must	B	have	C	ought	D	should
2	A	fetch	B	get	C	bring	D	put
3	A	would	B	could	C	should	D	must
4	A	possible	B	managed	C	able	D	successful
5	A	Owing	B	Since	C	Because of	D	As a result
6	A	have	B	had	C	be	D	to
7	A	mustn't	B	couldn't	C	oughtn't	D	didn't have to
8	A	owing to	B	due to	C	as	D	as a result
9	A	sadly	B	secondly	C	unfortunately	D	consequently
10	A	investigation	B	intention	C	demonstration	D	application
11	A	part	B	place	C	time	D	control
12	A	bring	B	do	C	take	D	have

SCORE / 12

Part 2

For questions **13–24**, read the text below and think of the word which best fits each gap. Use only **one** word in each gap. There is an example at the beginning (**0**).

Testing times

We always (0) ....take.... a lot of tests at school and although I am generally a good student, I don't do very (13) .... in exams. I don't know why. I generally (14) .... all my homework and I am very accurate but in tests I (15) .... a lot of mistakes. I always do (16) .... best, but I get very nervous and as a (17) ...., I don't think very clearly. After the test, I can usually correct my own mistakes, so it can't be because I don't know enough – it must (18) .... something to do (19) .... the lack of confidence I feel in exam situations. If I am (20) .... to answer all the questions at home but not under exam conditions, the problem (21) .... be stress related. If students receive poorer marks due (22) .... stress, wouldn't it be a good idea to have fewer exams? Do schools really (23) .... to test us all the time in (24) .... to find out how much we know? Surely there are other ways.

SCORE _____ / 12

Part 3

For questions **25–34**, read the text below. Use the word given in capitals at the end of some of the lines to form a word that fits in the gap **in the same line**. There is an example at the beginning (**0**).

I have been unemployed for a year. I've sent dozens of job ⁽⁰⁾ **applications**, with a detailed CV listing all my ⁽²⁵⁾.........., but I still haven't received a single phone call or ⁽²⁶⁾.......... to attend an interview. Sometimes employers don't even bother to reply to my emails. I know there's a lot of ⁽²⁷⁾.......... and that ⁽²⁸⁾.......... is really hard to find but I do have a Master's Degree in Energy and Environmental Studies.

APPLY
QUALIFY
INVITE

COMPETE
EMPLOY

For my dissertation, I did original research into energy ⁽²⁹⁾.......... in buildings. On the course, we also studied ways of saving animals in danger of extinction. So, I would be ideally suited to a position in a ⁽³⁰⁾.......... company or an ecological ⁽³¹⁾..........

CONSERVE

CONSTRUCT
ORGANISE

Although it is true that I am inexperienced, it isn't my fault I have never had a job. I actually like work: I think one of my personal ⁽³²⁾.......... is my enthusiasm and my ⁽³³⁾.......... to the environment. I'm approaching my ⁽³⁴⁾.......... birthday now and I'm beginning to wonder if I will ever find a job.

STRONG
COMMIT
THIRTY

Part 4

For questions **35–42**, complete the second sentence so that it has a similar meaning to the first sentence, using the word given. **Do not change the word given.** You must use between **two** and **five** words, including the word given. Here is an example (0).

Example:

0 She put on thick socks because she wanted to keep warm.
   AS
   She put on thick socks .... *so as to keep* .... warm.

35 A friend is looking after the baby while we're out.
   CARE
   A friend .... the baby while we're out.

36 It's possible that she didn't hear what I said.
   MIGHT
   She .... what I said.

37 The noise outside made it difficult for me to concentrate.
   BECAUSE
   I couldn't .... the noise outside.

38 The burglar wore gloves so as not to leave any fingerprints.
   ORDER
   The burglar wore gloves .... avoid leaving fingerprints.

39 Why didn't you have your bicycle brakes repaired immediately?
   OUGHT
   You .... your bicycle brakes repaired immediately.

40 It was raining, so they cancelled the match.
   OWING
   The match was cancelled .... rain.

41 An accident led to the road being closed.
   RESULT
   There was an accident and ...., the road was closed.

42 They let me take the rest of the day off.
   ALLOWED
   I .... the rest of the day off.

SCORE / 16

TOTAL SCORE / 50

5

AGENDA

Grammar
- **5a** Zero, first and second conditionals
- **5b** Third conditional, mixed conditionals
- **5c** wish, if only

Vocabulary
- **5d** want, expect, love, can't bear, etc.
- **5e** Prefixes (2)

Entry test

1 Choose the correct answer.

1 If you *don't / won't* hurry, you'll miss the train.
2 What *do / can* I do if she refuses to listen to me?
3 His French won't improve *provided / unless* he studies harder.
4 If I *have / had* more time, I would take up tennis.
5 If I *were / would be* you, I'd buy a new suit.

Now look at **5a** on pages 82–83.

SCORE /5

2 Choose the correct answer, A, B, C or D.

6 I .... be happy to advise you if you'd asked me.
   A will be   B would be   C had been   D would have been
7 If she .... her driving test, she would have bought a car.
   A passed   B has passed   C had passed   D would have passed
8 I wouldn't have lent him the money if he .... desperate.
   A isn't   B hasn't been   C hadn't been   D wouldn't have been
9 If you'd run faster, you .... the bus.
   A might catch   B would catch   C will have caught   D could have caught
10 If I hadn't worked hard when I was young, I .... where I am now.
   A wouldn't be   B haven't been   C won't have been   D hadn't been

Now look at **5b** on pages 84–85.

SCORE 2 /5

80

3 Choose the correct answer, A, B, C or D.

11 I wish I .... more money.
   A have   **B** had   **C** have had   **D** will have

12 If only I .... a little bit taller.
   A be   **B** will be   **C** were   **D** have been

13 I do wish you .... make less noise.
   A to   **B** will   **C** did   **D** would

14 I wish we .... on the same flight tomorrow.
   A will travel   **B** would travel   **C** had travelled   **D** were travelling

15 If only I .... the chance to study when I was younger.
   A had   **B** would have   **C** was having   **D** had had

Now look at **5c** on pages 86–88.

SCORE /5

4 Choose the correct answer, A, B, C or D.

16 I'm .... to pass all my exams at the first attempt.
   A wishing   **B** hoping   **C** wanting   **D** desiring

17 Farmers are .... a good harvest this year.
   A waiting   **B** expecting   **C** hoping   **D** looking forward

18 I'm really looking forward .... to camp again this summer.
   A to go   **B** to going   **C** for going   **D** for me going

19 She's very keen .... tennis.
   A for   **B** in   **C** on   **D** at

20 I can't stand .... to people complaining!
   A listen   **B** listening   **C** to listening   **D** for listening

Now look at **5d** on pages 89–91.

SCORE /5

5 Complete the words in the following sentences. Use the prefixes in the box.

   de   ex   mono   multi   semi

21 The detective managed to ....code the message.
22 Samantha is through to the ....-final of the women's singles.
23 Sarah is his ....-wife. They got divorced five years ago.
24 This is a(n) ....lingual English dictionary – all the definitions are in English.
25 Jamie was wearing a(n) ....coloured shirt.

Now look at **5e** on pages 92–93.

SCORE /5

TOTAL SCORE /25

Grammar

5a Zero, first and second conditionals

Conditional sentences have two parts: the conditional clause, which begins with *if* (or other words such as *when*, *unless*, etc.), and the main clause. Conditional sentences follow basic patterns.

See also: 5b

Zero conditional

- We use the zero conditional to talk about things that are always or generally true as a result of an action.
- To form zero conditional sentences, we use:
  if + present simple → present simple:
  When water **freezes**, it **turns** to ice.
  If you **mix** red and blue, you **get** purple.
- The conditional clause can come before or after the main clause. When it comes first, we put a comma after it:
  When I travel by boat, I often get sick.
  I often get sick when I travel by boat.

First conditional

- We use the first conditional to talk about possible actions or events in the future.
- To form first conditional sentences, we use:
  if + present simple → *will* + infinitive:
  If it **rains**, we**'ll stay** at home.
- Other structures are also possible in first conditional sentences:
  - *if* + present simple → modal verb
    If you **promise** to behave yourself, you **can come**.
  - *if* + present simple → *be going to*
    If you **don't work** hard, you**'re going to fail**.
  - *if* + present simple → imperative
    If you **need** anything, just **ask**.
  - *if* + present continuous → *will*/modal verb/imperative
    If you**'re leaving**, I**'ll come** with you.
  - *if* + present perfect → *will*/modal verb/imperative
    If you**'ve finished** your homework, you **can go** out.
  - *if* + present perfect continuous → *will*/modal verb/imperative
    If she**'s been waiting** for ages, she **may get** worried.
  - imperative + *and*/*or* → *will*/modal verb
    Eat less **and** you**'ll lose** weight.
- We can also use the following words and phrases in first conditional sentences:
  - (*just*) *in case*: This means 'because it is possible that' and it usually comes after the main clause:
    Ann will bring you a coat **in case** it gets cold.
  - *provided*/*providing* (*that*), *as long as*: These phrases mean 'on condition that':
    Provided you rest, you'll feel better soon.
  - *unless*: This means 'if not':
    If you **don't leave** now, you'll be late.
    → **Unless** you **leave** now, you'll be late.

Second conditional

- We use the second conditional to talk about unlikely events or situations in the future, or improbable/impossible events or situations in the present.
- To form second conditional sentences, we use:
  if + past simple + *would* + infinitive:
  If I **had** enough money, I **would retire**.
- In the main clause, we can also use *could* or *might* instead of *would*:
  If I **lost** my job, I **might go** abroad for a while.
- In the *if* clause, we can use *were* instead of *was*:
  I'd quit my job if I **were** rich.

82

ZERO, FIRST AND SECOND CONDITIONALS

5

PRACTICE

1 Complete the sentences. Use the correct form of the verbs in brackets.

0 If she *phones* (phone), I'll let you know.
1 If I .... (not be) busy, I'll come.
2 If he .... (be) careful, he wouldn't break so many things!
3 If we didn't have to work late, we .... (join) you.
4 If she breaks that vase, Grandma .... (be) furious!
5 Unless you .... (stop) wasting time, I'm leaving right now!
6 I can't help you if you .... (not give) me more information.
7 If a fire .... (start), the alarm goes off.
8 You .... (should / make) your own food if you don't like my cooking!
9 .... (take) more exercise and you'll feel much better soon.
10 If it wasn't raining, we .... (go) for a walk.

2 Write two sentences for each item.

0 we / leave at eight, we / arrive on time
likely: *If we leave at eight, we'll arrive on time.*
less likely: *If we left at eight, we'd arrive on time.*
1 I / not be busy, I / pick you up
likely: ....
less likely: ....
2 you / fall, you / break your leg
likely: ....
less likely: ....
3 we / not leave now, we / be late
likely: ....
less likely: ....
4 you / get the job, we / have a party
likely: ....
less likely: ....
5 the questions / be easy, everyone / pass the test
likely: ....
less likely: ....

3 Complete the second sentence so that it has a similar meaning to the first sentence, using the word given. Use between two and five words. Do not change the word given.

0 She has to do this herself because she doesn't have a secretary.
HAVE
She *wouldn't have to do* this herself if she had a secretary.
1 I'll let you borrow my laptop if you promise to be careful.
LONG
You can borrow my laptop .... to be careful.
2 I can't help you with your homework because I'm not very good at maths.
COULD
If I were better at maths, ... you with your homework.
3 If we win the elections, we will build more schools.
PROVIDED
We will build more schools .... the elections.
4 They won't let you into the theatre without a ticket.
UNLESS
They won't let you into the theatre .... a ticket.
5 Bring your sun cream because we may decide to go for a swim.
CASE
Bring your sun cream .... to go for a swim.

83

5b Third conditional, mixed conditionals

Third conditional

- We use the third conditional to talk about events that were possible in the past but did not happen.
- To form third conditional sentences, we use: *if* + past perfect + *would have* + past participle:
  *If Bruce **had asked** me, I **would have said** yes.*
  *If I **hadn't become** a teacher, I **would have liked** to be an actor.* ✓
  *If I **wouldn't have become** a teacher, I **would like** to be an actor.* ✗
- Notice how changing the clauses from positive to negative changes the meaning:
  *If I **had taken** an umbrella, I **wouldn't have** got wet.* (= I did get wet.)
  *If I **hadn't taken** an umbrella, I **would have** got wet.* (= I didn't get wet.)
- Both clauses can be negative:
  *They **wouldn't have** missed their plane if they **hadn't** overslept.* (= They did oversleep and they did miss their plane.)
- In the main clause, we can use *could* or *might* instead of *would*:
  *If you'd asked, I **could** have told you the answer.*
  *I **might** have got the job if I had applied for it.*

Mixed conditionals

Sometimes we use the second and third conditionals in the same sentence. We call these sentences mixed conditional sentences and we use them when a past event has an effect on the present. The conditional clause (third conditional) refers to the past and the main clause (second conditional) refers to the present or future. Compare the following sentences:
*If you **hadn't invited** me, I **wouldn't have gone** to the party.* (third conditional; I did go to the party.)
*If you **hadn't invited** me, I **wouldn't be** here now.* (third conditional + second conditional; I'm here now.)

PRACTICE

1 Complete the sentences. Use the correct form of the verbs in brackets.

0 If you **had come** (come) to the theatre yesterday, you **would have enjoyed** (enjoy) the play.
1 If I ………. (come) to Athens last year, I ………. (visit) you.
2 If we ………. (know) you already had tickets, we ………. (not get) any for you.
3 If you ………. (not destroy) my computer, I ………. (not need) a new one now!
4 If you ………. (not leave) the party so early on Saturday, you ………. (might / meet) Joe.
5 If you ………. (not spend) all your money, your father ………. (not be) angry now.
6 I ………. (could / become) an accountant if I ………. (be) good at maths.
7 If she ………. (try) harder, she ………. (get) that promotion last year.
8 He ………. (not get) the job if he ………. (miss) his interview.
9 If I ………. (meet) you before, my life ………. (be) different now.
10 If he ………. (not see) that car, there ………. (be) an accident.

84

THIRD CONDITIONAL, MIXED CONDITIONALS 5

2 Write third conditional sentences.

0 I felt tired. I went to bed early.
   If I hadn't felt tired, I wouldn't have gone to bed early.
1 I didn't have enough money. I didn't take a taxi.
   If ....
2 I wasn't interested in the film. I didn't go to the cinema.
   If ....
3 We took the wrong turning. We arrived late.
   If ....
4 Romeo thought Juliet was dead. He committed suicide.
   Romeo ....
5 Oliver lied. He was punished.
   Oliver ....
6 I didn't go to the wedding. I wasn't invited.
   I ....
7 I was afraid of the dark. I didn't go downstairs.
   If ....
8 You didn't train hard enough. You didn't win.
   If ....
9 He didn't apologise. She didn't forgive him.
   If ....
10 She didn't have a car. She had to take a taxi.
   If ....

3 Complete the article. Use one word in each gap.

The millennium bug

If you were around at the end of 1999, you've probably heard about the 'millennium bug' affecting the world's computer systems and its catastrophic effects. We waited and nothing happened. But what would (0) **have** happened if there really had (1) .... a millennium bug? Some experts claimed that it (2) .... have created chaos on the Internet, the whole system would have collapsed and all kinds of disasters would (3) .... followed: there (4) .... have been massive power failures, telephones would (5) .... stopped working, banks (6) .... have closed and so on.

What will happen if there (7) .... a similar bug in the future? Experts say that it is unlikely, but (8) .... it did happen, it (9) .... pose a serious problem. And if it happened unexpectedly, technicians (10) .... not have time to take the necessary action to prevent all possible problems. It is an unlikely scenario but (11) .... we plan ahead, we may live to find out.

85

5c wish, if only

wish + past simple/continuous

- We use *wish* + past simple/continuous to express our dissatisfaction with present situations:
  I **wish** I **was** tall. (= but I'm not)
  I **wish** I **was going** on holiday with you. (= but I'm not)
  Harry **wishes** his brother **were** here. (= but he isn't)
- We can use *were* instead of *was* after *wish*:
  I **wish** I **were** tall.
- We often use *wish* + *could* to talk about things we are unable to do:
  I wish I **could** help you. ✓
  I wish I **would** help you. ✗

wish + would

We often use *wish* + *would* to express our dissatisfaction and annoyance about something that we would like to be different:
I wish this car **would go** faster!
I wish you **would stop** talking! ✓
I wish you **to stop** talking! ✗
I wish they **would stop** arguing. ✓
I wish they **will stop** arguing. ✗

wish + past perfect

- We use *wish* + past perfect to express regret about the past:
  I wish I **hadn't taken** your advice. (= but I did)
- We can also use *wish* + *could have* + past participle:
  I wish she **could have come**. (= but she didn't)

Here is a summary of the patterns we use with *wish*:

Pattern after *I wish*	Time reference	Example
Past simple	present	I wish I **knew** the answer. (= I don't)
Past continuous	present	I wish I **was/were going** with you. (= I'm not)
could	present	I wish I **could give** you an answer. (= I can't)
would	present/future	I wish you **would be** quiet! (= Be quiet!)
Past perfect	past	She wishes she **had known** us then. (= she didn't)
could have + past participle	past	I wish I **could have explained**. (= I wasn't able to)

if only

If only can be used in the same way as *wish*. It is usually more emphatic. The patterns after *if only* are the same as those after *wish*:
If only I **had** more money. (= but I don't)
If only I **was going** with you. (= but I'm not)
If only you **could come**, too. (= but you can't)
If only the sun **would come** out!
If only I **had listened** to you. (= but I didn't)
If only he **could have joined** us. (= he wasn't able to)

5 WISH, IF ONLY

PRACTICE

1 Complete the sentences. Use the correct form of the verbs in brackets.

0 My grandad wishes he **could use** (can / use) a computer.
1 Bruce wishes he ………. (have) more money so he could buy a new sweater.
2 If only I ………. (be) taller! I'd love to be in the basketball team.
3 I wish I ………. (not spend) all my money. Now I don't have enough for my bus fare!
4 I wish you ………. (not watch) TV while I'm talking to you!
5 I wish you ………. (not do) that. It's really annoying!
6 Ella wishes she ………. (not speak) to her friend like that last night.
7 If only they ………. (not build) that block of flats right in front of our window!
8 Of course Tom wishes he ………. (can / come) with us but he has to stay here and work.
9 I wish we ………. (can / go) to the match on Saturday but we're visiting my uncle.
10 I really wish you ………. (not tell) Mary. Now she knows everything!
11 If only you ………. (not lose) all our money. Now we're broke.
12 Peter's always late. If only he ………. (turn up) on time for a change!

2 Write two sentences for each item. Use *I wish* or *if only* and the phrases in the box.

> drive more carefully   get to the bus stop five minutes earlier   let someone else drive
> not be so rude to her   ~~not eat so much~~   not forget to set the alarm   not lose my temper
> play fewer computer games   recycle more paper   respect the environment
> revise for it   ~~take more exercise~~   use their bikes instead   use their cars less often
> watch less TV   work harder

0 I've gained a lot of weight.
   I wish **I hadn't eaten so much.**
   If only **I'd taken more exercise.**
1 He crashed his car.
   I wish ………………………………… .
   If only ………………………………… .
2 I had a row with my best friend.
   I wish ………………………………… .
   If only ………………………………… .
3 Children don't read enough nowadays.
   I wish ………………………………… .
   If only ………………………………… .
4 We're cutting down too many trees.
   I wish ………………………………… .
   If only ………………………………… .
5 I failed my science test.
   I wish ………………………………… .
   If only ………………………………… .
6 I missed my bus.
   I wish ………………………………… .
   If only ………………………………… .
7 People use their cars when they don't need to.
   I wish ………………………………… .
   If only ………………………………… .

5 WISH, IF ONLY

3 Write a sentence for each item. Use *I wish* or *if only* and the words in brackets.

0 The weather is awful. (improve)
   If only the weather would improve!

1 He leaves the tap running all the time. (turn off)
   ....

2 Jamie is very angry. (calm down)
   ....

3 People hunt animals for sport. (stop)
   ....

4 The people next door have their TV on and it's too loud. (turn down)
   ....

5 Your friend keeps complaining about everything all the time. (stop)
   ....

6 Your favourite team has lost every match so far. (win)
   ....

7 Too much rubbish is thrown away. (recycle)
   ....

8 It doesn't rain enough. (more)
   ....

4 What are these people wishing? Complete the sentences.

0 If only *I'd taken an umbrella with me.*

1 If only ....

2 If only ....

3 If only ....

4 If only ....

5 If only ....

6 If only ....

7 If only ....

Vocabulary

5d want, expect, love, can't bear, etc.

want, wish, hope

Pattern	Meaning/Use	Example
want + noun	desire sth	I really **want** some **chocolate**.
want (*sb*) + *to*-infinitive	desire (sb) to do sth	I **want to go** on holiday.
wish + past simple *wish* + *could*	want sth to be true even though it is unlikely or impossible	I **wish** I **had** a dog. I **wish** I **could** fly.
wish + *to*-infinitive	want to do sth (formal)	I **wish to make** a complaint.
wish sb + noun	hope sth for sb	I **wish you luck** in your career.
hope + clause	want sth and believe it is possible or likely	I **hope** you're coming with us.
hope + *to*-infinitive	want to do sth	I **hope to see** you on Saturday.

- *Want* can have a direct object immediately after it. We cannot use *wish* or *hope* in this way:
  I want a drink. ✓
  I wish a drink. ✗
  I hope a drink. ✗
- We can use *wish* and *hope* (but not *want*) with a *that* clause:
  I hope (that) you will be happy. ✓
  I wish (that) you could be happy. ✓
  I want (that) you are happy. ✗

expect, (can't) wait, look forward to

Pattern	Meaning/Use	Example
expect + noun	demand sth	I **expect respect** from my children.
expect (*sb*) + *to*-infinitive	think or demand that sth will happen	I **expected him to phone** me.
expect + *that* clause	believe that sth will happen	I **expect** (**that**) **she'll do** well.
wait for sb/sth	stay somewhere or not do sth until sth else happens, sb arrives, etc.	They're **waiting for** a taxi.
can't wait/can hardly wait + *to*-infinitive; *can't wait/can hardly wait for sth*	be very excited about sth and eager for it to happen	I **can hardly wait to see** you! I **can't wait for** my birthday!
look forward to (*doing*) *sth*	be very excited about sth that is going to happen	I'm **looking forward to Saturday**. I'm **looking forward to seeing** you.

5 WANT, EXPECT, LOVE, CAN'T BEAR, ETC.

like, love, be fond of, be keen on

Pattern	Meaning/Use	Example
like sth	enjoy sth or think it is nice	I **like** your new dress.
like sb	think sb is nice and enjoy being with them	I don't think he **likes** me.
like + to-infinitive like + -ing	enjoy or prefer to do sth	I **like to take** a walk in the morning. I **like looking** at clouds.
love sb	have strong feelings of affection for sb; care very much about sb	I **love you**, Jane!
love + to-infinitive love + -ing	like sth very much; enjoy doing sth very much	He **loves to talk** about himself. I **love gardening**.
be fond of sb/sth	like sb/sth very much	John's quite **fond of Mary**, isn't he?
be fond of + -ing	like doing sth very much	I'm not very **fond of cooking**.
be keen on sb/sth	like sb/sth	He's pretty **keen on her**.
be keen on (doing) sth	be very interested in sth and enjoy doing it very much	She's **keen on tennis**. He's very **keen on gardening**.
be keen + to-infinitive	want to do sth or want sth to happen very much	She **was** very **keen to help**.

- Both *be fond of* and *be keen on* can be followed by *-ing*:
  I'**m fond of swimming**.
  I'**m keen on swimming**.
- We can use *be keen* (but not *be fond of*) with a *to*-infinitive:
  She'**s keen to get** back to work.
- Note that *be keen on* + *-ing* means 'be very interested in doing sth' but *be keen to do sth* means 'want very much to do sth' or 'want sth to happen very much'.

can't stand, can't bear

Pattern	Meaning/Use	Example
can't stand sb/sth	find sb/sth very unpleasant	I **can't stand** rock music.
can't/won't stand sth	can't/won't accept an unpleasant situation	I don't think I **can stand** the tension any longer.
can't stand + -ing	not be able to accept or not like doing sth	Anne **can't stand working** in that office.
can't/couldn't bear sb/sth	find sb/sth extremely unpleasant	Oh, I **can't bear** that man! Please don't leave me alone – I **couldn't bear** it!
can't bear (sb) doing sth	not be able to accept or not like (sb) doing sth	He **can't bear people being** late. I **can't bear watching** sport on TV.
can't bear + to-infinitive	not be able to accept or like sth	I **can't bear to see** her cry.

5 WANT, EXPECT, LOVE, CAN'T BEAR, ETC.

PRACTICE

1 Choose the correct answer.

0 Jason must be pretty keen *for* / *on* Miranda – they've been dancing all night.
1 I just *wanted* / *wished* to say how much I enjoyed our chat last night.
2 I *want* / *hope* everything goes well and that you arrive safe and sound.
3 Congratulations! We all *wish* / *hope* you every happiness!
4 I'm *wishing* / *hoping* to go and study abroad next year.
5 I'm *waiting* / *expecting* the postman any minute now.
6 I've been *waiting for* / *expecting* you in the rain since nine o'clock! Where have you been?
7 She's still getting over her illness, so don't *wait for* / *expect* too much from her.
8 I'm so *expecting* / *looking forward to* seeing my friends again after all this time.
9 He told her he *liked* / *loved* her with all his heart.
10 I *like* / *am fond on* David but we've never been close friends.
11 I quite *like* / *love* my neighbours and we do seem to get on quite well.
12 I can't *stand* / *wait* to get out of hospital!
13 He couldn't bear *to see* / *of seeing* his dog in pain.
14 I can hardly wait *to see* / *for seeing* her.

2 Complete the article. Use one word in each gap.

Teen trends

According to a new poll, the most popular leisure time activity for teenagers is watching TV. Nine out of ten teens said they are very (0) *keen* on watching TV and do so for several hours every day. Teens also enjoy (1).......... to music and are particularly fond (2).......... MP3s, which is how most young people listen to music.

After school, kids (3).......... forward to going home and surfing the Internet or (4).......... video games, sometimes for hours. One of the most popular free time activities is, of course, going out with friends – teens can't (5).......... for the weekend to come so they can sit around in cafés, chilling out. They are also very keen (6).......... going to the cinema with friends – but not with parents! Every teen wants (7).......... have lots of friends to hang out with but it's not cool to go out with parents – teens can't bear (8).......... be seen with their parents in public.

Finally, teens wait impatiently (9).......... the school year to be over so they can go on holiday, and ninety percent wish they (10).......... go on holiday with their friends rather than their mum and dad.

5e Prefixes (2)

- We have seen that we use prefixes to change the meaning of a word. Prefixes do not change the part of speech (but most suffixes do).
- Many prefixes give a word a meaning which is the opposite or negative of the original word. For example, we can use the prefixes *dis-*, *in-* or *un-*. Other prefixes change the meaning of a word in different ways. For example:
  multi- + *ethnic* → *multi-ethnic* (= made up of many different ethnic groups)
- Here are some more prefixes:

Pattern	Meaning/Use	Example
de- + verb/noun	opposite	*decentralise*
	shows that sth is removed	*debone*
	shows that sth is reduced	*devalue*
ex- + noun	former	*ex-husband*
macro- + noun	large; on a large scale	*macroeconomics*
micro- + noun	small; on a small scale	*microelectronics*
mini- + noun	very small or short	*mini-break*
mono- + noun	one	*monolingual*
multi- + noun/adjective	many	*multi-purpose*
semi- + noun/adjective	half; partly	*semicircle, semi-literate*
sub- + noun/adjective	under, below; less, lower	*subzero, subnormal*

She went to great trouble to **debone** *the fish.*

PRACTICE

1 Complete the words. Use the prefixes in the table above. Then write down the meaning of each word. You can use a dictionary to help you.

0 ......**de**value: reduce the value of something
1 ......semi...final: ....
2 ......ex...partner: former partner
3 ......sub...standard: ....
4 ......multi...national: ....
5 ......sub...section: ....
6 ......mini...bus: small bus
7 ......de...caffeinated: ....
8 ......de...frost: ....
9 ......multi...coloured: ....
10 ......de...regulate: ....
11 ......sub...zero: ....
12 ......ex...wife: former wife
13 ......de...nationalise: ....
14 ......micro...organism: ....
15 ......de...rail: (off a train)
16 ......mini...skirt: ....
17 ......sub...soil: ....
18 ......micro...chip: ....
19 ......de...code: ....
20 ......semi...circle: half a circle

92

PREFIXES (2) 5

2 Choose the correct answer, A, B, C or D.

0 Unless you .... the fish first, your guests won't enjoy it.
  A unbone   B debone   C sub-bone   D pre-bone
1 I think the government should .... the post office.
  A denationalise   B innationalise   C ex-nationalise   D subnationalise
2 I wish my .... and I were still on speaking terms.
  A pre-partner   B ex-partner   C semi-partner   D sub-partner
3 This .... tool is ideal for a variety of uses.
  A macro-purpose   B mono-purpose   C micro-purpose   D multi-purpose
4 Let's form a .... and do something about the problem.
  A subcommittee   B micro-committee C macro-committee D multi-committee
5 These .... can only be seen under a microscope.
  A macro-organisms   B micro-organisms C mini-organisms   D semi-organisms
6 Ours was the only room in the hotel that didn't have a ....
  A micro-bar   B mini-bar   C multi-bar   D semi-bar
7 .... were an early type of plane with only one set of wings.
  A Microplanes   B Semiplanes   C Monoplanes   D Subplanes
8 .... is destroying large areas of tropical rain forest.
  A Subforestation   B Semiforestation C Macroforestation D Deforestation
9 At the time, we were living in a nice .... house with a garden.
  A micro-detached   B semi-detached   C macro-detached   D sub-detached
10 She only drinks .... tea.
  A uncaffeinated   B decaffeinated   C incaffeinated   D discaffeinated

3 Complete the sentences. Use the words in the box with the correct prefixes.

bug   chip   code   cultural   economics   final   husband   national   zero

0 I enjoy living in a *multi-cultural* society.
1 That year, he took me to see England play in the .... of the European Cup.
2 Nick and Amanda both work for a large .... company.
3 He was so stingy! He would sit in .... temperatures because he refused to switch on the central heating!
4 James is Lisa's .... And that's their daughter, Emily.
5 .... is the study of large economic systems such as those of a whole country or area of the world.
6 When you've finished writing the computer program, you will need to check for errors and .... it.
7 This electronic card has a .... which contains the cardholder's name and address.
8 Nobody knows what those symbols stand for. We haven't been able to .... the message yet.

93

6

AGENDA

Grammar
- **6a** Time and condition clauses with future reference
- **6b** More future forms
- **6c** Expressions of time and preference

Vocabulary
- **6d** *afterwards, after, until, as far as*, etc.
- **6e** Phrases with *time*

Entry test

1 Choose the correct answer, A, B, C or D.

1 As soon as you .... what you're doing, I'd like a word with you, please.
   A finish   B are finishing   C will finish   D will have finished

2 I'll write to her when I .... time.
   A have   B will have   C would have   D have had

3 Don't interrupt me .... I'm talking.
   A until   B after   C while   D by the time

4 Give him a ring before you go .... he's out.
   A whether   B as long as   C on condition that   D in case

5 .... you could visit another planet, would you go?
   A Provided   B Suppose   C Whether   D Whenever

Now look at **6a** on pages 96–98.

SCORE .... / 5

2 Choose the correct answer, A, B, C or D.

6 I was on the .... of giving up when Ken offered to help.
   A edge   B point   C matter   D moment

7 The film is .... start, so please take your seats.
   A about to   B ready for   C coming to   D on the verge of

8 The meeting isn't .... start till three.
   A on the point   B about to   C about for   D due to

9 The President .... address the nation on TV later.
   A is for   B is owing to   C is to   D is in to

10 .... I suggest, I know he'll disagree.
   A No matter   B No matter if   C However   D Whatever

Now look at **6b** on pages 99–100.

SCORE .... / 5

94

ENTRY TEST 6

3 Choose the correct answer, A, B, C or D.

11 Have you packed? It's time ………… .
    A for leaving   B we must leave   C we left   D we are leaving
12 It's time ………… your medicine.
    A you will take   B for your taking   C for you to take   D for you are taking
13 It's late – it's about time ………… .
    A we leave   B for us leaving   C we were leaving   D we've left
14 I'd rather ………… a taxi if you don't mind.
    A take   B to take   C I'll take   D I'd take
15 I'd sooner we ………… tonight.
    A won't go out   B don't go out   C wouldn't go out   D didn't go out

Now look at **6c** on pages 101–103.   SCORE ____ / 5

4 Choose the correct answer, A, B, C or D.

16 The speech will last for an hour. ………… , there's a reception.
    A After   B Afterwards   C Following   D After then
17 She came but left ………… fifteen minutes.
    A after   B afterwards   C later   D by
18 We must wait ………… Friday for our exam results.
    A after   B afterwards   C until   D by
19 I'd like the room to be ready ………… next Monday.
    A until   B to   C as far as   D by
20 Why not give Harry a ring ………… he's not at home?
    A in case   B in the case   C in case of   D in the case of

Now look at **6d** on pages 104–105.   SCORE ____ / 5

5 Complete the phrases with *time* in the following sentences. Use one or two words in each gap.

21 Parents should spend …………… with their children than they do now.
22 We watched TV to pass …………… until dinner was ready.
23 I think learning something you're never going to use is …………… of time.
24 We …………… amazing time in London! It was fantastic!
25 …………… time with the test – if you rush, you'll make mistakes.

Now look at **6e** on pages 106–107.   SCORE ____ / 5

TOTAL SCORE ____ / 25

95

Grammar

6a Time and condition clauses with future reference

When we talk about the future, we often use time words or phrases like *when*, *after*, *as soon as*, etc., or words/phrases describing a condition (for example *whether*, *as long as*, etc.). We use the present simple (not *will*) after these words and phrases.

Time clauses

Here are some time words and phrases we use in future time clauses:

Pattern	Meaning/Use	Example
after + present simple	when sth has happened	I'll see you **after** I get back from my holiday.
as soon as + present simple	immediately after	**As soon as** he arrives at the hotel, call a taxi.
before + present simple	earlier than	Finish your work **before** Mum gets home.
by the time + present simple	during the time before sth happens	He will have left **by the time** you get there.
once + present simple	from the time when sth happens	**Once** she arrives, we'll start.
suppose/supposing + present simple	imagine that	**Supposing** she asks for your help, what will you do?
until + present simple	up to the point in time that	I won't leave **until** you tell me what happened.
when + present simple	at or during the time that	I'll call you **when** I'm free.
whenever + present simple	at any time	Phone me **whenever** it's convenient.
while + present simple	during the time that	Let's forget about work **while** we're on holiday.

- We can use the present perfect instead of the present simple to refer to an action that will be complete in the future:
  I'll take up gardening as soon as I **'ve retired**.
- Sometimes there is a change in meaning. Compare:
  When I phone Mary, I'll ask her. (= I'll phone Mary and ask her at the same time.)
  When I've phoned Mary, I'll let you know. (= First I'll phone Mary and then I'll let you know.)
- We can use the present continuous after *while*, to refer to an action that will be in progress in the future:
  I'll go for a walk while they **'re having** lunch.
- We can use the past simple after *suppose/supposing*, to talk about unlikely or imaginary events in the future:
  Supposing you **failed**, would you try again?

96

6 TIME AND CONDITION CLAUSES WITH FUTURE REFERENCE

Condition clauses

Pattern	Meaning/Use	Example
if + present simple	used to talk about sth that might happen or might be true	**If** I see her, I'll let you know.
as/so long as + present simple	only if	I'll come **as long as** you pay.
(just) in case + present simple	because it is possible that	Take an umbrella **in case** it rains.
on condition that + present simple	only if	I'll lend you the money **on condition that** you pay me back by Friday.
provided/providing (that) + present simple	only if	We'll get there on time **provided** we leave now.
unless + present simple	if not	We won't go for a walk **unless** it's sunny.
whether + present simple (*+ or not*)	used to say that something will or will not happen whatever the situation is	**Whether** we win **or not** depends on how hard we train.

See also: **5a**

When a clause beginning with *if, whether, when,* etc. is the object of the sentence, we can use *will*:
I doubt if/whether David **will come**.
I don't know when they**'ll come back**.

PRACTICE

1 **Choose the correct answer.**

0 You can drop in *whenever* / *on condition that* you like.
1 *When* / *Until* he arrives, everyone must stand.
2 We're not going to stop digging *until* / *as soon as* we find the ancient ruins.
3 They're going to check the building *before* / *supposing* the President arrives.
4 *While* / *By the time* we get to the cinema, the film will have started.
5 Please phone your father *until* / *as soon as* you see this message.
6 *In case* / *Supposing* you had a baby girl, what would you call her?
7 *Whether* / *Unless* they win or not depends on Dennis being on good form.
8 *When* / *Before* the Smiths arrive, ask them to wait outside, please.
9 *As soon as* / *Before* you hear the alarm, run for the exit.
10 You'll recover quickly *whenever* / *provided* you rest.

6 TIME AND CONDITION CLAUSES WITH FUTURE REFERENCE

2 Complete the sentences. Use the present simple or the present perfect of the verbs in brackets. Sometimes more than one answer is possible.

0 As soon as I *save/have saved* (save) enough money, I'm going to go on a long holiday.
1 I hope you'll be awake when I .... (come) home.
2 Come whenever you .... (be) ready.
3 I'll stay until you .... (finish).
4 They will have sold all the tickets by the time we .... (get) there.
5 Don't open your eyes until I .... (tell) you to.
6 Whether she .... (play) on Saturday depends on what her doctor says.
7 I'll tell you a secret as long as you .... (promise) not to tell anyone else.
8 I'll lend you the book on condition that you .... (bring back / it) on Monday.
9 Let's get our swimming things in case we .... (get) a chance to go swimming.
10 We'll go to bed as soon as the programme .... (finish).

3 Complete the text. Use one word in each gap.

What to do in a tsunami

Tsunamis are a mass of sea waves that are usually caused by an earthquake in the floor of the sea. (0) *Once* the tsunami reaches the coast and hits shallow water, the height of the waves will rise rapidly and cause destruction to the land near the shore where it hits. Whether you survive a tsunami or (1) .... could depend on following these simple instructions.

(2) .... the earthquake that causes the tsunami occurs far out in the ocean, there should be plenty of time to find somewhere safe to go. If, however, the earthquake (3) .... close to shore, there may only be minutes between the earthquake and the arrival of the first wave. As (4) .... as you feel the ground shake and you know an earthquake has occurred, go to high ground immediately. (5) .... that you are at least fifty feet above sea level, you should be clear of any waves that are heading your way. Wait there (6) .... the crisis is over.

Do not return to shore – stay where you are (7) .... case there are more waves coming – do not assume that it is safe to return to shore because the first wave is over. As long (8) .... you are on high ground, you should be safe.

'*As soon as* you *start* talking sense, people will say you're an old fool.'
BOB HOPE

98

6b More future forms

We can use different ways to talk about the future in English.
Here are some more future forms:

Form	Meaning/Use	Example
be about to + infinitive	be going to do sth very soon	The train **is about to leave**. Let's hurry.
be due to + infinitive	be expected to do sth already arranged	She **is due to start** her new job next week.
be to + infinitive	be expected to do sth arranged or officially ordered	The Pope **is to visit** Cuba this month.
be not to + infinitive	be expected or ordered not to do sth	You **are not to begin** until I give the order.
be on the verge of (doing) sth	be at the point where sth is about to happen	They **are on the verge of signing** a new contract.
be on the point of (doing) sth	be going to do sth very soon	We **were on the point of giving up** hope.

We also often use the following words when we talk about the future.
They are usually followed by the present simple:

- *whatever, whoever, whenever, wherever, however*:
  Wherever *you go, I'll follow.*
  However *hard he tries, he'll fail.*
- *no matter what/who/etc.*:
  No matter what *she says, they won't believe her.*

For future forms, see also: **2a** and **2b**

PRACTICE

1 Choose the correct answer.

0 They are (due) / *on the point* to leave tomorrow.
1 Fasten your seatbelts. We are about to *take / taking* off.
2 The boat is *due / on the verge* to leave at ten o'clock.
3 You *are not to / aren't due to* take the car without my permission.
4 Doctors claim they are on the *due / point* of a breakthrough.
5 He's thinking *to give up / of giving up* but you can help him.
6 *However / No matter* how much the painting costs, I'll buy it.
7 *Whatever / However* much it costs me, I'll do it.
8 I'm due *to be / for being* at a conference in Berlin on Monday.
9 *Whatever / Whoever* it is, I'll ask them to leave.
10 They *are / are on the point* to change the exam next year.

99

6 MORE FUTURE FORMS

2 Complete the sentences. Use the *to*-infinitive, the *-ing* form or the present simple of the verbs in the box.

> announce   arrive   burst   expire   ~~have~~   hide   hire   leave
> move   perform   run   see   try

0 I think Eric is due **to have** his operation in two weeks.
1 Mrs Bower is on the point of .... her resignation.
2 Martha was on the verge of .... into tears.
3 The Prime Minister is .... in Brussels at noon.
4 I am about .... my last trick, ladies and gentlemen.
5 Your subscription to our website is due .... next month.
6 You are not .... your room until I tell you to!
7 No matter how hard he ...., he'll never be a successful actor.
8 Whenever you .... Jane, will you tell her to give me a ring?
9 No matter who they .... for the job of manager, the factory will still close.
10 Wherever the burglars ...., the police will find them.
11 She won't break the world record however fast she ....
12 No matter where we ...., we will still have to travel to get to work.

3 Complete the text. Use one word in each gap.

Polly: pop music phenomenon

Polly is just twenty-three years old and she's already sold millions of albums. Now she (0) **is** about to make pop music history. She's already got two singles in the top twenty and she is (1) .... the verge of getting a third single in the charts. No other solo artist has ever achieved this – not even Madonna. Polly has won three Grammy Awards. She (2) .... soon to be awarded her fourth Grammy for Best Female Pop Vocal Performance.

She is (3) .... to fly to China next week, where she will give her first concert ever in Beijing. (4) .... Polly performs – whether it is in China, Europe or the USA – she causes a sensation.

Now her career (5) .... about to get another boost when she appears on a popular music show in the USA next month. While in the States, she is (6) .... meet the President of the USA in the White House. And that's not all: Polly is on the point (7) .... signing a new contract – this time to star in a Hollywood film as a country singer! Filming is due (8) .... start in the autumn of next year.

What next for Polly? (9) .... she does, she will continue to attract media attention. And no matter (10) .... she does, millions of fans around the world will continue to follow her.

> *So there I am, sitting in my seat, **on the verge of** a nervous breakdown. 'We **are about to leave**,' says the man next to me, grinning. The noise of the engines is deafening and I***'m on the point of being** *sick. The steward bends over me and says, 'We***'re due to take off** *soon, sir. Would you like sweets or cotton wool?' 'I'd rather have the cotton wool, please,' I reply. 'Sweets always fall out of my ears.'*

6c Expressions of time and preference

it's time

- We can talk about what we think should happen using *it's time* in the following patterns:
  - *it's time* + *to*-infinitive:
    It's time to go to bed. ✓
    It's time we go to bed. ✗
  - *it's time for* + noun:
    It's time for bed.
  - *it's time for* + sb + *to*-infinitive:
    It's time for you to go to bed.
- In the following patterns, we use *it's time* with a past tense to refer to things that we think should happen now or very soon:
  - *it's time* + sb + past simple:
    It's time you went to bed. ✓
    It's time you will go to bed. ✗
  - *it's time* + sb + past continuous:
    It's time we were leaving.
  - *it's high time* + past simple (or past continuous for emphasis):
    It's high time we left.
    It's high time you were earning your own living!
  - *it's about time* + past simple (or past continuous for emphasis), often suggesting criticism:
    It's about time we took global warming seriously.

would rather

- We use *would rather* to express preference, in the following patterns:
  - *would rather* + infinitive (+ *than* + infinitive)
    I'd rather stay in. ✓
    I'd rather to stay in. ✗
    I'd rather stay in **than go** out with Nick.
    Would you **rather go** with them or stay with me?
  - *would rather* + sb + past simple:
    I'd rather you stayed a little longer. ✓
    I'd rather you to stay a little longer. ✗
    I'd rather Anne didn't come to the meeting.
- We also use *would rather* to express criticism – to talk about something we think should have been done differently in the past. We use it in the following pattern: *would rather* + sb + past perfect:
  I'd rather you had asked me before buying that shirt. (= but you didn't)

would sooner

We use *would sooner* in the same way as *would rather*. It follows the same patterns:
I'd sooner die than marry Ted!
I'd sooner you didn't wait for us.

would prefer

We use *would prefer* to express preference, in the following patterns:
- *would prefer* + *to*-infinitive:
  She'd prefer not to watch the film.
- *would prefer* + *to*-infinitive + *rather than* + infinitive/-*ing*:
  I'd prefer to stay in **rather than go** out/**going** out with Nick.
- *would prefer* + sb + *to*-infinitive:
  We'd prefer you to stay.
  I'd prefer you not to come.
- *would prefer it if* + sb + past simple:
  She'd prefer it if you didn't come.

Isn't it time you had your hair cut?

101

6 EXPRESSIONS OF TIME AND PREFERENCE

PRACTICE

1 Match 1–12 with a–m to make sentences.

0 It's high time she — **9**
1 It's time to
2 I'm sorry but I'd rather
3 Would you really prefer to
4 Actually, I'd rather be
5 It's about time
6 I'd prefer it
7 I'd sooner play football
8 Don't you think it's time we
9 Marry you?
10 I would
11 It's time for
12 I'd prefer

a if you didn't tell anyone about this.
b bed, young lady.
c not talk about what happened.
d told Emma what's going on?
e beautiful than rich.
f leave for the airport.
g took her exams seriously.
h rather stay here if you don't mind.
i you got down to work.
j it if you didn't invite Wayne to the party.
k fail rather than ask Fred for help?
l I'd rather die!
m than watch it on TV.

2 Choose the correct answer, A, B or C.

0 It's eight o'clock. Isn't it time ....?
   A we get up   **B to get up** (circled)   C for us getting up
1 It's late. It's high time we ....
   A go home   B must go home   C went home.
2 No coffee for me, thanks. I'd rather .... some water.
   A have   B to have   C having
3 She says she'd prefer .... tomorrow.
   A you come   B it if you come   C it if you came
4 Look at your room! It's about time .... it up!
   A you tidy   B you tidied   C for you tidying
5 Isn't it time .... lunch yet? I'm starving!
   A for   B we have   C for having
6 Ben would rather you .... now. Can you come later?
   A don't come   B didn't come   C hadn't come
7 I'd prefer .... a jacket and tie.
   A I wear   B wearing   C to wear
8 I think it's time we .... goodbye.
   A say   B are saying   C said
9 I'd sooner you .... this with me first.
   A discussed   B have discussed   C had discussed
10 I'd prefer to watch a film .... a game.
   A from playing   B rather than to play   C rather than play

102

EXPRESSIONS OF TIME AND PREFERENCE **6**

3 Complete the conversations. Use the correct form of the verbs in the box.

> do   fix   ~~get~~   go   help   keep   not stop   paint   ~~phone~~
> spend   stay   take   tell   visit

0 **A:** It's time *to get* the dinner ready.
  B: I'd rather we *phoned* for a pizza.
1 **A:** I think it's time we ………….. our cousins in Camden.
  B: I'd prefer ………….. the money on a holiday in Brighton.
2 **A:** It's time we ………….. that hole in the fence.
  B: I'd rather we ………….. the bedroom.
3 **A:** I think it's time ………….. home.
  B: I'd rather ………….. a bit longer if that's OK with you.
4 **A:** It's about time he ………….. you with the housework.
  B: To be honest, I'd sooner ………….. it myself.
5 **A:** It's high time you ………….. Jenny what really happened.
  B: Well, I'd rather ………….. this to myself!
6 **A:** I think it's time for us ………….. a break.
  B: I'd sooner we ………….. until we've finished.

'What time is it when an elephant sits on your car?'
'*It's time to get* a new one.'

4 Complete the second sentence so that it has a similar meaning to the first sentence, using the word given. Use between two and five words. Do not change the word given.

0 You really ought to start work on that project.
  HIGH
  It's *high time you started* work on that project.
1 You should buy a new car.
  TIME
  It's ………….. new car.
2 She thinks it would be better if you stayed at home tonight.
  PREFER
  She ………….. if you stayed at home tonight.
3 Stop spending all our money on clothes.
  RATHER
  I'd ………….. all our money on clothes.
4 I would prefer to study drama than engineering.
  SOONER
  I ………….. drama than engineering.
5 We think it would be better if you slept in the living room.
  PREFER
  We'd ………….. in the living room.
6 I really think you should tell her what you think.
  HIGH
  It ………….. her what you think.
7 I have to pick up the kids from school now.
  FOR
  It's time ………….. the kids from school.
8 I don't want you to come to the doctor with me.
  WOULD
  I ………….. come to the doctor with me.
9 Your hair's too long.
  HAD
  It's about ………….. a haircut.
10 Let's walk to the station instead of going by car.
  THAN
  I'd prefer to walk to the station ………….. by car.

103

Vocabulary

6d afterwards, after, until, as far as, etc.

afterwards

- *Afterwards* is an adverb. It means 'following the event that has just been mentioned':
  The play lasts for two hours. **Afterwards**, *you can meet the actors.*
- We can also use *afterwards* at the end of a sentence, to mean 'later':
  We left at six. Carol arrived shortly **afterwards**.

afterwards and then

- When we are talking about an action that follows another action, we can use either *afterwards* or *then*:
  We all had lunch together. **Then/Afterwards** *we went to the beach.*
- To introduce the next step in a series of instructions, we usually use *then*:
  Check that the paper is properly loaded. **Then** *press the start button.* **Then** …

afterwards and later (on)

- *Afterwards* often suggests that the second event occurs quite soon after the first one has finished:
  I went to see Adrian in the morning. **Afterwards**, *I drove into town to do some shopping.*
- If there is a longer interval between the two events, we usually use *(much) later* or *later on*:
  I couldn't understand why she hadn't answered my letters. **Later**, *I realised she'd moved house.*
  I saw a woman on the stairs. **Later on**, *I found out that she was my neighbour.*
  My main aim is to graduate. **Afterwards**, *I'd like to go and work in Canada.*

after and in

- We can use *after* as a preposition, to mean 'following something'. In this case, *after* is followed by a time word or phrase (e.g. *after a week*):
  After a few days, *I felt much better.*
  She left **after an hour**.
- We cannot use *after* on its own. It is followed by a time word or phrase, or a noun. We can also use *after that* (= *afterwards*):
  We're leaving **after lunch**.
  I'm hoping to visit the States. **After that/ Afterwards**, *I'd like to travel to Mexico.* ✓
  ~~*I'm hoping to visit the States.* **After**, *I'd like to travel to Mexico.*~~ ✗
- Compare the use of *after* and *in*:
  She left **after five minutes**.
  She'll be leaving **in an hour**.

by and until/till

- We use *by* for an action that happens before or no later than a certain time:
  Could you let us know your decision **by** *Friday?*
- We use *until/till* for an action continuing up to the time mentioned:
  Let's wait here **until** *the rain stops.*

until/till, to and as far as

- We use *until/till* in connection with time:
  The shops are open **until** *six.*
  I'll be here **until** *five.*
- We use *as far (as)* to talk about direction towards or distance from a place. We use *to* to mean 'towards and stopping at a particular place'.
  Do you know which bus goes **to** *Marble Arch?*
  We went **as far as** *London.*

6 AFTERWARDS, AFTER, UNTIL, AS FAR AS, ETC.

PRACTICE

1 Choose the correct answer.

0 She had her baby in June. Not long *after* / *after that*, she resigned.
1 I have to submit my report *by* / *until* the end of the month.
2 They came in June and left two months *later* / *lately*.
3 We had a quick coffee and *after* / *then* went shopping.
4 Owen arrived *after* / *afterwards* five minutes.
5 We stayed at the library *till* / *as far as* it closed.
6 I saw him enter the bank at about one o'clock. Ten minutes *after* / *later*, he ran out with a bag full of money.
7 We need your response *by* / *until* tonight.
8 You can stay *by* / *till* the weekend.
9 *After* / *Afterwards* a few hours, the mist cleared.
10 We're going to leave Italy *by* / *in* a couple of months to go and live in the States.

2 Complete the sentences. Use the words and phrases on page 104.

0 Do you always walk ...*to*... work?
1 I'll see you .... a couple of hours.
2 I was bored at first but .... on I enjoyed it.
3 To start the machine, switch it on. .... press the red button.
4 On Sunday morning, we went for a stroll around the park. ...., we went for a meal.
5 I felt really sick when we got there but .... a few days I was fine.
6 I'll need the translation .... January 28th, please.
7 We waited .... ten o'clock and then we decided to go home.
8 We ran .... as the bridge and then stopped.

3 Complete the story. Use one word in each gap.

My first encounter with Dracula

I had been riding all day and it had already got dark. I was on my way to Count Dracula's castle but I had only got (0) ...*as*... far as the first village. I wanted to get (1) .... my destination before midnight. The mountain was steep and the forest all around was black and silent. Suddenly, I heard a strange sound in the distance. A few seconds (2) ...., I heard a terrible howl and realised that there were wolves in the forest. I was beginning to wish I had stopped at the village inn and waited (3) .... morning before continuing with my journey but I had been hoping to reach the castle just (4) .... eleven – no later than midnight. In his letter, the Count had said he would wait up (5) .... I arrived. I rode on.

(6) .... a while, I came to a fork in the road. On my left, through the trees, I could see the castle. Excited, I took the road that led (7) .... Dracula's castle. Soon, I was outside the gate. I knocked and waited. (8) .... a few seconds, I heard a key turning. The door opened and (9) .... I saw him. 'Good evening,' he said. 'Come in. I have been waiting for you. We'll have some wine and after (10) .... I'll show you to your room.' I made polite conversation with the count for an hour or so and (11) .... I was shown upstairs. I was so tired I slept (12) .... midday the next day.

105

6e Phrases with *time*

Phrase	Meaning	Example
there's time (for sth)	there is enough time (to do sth)	**There's time for** one more question.
have time (for sth/to do sth)	have enough time (to do sth)	Do you **have time for** a coffee? I don't **have time to talk** right now.
have a good/great/etc. time	enjoy yourself very much	Thanks for the party – we both **had a wonderful time**.
in time (for sth/to do sth)	early enough (to do sth)	If we hurry, we'll be there **in time for** the last train. We got there just **in time to see** the Queen.
lose time (doing sth)	fall behind because of delays	We **lost** a lot of valuable **time waiting** for the others to arrive.
on time	at the planned time	I drove quickly and got there right **on time**. They had to rush to get to work **on time**. ✓ They had to rush to get to work **in time**. ✗
pass the time	spend time, especially when you are bored or waiting for sth	We played games to **pass the time** until the train arrived. ✓ We played games to **spend the time** until the train arrived. ✗
pass the time of day (with sb)	talk to sb for a short time in order to be friendly	I was just **passing the time of day with** him.
the right time (to do sth)	the time when sth should happen	I think now is **the right time** for you **to buy** your own house.
spend time (on sth/doing sth/with sb)	use time doing a particular thing or with a particular person	I've **spent** a lot of **time on** this project. We **spent** the whole **time lying** on the beach. You should **spend** more **time with** your brother.
spend + time expression	stay somewhere for a stated period of time	We'll have to **spend the night** in a hotel.
spend + time expression doing sth	do sth for a stated period of time	I **spent the whole weekend cleaning** up.
take (sb) time	to need or require a lot of time	Learning a language **takes time**.
take (sb) + time expression	to need or require a particular amount of time	The journey **takes four hours**.
take your time	do sth without hurrying	**Take your time** – there's no rush.
time flies	time passes very quickly.	Doesn't **time fly** when you're having fun?
waste (one's) time (on sth/with sth/doing sth)	use more time than is useful or sensible	Stop **wasting time** watching TV and get on with your homework!
be a waste of time	not be worth the time you use because there is little or no result	Arguing with her **is** a complete **waste of time**.

6 PHRASES WITH TIME

PRACTICE

1 Match 1-12 with a-m to make sentences.

0 How time — k
1 How much time
2 They spent more time
3 Unless you leave now, you won't get there
4 Don't waste
5 Don't spend too much time
6 She ran and managed to get there just in time
7 Take your time –
8 Hurry up! We can't afford to
9 We'll have to spend
10 What shall we do
11 There isn't time to
12 Enjoy your holiday. I hope you

a on time.
b for the meeting.
c explain – just do it.
d lose any more time.
e on the first question.
f have a wonderful time.
g we don't mind waiting.
h to pass the time until dinner?
i the night in the car, I'm afraid.
j your time with computer games.
k flies! We've really got to go now.
l in their hotel room than on the beach.
m does it take to get from your house to the airport?

Time flies!

2 Complete the sentences. Use one word in each gap.

0 Bye! Have a wonderful ....*time*....
1 How on earth am I going to .... the time in this boring place?
2 We were just passing the time of .... when her mobile rang.
3 I don't go out much. I .... most evenings at home, reading.
4 It's been at least two weeks. The builders are certainly .... their time with our roof!
5 No, the report isn't ready yet. These things .... time, you know.
6 Stop trying to change her mind. You're .... your time.
7 Be patient. It .... time for someone to change.
8 We .... the whole weekend decorating the living room.
9 Do we .... time for a quick game of basketball before lunch?
10 No, there were no delays – our train arrived right .... time.
11 You're just .... time to catch the last few minutes of the game.
12 I think we .... time for a quick coffee before our bus leaves.

3 Complete the phrases with *time* in the following sentences.

0 When you're in a long queue, what do you do to ....*pass the time*.... ?
1 I really think you should .... time with her. She really needs you.
2 I expect they'll be late – they hardly ever turn up ....
3 It usually .... to learn a new skill.
4 I'm sorry, I don't have .... chat now.
5 Surely there .... one last dance. Come on you two!
6 Did you .... at the party last night?
7 It's a complete .... trying to change his mind. He just won't listen.
8 Don't .... trying to explain. She'll never understand.
9 Do you .... install this program on my laptop before you go?
10 If we take a taxi, we'll be there .... for the meeting.

107

Exam practice 3

Part 1

For questions **1–12**, read the text below and decide which answer (**A**, **B**, **C** or **D**) best fits each gap. There is an example at the beginning (**0**).

EXAM TIPS

Taking exams is tough. But examiners are not insensitive people, **(0)**.......... candidates may think. Most examiners are ordinary people who do their best to pass candidates, as **(1)**.......... as candidates follow certain basic rules of the exam process. **(2)**.......... you know what is expected of you, you **(3)**.......... well.

First of all, you **(4)**.......... know how much time to spend on each question **(5)**.......... you look at the whole paper first. So, before you **(6)**.......... the test, make sure you know what is expected of you.

Do not start writing as **(7)**.......... as you get the paper: think first, **(8)**.......... write. Secondly, you are unlikely to do well unless you **(9)**.......... ALL the questions. And if you **(10)**.......... the instructions carefully, you will slip up. Thirdly, make sure you have an eraser **(11)**.......... you need to correct your mistakes. Finally, remember that **(12)**.......... your answer is right or not, the examiner cannot give you a mark for it if your handwriting is illegible!

0	**A** however	**B** (whatever)	**C** whoever	**D** whenever
1	**A** much	**B** far	**C** long	**D** soon
2	**A** Provided	**B** Whether	**C** Unless	**D** In case
3	**A** should do	**B** would do	**C** might do	**D** would have done
4	**A** don't	**B** won't	**C** wouldn't	**D** didn't
5	**A** unless	**B** if	**C** as long as	**D** whether
6	**A** sit	**B** will sit	**C** would sit	**D** could sit
7	**A** quickly	**B** immediately	**C** fast	**D** soon
8	**A** after	**B** afterwards	**C** then	**D** then later
9	**A** answer	**B** don't answer	**C** will answer	**D** won't answer
10	**A** read	**B** don't read	**C** will read	**D** won't read
11	**A** as if	**B** in case	**C** unless	**D** if only
12	**A** however	**B** if	**C** even if	**D** whether

SCORE / 12

Part 2

For questions **13-24**, read the text below and think of the word which best fits each gap. Use only **one** word in each gap. There is an example at the beginning (**0**).

DIGITAL NOISE

We live in a time of constant digital noise. Take the mobile phone. First, there are all those silly ringtones which keep going off ⁽⁰⁾ ..**wherever**.. you happen to be: on the bus, in the train, in the cinema – everywhere. It's ⁽¹³⁾........................ time something was done about it.

I don't dislike mobile phones; on the contrary, I'm very fond ⁽¹⁴⁾........................ mine, and if I didn't have it, I ⁽¹⁵⁾........................ feel lost. However, I wish people ⁽¹⁶⁾........................ not force complete strangers to listen to their endless mobile chats; ⁽¹⁷⁾........................ only they'd realise how annoying this is! I used to ⁽¹⁸⁾........................ forward to going places by train until the mobile phone appeared on the scene. Now every morning, on my way ⁽¹⁹⁾........................ work, I have to listen to people's private conversations! I can't ⁽²⁰⁾........................ listening to people chatting to their friends! If only they ⁽²¹⁾........................ something important to say! I can't bear ⁽²²⁾........................ to this junk. I ⁽²³⁾........................ sooner buy a car ⁽²⁴⁾........................ have to put up with this noise any more. I just hate noise pollution!

SCORE ____ / 12

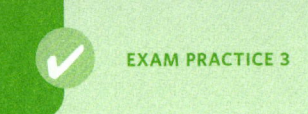

Part 3

For questions **25–34**, read the text below. Use the word given in capitals at the end of some of the lines to form a word that fits in the gap **in the same line**. There is an example at the beginning (**0**).

AYRTON SENNA

Ayrton Senna da Silva, the great Brazilian racing (0) *driver*, was born in Santana, a poor (25).......... of São Paulo, in 1960. Senna developed an interest in cars at an early age. He entered his first karting (26).......... at the age of thirteen, and in 1977 he won the South American kart (27).......... . At the time of his tragic death in 1994, he had already achieved his reputation as a great sports (28).......... .

Although Senna is remembered for his (29).......... in Formula One, for some people, his (30).......... in life was more important than his genius on the track. As Senna became more famous, he never forgot the (31).......... of so many children in Brazil. He used his (32).......... to help people less fortunate than himself. Shortly before his death, he founded an (33).......... dedicated to poor Brazilian children. Both as an athlete and as a philanthropist, he is an (34).......... to young people everywhere.

DRIVE
NEIGHBOUR

COMPETE
CHAMPION

PERSONAL
ACHIEVE
GREAT

POOR
AFFLUENT

ORGANISE

INSPIRE

SCORE ____ / 10

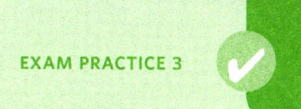

Part 4

For questions **35–42**, complete the second sentence so that it has a similar meaning to the first sentence, using the word given. **Do not change the word given.** You must use between **two** and **five** words, including the word given. Here is an example (0).

Example:

0 He's supposed to be here any moment now.
   DUE
   He .... *is due to* .... arrive any moment now.

35 My dad will be back when he's done with the shopping.
   UNTIL
   My dad won't be back .... finished the shopping.

36 We may have to take a taxi, so take some extra money with you.
   CASE
   Take some extra money with you .... take a taxi.

37 I can't wait to see them again next summer.
   FORWARD
   I'm really .... them again next summer.

38 Let me know the moment Penny arrives, will you?
   SOON
   Let me know ...., will you?

39 I'd prefer to read a book than surf the net all day.
   RATHER
   I .... a book than surf the net all day.

40 Without a password, we won't be able to log onto the site.
   UNLESS
   We won't be able to log onto the site .... a password.

41 If you arrive before seven, I can meet you outside the cinema.
   LONG
   I can meet you outside the cinema .... you arrive before seven.

42 Luke arrived late because his train was late.
   TIME
   If the train had ...., Luke wouldn't have arrived late.

7

AGENDA

Grammar
- 7a The passive: form
- 7b The passive: use, agent
- 7c The causative

Vocabulary
- 7d *get* and *have* (*got*)
- 7e Compound nouns

Entry test

1 Choose the correct answer.

1 At the moment he *is treating / is being treated* for his injuries.
2 The date of the exam *was / has* announced yesterday.
3 When they got home, the fence between the two houses *had / had been* removed.
4 A new hospital will *be / have* built here soon.
5 Dinner *isn't / hasn't* included in the price.

Now look at **7a** on pages 114–116.

SCORE /5

2 Choose the correct answer, A, B, C or D.

6 She .... in a small village in the south of Spain.
   A grew up   **B** was grown up   **C** has grown up   **D** has been grown up
7 Breakfast .... at seven o'clock.
   A serves   **B** is serving   **C** is served   **D** has served
8 It .... that five people died in the explosion.
   A is reporting   **B** is reported   **C** has reported   **D** was reporting
9 The road had been blocked .... a tree.
   A through   **B** of   **C** by   **D** with
10 The message had been written in the sand .... a stick.
   A through   **B** of   **C** by   **D** with

Now look at **7b** on pages 117–119.

SCORE /5

3 Choose the correct answer, A, B, C or D.

11 Bill .... last week.
 A had cut his hair   **B** had his hair cut   **C** got cut his hair   **D** got cutting his hair
12 Shall I have my assistant .... for a taxi?
 A phone   **B** to phone   **C** phoned   **D** phoning
13 .... our house broken into while we were away.
 A Robbers had   **B** We had   **C** It was   **D** It's been
14 We .... the roof painted yet.
 A haven't   **B** haven't had   **C** didn't get   **D** didn't have
15 We're .... a new swimming pool built.
 A doing   **B** asking   **C** making   **D** having

Now look at 7c on pages 120–121.   SCORE / 5

4 Choose the verb (A, B, C or D) that best describes the meaning of *get* in the following sentences.

16 You can *get* a second-hand mobile phone for under ten pounds.
 A buy   **B** sell   **C** hold   **D** pay
17 Could you *get* here a little sooner?
 A go   **B** leave   **C** arrive   **D** move
18 How much do you expect to *get* for your car?
 A sell   **B** buy   **C** pay   **D** receive
19 You have to press this key first. *Got* it?
 A find   **B** know   **C** understand   **D** push
20 Will you go and *get* the key, please?
 A find   **B** use   **C** bring   **D** leave

Now look at 7d on pages 122–123.   SCORE / 5

5 Complete the compound nouns in the following sentences. Use one word in each gap.

21 They've bought a new ....washer but it doesn't seem to work.
22 The house was cold, so we had a new central .... system installed.
23 We fight for .... rights such as freedom of speech.
24 There was a(n) ....-in at the office last night; the thieves stole some paintings and £5,000.
25 Mr Edwards is in hospital. He had a heart .... last night.

Now look at 7e on pages 124–127.   SCORE / 5

TOTAL SCORE / 25

Grammar

7a The passive: form

We form the passive using the following pattern: subject + *be* + past participle. The tense of the verb *be* each time is the same as the tense of the verb in the active sentence.

Tense/Form	Passive pattern	Example: passive	Example: active
Present simple	am/is/are + past participle	Champagne **is made** in France.	They make champagne in France.
Present continuous	am/is/are being + past participle	The matter **is** still **being considered**.	They are still considering the matter.
Past simple	was/were + past participle	The date **was announced** yesterday. The school **was built** by the local government. ✓ The school **has built** by the local government. ✗	They announced the date yesterday. The local government built the school.
Past continuous	was/were being + past participle	Every effort **was being made** to end the strike.	They were making every effort to end the strike.
Present perfect	have/has been + past participle	A new stadium **has been built** in London.	They've built a new stadium in London.
Past perfect	had been + past participle	The work **had been finished** by 2011.	They had finished the work by 2011.
Future simple	will be + past participle	You **will be examined** by Mr Roberts.	Mr Roberts will examine you.
Future perfect	will have been + past participle	The project **will have been completed** by June.	They will have completed the project by June.
be going to	am/is/are going to be + past participle	A new hospital **is going to be built** here.	They're going to build a new hospital here.
Modal verb	modal + *be* + past participle	The house **must be cleaned**.	They must clean the house.

- We do not usually use the passive in the present perfect continuous, the past perfect continuous, the future continuous or the future perfect continuous:
  We **will be being watched**. ✗
  They **will be watching** us. ✓
- We form passive questions and negative sentences in the same way as in the active:
  When **are** important subjects usually **discussed**?
  Experiments **are not carried out** in this room.

- In passive sentences, we place adverbs of frequency, time, etc. (e.g. *always, sometimes, just,* etc.) after the first auxiliary verb (*is, has, will,* etc.):
  It is **usually** made of wood.
  They have **just** been found.
  She will **never** be forgotten.

THE PASSIVE: FORM 7

PRACTICE

1 Complete the sentences. Use the correct passive form of the verbs in brackets.

0 The police report that the missing person *has already been found* (already / find).
1 The news .... (broadcast) at six o'clock every day.
2 At the moment, the suspect .... (interview) by the police.
3 The cinema .... (close down) four years ago.
4 A new security system .... (install) in all our offices in the next few weeks.
5 A new government .... (elect) by the end of next month.
6 There must be a mistake – the hotel bill .... (already / pay) by my wife.
7 When we got home, we realised that the house .... (burgle).
8 The second bomb went off while the building .... (evacuate).
9 The government says tax reforms .... (introduce) next year.
10 In some countries, newspapers .... (sell) in kiosks as well as supermarkets.

2 Rewrite the sentences in the passive.

0 We do not add preservatives to our products.
  Preservatives are not added to our products.
1 They are building a new school in West Street.
  ....
2 They have just arrested him on suspicion of murder.
  ....
3 They will publish her new book next month.
  ....
4 They will have completed the new motorway by Christmas.
  ....
5 They've just cleaned the hotel rooms.
  ....
6 Someone stole her bike last night.
  ....
7 They're going to repair the machine tomorrow.
  ....
8 They were servicing her car when I called her.
  ....
9 They had finished the project by Friday.
  ....
10 They may invite him to the wedding.
  ....

> *The service in the hotel was so bad that when I asked for a hot towel, I **was told** to put a cold one on the radiator.*

115

7 THE PASSIVE: FORM

3 **Complete the article. Use the correct passive form of the verbs in brackets.**

Credit card fraud

A type of con trick which **(0)** *is designed* (design) to skim your credit card number, PIN and other information when you swipe has been growing in popularity. The con, which **(1)**............... (know) as skimming, allows thieves to steal your information by the use of a device which **(2)**............... (insert) through the card slot of an ATM, allowing the data on your card to be read.

The latest European ATM Crime Report **(3)**............... (just / publish) and it shows a twenty-four percent increase in card skimming attacks at European ATMs in the last year. 5,743 attacks **(4)**............... (report) for the period January to June this year. This is the largest number of such attacks which **(5)**............... (record) in any six-month period so far. Already, millions of pounds **(6)**............... (lost) through skimming and more **(7)**............... (lose) if effective measures **(8)**............... (not take).

The theft of personal details **(9)**............... (may / avoid) by using secure ATMs or being very careful when you use an ATM. Anti-skimming measures **(10)**............... (already / install) at many European ATMs. Fortunately, in some countries, a drop in skimming attacks **(11)**............... (report). Cardholders should know that even if their card details **(12)**............... (skim), they will not lose out. This is good news for members of the public.

*Most of the staff **had been** poorly **trained**.*

116

7b The passive: use, agent

Use

We often use the passive in the following situations:

Use	Example
when it is obvious or not important to say who did the action	He **has** just **been arrested**. A cure **has** just **been found.**
to avoid using a vague subject (e.g. *they, someone*)	The job **will be finished** by tonight.
to describe a process	The beans **are separated** from the shells and then they **are put** into sacks.
in official announcements	Fees **must be paid** in advance.
in scientific texts	The liquid **is heated** to a temperature of 90°C.
in written reports	The meeting **was held** on 21 January.

- We often use the passive with verbs like *think, suggest, believe, expect, know*, etc. in the following patterns:
  - *it* + passive + *that* clause
    It was reported that five people died in the accident.
  - subject + passive + *to*-infinitive
    She is thought to be one of the world's finest cellists.
- The structure *be supposed to* has a different meaning from *be thought to*:
  She's supposed to be your friend. (= but she isn't behaving like a friend)
- When an active verb has two objects, either object can be the subject of the passive sentence:
  They gave him **some money**. (= active)
  He was given **some money**.
  Some money was given **to him**.
- It is, however, more common for the indirect object (usually a person) to become the subject of the passive sentence:
  They gave us more time to finish the project.
  We were given more time to finish the project.
  More time was given to us to finish the project. (= possible but less common)
- Intransitive verbs (verbs that do not take an object) are never used in the passive:
  The job **seemed** easy at first. ✓
  ~~The job **was seemed** easy at first.~~ ✗

Agent

- In passive sentences, we often don't mention the doer of the action (the agent). We are more interested in the action itself. If, however, we want to mention the agent, we use *by*:
  This book was written **by Christopher Wallace**.
- If we want to mention a tool or instrument that was used for the action, we use *with*:
  The victim was killed **with a knife**.
- We only mention the agent when it adds important information to the sentence. If the agent is unknown, unimportant or obvious, we omit it:
  He was fined for driving without a licence. (It is clear who fined him: the police. We do not mention the agent.)
  The suspect was interviewed **by Detective Smith**. (The agent adds important information to the sentence.)
- We also omit the agent when we want to avoid saying who was responsible for an action:
  I've been told not to say anything.

7 THE PASSIVE: USE, AGENT

PRACTICE

1 Complete the sentences. Use *by* or *with*.

0 This church was designed ...**by**... Christopher Wren.
1 The dog had been shot .... a hunter.
2 A decision to strike was taken .... some of the workers.
3 The poor man had been stabbed .... a penknife.
4 The candidates' essays will be marked .... Professor Richards.
5 The room was filled .... smoke.
6 I think all the pictures were taken .... a professional photographer.
7 The man was beaten .... a stick.
8 The walls were covered .... posters of her favourite singers.

2 Rewrite the sentences in the passive in two ways.

0 They sent him a letter.
He was sent a letter.
A letter was sent to him.

1 They gave each of the children a bottle of milk.
....
....

2 They will pay the workers £50.
....
....

3 They may offer her the job.
....
....

4 They teach the students French.
....
....

5 They showed us the sights.
....
....

6 Someone's telling the children a story.
....
....

7 Someone gave them a lot of money.
....
....

8 They've just sent me an email.
....
....

7 THE PASSIVE: USE, AGENT

3 **Complete the second sentence so that it has a similar meaning to the first sentence, using the word given. Use between two and five words. Do not change the word given.**

0 Reports say that the plane has landed safely.
   IS
   It *is reported that* the plane has landed safely.

1 They say the country is on the verge of civil war.
   SAID
   The country .... on the verge of civil war.

2 People thought that the President was ill.
   BE
   The President .... ill.

3 The architect received £50,000 for his work.
   WAS
   £50,000 .... for his work.

4 People believe that he escaped.
   HAVE
   He is .... escaped.

5 They thought that he was the best actor for the part.
   CONSIDERED
   He .... the best actor for the part.

6 People thought she was very good at maths, but she failed her last test.
   SUPPOSED
   She .... very good at maths, but she failed her last test.

7 They decided to discuss the matter at the next meeting.
   AGREED
   It .... the matter would be discussed at the next meeting.

8 They showed the new science lab to the students.
   WERE
   The .... the new science lab.

9 Everything I know about art, I learnt from Mrs Robinson.
   TAUGHT
   I .... about art by Mrs Robinson.

10 They used a digital camera to take these photos.
   WITH
   These .... a digital camera.

> 'I **am informed** from many quarters that a rumour **has been put about** that I died this morning. This is quite untrue.' WINSTON CHURCHILL

119

7c The causative

have/get something done

- The pattern for the causative form is *have/get* + object + past participle:
  I'm **having my house decorated** at the moment.
  You ought to **get your blood pressure checked**.

- We use the causative form when we arrange for somebody else to do something for us:
  We've just **had the air-conditioning installed**. (= We didn't do it ourselves. Somebody else did it for us.)

- We also use the causative form to talk about something unpleasant. In this case, we use *have* but not *get*:
  I **had my wallet stolen** last night. ✓
  I ~~got my wallet stolen last night~~. ✗
  He **had his house broken into** last week. ✓
  ~~He got his house broken into last week~~. ✗

- Sometimes, *have/get something done* suggests the need to deal with a difficulty:
  I'm afraid you'll have to **get the whole house rewired**.

have somebody do something, get somebody to do something

We use the following patterns to mean 'make, persuade or cause someone to do something':

- *have* + sb + infinitive
  Shall I **have my secretary send** you the details?
  I'll **have my assistant bring** you a copy.

- *get* + sb + to-infinitive
  Shall I **get my secretary to send** you the details?
  I'll **get my assistant to bring** you a copy.

get + past participle

We often use *get* + past participle to mean 'become':
She **got dressed** and went downstairs.
My dog **got run over** by a van.

7 THE CAUSATIVE

PRACTICE

1 Complete the conversations. Use the causative form of *have* and the verbs in brackets.

0 **A:** Your hair looks nice.
  B: Thanks, I *have just had it cut*. (just / it / cut)

1 **A:** I'm finding it difficult to read small print nowadays.
  B: Why don't you go and .... (your eyes / test)?

2 **A:** What a lovely dress!
  B: Thanks, I .... (it / make) for my birthday last year.

3 **A:** My car's been making some funny noises lately.
  B: You should .... (it / service).

4 **A:** I'm freezing!
  B: We really need to .... (central heating / install).

5 **A:** The living room looks lovely.
  B: I'm glad you like it. We .... (just / it / redecorate).

6 **A:** Why aren't you wearing your watch?
  B: Actually, I .... (it / repair) at the moment.

7 **A:** Oops! Sorry, I've just spilt my coffee on the tablecloth!
  B: Don't worry. I was going to .... (it / dry-clean) anyway.

8 **A:** That tree is blocking the view from my front window.
  B: Well, you don't expect me to .... (it / cut down), do you?

9 **A:** I've got a terrible toothache!
  B: Well, you really should .... (that cavity / fill).

10 **A:** We .... (a swimming pool / build) last weekend.
   B: Really? How much did it cost you?

2 Complete the text. Use one word in each gap.

Well, we (0) *had* our house broken into last week. It was awful – they wrecked the place. Not only did we (1) .... things taken, not only did I have my beautiful iPhone and camera (2) .... but a lot of things also (3) .... broken as they searched the house. Some of the windows (4) .... smashed as they tried to break in, so now we've got to get all the damage (5) ....

So we've decided to give the house a complete makeover. We're going to (6) .... the whole house redecorated. The first place we're going to start is the living room. We're going to have (7) .... repainted. I want to have one of the walls (8) .... green, something I've always wanted. I'll also get my housemate (9) .... build a new TV stand and CD tower – both green, of course!

Since the burglary, I've also become more active in the community and have campaigned to (10) .... new surveillance cameras installed in our street. This means a lot of trees will (11) .... chopped down to make people's houses visible to the camera but it is a small sacrifice compared with the safety and security of our homes.

WAITER: How would you like **to have your eggs cooked**, sir?
CUSTOMER: Is there any difference in the price?
WAITER: No, sir.
CUSTOMER: Then please **have the chef cook** them with ham, potatoes and sausages.

121

Vocabulary

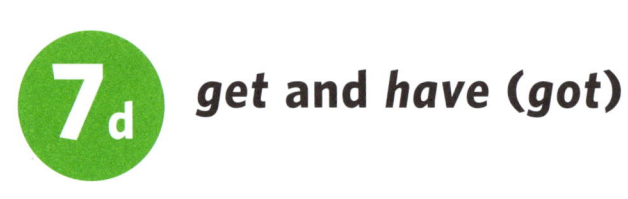

7d get and have (got)

get

Meaning/Use	Example
receive, experience	Sharon always seems to **get** loads of mail. He'll **get** a shock when he sees the bill.
obtain	Where did you **get** that painting? He's gone to **get** help.
buy	I **got** the plant from Columbia Road Market. I **got** this pullover for £30.
receive (money)	I only **got** £50 for my old bike. She **gets** £300 a week.
catch (an illness)	It's fairly unusual for adults to **get** measles. When I was five, I **got** the mumps.
arrive	What time will we **get** there?
move	I can't **get** the car out of the garage. ~~Leave out of~~ my house! ✗ **Get out of** my house! ✓
become (get + adjective/past participle – see page 120)	When I tried to talk to him about it, he just **got** really **angry**. **Get dressed** and come downstairs immediately!
make sb/sth do something (get + sb + to-infinitive – see page 120)	Why don't you **get Chris to wash** the car? I wonder if Frank can **get the DVD player to work**.
begin doing sth	Let's **get** moving – what are we waiting for?
understand	Oh, I **get it**. You put the paper in here and then press the button.
bring	Run upstairs and **get** a pillow.
reach (get to + noun)	I haven't **got to** the end of the book yet.

have (got)

We can use *have* or *have got* for the meanings below:

Meaning/Use	Example
own, possess	What kind of car **has** she **got**/does she **have**? I'**ve got** two sisters. ✓ ~~I got two sisters.~~ ✗
possess particular characteristics	She'**s got**/**has** an awful temper.

For *have (got) to*, see **3a**

7 GET AND HAVE (GOT)

PRACTICE

1 Match 1–8 with a–i to make sentences.

0 Why do I always get — **d**
1 I'm still in shock – I got
2 Is there anywhere I can get
3 Ewan's just popped out to get
4 In the sales, I got
5 He's in bed because he's got
6 How on earth are you going to get
7 Four hours later, we finally got
8 It's getting late – we should get

a such a surprise when I opened the door!
b a cold off one of the kids at school.
c some groceries.
d socks for Christmas?
e going.
f a great DVD player for less than £200.
g that piano down the stairs?
h a good haircut?
i to the camp, tired and hungry.

2 Complete the sentences. Use the words and phrases in the box.

> cold   going   it   ~~silly~~   the car   the joke   the kids
> those wet clothes   to the end

0 This game is getting ...**silly**... – let's stop it.
1 It's getting .... outside. Let's go inside.
2 I can't get .... to start.
3 Let's get .... – we're already late as it is.
4 You need to press the green button and wait – got ....?
5 She's just gone to get .... from school.
6 You'd better get .... off or you'll catch a cold.
7 When you get .... of the test, let me know.
8 I still don't get .... – it must be my sense of humour!

3 Choose the verb that best describes the meaning of *get* in each case. You can use some of the verbs more than once.

> become   buy   make   obtain   receive   understand

There are four kinds of 'junk' in my life that get on my nerves. The first is junk mail that I (0) **get** by email, the second is traditional junk mail the postman brings; the third is phone calls I (1) **get** from people I don't know – just when I'm trying to (2) **get** a nap in the afternoon. In most cases, a stranger is trying to (3) **get** me to buy something – they tell me to (4) **get** a new credit card or (5) **get** something at a bargain price. I (6) **get** really annoyed when I'm woken up by these calls! I try and (7) **get** them to stop by putting the phone down but that doesn't always work because I also (8) **get** recorded messages!
The fourth kind of junk is emails I (9) **get** from Kate. Kate is a friend who spends most of her free time surfing the net and finding jokes. So all her friends (10) **get** lots of cyber jokes from her every day. She just doesn't (11) **get** it: I'd rather not (12) **get** links to every Internet site she finds funny! I usually don't even (13) **get** the joke. To me, it's just all junk.

0 ...**receive**...
1 ....
2 ....
3 ....
4 ....
5 ....
6 ....
7 ....
8 ....
9 ....
10 ....
11 ....
12 ....
13 ....

123

7e Compound nouns

Form

- A compound noun consists of two or three words that function like one word.

Form	Example
noun + noun	notebook, timetable, science fiction
adjective + noun	fast lane, fast food, first aid
verb + particle	breakup, checkout, takeover
three words, with the first two words used adjectivally and usually joined with a hyphen	back-seat driver, one-parent family, ready-made meal, three-piece suite

- We can write compound nouns as one word, as two words or as two words with a hyphen (-). There are no definite rules for this. If in doubt, consult a dictionary:

  babysitter   mother tongue
  sunglasses   youth hostel
  roadworks   human being
  address book   break-in

Countable or uncountable?

Compound nouns may:
- be countable:
  one alarm clock – two alarm clocks
  a car park – several car parks
  a compact disc – ninety compact discs
- be uncountable:
  air traffic control   chewing gum
  mineral water   table tennis
- only have a plural form:
  armed forces   human rights
  roadworks   sunglasses

For compound adjectives, see 9e

Here is a list of common countable, uncountable and plural compound nouns:

Countable	Uncountable	Plural
baggage hall	air conditioning	bagpipes
bank account	blood pressure	bedclothes
break-in	cardboard	civil rights
breakout	central heating	current affairs
burglar alarm	common sense	denim jeans
can opener	cotton wool	French fries
car park	dry cleaning	high heels
clothes peg	fancy dress	inverted commas
computer game	fast food	last orders
credit card	feedback	legal proceedings
cutback	first aid	luxury goods
database	food poisoning	modern languages
dining room	higher education	nail scissors
dishwasher	iced tea	natural resources
drawing pin	ill-treatment	nutcrackers
driving licence	job sharing	Olympic Games
fairytale	junk food	opening hours
film star	keyhole surgery	outskirts
frying pan	lateral thinking	party politics
letterbox	make-up	race relations
life support system	metalwork	reading glasses
minimum wage	mineral water	roadworks
mirror image	New Year's Day	roller skates
mobile phone	ovenware	scare tactics
motorway	peacetime	sunglasses
number plate	power dressing	swimming trunks
painkiller	rainwater	taste buds
penalty shoot-out	realestate	traffic lights
pepper grinder	software	underpants
question mark	stomachache	walking boots
road map	sunshine	winter sports
skateboard	toilet paper	waterworks
television series	tomato ketchup	
throwback	whooping cough	
trial run	work experience	
washing-up	writing paper	
word processor		

124

7 COMPOUND NOUNS

PRACTICE

1 Complete the table. Write the words in the box in the correct column.

> air conditioning   heart attack   high school   human nature   letterbox   news bulletin   old age
> parking meter   personal computer   pocket money   police station   post office   remote control
> show business   sleeping bag   social work   soda water   swimming pool   toilet paper
> washing machine   washing powder   washing-up liquid   water skiing   writing paper

Countable		Uncountable	
heart attack	high school	air conditioning	human nature

2 Match the two parts of the compound nouns in each list. Then complete the sentences with compound nouns from the two lists.

noun + noun
- 0 fire — e — a crossing
- 1 zebra — b card
- 2 pocket — c washer
- 3 dish — d opener
- 4 lap — e brigade
- 5 credit — f alarm
- 6 burglar — g money
- 7 can — h case
- 8 suit — i top

adjective + noun
- 0 remote — c — a school
- 1 social — b sense
- 2 high — c control
- 3 central — d food
- 4 common — e fries
- 5 French — f rights
- 6 dry — g heating
- 7 human — h cleaner's
- 8 fast — i worker

0 Quick! Phone the *fire brigade*! The house next door is on fire!
1 They should put a .... outside the school so that children can cross the road safely.
2 It's freezing in here! Why don't you get .... installed?
3 Is the .... you get from your parents enough for your needs?
4 When you leave primary school and get to ...., lessons get much more difficult.
5 He'll never think of such a simple solution because he hasn't got any ....
6 Who's got the ....? Will you please change the channel?
7 Could you pick up my suit from the .... on your way home?
8 After the last break-in, they decided to get a .... installed.
9 Do you usually pay in cash or by ....?
10 No, he isn't a police officer – he's a ....

125

7 COMPOUND NOUNS

3 Complete the crossword. The missing words are parts of compound nouns.

Across

1. My .... cleaning has to be picked up before six.
2. Eric thinks wearing .... glasses even when it's raining makes him look cool.
7. At our school, they didn't turn on the central .... until October.
8. We can omit .... commas when we report what someone says.
9. You don't need to wear ....-up. You look beautiful without it!
10. Did you know that chewing .... is illegal in Singapore?
11. It's just common .... not to walk home on your own.

Down

1. We could hire a van. Do you have a valid .... licence?
2. He's a student at the Manchester School of Economic and Social ....
3. You should avoid .... food like hamburgers if you want to lose weight.
4. I'd like a cheeseburger and some French ...., please.
5. The multi-storey car .... is going to be knocked down.
6. I stood at the bus .... for over an hour and then six buses came along at once!
7. It's about time the world paid more attention to .... rights issues.

4 Complete the sentences. Use the compound nouns in the box.

> ~~break-in~~   breakout   breakup   check-in   checkout   getaway
> hold-up   printout   setback   takeaway   take-off

0. Since the *break-in*, we've had all our locks changed.
1. I'm afraid there's been a slight .... in our plans.
2. Come on, let's go! What's the ....?
3. The thieves made their .... in a black car.
4. Carol works on the .... at the local supermarket.
5. There was a mass .... from Winston Prison last night.
6. The .... of her marriage was also the end of her career.
7. Let's have a .... tonight. I'm too tired to cook.
8. Please fasten your seatbelts. The plane is ready for ....
9. I'd give you a .... of Joe's email but my printer's not working.
10. You need to be at the .... at least two hours before departure.

126

COMPOUND NOUNS 7

5 **Complete the text. Use the words in the box.**

> common   fast   heels   hot   junk   licence   make-up
> mobile   roller   ~~schoolmates~~   skateboards   stomach
> sunglasses   text   tomato   traffic

My best friend Beryl was always a bit different from my other ⁽⁰⁾ _schoolmates_. She was very intelligent but she didn't have much ⁽¹⁾............. sense. For example, she wore ⁽²⁾............. indoors, even when it was cloudy. And she wore high ⁽³⁾............. when everybody else was wearing trainers. It was against the rules to wear ⁽⁴⁾............. at school but she wore it anyway. We were also not allowed to use our ⁽⁵⁾............. phones but she would secretly send ⁽⁶⁾............. messages while the teacher was talking. She always did the opposite of what everyone else did. So when we all had ⁽⁷⁾............. or bikes, she would prefer ⁽⁸⁾............. skates and so on.

We were always advised to eat healthy food but Beryl always ate ⁽⁹⁾............. food – usually ⁽¹⁰⁾............. dogs covered in ⁽¹¹⁾............. ketchup and mustard – until she got a terrible ⁽¹²⁾............. ache.

Beryl was also in love with speed. As soon as she was old enough to have a driving ⁽¹³⁾............., she got a car and always drove fast. Once she went straight through the red ⁽¹⁴⁾............. lights and had to pay a fine. Yes, Beryl always drove in life's ⁽¹⁵⁾............. lane. I wonder where she is now.

> **Grandma** would often **babysit** her **grandchildren** but she would always fall asleep in her **armchair** before they did. Once, her five-year-old **grandson** woke her up saying, 'Wake up, Granny! It's past my **bedtime**!'

127

8

AGENDA

Grammar
- 8a Reported speech (1)
- 8b Reported speech (2)
- 8c -ing forms and infinitives after verbs

Vocabulary
- 8d say, tell, talk, speak, etc.
- 8e -ed and -ing adjectives

Entry test

1 Choose the correct answer.

1 'Let's go to the cinema,' Amy *suggested / announced*.
2 She *told / explained* that she had been feeling unwell.
3 Sue *insisted / begged* John to help her.
4 They warned the children *not to go / do not go* near the river.
5 She said she *was / had been* trying to phone you all day.

Now look at 8a on pages 130–133.

SCORE ___ / 5

2 Choose the correct answer, A, B, C or D.

6 The judge asked the witness .... give her more information.
 A that he **B** if he could **C** that he could **D** whether he

7 They asked if .... always wanted to be a doctor.
 A did she **B** has she **C** had she **D** she had

8 Mark asked .... going to lend them the money.
 A that I was **B** if I was **C** was I **D** whether was I

9 They wanted to know what .... the money on.
 A she'd spent **B** had she spent **C** did she spend **D** she did spend

10 I asked Jo .... in a flat.
 A if she live **B** does she live **C** whether she lived **D** did she live

Now look at 8b on pages 134–136.

SCORE ___ / 5

128

3 Choose the correct answer, A, B, C or D.

11 The car swerved to avoid .... the pedestrian.
   A hit   B to hit   C hitting   D that it hit

12 Emily admitted .... know the answer to the question.
   A to not   B not to   C of not   D that she didn't

13 Would you like .... with us tonight?
   A you come   B to come   C coming   D to coming

14 Jamie is hoping .... law at Harvard.
   A he studies   B to study   C studying   D to studying

15 I'd rather .... the children decide for themselves.
   A I let   B that I let   C let   D letting

Now look at 8c on pages 137–139.   SCORE ___ / 5

4 Choose the correct answer, A, B, C or D.

16 What did the newspaper .... about the accident?
   A tell   B refer   C say   D speak

17 I was persuaded .... on the trip at the last minute.
   A to go   B me to go   C that I go   D for going

18 She convinced the court .... innocent.
   A to be   B for being   C being   D that she was

19 The suspect .... that he had been to the bank that day.
   A refused   B rejected   C denied   D told

20 We made her an excellent offer but she .... it.
   A refused   B rejected   C denied   D accepted

Now look at 8d on pages 140–142.   SCORE ___ / 5

5 Choose the correct answer.

21 I'm sorry but I don't find her jokes at all *amused / amusing*.
22 We were all really *disappointed / disappointing* when the concert was cancelled.
23 He's got some really *annoyed / annoying* habits!
24 The lecture was so *bored / boring* I nearly fell asleep.
25 She has the most *charmed / charming* little cottage I've ever seen.

Now look at 8e on pages 143–145.   SCORE ___ / 5

TOTAL SCORE ___ / 25

129

Grammar

8a Reported speech (1)

Direct speech

- When we quote someone's actual words, we can use reporting verbs like *say, reply, suggest, shout*, etc.:
'Let's go swimming,' Peter **suggested**.
- The speaker's words can come before or after the reporting verb:
'I knew the answer,' she said.
She said, 'I knew the answer.'
- Notice the punctuation in direct speech: the speaker's words are put in inverted commas. The comma, full stop, question mark or exclamation mark come before the closing quotation mark:
'You mustn't give up,' his mother insisted.
'Do you take sugar?' she asked.
'Help!' she shouted.

Reported statements

- In reported speech, we report what someone said earlier, without quoting their actual words.
- When we report someone's words, we often use a past tense reporting verb like *said, told, suggested*, etc.:
She **said** (that) she knew the answer.
- After a past tense reporting verb, we usually make changes to verb tenses, pronouns and possessive adjectives, as well as place and time references:
'I'm visiting my cousins tomorrow,' Penny said.
Penny said that **she was visiting her** cousins **the following day**.

Changes in reported speech

- In reported speech, tenses and modal verbs change as follows:

Direct speech → Reported speech	Example	
present simple → past simple	'I **want** to buy it.'	He said (that) he **wanted** to buy it.
present continuous → past continuous	'I**'m leaving**.'	He said (that) he **was leaving**.
past simple → past perfect simple	'I **saw** her.'	He said (that) he **had seen** her.
past continuous → past perfect continuous	'I **was working**.'	He said (that) **he had been working**.
present perfect simple → past perfect simple	'I**'ve finished**.'	He said (that) he **had finished**.
present perfect continuous → past perfect continuous	'I**'ve been running**.'	He said (that) he **had been running**.
am/is/are going to → was/were going to	'I**'m going to** stay.'	He said (that) he **was going to** stay.
will → would	'I**'ll** help you.'	He said (that) he **would** help me.
can → could	'I **can** do it.'	He said (that) he **could** do it.
may → might	'I **may** do it.'	He said (that) he **might** do it.
must → had to	'I **must** go.'	He said (that) he **had to** go.

REPORTED SPEECH (1) 8

- The past perfect simple and past perfect continuous don't change in reported speech:
'I **had finished**.' → He said (that) he **had finished**.
'I **had been running**.' → He said that he **had been running**.

- *Could, would, might, should* and *ought to* don't change in reported speech:
'I **might** join you.' → He said (that) he **might** join us.

- When the reporting verb is in a present tense, there is no change in reported speech:
'I **may** be late.' → He **says** (that) he **may** be late.

- We do not need to change the verb tense when we are reporting things that are still true:
'I**'ve got** a brother.' → He told me (that) he**'s got** a brother.
However, after past reporting verbs, we usually change the tenses, even if the things we are reporting are still true.

- These words and phrases also change in reported speech:

Direct speech	Reported speech
here	there
this/these	that/those
this/that + noun	the + noun
ago	before
last week	the week before, the previous week
next week	the week after, the following week
now	then
today, tonight	that day, that night
this morning	that morning
tomorrow	the next/following day, the day after
yesterday	the day before, the previous day

Reported commands and requests

- When we report commands and requests, we use the following pattern: reporting verb + sb + *to*-infinitive:
'Please stay, John,' she said. → She **asked John to stay**.

- *Tell, order* and *ask* are some common reporting verbs for commands and requests:
'Be quiet!' she told them. → She **told** them to be quiet.
'Stop!' the police officer told him. → The police officer **ordered** him to stop.
'Please let me stay, Dad,' Anne said. → Anne **asked** her dad to let her stay.

- Note that when we report negative commands and requests, we use *not* before the *to*-infinitive.
'Please don't do it,' she told him. → She told him **not to do** it.

Reporting verbs

- We often use different reporting verbs to summarise what someone said.
'Why don't you stay with us?' → They **invited** me to stay with them.

- Reporting verbs can describe the speaker's intention, or tell us more about the way someone says something:
'I'll call the police.' → She **threatened** to call the police.
'I'll carry the books.' → He **offered** to carry the books.

- Different reporting verbs are used with different structures. Below are some common ones. Note that some verbs can be used with more than one structure:

131

8 REPORTED SPEECH (1)

Verbs	Examples
verb + *to*-infinitive agree, decide, demand, offer, promise, propose, refuse, swear, threaten, volunteer	'No, I won't do it!' → He **refused to do** it. 'Can I help you?' → She **offered to help** me. 'I'll come back.' → He **promised to come back**.
verb + sb + *to*-infinitive advise, beg, encourage, forbid, instruct, invite, order, persuade, urge, warn	'Please don't go!' → She **begged him** not **to go**. 'Don't cross that bridge!' → She **warned me** not **to cross** the bridge. 'You should talk to Nikki.' → He **advised me to talk** to Nikki.
verb + *-ing* admit, deny, recommend, suggest	'I stole the money,' → He **admitted stealing** the money. 'I didn't steal the money.' → He **denied stealing** the money.
verb (+ sb) + preposition + *-ing* accuse sb of, agree (with sb) on/about, apologise (to sb) for, complain (to sb) about, congratulate sb on, insist on	'You stole the money.' → She **accused me of stealing** the money. 'I'm sorry I'm late.' → He **apologised for being** late. 'You won! Well done!' → She **congratulated me on winning**.
verb (+ sb) + *that* clause add, admit, agree, announce, boast, claim, complain, decide, deny, explain, inform (sb), persuade (sb), promise (sb), remind (sb), report, suggest, threaten, warn (sb)	'Yes, it's a good idea.' → He **agreed that** it was a good idea. 'My soup is cold!' → She **complained that** her soup was cold. 'I'll come back.' → He **promised** (me) **that** he would come back. 'It's Jane's birthday.' → She **reminded me that** it was Jane's birthday.

- *Suggest* can be followed by the following structures:
  - suggest + *-ing*:
    'Let's go to the cinema.' → I suggested going to the cinema.
  - suggest + that + past simple:
    I suggested that we went to the cinema.
  - suggest + that + sb + should + infinitive:
    I suggested that we should go to the cinema.

For reported questions, see 8b

PRACTICE

1 Report the statements.

0 'Let me help you.'
  My friend offered to help me.

1 'I wasn't anywhere near the scene of the crime.'
  The accused claimed ....

2 'This spot is the best place for a picnic.'
  My father said ....

3 'We're leaving tomorrow.'
  Ella said ....

4 'Please answer the phone.'
  He asked his son ....

5 'I gave you the money last week.'
  She insisted ....

6 'Put your hands up!'
  The man ordered me ....

7 'If I were you, I wouldn't work so hard.'
  My friend advised me ....

8 'No, I won't lend him the money.'
  Joan refused ....

132

REPORTED SPEECH (1) 8

2 Match the statements (1–10) with the reporting verbs (a–k).

0 'If you do that again, I'll leave,' she told me.   i   a ask
1 'I'm going to retire soon,' he said.   h   b beg
2 'Please bring us the wine list,' she told the waiter.   a   c explain
3 'Our team will easily beat yours,' he told us.   k   d warn
4 'Please, please give me another chance,' she told him.   b   e remind
5 'I'm innocent, Your Honour,' he told the judge.   g   f advise
6 'I was late because I missed my bus,' she said.   c   g claim
7 'Why don't we play a game?' he said.   j   h announce
8 'Don't forget to phone Alex,' she told him.   e   i threaten
9 'Careful! The water's deep!' he said.   d   j suggest
10 'You should be more careful in the future,' she told the student.   f   k boast

3 Report the statements in Exercise 2.

0 She threatened to leave if I did that again.
1 ....
2 ....
3 ....
4 ....
5 ....
6 ....
7 ....
8 ....
9 ....
10 ....

4 Complete the text. Use one word in each gap.

Logged in

Monday, 17 October

A new teacher

The first day back at school. We were waiting for our new teacher and I wondered what he or she would be like. Suddenly, the door opened and a tall thin man walked in. He looked at us, smiled and told (0) **us** to sit down and be quiet. Billy O'Reilly (1) ...., 'Good morning, sir! What's your name?' in his loud cheery voice but the new teacher (2) .... him to put his hand up and (3) .... to shout out without permission. He told us that his name (4) .... Mr John Walker. Billy giggled. 'What are you laughing at?' (5) .... Mr Walker. Billy said he (6) .... a cough and he followed this with a loud cough; the whole class laughed. The teacher smiled and said we (7) .... call him John. He explained (8) .... he wanted us to work hard and play hard. He said that the text we (9) .... do together for the English exam was Shakespeare's *Romeo and Juliet*. He said we (10) .... to read the first two scenes before the (11) .... week's lesson. He smiled again and said he (12) .... sure we would get on very well. Then he asked if we had any questions.

133

8b Reported speech (2)

Reported questions

- In reported questions, the word order is the same as in statements:
 '*Can I leave the room?*' *I asked.* → *I asked if* **I could leave** *the room.*
 She asked me **where I was** *from.* ✓
 ~~*She asked me* **where was I** *from.*~~ ✗

- We do not use the auxiliary *do/does/did* in reported questions:
 '*What do you want?*' *he asked me.* → *He asked* **what I wanted**.

- We do not use a question mark in reported questions:
 '*How is Johnny getting on at school?*' *she asked.* → *She asked how Johnny was getting on at school.*

- Some reporting verbs we often use in reported questions are: *ask, inquire, wonder, want to know*:
 She **wanted to know** *where I was going.*

- In reported questions, the tense changes and the changes to place/time references are the same as those for reported statements:
 '**Are** *you OK?*' → *She asked if I* **was** *OK.*
 '*Is Jamie* **here**?' → *He asked if Jamie was* **there**.

Yes/No questions

- When we report questions that can be answered with 'yes' or 'no' (e.g. *Are you happy here? Do you live in a flat?*), we use *if* or *whether* after the reporting verb:
 '*Are you happy here?*' *he asked.* → *He asked* **if/whether** *I was happy there.*
 '*Does he live in a big flat?*' *she asked.* → *She asked* **if/whether** *he lived in a big flat.*

- We can use *if* and *whether* in the same way:
 '*Are the summers very hot there?*' *he inquired.* → *He asked* **if /whether** *the summers were very hot there.*
 '*Have you always lived in the old town?*' *she asked him.* → *She asked him* **if/whether** *he had always lived in the old town.*

- However, when we are asking someone to make a choice, we usually use *whether*:
 '*Do you want coffee or tea?*' *they asked me.* → *They asked me* **whether** *I wanted coffee or tea.*

- We use *whether* (not *if*) when the reported question includes the phrase *or not*:
 '*Are you going to tell me the answer or not?*' *she asked.* → *She asked* **whether** *I was going to tell her the answer* **or not**.
 '*Is he coming or not?*' *I asked.* → *I asked* **whether** *he was coming* **or not**.

Wh- questions

- When we report questions that begin with a question word (*who, where, why, what, when, how, how long,* etc.), we use the question word in the reported question:
 '*Who built that castle?*' *she asked.* → *She wanted to know* **who had built** *the castle.*
 '*Where did you go this summer?*' *he asked.* → *He asked* **where** *we had gone that summer.*
 '*Why are you laughing?*' *she asked us.* → *She asked us* **why we were** *laughing.*

REPORTED SPEECH (2) 8

Practice

1 Choose the correct answer.

0 The interviewer wanted to know where *(I was)/ was I* from.
1 He also asked if *I had / did I have* any work experience.
2 He asked how old *am I / I was*.
3 He wanted to know what *have I / I had* been doing since I left school.
4 He asked *when / whether* I had had a nice trip down from Liverpool.
5 He also asked how long *the journey had taken / did the journey take*.
6 He asked me what *I liked / did I like* most about my job.
7 He wanted to know who *had told / had they told* me about their company.
8 He asked me what *I thought / did I think* the qualities of a good manager were.
9 He *told / inquired* how much money I was hoping to earn.
10 Finally, he asked me when *can I / I could* start work.

2 Report the questions.

0 'Can I have some more pocket money?'
   The boy asked *if he could have some more pocket money*.
1 'Are you still living in London?'
   I asked him ....
2 'Do you work in the central branch or in the provinces?'
   She asked me ....
3 'Are you going to give me the money or not?'
   She asked him ....
4 'Has he brought the book back?'
   I wanted to know ....
5 'Is it snowing in Manchester?'
   He asked ....
6 'Are you married?'
   The man asked me ....
7 'Have you been eating properly?'
   The doctor asked him ....
8 'Would you like to join us tomorrow?'
   They asked me ....
9 'Do you speak French?'
   She asked the girl ....
10 'Have you finished?'
   The teacher asked him ....

8 REPORTED SPEECH (2)

3 **Report the questions.**

0 'Where were you born?' I asked Emmy.
I asked Emmy where she had been born.

1 'How far is the stadium?' the man asked us.
The man asked how far the stadium was.

2 'Who bought the Picasso painting?' she asked.
She asked who had bought the Picasso painting.

3 'What were they doing?' Mrs Fox asked.
Mrs Fox asked what they had been doing.

4 'How long have you lived here?' Jo asked Ben.
Jo asked Ben how long he had lived there.

5 'How often do you visit your cousins?' I asked Pam.
I asked Pam how often she visited her cousins.

6 'Why are you laughing?' she asked me.
She asked me why I was laughing.

7 'How long have you been waiting?' I asked them.
I asked them how long they had been waiting.

8 'What did she say?' Harry asked.
Harry asked what she had said.

9 'What should I do?' she asked her friend.
She asked her friend what she should do.

10 'Where are you going to stay?' I asked them.
I asked them where they were going to stay.

4 **Complete the text. Use one word in each gap.**

A difficult day at school

Mrs Evans, our history teacher, decided to give us an oral test about the American War of Independence yesterday. I hadn't done my homework because I had had a stomachache the night before and I (0) **wondered** if I would be able to answer any of her questions. First, she asked when the war (1) had started – I had no idea. Then she (2) wanted to know if we knew the name of the English king at the time. Then she (3) asked who the author of the Declaration of Independence (4) was. She asked me if I (5) knew the answer. By then, I wasn't feeling very well again, so I asked Mrs Evans if I (6) could be excused. She didn't hear me though and continued with the next question, so I got up and walked towards the door; Mrs Evans asked me (7) where I was going. I asked her (8) if/whether I could leave the room and she said I had to wait till the test was over. I explained I wasn't feeling well and asked how long the test was (9) going to take. Luckily, it only took five more minutes! I was so glad when the lesson ended!

8c -ing forms and infinitives after verbs

Verbs can be followed by an infinitive (with or without *to*), an *-ing* form, a noun or a *that* clause:
I want **to tell** you something.
I must **go** now.
They started **laughing**.
I fancy **an ice cream**.
She admitted **that she had been wrong**.

Verb + *-ing* form

- Here are some verbs that are followed by an *-ing* form:

avoid	feel like	miss
be worth	finish	postpone
delay	involve	practise
dislike	keep	propose
enjoy	mention	risk
fancy	mind	

I **avoid going** to noisy bars.
The castle **is worth visiting**.

- We always use the *-ing* form after verbs that are followed by prepositions (e.g. *insist on, succeed in, apologise for*):
She **insisted on coming** with me to the lawyer.
He **succeeded in breaking** the world record.
He **apologised for letting** me down.

- Phrasal verbs (e.g. *keep on, put off, look forward to*) are also followed by an *-ing* form:
They were **looking forward to meeting** him.

- Some verb phrases that are followed by prepositions are also followed by an *-ing* form. Here are some examples: *be good at, be keen on, be fed up with, be tired of*:
She's **good at getting** people to do things.
He's very **keen on travelling**.

- The verbs above can also be followed by a noun:
I avoid **noisy bars**.
They were looking forward to **their holiday**.

- Remember: we always use the *-ing* form of a verb after prepositions.

Verb + *-ing* form/*that* clause

- Here are some verbs that are followed by an *-ing* form or a *that* clause:

admit	deny	report
consider	imagine	suggest

He **admitted lying** to the police.
He **admitted that he had stolen** the goods.

- These verbs can also be followed by a noun:
He admitted his **crimes**.

- We cannot use an infinitive after these verbs:
He **denied doing** it. ✓
He ~~denied to do it~~. ✗

- When these verbs are followed by a *that* clause, we can omit *that*:
He **admitted he had stolen** the goods.

Verb + *to*-infinitive

- Here are some verbs that are followed by a *to*-infinitive:

agree	hope	promise
appear	intend	refuse
can afford	learn	seem
choose	manage	threaten
decide	offer	want
expect	plan	wish
fail	prepare	
hesitate	pretend	

I **agreed to stay** with her.
The animal **appears to be** dead.
We **can't afford to go** on holiday this year.

- Some of these verbs can also be followed by a noun, an adjective or a *that* clause:
She **failed the exam**.
He **seems frightened**.
I **agree that it is** difficult.

137

8 -ING FORMS AND INFINITIVES AFTER VERBS

Verb + bare infinitive

- The verbs *make*, *let*, *would rather*, *would sooner* and *had better* are followed by a bare infinitive (= infinitive without *to*):
  They **let us leave** early.
  They **made us wait** for two hours.
  I'**d rather go** to Italy this year.
  I'**d sooner die** than give the secret away!
- In the passive, we use a *to*-infinitive after *make*:
  We **were made to wait** for two hours.
- We do not use *let* in the passive. We use *allow* instead:
  We **were allowed to leave** early.
- We also use a bare infinitive (= infinitive without *to*) after modal verbs:
  I **can't help** you.
  We **might be** a bit late.

Verb + -ing form/to-infinitive with no change in meaning

- Some verbs can be followed by an *-ing* form or a *to*-infinitive without a change in meaning. Here are some of these verbs:

  begin   continue   love
  can't bear hate   prefer
  can't stand like   start

  I **began training** as soon as I heard about the hockey match.
  I **began to train** as soon as I heard about the hockey match.
- These verbs can also be followed by a noun:
  I **began French** when I was twelve.
  I **don't like pop music** very much.
- *Can't bear* and *can't stand* both mean 'not be able to accept or not like something'. *Can't bear* is common in both written and spoken English. *Can't stand* is more common in spoken English. Both *can't bear* and *can't stand* can be followed by an *-ing* form, a *to*-infinitive or a noun:
  I **can't bear/can't stand listening** to this music!
  I **can't bear/can't stand to hear** them arguing!
  I **can't bear/can't stand TV commercials**!

Verb + -ing form/to-infinitive with change in meaning

Some verbs can be followed by an *-ing* form or a *to*-infinitive but with a change in meaning.

Here are some of them:

Verb	Meaning	Example
remember + *to*-infinitive	not forget sth you must do	I **remembered to turn off** the oven.
remember + *-ing* form	have a memory of sth you did in the past	I **remember turning off** the oven.
forget + *to*-infinitive	not remember sth you must do, get or bring	I **forgot to phone** Kevin.
forget + *-ing* form	not remember sth you did in the past	I'll never **forget visiting** Venice for the first time.
try + *to*-infinitive	make an effort	They **tried to help** her.
try + *-ing* form	do sth to see what happens	**Try closing** the file and then opening it again.
stop + *to*-infinitive	stop in order to do sth	I **stopped to tie up** my shoelace.
stop + *-ing* form	no longer do sth	He **stopped wearing** ties years ago.
go on + *to*-infinitive	do sth after you've finished doing sth else	He told us about his childhood. Then he **went on to describe** his experiences in the army.
go on + *-ing* form	continue doing sth	She **went on talking** for hours!
regret + *to*-infinitive	feel sorry or sad about sth you have to do	We **regret to inform** you that we cannot offer you the post.
regret + *-ing* form	feel sorry about something you have or haven't done	She **regretted accepting** the job.
mean + *to*-infinitive	intend	I didn't **mean to hurt** you.
mean + *-ing* form	involve sth or have a particular result	His new job will **mean travelling** a lot.

138

-ING FORMS AND INFINITIVES AFTER VERBS **8**

PRACTICE

1 Choose the correct answer.

0 He denied *to lie* / *lying*.
1 I learnt *to drive* / *driving* when I was twenty.
2 They suggested *to postpone* / *postponing* the basketball match.
3 The bad weather delayed *that they arrived* / *their arrival*.
4 I can't bear *see* / *to see* children suffer.
5 We really can't afford *to buy* / *buying* a new washing machine.
6 I look forward to *see* / *seeing* you at the party.
7 I'd rather *stay* / *to stay* at home if that's ok.
8 I don't remember *to see* / *seeing* Al at the gym.
9 His mum always makes him *tidy* / *to tidy* his room before he goes out.
10 I'm really sorry, I didn't mean *to upset* / *upsetting* you.

2 Complete the article. Use the correct form of the verbs in brackets.

Pablo Picasso

From the age of seven, Picasso started (0) *having* (have) artistic training from his painter father. He was very keen on (1) .... (paint) and it was obvious that he was very good at it. He began (2) .... (miss) classes at school and insisted on (3) .... (paint) pictures instead. His father saw the thirteen-year-old Picasso painting like a master, so he gave up (4) .... (paint) in order to help his son become a great artist. Picasso's father then persuaded the art academy (5) .... (allow) his son to take the entrance exam. Later, he decided (6) .... (send) the young artist to Madrid's Royal Academy. Thus, at the age of sixteen, Picasso started (7) .... (go) to classes in Madrid. However, he disliked formal instruction, so he soon stopped (8) .... (turn up) for classes and spent hours in the Prado Museum instead.

3 Complete the second sentence so that it has a similar meaning to the first sentence, using the word given. Use between two and five words. Do not change the word given.

0 We were forced to give them the money.
   MADE
   They *made us give them* the money.
1 Unfortunately, we cannot accept your application.
   INFORM
   We regret .... your application has not been accepted.
2 I'd prefer to work in an office.
   RATHER
   I .... in an office.
3 We were not allowed to enter the lab.
   LET
   They .... the lab.
4 I said it would be a good idea to start our own website.
   SUGGESTED
   I .... our own website.
5 She managed to get a place at York University.
   SUCCEEDED
   She .... a place at York University.
6 It looks as if this door is locked after all.
   APPEARS
   This door .... after all.
7 We can't wait for our holiday next month.
   FORWARD
   We're really .... on holiday next month.
8 Tony refused to let me pay for our meal.
   INSISTED
   Tony .... for our meal himself.

139

Vocabulary

8d say, tell, talk, speak, etc.

say

- We can use *say* as a reporting verb in direct speech, before or after the speaker's actual words:
  Tom **said**, 'This is great!'
  'I'm so tired,' she **said**.
- We use *say* (*that*) in reported speech:
  She **said** (**that**) she might be late.
- Certain objects can 'say' things:
  The clock **says** it's five past ten.
  The email **says** we've won first prize!
  The newspaper **says** there's been a hijacking.
  The label **says** it was produced in Argentina.
- *Say* cannot have a person as a direct object. We must use *to*, followed by the person:
  She said goodbye **to her parents**.
- Here are some common phrases and expressions with *say*:

Phrase	Example
say your prayers	The children **said their prayers** and got into bed.
say yes/no	He asked her to marry him and she **said yes**.
say hello/goodbye	I'll just go and **say hello** to Amanda.
say a few words	I'd like to **say a few words**.
have sth to say	If you **have something to say**, say it now.
People say …	**People say** he used to be a spy.
Let's just say (that) …	**Let's just say** he doesn't always tell the truth.
(Let's) say … (that) (= suppose)	**Say** they offered you the job – would you take it?

tell

- *Tell* is followed by a direct object:
  He **told us** the answer.
- We can use *tell* as a reporting verb in direct speech:
  'Come here,' she **told** me.
  She smiled and then **told** me, 'Of course I'll help you.'
- We use *tell sb* (*that*) in reported speech:
  She **told them** (**that**) she might be late.

tell sb about sth

Compare *tell sb about sth* and *say sth* (*to sb*):
She **told us about** her trip to North America. (= talked about)
I'd like to **say something about** my trip to North America. (= talk about)
She **told the neighbours about** the burglary. (= reported)
I'm going to **say something to the neighbours** about the noise. (= complain)

tell sb to do sth

We use *tell* (not *say*) with a *to*-infinitive to report commands:
The policeman **told me to go** with him. ✓
The policeman **said me to** go with him. ✗
'Close the door,' he said. → He **told me to close the door**.

tell sb what/how/where/etc.

Tell sb what/how/where/etc. can be followed:
- by a clause:
  Tell me **what you need**.
  I can't tell you **where he is**.
  I'll tell you **how I managed to** convince him.
- by a *to*-infinitive:
  Tell me **what to do**.
  I told them **where to go**.
  I'll tell you **when to stop**.

Common phrases and expressions with *tell*

Phrase	Example
tell a lie/lies	I've never **told a lie** in my whole life.
tell the truth	He never **tells the truth**.
tell a story/ a joke	If you're quiet, I'll **tell you a story**.
tell yourself that	I keep **telling myself that** there was nothing else I could have done.
tell sb/sth apart	It's impossible to **tell the twins apart**.
tell a mile off (that)	You could **tell a mile off that** she was lying.
tell tales	I didn't do it – somebody's been **telling tales**.

Be careful: we use *give* (not *tell*) with the following nouns:

give advice
give orders
give an opinion
give information
give directions
give the details (*of sth*)

*Could you **give** me some **advice** on how to prepare for the exam?*

talk about and speak about

- *Talk about* means the same as *discuss*:
  *Let's **talk about** the problem.* (= Let's discuss the problem.)
- We use *speak about* in more formal contexts:
  *The lecturer is going to **speak about** the modern novel.* (= give a talk on)
- We often use *talk about* to mean 'describe' or 'tell stories about':
  *She often **talked about** her days as a student.*

persuade and convince

- *Persuade* means 'make someone decide to do something, especially by giving them reasons why they should do it, or asking them many times to do it'.
  *I'll **persuade** her to buy me a pony.*
- *Persuade* is followed by a *to*-infinitive:
  *He finally **persuaded** her **to go out** with him.*
- *Convince* can be used in the same way as *persuade*:
  *We've been trying to **convince** Heather **to come**.*

- It can also mean 'make someone feel certain that something is true'. When used in this way, *convince* may be followed by a noun or pronoun, by a *that* clause, or by *of* + noun:
  *Her evidence **convinced the court**.*
  *Her arguments **convinced me**.*
  *I **convinced them that** the story was true.*
  *We finally **convinced** them **of** our innocence.*

deny, refuse, reject and turn down

Form	Meaning	Example
deny + noun	say that sth is not true	He **denied the claims**.
deny + *that* clause		She **denied that she had stolen** the money.
deny + -ing		She **denied stealing** the car.
refuse + noun	not accept sth	They **refused our help**.
refuse + *to*-infinitive	say you will not do sth	He **refused to apologise**.
reject + noun	refuse to accept, believe in or agree with sth	They **rejected her ideas**.
turn down	refuse an offer, request or invitation	I **turned down** their offer.

- *Deny* means 'say that something is not true'.
  *He was accused of stealing a car but he **denied it**.*
  *He **denied taking** the money.*
- *Refuse* means 'say you will not do something that someone asks you to do'.
  *She **refused to help** us.*
- *Reject* means 'refuse to accept, believe in or agree with something'. It can only be followed by a noun (or pronoun).
  *I made a suggestion but they **rejected it**.*
- *Turn down* is a phrasal verb. We can use it instead of *refuse* or *reject*.
  *She **turned down** her brother's **offer** of help.*

8 SAY, TELL, TALK, SPEAK, ETC.

Practice

1 Complete the conversations. Use the correct form of the verbs in the box. You can use some of the verbs more than once.

| convince | deny | give | persuade | say | talk | tell | turn down |

0 **A:** People ..*say*.. that he's been all round the world.
  B: Yes, he often ..*talks*.. about his travels.
1 **A:** I think he has just .... us another one of his stories.
  B: I know! Does he ever .... the truth?
2 **A:** Rose is brilliant at .... jokes.
  B: I hope we can .... her to tell us some tonight.
3 **A:** Why don't you ask Dr Roberts to .... you a second opinion?
  B: Yes, I ought to .... to someone else about this.
4 **A:** Doctor, they .... it's urgent!
  B: Very well, ... them I'm on my way.
5 **A:** They .... the Prime Minister will be talking about the new law in Parliament today.
  B: I wonder what he's going to .... this time!
6 **A:** You .... me you were my friend!
  B: What are you .... about?
7 **A:** I .... a lie when I said I believed him.
  B: Really? I believe what he ....
8 **A:** You .... him some good advice about his interview.
  B: But he didn't get the job. I wonder why he was ....
9 **A:** I accused him of stealing and he didn't .... it.
  B: I think you should .... your boss!
10 **A:** I couldn't .... her to come with us.
   B: Did you .... her that Ken is coming, too?

2 Choose the correct answer.

A BIG STEP TOWARDS A BETTER WORLD?

Key states say they have reached an agreement at the Canberra Summit on Climate Change. The President of the USA ⁽⁰⁾*(said)*/*told* the agreement would be a foundation for global action. 'Let's just ⁽¹⁾*say*/*tell* we have taken a big step towards a better world,' he told reporters. However, the deal was ⁽²⁾*rejected*/*denied* by a number of dissatisfied nations who had earlier ⁽³⁾*turned down*/*denied* a proposal by the USA to adopt a 'carbon swap' policy. Likewise the representative from Venezuela ⁽⁴⁾*refused*/*denied* rumours that an agreement had been reached at the last minute, while the Chinese representative ⁽⁵⁾*told*/*told to* reporters that there were still a lot of issues to ⁽⁶⁾*speak*/*talk* about. She admitted there were disagreements between large and small nations but they would try and ⁽⁷⁾*refuse*/*persuade* all countries ⁽⁸⁾*to sign*/*of signing* the agreement. 'We haven't ⁽⁹⁾*turned down*/*convinced* everybody that we've got the best deal yet but we refuse ⁽¹⁰⁾*to accept*/*accepting* defeat.' The European Union Commission President said: 'I cannot deny ⁽¹¹⁾*that there are*/*of* a few issues with the agreement but we will not ⁽¹²⁾*tell*/*give* any further details at this time.' 'I do not want to ⁽¹³⁾*tell*/*give* an opinion yet – the talks are not over,' ⁽¹⁴⁾*said*/*told* the French representative.

8e -ed and -ing adjectives

-ed adjectives

- Adjectives ending in -ed usually tell us how a person feels. They are the past participle forms of regular verbs, used as adjectives:
  *The **worried** parents waited anxiously for news.*
  *I was **exhausted**, so I went straight to bed.*
- We can also use the past participles of irregular verbs as adjectives. These do not end in -ed:
  *She died of a **broken** heart.*

-ing adjectives

- Adjectives ending in -ing usually describe the effect something or someone has on us. They are the -ing forms of verbs, used as adjectives:
  *It was a **disappointing** film.*
  *This game's so **boring**.*
  *The journey was really **exciting**.*
  *My job is **exhausting**.*
- Here are some common -ed/-ing adjectives. You can check their meaning in a dictionary:

  amused/amusing   fascinated/fascinating
  annoyed/annoying   frightened/frightening
  bored/boring   interested/interesting
  confused/confusing   irritated/irritating
  disappointed/disappointing satisfied/satisfying
  disgusted/disgusting   surprised/surprising
  embarrassed/embarrassing   terrified/terrifying
  encouraged/encouraging tired/tiring
  excited/exciting

- There are many -ed/-ing adjectives which are not connected with feelings. Here are some examples:
  *a **falling** leaf   a **burning** building*
  *a **locked** door   a **computerised** database*

PRACTICE

1 Complete the article. Use -ed or -ing adjectives formed from the verbs in brackets.

This year's Oscars ceremony was not, in my view, one of the most **(0)** ..exciting.. (excite) ever. Presenter Jeremy Hayman is a first-rate entertainer, who knows how to tell **(1)** .... (amuse) jokes but doesn't know when to stop. He is the kind of comedian who can make introducing someone **(2)** .... (interest) but I began to get **(3)** .... (annoy) with the less than **(4)** .... (flatter) remarks about famous stars present in the audience.

However, there were more **(5)** .... (bore) moments, particularly when the speeches of thanks went on for too long. Not many people are **(6)** .... (interest) in hearing stars making long speeches thanking their mum!

Best Actress Jane Taylor must have felt really **(7)** .... (embarrass) when she forgot her director's name. Best Actor Howard Harris, however, made a **(8)** .... (move) speech about his recent struggle with illness. The audience were **(9)** .... (surprise) by his frankness and he kept his speech short, so we didn't have time to get **(10)** .... (bore). But really, the most **(11)** .... (annoy) moment of the whole evening was the long introduction to the ten best films. I got very **(12)** .... (irritate) when they got to the fifth film after ten minutes and were still only half way.

8 -ED AND -ING ADJECTIVES

2 Complete the sentences. Use *-ed* or *-ing* adjectives formed from the verbs in the box.

> annoy   bore   confuse   depress   disgust   embarrass
> frighten   interest   ~~irritate~~   relax   surprise

0 I was getting more and more ...*irritated*... at her questions – she just wouldn't stop asking about my private life!
1 He's had a lot of bad news recently and is feeling a bit .... – let's go and cheer him up.
2 Would you be .... in coming to the theatre this evening?
3 Can't you fix that dripping tap? It's getting on my nerves – it's really ....!
4 I didn't expect to see Peter at the party – I was really .... to see him there.
5 I don't find horror films ....; in fact, I find them quite funny.
6 I find it .... to lie on the sofa and listen to music after a hard day's work.
7 Leo was getting really .... with doing the same thing every day.
8 The instructions were very complicated and the students were ....
9 And then I dropped the cake and everybody started laughing. It was really ....!
10 No, of course I won't eat that! It looks ....!

3 Answer the questions using *-ed* or *-ing* adjectives. Use your own ideas.

0 If you failed your next exam, how would you feel?
   I'd be really disappointed.
1 How would you feel if you climbed Mount Everest?
   ....
2 What do you think about the destruction of the rain forests?
   ....
3 What do you think of people who drop litter?
   ....
4 What do your parents think of your friends?
   ....
5 If you were flying to New York tomorrow, how would you feel?
   ....
6 Whenever you see a beggar, how do you feel?
   ....
7 What do you think of sport on television?
   ....
8 When a bus or train is late, how do you feel?
   ....
9 How would you feel if you were caught cheating in an exam?
   ....
10 How would you feel if a friend organised a surprise party on your birthday?
   ....

-ED AND -ING ADJECTIVES   8

4 Complete the sentences using *-ed* or *-ing* adjectives. Use your own ideas.

0 I find science fiction stories *very interesting*.
1 I'd feel .... if I failed my English test.
2 I'd feel really .... if I met my favourite singer.
3 The thought of travelling to the moon is ....
4 I'd be .... if my best friend forgot my birthday.
5 I wouldn't be .... if the economy collapsed.
6 I find lying on the beach on a hot summer day ....
7 I agree that television is ....
8 Football couldn't be more ....

5 Complete the crossword. Use *-ed* or *-ing* adjectives formed from the verbs in the box.

age	interest
amuse	reward
arm	surprise
captivate	terrify
freeze	touch
heat	trust
humiliate	

Across

2 I hear you want to buy a car. Would you be .... in a second-hand Honda?
5 What began as a friendly discussion, soon became a .... argument.
6 I wasn't at all .... by his jokes. I found them rather insulting.
8 I was really .... to see Eric there – I thought he was in China!
9 It's .... in here! Will you turn the heater on, please?
10 Are .... aircraft, say those older than ten years, safe to fly in?
11 Nursing can be a very .... career, can't it?
12 I thought someone had broken into our house – I was absolutely ....!

Down

1 The countess won over the nation with her .... smile.
3 You shouldn't have believed him – you're far too ....
4 My family were deeply .... by your offer of help and sympathy.
7 I felt utterly .... when you criticised me in front of all my friends last night.
10 The army, navy and air force are known as the .... forces.

145

Exam practice 4

Part 1

For questions **1–12**, read the text below and decide which answer (**A**, **B**, **C** or **D**) best fits each gap. There is an example at the beginning (**0**).

SHAKESPEARE

Everyone was looking forward ⁽⁰⁾.......... *The Taming of the Shrew* at the theatre. The reviews had been very good – it had been described ⁽¹⁾.......... the critics as one of the most ⁽²⁾.......... shows in town. One critic said it was one of the most engaging productions of Shakespeare he ⁽³⁾.......... in years. *The Taming of the Shrew* is one of Shakespeare's earliest plays, which he ⁽⁴⁾.......... written at the beginning of his career, and which most agree is not a masterpiece.

Most people in Britain remember ⁽⁵⁾.......... a Shakespeare play at school and for the majority it was a boring experience. Many years later, most will struggle to tell you ⁽⁶⁾.......... the texts or the teachers were to blame, but a lack of understanding played a large part. Some teachers didn't encourage their students to ⁽⁷⁾.......... about the meaning of the plays or allow them to ⁽⁸⁾.......... their own opinion or interpretation of the play, and so many students simply weren't interested. However, some students are ⁽⁹⁾.......... enough in literature to spend the extra time studying the peculiar Elizabethan language, and these are the ones that succeeded ⁽¹⁰⁾.......... why Shakespeare is so special. These are the students who insisted ⁽¹¹⁾.......... the meaning of all the unknown words as if it was a foreign language and go ⁽¹²⁾.......... to appreciate Shakespeare throughout their adult lives.

0	A	see	B	seeing	C	to see	D	to seeing
1	A	of	B	as	C	by	D	from
2	A	annoying	B	entertaining	C	disgusting	D	exhausting
3	A	saw	B	was seeing	C	has seen	D	had seen
4	A	was	B	had	C	has been	D	had been
5	A	study	B	to study	C	studying	D	of studying
6	A	why	B	whether	C	about	D	that
7	A	talk	B	speak	C	say	D	discuss
8	A	talk	B	tell	C	say	D	give
9	A	fond	B	excited	C	keen	D	interested
10	A	to understand	B	of understanding	C	in understanding	D	for understanding
11	A	to translate	B	on translating	C	in translating	D	at translating
12	A	up	B	back	C	forward	D	on

SCORE / 12

Part 2

For questions **13-24**, read the text below and think of the word which best fits each gap. Use only **one** word in each gap. There is an example at the beginning (**0**).

SHOPLIFTER

The young man was wearing a large bulky jacket. He had filled up his basket, paid for his shopping and was about to leave the shop when a woman approached him and (0) ....*told*.... him (13) .... wait one minute. 'What's up?' asked the young man. The shop detective asked him (14) .... he intended to pay for the ham. 'What ham?' replied the young man, seemingly surprised. 'The one you managed (15) .... hide inside your jacket when you thought I wasn't looking,' (16) .... the detective. 'I don't know what you're talking (17) ....!' said the shopper. 'I suggest (18) .... cooperate,' said the detective. 'I'd rather (19) .... call the police.' The young man couldn't deny (20) .... a packet of ham and stuffing it inside his jacket.

The store detective told (21) .... to follow her into the office. She closed the door and (22) .... the thief why he had not paid for the ham. On the verge of tears, the young man explained that he (23) .... been unemployed for a year and begged the detective to (24) .... him go. 'And if I allow you to go, do you promise not to do it again?' asked the detective. The young man, now visibly upset, nodded.

SCORE _____ / 12

Part 3

For questions **25–34**, read the text below. Use the word given in capitals at the end of some of the lines to form a word that fits in the gap **in the same line**. There is an example at the beginning (**0**).

MRS COOPER

I'll never forget my primary school teacher, Mrs Cooper. She was one of the most **(0)** *motivating* teachers I've ever had. But what made dear old Mrs Cooper such an **(25)** .... and memorable teacher? Well, first of all, she had a class of thirty nine-year-olds and she was always very **(26)** .... Her lessons weren't necessarily exciting but we were never **(27)** .... either. She was very active and worked very hard to keep us all **(28)** .... in whatever it was she was trying to teach us; she ran around and jumped up and down – she must have been **(29)** .... by the end of the day. She was also a great storyteller – she would put on her round **(30)** .... glasses, open her big book and begin another **(31)** .... story.

As for me, it's because of her that I became a professional athlete. I remember being **(32)** .... of water and her running along the edge of the **(33)** .... pool as I learnt to swim my first 100 metres, shouting, 'You can do it! You can do it!' What an **(34)** .... teacher!

MOTIVATE

INSPIRE

ENCOURAGE
BORE
INTEREST

EXHAUST

READ
FASCINATE

TERRIFY
SWIM

AMAZE

Part 4

For questions **35–42**, complete the second sentence so that it has a similar meaning to the first sentence, using the word given. **Do not change the word given.** You must use between **two** and **five** words, including the word given. Here is an example (0).

Example:

0 You ought to ask someone to paint the fence soon.
   HAVE
   You ought to ...... *have the fence painted* ...... soon.

35 We refer to people who are good with computers as 'techies'.
   KNOWN
   People who are good with computers .... 'techies'.

36 Harold Edwards directed this film.
   BY
   This film .... Harold Edwards.

37 Nobody can deny that her voice is beautiful.
   BE
   It .... her voice is beautiful.

38 A mechanic repaired her car for 200 euros.
   BY
   She .... a mechanic for 200 euros.

39 My car really needs to be serviced pretty soon.
   GET
   I really need .... pretty soon.

40 We won't be allowed to bring coffee into the lab.
   LET
   They .... coffee into the lab.

41 People say that Rome is the most beautiful city in Europe.
   SUPPOSED
   Rome .... the most beautiful city in Europe.

42 They're going to pull down that old building soon.
   PULLED
   That old building .... down soon.

SCORE / 16

TOTAL SCORE / 50

9

AGENDA

Grammar
- **9a** Comparative and superlative adjectives
- **9b** Adjectives followed by prepositions
- **9c** Order of adjectives

Vocabulary
- **9d** Easily confused adjectives
- **9e** Compound adjectives

Entry test

1 Choose the correct answer.

1 Some think that cats are *as / more* intelligent than humans.
2 This is the *lovelier / loveliest* dress I've ever seen!
3 It was the *worse / worst* film I've seen all year.
4 Email is a *much / lot* more efficient than sending a fax.
5 Don't you think the last hotel was *slightly less / more least* modern than this one?

Now look at 9a on pages 152–154.

SCORE ___ / 5

2 Choose the correct answer, A, B, C or D.

6 She was grateful .... the help we had given her.
  A of **B** with **C** to **D** for
7 The bath is full .... water!
  A with **B** of **C** up **D** from
8 I will not be responsible .... what happens.
  A of **B** at **C** for **D** by
9 I didn't know he was married .... Barbara.
  A with **B** to **C** of **D** in
10 They're very proud .... their daughter's success.
  A for **B** on **C** of **D** with

Now look at 9b on pages 155–156.

SCORE ___ / 5

3 Choose the correct answer.

11 Keith bought Emma a pair of *black leather / leather black* gloves.
12 A *Japanese new / new Japanese* car factory will be opened in the north.
13 She was wearing a *red lovely / lovely red* dress.
14 He's just bought a *posh German sports / German posh sports* car.
15 They live in *an old beautiful / a beautiful old* house.

Now look at 9c on page 157.

SCORE ___ / 5

4 Choose the correct answer, A, B, C or D.

16 As chairperson, she's the .... person on the committee.
   A strongest   B most strong   C biggest   D most powerful
17 Are you .... enough to lift that box?
   A large   B strong   C great   D big
18 The boys are getting .... – they need new clothes.
   A greater   B higher   C taller   D stronger
19 She's so .... that she finds it hard to say no.
   A thin   B fragile   C weak   D slender
20 I think it's perfectly .... to want to be with friends on holiday.
   A strange   B foreign   C odd   D natural

Now look at 9d on pages 158–163.

SCORE ___ / 5

5 Choose the correct answer, A, B, C or D.

21 She's so ....-minded! She's always forgetting her keys.
   A loose   B absent   C distant   D weak
22 She wears glasses because she's ....-sighted.
   A little   B low   C short   D close
23 He's very ....-going and gets on with everyone.
   A happy   B open   C friendly   D easy
24 She was such a(n) ....-hearted person – always willing to help!
   A kind   B open   C friendly   D nice
25 Mr Simms is a ....-known local artist.
   A highly   B well   C generally   D very

Now look at 9e on pages 164–165.

SCORE ___ / 5

TOTAL SCORE ___ / 25

151

Grammar

9a Comparative and superlative adjectives

Use

- We use comparative adjectives to compare one person, thing, place, etc. with another person, thing, place, etc.
- We use superlative adjectives to compare one person, thing, place, etc. with a whole group of people, things, places, etc.

Form

- To form the comparative, we add *-er* to the adjective. We often use the word *than* after the adjective:
  Bill is **taller** (**than** John).
- To form the superlative, we add *the* before the adjective and *-est* to the adjective. We often use phrases beginning with *of* or *in* after superlative adjectives:
  Jane is **the youngest of** the three sisters.
  Bill is **the tallest** boy **in** the class.
- In some cases, we can omit *the* before superlative adjectives:
  Her **biggest** fear is being left alone.

One-syllable adjectives

For most one-syllable adjectives, we add *-er* to form the comparative and *-est* to form the superlative:

Adjective	Comparative	Superlative
cheap	cheaper	the cheapest
fast	faster	the fastest
young	younger	the youngest

Two-syllable adjectives

- Some two-syllable adjectives form the comparative and superlative with *-er* and *-est*:

Adjective	Comparative	Superlative
busy	busier	the busiest
narrow	narrower	the narrowest

- Other two-syllable adjectives do not take *-er* or *-est*. We use *more/the most* before the adjective instead:

Adjective	Comparative	Superlative
careless	more careless	the most careless
handsome	more handsome	the most handsome

- With some two-syllable adjectives, both *-er/-est* and *more/the most* are possible:

Adjective	Comparative	Superlative
friendly	friendlier/more friendly	the friendliest/the most friendly
simple	simpler/more simple	the simplest/the most simple

Adjectives ending in -e

For adjectives ending in *-e*, we add *-r* to form the comparative and *-st* to form the superlative.

Adjective	Comparative	Superlative
close	closer	the closest
safe	safer	the safest

Adjectives ending in one vowel + one consonant

- For adjectives that end in one vowel + one consonant, we double the consonant before adding *-er* or *-est*:

Adjective	Comparative	Superlative
big	bigger	the biggest
fat	fatter	the fattest

- Be careful: if there are two vowels before the consonant, we do not double the consonant:

Adjective	Comparative	Superlative
cheap	cheaper	the cheapest
great	greater	the greatest

COMPARATIVE AND SUPERLATIVE ADJECTIVES

Adjectives ending in *-y*
For adjectives that end in *-y*, we change the *-y* to *-i* before adding *-er/-est*:

Adjective	Comparative	Superlative
angry	angrier	the angriest
busy	busier	the busiest

Longer adjectives
To form the comparative and superlative of adjectives with three or more syllables, we use *more/the most*:

Adjective	Comparative	Superlative
expensive	more expensive	the most expensive
intelligent	more intelligent	the most intelligent

Adjectives ending in *-ed*, *-ing*, *-ful* and *-less*
Adjectives that end in *-ed*, *-ing*, *-ful* and *-less* do not take *-er* or *-est*. We use *more/the most* instead:

Adjective	Comparative	Superlative
boring	more boring	the most boring
careless	more careless	the most careless
forgetful	more forgetful	the most forgetful
worried	more worried	the most worried

Irregular adjectives
These adjectives are irregular:

Adjective	Comparative	Superlative
bad	worse	the worst
far	farther/further	the farthest/furthest
good	better	the best
old	older/elder	the oldest/eldest

farther/further, farthest/furthest

- *Far* has two comparative and superlative forms: *farther/farthest* and *further/furthest*. We use them to talk about distances:
  Chris swam to the **farther** end of the lake.
  Jennie sat at the **further** end of the room.
- *Further* can also mean 'more' or 'extra'. We cannot use *farther* in the same way:
  For **further** information, please write to the above address. (= more information)

older/elder, oldest/eldest

- *Old* has two comparative and superlative forms: *older/oldest* and *elder/eldest*. We use *elder/eldest* for family members:
  David's **elder** son is studying law at Harvard.
- We cannot use *than* with *elder*:
  He is **elder than** me. ✗
  He is **older than** me. ✓

Determiners

- Note the comparative and superlative forms of the determiners below:

Determiner	Comparative	Superlative
many	more	the most
much	more	the most
little	less	the least

'How **much** did you spend?' '**More** than you did!'
We know **little** about his parents and **less** about his younger brother.

less (than), the least

We can use *less* + adjective (+ *than*) and *the least* + adjective (+ *of/in/*etc.) to make negative comparisons:
This film was **less successful** (**than** original).
It was **the least successful** of all his films.

far/much/a lot + comparative

We use *far*, *much* or *a lot* before a comparative adjective for emphasis. There is little difference in meaning, although *far* is often stronger:
Bill is **far/much/a lot richer than** Tom.

the + comparative, *the* + comparative

The structure *the* + comparative, *the* + comparative can be used to show that things change or vary together:
The older I get, **the more forgetful** I become.

For more comparative structures, see **10a**

9 COMPARATIVE AND SUPERLATIVE ADJECTIVES

PRACTICE

1 Complete the sentences. Use the comparative or superlative form of the adjectives in the box. Add any other words necessary.

> bad   careful   comfortable   ~~difficult~~   far   friendly   good
> happy   hot   intelligent   lucky   old (x2)   simple   suitable

0 This exercise is too easy. Can we try a(n) ...*more difficult*... one?
1 She comes top in all the exams – she must be ………. girl in the class.
2 The temperature in July reaches forty-four degrees; it's ………. month of the year.
3 You made too many mistakes, which is why you failed. You should be ………. in the future.
4 This pen's not very good – I'd like a(n) ………. one, please.
5 My wedding day was ………. day of my life.
6 Lying down in bed is ………. sitting on a hard chair.
7 Our youngest son doesn't want to be a teacher, unlike his ………. brother.
8 Now, before we continue, are there any ………. questions?
9 I have a(n) ………. headache today than I did yesterday.
10 The rules of this game are too complicated – can we play something ……….?
11 She's ………. person I know. She's always winning prizes in lotteries!
12 Don't worry, my dog won't bite you. He's much ………. you think – he loves people!
13 I wouldn't wear jeans if I were you – a suit would be ………. for the occasion.
14 That castle is ………. building in our town; it's more than 500 years old.

2 Complete the text. Use the comparative or superlative form of the adjectives in brackets. Add any other words necessary.

Canada v. the USA   Monday, 17 October

I've just got back from a tour of the USA and Canada. I used to think they were very similar countries but I now realise they are very different. I think Canadians are (0) *more polite* (polite) and (1) ………. (gentle) their southern neighbours. They are generally (2) ………. (modest) in their behaviour than the Americans who tend to be a bit (3) ………. (loud).

I used to think the USA was a (4) ………. (nice) place to live than Canada but I have changed my mind. Even though the USA is a (5) ………. (rich) nation than Canada, the standard of living appears to be (6) ………. (good) in Canada. The World Health Organization ranks Canada (7) ………. (high) the USA for its health service and Canadians have a (8) ………. (long) life expectancy than their American friends. However, things are much (9) ………. (cheap) in the USA.

The USA is one of (10) ………. (violent) countries in the world and I felt (11) ………. (safe) on the streets of Toronto than in New York. The USA has a much (12) ………. (bad) crime rate than Canada. I had a (13) ………. (pleasant) time in Canada. The people genuinely seemed to be (14) ………. (happy) and (15) ………. (relaxed). All in all, I think Canada is one of (16) ………. (beautiful) countries in the world to visit and probably one of (17) ………. (good) to live in, too.

> *The best things in life are free.*

9b Adjectives followed by prepositions

- The following are some common adjective + preposition combinations:

Adjectives	+ Preposition
angry, annoyed, anxious, certain, confident, excited, happy, nervous, pleased, right, sorry, upset	about
amazed, angry, annoyed, bad, excellent, good, hopeless, lucky, skilful, skilled, surprised, useless I'm **surprised for** his behaviour. ✗ I'm **surprised at** his behaviour. ✓	at
amazed, amused, bored, impressed, shocked, surprised	by
famous, late, ready, responsible, sorry, suitable	for
absent, different, safe	from
disappointed, interested, involved I'm **interested for** buying a new computer. ✗ I'm **interested in** buying a new computer. ✓	in
keen, reliant	on
afraid, ashamed, aware, capable, certain, confident, critical, envious, fond, full, guilty, incapable, jealous, kind, nice, proud, scared, short, stupid, sure, suspicious, terrified, tired, typical I'm **proud for** my son. ✗ I'm **proud of** my son. ✓ I'm **tired from** my job. ✗ I'm **tired of** my job. ✓	of
accustomed, engaged, friendly, generous, inferior, kind, married, polite, rude, superior, similar	to
friendly, patronising	towards
angry, annoyed, bored, busy, careful, content, crowded, delighted, disappointed, familiar, friendly, furious, happy, occupied, pleased, satisfied	with

- Some adjectives can be followed by more than one preposition. Here are some examples:
  - *angry about* = angry because of a situation or action
    angry at/with sb = angry because of sb
  - *tired from* = physically tired as a result of an activity
    tired of = bored or irritated by sth
  - *friendly to/towards* = behaving in a friendly way
    friendly with = friends with sb
  - *sorry for* = feeling pity or sympathy for
    sorry about = feeling unhappy or ashamed about

Are those clothes really **suitable for** a job interview?

9 ADJECTIVES FOLLOWED BY PREPOSITIONS

PRACTICE

1 Choose the correct answer, A, B, C or D.

0 I'm sorry .... the mess – I've just finished making dinner.
   A about   **B** for   **C** with   **D** at

1 Jackie was furious .... Gary for being late again.
   A of   **B** for   **C** with   **D** on

2 Don't ask me to play – I'm useless .... computer games!
   A in   **B** at   **C** in   **D** on

3 This new washing machine is completely different .... the other one.
   A of   **B** with   **C** on   **D** from

4 I'm afraid I'm not very keen .... cabbage.
   A towards   **B** in   **C** on   **D** at

5 I'm tired .... listening to your excuses!
   A at   **B** with   **C** on   **D** of

2 Complete the sentences. Use the adjectives in the box and the correct prepositions.

| absent | amused | ashamed | crowded | different | engaged | excited | famous |
| good | guilty | interested | involved | proud | right | shocked | typical |

0 The jury found him *guilty of* murder.
1 Stop hitting that little boy! You should be .... yourself!
2 I used to love watching football but I'm just not .... it any more.
3 Dave's been .... school for four days now; is he OK?
4 It's .... him to arrive late – he's hardly ever on time.
5 I'm afraid I'm not .... his jokes – I find them in rather poor taste.
6 The kids are really .... their holiday – they can't wait!
7 He got .... too many clubs and societies and had no time to study.
8 She used such bad language I was really .... what I heard!
9 He's very .... maths and physics but hopeless at languages.
10 Soon, the young man became internationally .... his novels.
11 The streets were .... shoppers and you could hardly move.
12 Congratulations on passing the exam! We're so .... you!
13 She was .... John for a long time but then she married someone else!
14 You were .... the party; you had said it would be great fun, and it was!
15 Although they're twins, they're very .... each other.

> 'When a man is **tired of** London, he's **tired of** life.' SAMUEL JOHNSON

9c Order of adjectives

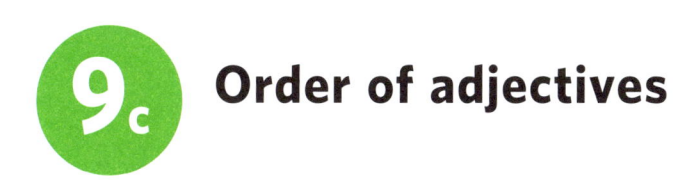

When there is more than one adjective before a noun, this is the most common order:

Opinion	Size	Other qualities	Age	Shape	Colour	Origin	Material	Purpose/Type
nice	big	cold	old	round	blue	French	glass	electric

- The order of adjectives of size, shape, age and colour may vary, especially when we focus on a particular feature. For example, we can say:
  a **round black** table (= normal order) or
  a **black round** table (= focus on colour)
- We generally use commas between adjectives (especially in longer sequences):
  There was a **big, round, red** Persian carpet on the floor.
- When there is more than one adjective of the same type in a sentence, we often join them with *and*. When there are more than two adjectives, we use commas and *and* before the last adjective:
  The children were **cold and hungry**.
  The house was **large and impressive**.
  He was **tall, dark, handsome**. ✗
  He was **tall, dark and handsome**. ✓

- We can put a comma or *and* between two adjectives that describe someone's character:
  He was a clever **and** imaginative young man.
  He was a clever, imaginative young man.
- When there are two colour adjectives before the noun, we have to use *and* between them. When there are more than two colour adjectives, we have to use *and* before the last one:
  They own a **red and white** car.
  They were waving a **blue, white, red** flag. ✗
  They were waving a **blue, white and red** flag. ✓

PRACTICE

1 Put the adjectives in the correct order. If the order is correct, put a tick (✓) on the line.

0	old English textbooks	✓
00	wool thick socks	thick, wool socks
1	a wooden big spoon	
2	a small nylon bag	
3	a big delicious birthday cake	
4	a round plastic small button	
5	a(n) large frying old pan	
6	a pair of black leather riding boots	
7	a pink silk beautiful blouse	
8	a round large ball	
9	a(n) big old brick factory	
10	a(n) wooden ugly old desk	

'Life is **nasty**, **brutish** and **short**.'
HOBBES

Vocabulary

9d Easily confused adjectives

Here are some adjectives we frequently confuse:

strong or powerful?

Adjective	Meaning	Example	Collocations
strong	of physical strength: great	I'm not **strong** enough to lift that bag.	strong hands, a strong back
	of things: not easily broken or destroyed	You will need a **strong** metal ladder.	a strong branch/pair of scissors
	of a person: important, effective or determined	We need a **strong** leader.	a strong member of the team/candidate
	of feelings and opinions: great	He has **strong** feelings about this issue.	strong feelings/emotions, a strong belief
	of level or intensity: great	The street lights are not **strong** enough here.	a strong influence/connection
	of a taste or smell: very great or intense	I'd love a cup of **strong** coffee.	a strong taste/flavour/smell
powerful	important and able to control and influence	The President is the most **powerful** man in the US.	a powerful person/politician/organisation/country
	physically strong	Joe was a **powerful**, well-built, young man.	powerful jaws/shoulders
	of actions: having a great physical effect	Ali had a **powerful** punch.	a powerful kick/blow/explosion
	of actions: having a great effect on feelings or thoughts	The lawyer outlined a **powerful** defence.	a powerful speech/argument/film
	of a machine/weapon: very effective	The Jaguar has a very **powerful** engine.	a powerful bomb/computer/weapon
	of medicine: having a very strong effect	The drug is very **powerful**.	a powerful medicine/remedy
	of sound or light: very easy to hear or see	This musical instrument produces a **powerful** sound.	a powerful light/lamp

big, large or great?

Adjective	Meaning	Example	Collocations
big	of more than average size or amount	He's got a **big** room.	a big house/crowd
	important	Deciding on a new house is a **big** decision.	a big day/occasion/star
	old or older	You're a **big** girl now.	a big boy/brother/sister
	successful	Rap music was **big** in the 1980s.	big in Hollywood/in business/in the show business/in the city
	to a large degree	He's a **big** gambler.	a big eater/drinker
large	big in size, amount or number	Los Angeles is the second **largest** city in the US.	a large shirt/family/amount/number/area/population
	tall and often fat	He was **large** for his age.	a large person/woman/man
great	very large in amount or degree	His last film was a **great** success.	a great number/shock/deal
	very large in size	A **great** crowd had gathered outside the theatre.	a great wall/mountain/estate
	very important and influential	Einstein was a **great** scientist.	a great painter/statesman/achievement/woman
	very serious	The result was a **great** disappointment to me.	a great mistake/problem
	very good or pleasant	What a **great** idea!	a great film/time/view
	extremely good in ability or quality	He was one of the **greatest** artists of all time.	a great musician/detective/composer/athlete

little, small or short?

Adjective	Meaning	Example	Collocations
little	small in size	The ring came in a **little** box.	a little house/dog, little bits
	short in time or distance	Shall we walk a **little** way?	a little while
	young	Come and meet my **little** sister.	a little boy/girl/brother
small	not large in size or amount	It's a **small** city.	a small family/amount/size/area/town/car
	not important	It's only a **small** problem.	a small wound/error/mistake/change/difference
	not doing business on a large scale	The government should help **small** businesses.	a small firm/farmer/businessman
short	measuring a small amount in length or distance	You look nice with **short** hair.	a short skirt/distance/drive/journey/walk
	of a person: not tall	She's much **shorter** than her sister.	a short man/woman/boy/girl
	happening or continuing for only a little time	Our holiday seemed so **short**.	a short time ago/meeting/course/while/period
	not having many words or pages	I'll just send him a **short** email.	a short book/novel/letter

9 EASILY CONFUSED ADJECTIVES

high or tall?

Adjective	Meaning	Example	Collocations
high	measuring a long distance from bottom to top	The **highest** mountain in Scotland is Ben Nevis.	a high wall/fence/tower/heel
	a long way above the ground, floor, etc.	It was a huge room with a **high** ceiling.	a high shelf/branch/window/cloud
	of an amount, number, etc.: large or larger than usual	Many cities suffer from **high** levels of pollution.	a high salary/price/temperature
	having an important or powerful position	What is the **highest** rank in the army?	high society/honour
tall	having a greater height than normal	Your son's getting **taller**.	a tall man/building/tower/tree

weak, thin, slim or skinny?

Adjective	Meaning	Example	Collocations
weak	not physically strong	The illness had left her feeling tired and **weak**.	a weak man/woman/heart
	easily influenced	She has such a **weak** personality.	a weak character
	not very good at something	He's **weak** at physics.	a weak team
	not likely to make people believe that sth is true	That's such a **weak** excuse!	weak point/argument/ending
	containing a lot of water	This tea is rather **weak**, isn't it?	weak coffee/soup/juice
thin	of things: not thick	We need **thin** nylon rope.	a thin slice/layer/jacket, thin cloth
	of people: not fat	He was tall and **thin**.	a thin man/girl, thin legs/arms
	of liquids: not thick	The soup was **thin** and tasteless.	thin paint/milk/sauce
	easy to see through	The early morning landscape was covered with a **thin** mist.	a thin fog, thin smoke/clouds
slim	very small in amount or number	There's only a **slim** chance of getting a place at Harvard.	slim hopes/prospects
	attractively thin	I wish I were as **slim** as you.	a slim girl/model/figure/waistline
skinny	too thin	You should eat more – you're far too **skinny**!	a skinny person/model, skinny arms/legs

160

last or latest?

Adjective	Meaning	Example	Collocations
last	the most recent	I met him **last** April.	last week/night/year
	happening or existing at the end	I'm reading the **last** chapter.	the last train/flight/bus/dance
	the only remaining	You're my **last** hope!	the last chance/opportunity
latest	the most recent	She was dressed in the **latest** fashion.	the latest gossip/film/news/discovery

natural or physical?

Adjective	Meaning	Example	Collocations
natural	existing in nature and not made or caused by people	Is that the **natural** colour of your hair?	the natural world, a natural disaster/flavour, natural causes
	that you are born with or is part of your character	She shows a **natural** ability with figures.	a natural skill/tendency
	normal and as you would expect	It was **natural** for her to be concerned about her children's education.	a natural reaction/response
physical	related to sb's body	The accident affected both her **physical** and mental health.	physical strength/energy/exercise, in good physical shape, a physical examination
	relating to real objects that you can touch, see or feel	There was no **physical** evidence to suggest that he was guilty.	the physical world/environment, physical conditions

strange or foreign?

Adjective	Meaning	Example	Collocations
strange	unusual or surprising in a way that is difficult to explain	We heard a **strange** noise.	strange behaviour/events, in a strange way, for some strange reason
	not familiar	There I was, all alone in a **strange** city.	strange people, a strange country
foreign	from or relating to a country that is not your own	I thought she sounded **foreign**.	a foreign language/student/company, foreign currency
	involving or dealing with other countries	He's the **Foreign** Minister.	foreign affairs/policy/trade/news

9 EASILY CONFUSED ADJECTIVES

PRACTICE

1 Choose the correct answer.

0 For next time, I'd like you to write a *small* / *short* story.
1 It was eight o'clock and the sun was already *high* / *tall* in the sky.
2 He was a *slim* / *skinny*, handsome man.
3 The *last* / *latest* time I saw Rob was in Manchester.
4 I think it was a perfectly *natural* / *physical* reaction.
5 The trousers are made of *strong* / *powerful* material so they won't tear easily.
6 There was a *large* / *great* view from our hotel room.
7 How *big* / *great* is your house in the country?
8 Some supermodels are far too *slim* / *skinny* – they look as if they haven't eaten for weeks.
9 Have you heard the *last* / *latest* news?
10 The boys are getting *higher* / *taller* all the time.
11 I wish my legs were *thinner* / *skinnier*!
12 Have you met my *small* / *little* sister?
13 Does your country import a lot of *foreign* / *strange* goods?
14 I think we should have a *short* / *small* meeting and talk about this.
15 I felt a bit *strange* / *foreign* when I took the pills for the first time.

2 Complete the sentences. Use the words in the box.

| foreign | great | greatest | ~~high~~ | large | last |
| latest | natural | physical | thin | weak |

0 There were some ..*high*.. cliffs along the river bank.
1 The road was covered with a .... layer of ice.
2 Who was the .... person to see the man alive?
3 This is the .... model – it's much better than the previous one.
4 It's .... for a child of his age to miss his mother.
5 I don't feel very well. My legs feel really ....
6 We had a .... time at the party on Saturday.
7 The T-shirt comes in three sizes: small, medium and ....
8 Rembrandt was one of the .... artists who ever lived.
9 Do you speak any .... languages?
10 The book discusses the emotional and .... needs of young children.

162

9 EASILY CONFUSED ADJECTIVES

3 <u>Underline</u> the *one* word in each group that cannot be used with the adjective in bold.

0 **big:**	grin	crowd	<u>level</u>	sister	business	box	film star
1 **strong:**	faith	tree	friendship	tool	bomb	tea	muscles
2 **foreign:**	language	student	currency	news	affairs	policy	house
3 **tall:**	child	temperature	tree	giraffe	skyscraper	bottle	chimney
4 **high:**	speed	hopes	wall	rent	man	heels	mountain
5 **large:**	amount	collection	occasion	area	family	city	number
6 **thin:**	layer	soup	legs	person	figure	excuse	walls
7 **slim:**	girl	hope	waist	cloth	man	chance	body
8 **last:**	night	time	gossip	bus	chance	dance	semester
9 **latest:**	fashion	film	discovery	year	trend	novel	news
10 **short:**	man	money	dress	story	journey	hair	holiday
11 **physical:**	strength	world	exercise	energy	plants	effort	conditions
12 **small:**	distance	town	business	mistake	food	problem	cut
13 **weak:**	clothes	pulse	heart	argument	character	excuse	point

4 Complete the crossword. Use words from pages 158–161.

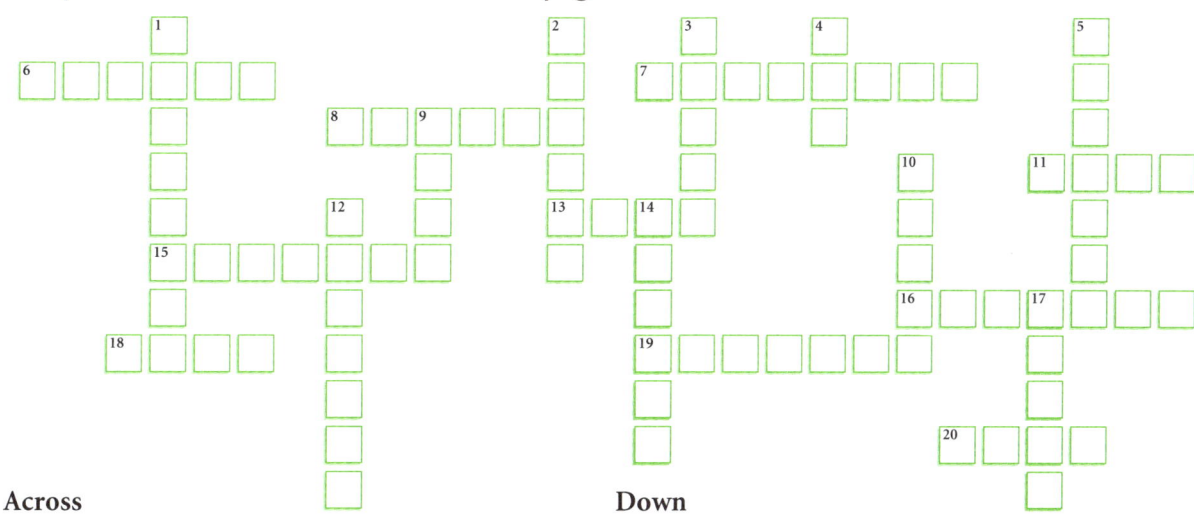

Across

6 Most onions have a ………. flavour.
7 Take plenty of ………. exercise and eat more fruit and vegetables.
8 Have you heard the ………. gossip? Sue's just broken up with Kevin.
11 We can say buildings, people and trees are ………. .
13 We met on holiday ………. year.
15 For Poles, English is a ………. language.
16 Glasgow is the ………. city in Scotland but Edinburgh is the capital.
18 They have only a ………. chance of winning.
19 Is fair hair your ………. colour?
20 Emily is still ………. after her illness.

Down

1 Ferrari produces cars with very ………. engines.
2 This is Sean, my ………. brother.
3 Doris Lessing has written excellent ………. stories.
4 Oh, stop crying, Tommy! You're a ………. boy now!
5 It can be lonely when you're on your own in a ………. town.
9 It was freezing and I was only wearing a ………. summer jacket.
10 He fell over but only got a ………. bruise on his arm.
12 Name the ………. mountain in the world.
14 Days without proper food had left them so ………. .
17 Shakespeare wrote such ………. plays!

*A chain is no stronger than its **weakest** link.*

163

9e Compound adjectives

Form

- A compound adjective consists of two words that function like one word. We often use a hyphen between the two words:
  red-haired   badly-maintained
- The second part of a compound adjective is often:
  - a present participle (the *-ing* form of a verb):
    tight-**fitting**   good-**looking**
  - a past participle:
    old-**fashioned**   well-**built**   blue-**eyed**
  - a preposition:
    broken-**down**   well-**off**
  - another adjective:
    brand-**new**   duty-**free**
- Note the following common errors:
  ~~She was an attractive **red-headed** woman.~~ ✗
  She was an attractive **red-head**. ✓
  She was an attractive **red-haired** woman. ✓
  ~~He's very **well-looking**.~~ ✗
  He's very **good-looking**. ✓
  ~~The furniture was **old-fashion**.~~ ✗
  The furniture was **old-fashioned**. ✓
  ~~I saw a **one-eye** sailor on the boat.~~ ✗
  I saw a **one-eyed** sailor on the boat. ✓
  ~~There was a **breaking-down** car on the motorway.~~ ✗
  There was a **broken-down** car on the motorway. ✓

Use

We use compound adjectives like all other adjectives. We often use them to describe:
- physical appearance
  broad-shouldered   dark-haired   good-looking
- personality:
  good-tempered   open-minded
- places:
  built-up   run-down   wide-open
- everyday objects:
  worn-out   hand-made   man-made

For compound nouns, see **7e**

Practice

1 Match 1–14 with a–o to make compound adjectives.

0	dark-	e	a	hand
1	absent-		b	legged
2	easy-		c	selling
3	second-		d	hearted
4	newly-		e	haired
5	well-		f	looking
6	long-		g	dressed
7	hard-		h	eyed
8	best-		i	minded
9	brand-		j	new
10	kind-		k	married
11	air-		l	conditioned
12	good-		m	working
13	self-		n	confident
14	green-		o	going

2 Complete the table. Use the compound adjectives from Exercise 1.

Physical appearance	dark-haired
Personality	
Other	

164

COMPOUND ADJECTIVES 9

3 Complete the sentences. Use compound adjectives from the table in Exercise 2.

0 Her hair? I'm not sure – I think she was *dark-haired*. No, wait – she was blonde.
1 Everyone congratulated the ………. couple.
2 She's always ………. and has a fine sense of style. She spends a lot of money on her clothes.
3 No, I don't think he's ugly! In fact, I find him quite ………. .
4 I'll have to buy a ………. computer; I can't afford a new one.
5 *The Last Sign* is the latest science fiction novel by ………. author Trevor Woods.
6 He never remembers anything. He's very ………. .
7 I wish I were as ………. as she is. I just wish I could believe in myself!
8 She was always very ………. at school, which is why she always got full marks in all the tests.
9 He's very ……….: always relaxed and happy to accept things without getting upset or worried.
10 Our room was small and dark but at least it was ………. .

4 Complete the compound adjectives in the following sentences. Use the words in the box.

badly	class	distance	fashioned	~~free~~	headed
known	made	off	sighted	tempered	up (x2)

0 We bought some duty-*free* perfume at the airport.
1 I made a long-………. call to London and it cost me a fortune!
2 They seem to be very well-……….; they have a great big house and two expensive cars.
3 I'm fed-………. with this exercise! Will you help me, please?
4 I usually travel second-………. because it's cheaper.
5 This vase is hand-………. – that's why it's so expensive.
6 He gets very bad-………. when he's tired and starts shouting at people.
7 I live in a built-………. area of the city, which is very noisy and full of traffic.
8 She's a well-………. TV personality – almost everybody recognises her in the street.
9 I've never met anyone as big-………. as Jim. He has a really high opinion of himself.
10 I have to get my eyes tested – I've become very short-………. lately.
11 A ……….-maintained car won't have a very reliable engine.
12 Will you ever get rid of those old-………. clothes?

> *There are three golden rules if you want to be a **first-class** public speaker: stand up, speak up, shut up.*

10

AGENDA

Grammar
- 10a Comparisons
- 10b *so* and *such*; *too, enough, very*
- 10c *quite, rather*, etc.; linking verbs

Vocabulary
- 10d Adjectives which are similar
- 10e Suffixes (4)

Entry test

1 Choose the correct answer.

1 She's not as intelligent *as / than* her sister.
2 The film wasn't *so / such* good as I had expected.
3 Maria is the same age *as / like* Kate.
4 She works *as / like* an accountant in a local bank.
5 He's getting richer *and / more* richer every year.

Now look at 10a on pages 168–169.

SCORE ___ / 5

2 Choose the correct answer, A, B, C or D.

6 We hadn't expected the trip to be .... exhausting.
  A such   B so   C such an   D like so
7 .... behaviour will get you into trouble with the director.
  A Such   B Such a   C So the   D Like
8 There were .... many people at the party there was no room to move.
  A so   B such   C such a   D that
9 The bill was much .... expensive for me to pay on my own.
  A very   B too   C more   D quite
10 I don't have .... time to speak now.
  A a   B plenty   C enough   D enough a

Now look at 10b on pages 170–172.

SCORE ___ / 5

166

ENTRY TEST 10

3 Choose the correct answer, A, B, C or D.

11 She's .... sensitive to other people's problems.
 A a quiet B a quite C quite D quite a
12 It was .... good result but you could have done better.
 A rather B a bit C a little D a fairly
13 It was .... difficult question.
 A very B too C rather D a rather
14 She's .... thin for her part in the play.
 A lot B a bit C little D little too
15 He .... rather moody at the moment.
 A behaves B grows C does D seems

Now look at **10c** on pages 173–175.

SCORE ____ / 5

4 Choose the correct answer, A, B, C or D.

16 I felt so .... when my parents turned up at Joe's party!
 A shy of B shameful C shamed D embarrassed
17 I felt so .... as I sat outside the dentist's, thinking it would be really painful!
 A bad-tempered B embarrassed C nervous D frightening
18 I would never cheat – I would be .... of being caught.
 A worried B anxious C nervous D afraid
19 His jokes always make me laugh – I find them quite ....
 A amusing B enjoying C tiring D sympathetic
20 My sister's always been scared .... heights.
 A to B of C from D in

Now look at **10d** on pages 176–178.

SCORE ____ / 5

5 Complete the sentences. Use words formed from the words in CAPITALS at the end of the lines.

21 Your handwriting's completely illegible; you shouldn't be so .... when you write. **CARE**
22 Do you have any books .... for young children? **SUIT**
23 Although she was told the operation would be ...., she still felt very nervous about it. **PAIN**
24 I didn't mean to upset you – perhaps you're just a little too .... **SENSE**
25 She ought to write things down if she's so .... **FORGET**

Now look at **10e** on pages 179–181.

SCORE ____ / 5

TOTAL SCORE ____ / 25

167

Grammar

10a Comparisons

as ... as, not as/so ... as

- To say that two things, people, places, etc. are the same or equal in some way, we use *as* + adjective/adverb + *as*:
  He's **as tall as** Harry.

- To say that two things, people, places, etc. are different, we use *not as/so ... as*:
  Mary is as tall as Jane but she is**n't as tall as** Andrew.
  The café is **not as** crowded as it was earlier.

- We cannot use *so ... as* in affirmative sentences:
  ~~She worked so hard as Pete.~~ ✗
  She worked **as hard as** Pete. ✓
  She didn't work **so hard as** Pete. ✓
  She didn't work **as hard as** Pete. ✓

- We can omit the second part of the comparison if it is clear who or what we are talking about:
  She's not **as tall** (**as him/as he is**).
  John didn't do **as well as** Helen in the exam.
  John didn't do **as well** (**as her/as she did**).

- Be careful: we use *as ... as*, not *as ... so*:
  ~~Tea isn't as strong so coffee.~~ ✗
  Tea isn't **as strong as** coffee. ✓

as many/much/little/few as

- We also use *as many/much/little/few as* in comparisons. Notice that we do not use *a*:
  Bill doesn't have **as much money as** Anne.
  If she had **as little money as** he did, she would think differently.
  Amy doesn't have **as many meals as** Fred.
  If Amy had **as few meals as** Fred, she would be thinner.

- We cannot use *more*, *less* or *several* in the same way.

the same (as)

- *Same* is followed by the preposition *as*. We always use *the* before *same*:
  Their car is **the same** (**as** ours).
  Peter is **the same age** (**as** George).

- We can use *exactly* before *the same* for emphasis:
  Their car is **exactly the same** (as ours).
  Peter is **exactly the same** age (as George).

like and as

Note the difference between *like* and *as*: we use *like* to say that things, people, places, etc. are similar. We use *as* to say what job, duty, use or appearance somebody or something has:

Form	Example
like + noun	He runs **like the wind**. **Like the Greeks**, Italians use olive oil a lot.
like + pronoun	My brother is just **like me**. **Like you**, I'm not very keen on football.
as + noun	She works **as a doctor**. **As your teacher**, I advise you to work harder. Don't use your shirt **as a towel**!

10 COMPARISONS

Repeating comparatives

In the following structures, we repeat the comparative adjective in a sentence:

Form	Meaning/Use	Example
comparative + and + comparative	changing all the time	She was getting **more and more** irritated. He's getting **taller and taller**.
the + comparative + clause + the + comparative + clause	to show that things change or vary together	**The older** I get, **the wiser** I become. **The harder** you work, **the better** you'll do.
the + comparative + the + comparative	used in common phrases	**the bigger the better** **the sooner the better**

Practice

1 Look at the table and complete the sentences about Bob and Tony, the twins.

	Bob	Tony
Date of birth	22 August	22 August
Time of birth	11.10 a.m.	12.30 a.m.
Weight at birth	3 kg	3.5 kg
Hair	fair	fair
Resembles	mum	dad
Height now	1.90 m	1.95 m
School	Central College	Central College
Geography	A	B
Maths	C+	B
English	D	D
History	A	A
Occupation	unemployed	coal miner

0 Date of birth: Bob was born on the same day **as Tony**.
1 Birthday: Tony's birthday is on .... Bob's.
2 Time of birth: Tony was not born at .... Bob.
3 Weight: At birth, Bob was not .... Tony.
4 Hair: Bob has the same .... Tony.
5 Appearance: Bob looks like .... but Tony looks ....
6 Height: Bob is not .... Tony.
7 School: Tony went to .... Bob.
8 Geography: Tony was not as good at ....
9 Maths: Bob was not as ....
10 English: Bob was just as bad .... Tony was.
11 History: Bob was .... Tony was.
12 Occupation: Tony works ....
13 Money: Bob doesn't have as ....
14 Success: Bob hasn't been ....

169

10b so and such; too, enough, very

so and such

We use *so* and *such* in different ways, in the following patterns:

Form	Meaning/Use	Example
so		
so + adjective/adverb	very, extremely	It's **so hot** in here! She could run **so fast**!
	to such a great degree or amount	Don't look **so angry**. Don't walk **so fast**!
so + adjective/adverb (+ *that*)	to emphasise the degree or amount of sth, by saying what the result is	My car is **so old** (**that**) I can't get any spare parts for it. She drives **so fast** (**that**) nobody can keep up with her.
so many/much/little/few	to emphasise the degree or amount of sth	How did you make **so much** money?
so many/much/little/few (+ *that*)	to emphasise the degree or amount of sth, by saying what the result is	There were **so many** people queuing outside the theatre (**that**) we went back home.
such		
such + adjective + plural/ uncountable noun	very, extremely	She's got **such lovely hair**! They're **such good friends**.
such + adjective + plural/ uncountable noun (+ *that*)	to emphasise the degree or amount of sth, by saying what the result is	They're **such good friends** (**that**) they tell each other everything.
such a/an + adjective + singular noun	very, extremely	It was **such a beautiful day**!
such a/an + adjective + singular noun (+ *that*)	to emphasise the degree or amount of sth, by saying what the result is	It was **such a hot day** (**that**) we decided to go for a swim.

too, enough, very

- *Too* means 'more than is acceptable or possible'. *Very* means 'a lot'. Compare:
  I was **too tired**. (= so I couldn't do any work)
  I was **very tired**. (= but I could still do some work)
  ~~I was **too happy** when I received your email.~~ ✗
  I was **very happy** when I received your email. ✓

- We do not use *very* with adjectives that already have a strong meaning:
  ~~Meno Park in Tokyo is **very huge**.~~ ✗
  Meno Park in Tokyo is **huge**. ✓
  Meno Park in Tokyo is **absolutely huge**. ✓

  See also: 10c

10 SO AND SUCH; TOO, ENOUGH, VERY

We use *too* and *enough* in the following patterns:

Form	Example
enough + noun	Do we have **enough cheese** for a pizza?
enough + noun + *to*-infinitive	Do you have **enough money to buy** the book?
not + adjective/adverb + *enough*	You're **not** driving **fast enough**! We'll be late!
not + adjective/adverb + *enough* (+ *for* sb) + *to*-infinitive	I'm **not clever enough to study** medicine. She did**n't** explain it **clearly enough for everyone to understand**.
too + adjective/adverb	I can't drink this – it's **too hot**.
too + adjective/adverb (+ *for* sb) + *to*-infinitive	The coffee was **too hot** to drink. He walked **too quickly for the children to keep** up with him.

PRACTICE

1 Match 1–6 with a–g to make sentences.

0 The pianist played so badly that — **e**
1 The kids were so tired that — **b**
2 The food was so bad that — **g**
3 She's got so many clothes that — **c**
4 It's such a tiny kitchen that — **a**
5 He eats so much sugar that — **d**
6 They were making so much noise that — **f**

a I don't have to do much to keep it clean.
b they went straight to bed.
c she never wears the same thing twice.
d his teeth will rot.
e the audience walked out.
f I couldn't concentrate.
g nobody could eat it.

2 Choose the correct answer.

0 We had to pay *a such* / **such a** high price for coffee in London!
1 Passing my driving test was *so* / **such** a relief!
2 We're having **such** / *such an* awful weather that we can't go for a swim.
3 We had *so* / **such a** terrible time that we swore we wouldn't do it again.
4 She loved him **so** / *such* deeply that she couldn't bear it when he was away.
5 There were **so** / *such* few people there they nearly cancelled the performance.
6 The film was *so* / **such a** boring I wanted to leave.
7 I had *so* / **such** many things to do I didn't know where to start.
8 It was *so* / **such a lovely** day we decided to have a picnic in the park.
9 There was **so** / *such* much noise I could hardly hear myself think!
10 Joe was **so** / *such an* angry that he started shouting at me.

171

10 SO AND SUCH; TOO, ENOUGH, VERY

3 Complete the sentences. Use *too*, *enough* or *very*.

0 It's much **too** hot in here – turn the heating down.
1 If you've had .... food, I'll take the plates away.
2 She doesn't speak Spanish well .... to order a meal on her own.
3 The food was much .... salty to eat.
4 That's a .... beautiful piece of music. What is it?
5 She was speaking .... fast for us to understand what she was saying.
6 It seems that she isn't good .... to be in the team.
7 I don't have .... room to put them up.
8 The film was .... good – I wouldn't mind seeing it again.
9 We're .... different characters; I don't know how we'll manage to get on.
10 Your test was .... good; well done!

4 Complete the second sentence so that it has a similar meaning to the first sentence, using the word given. Use between two and five words. Do not change the word given.

0 I was almost two hours late because there was heavy traffic.
   SUCH
   There was **such heavy traffic that** I was almost two hours late.

1 I didn't have the strength to carry the case on my own.
   HEAVY
   The case was .... carry on my own.

2 The shelf is too high for me to reach.
   TALL
   I'm .... the shelf.

3 I cried because the film was sad.
   THAT
   The film was .... I cried.

4 Nobody can believe she's Spanish because her English is very good.
   WELL
   She .... that nobody can believe she's Spanish.

5 My brother's too young to vote.
   OLD
   My brother .... vote.

6 Craig's marks were too low for a place at Harvard.
   HIGH
   Craig's marks .... for a place at Harvard.

7 If there had been fewer people in the queue, we would have waited.
   SO
   There .... in the queue that we decided not to wait.

8 He couldn't sleep because the coffee was very strong.
   SO
   The coffee .... he couldn't sleep.

9 If this soup was not so hot, I could eat it now.
   FOR
   This soup is .... eat now.

10 The ticket was too expensive for us.
   ENOUGH
   We didn't .... a ticket.

> *An acquaintance is someone you know **well enough to borrow** from but not **well enough to lend** to.*

10c quite, rather, etc.; linking verbs

a bit/a little, fairly, quite, rather, very

- These have meanings which range from 'slightly' (marked - below) to 'very strong' (marked +++):

She's **a bit/a little** tired.	She's **fairly** tired.	She's **quite** tall.	She's **rather** tall.	She's **very** tall.
-	+	+	++	+++

- They can be followed by a number of structures:

Form	Meaning/Use	Example
a bit + adjective/adverb	slightly	She's **a bit short** for the team.
a little + adjective/adverb		She's **a little short** for the team.
fairly + adjective/adverb	quite	She's **fairly tall**.
a fairly + adjective + noun		It's **a fairly long trip**.
quite + adjective/adverb	not very but more than slightly	He's **quite talented**.
quite a(n) + adjective + noun		It was **quite a rude answer**. ✓ It was **a quite rude answer**. ✗
quite a(n) + noun	to emphasise that something is very good, large, interesting, etc.	It was **quite a surprise**.
quite + verb	fairly but not very	I **quite like** coffee.
rather + adjective/adverb	fairly or to some degree	We were all **rather surprised**. He did **rather badly** in the test.
rather a(n) + adjective + noun		It came as **rather a/a rather big surprise**.
a(n) rather + adjective + noun		
rather a(n) + noun		It came as **rather a surprise**.
rather + verb		I **rather like** her.
very + adjective/adverb	a lot	I'm **very sorry**. You did **very well**.

- *Quite* isn't as strong as *very*. Compare:
  She's **very clever**.   She's **quite clever**.
- *Quite* is stronger than *a little*. Compare:
  She's **a little greedy**.   She's **quite greedy**.
- *Quite* + adjective/adverb can also mean 'completely':
  No, thanks, I won't have any more to eat. I'm **quite full**. (= completely full)
  Yes, I'm **quite certain** that he's the same man. (= completely certain)
- Here are some words we often use with *quite* to mean 'completely':
  quite amazing   quite clear   quite right
  quite safe   quite true   quite wrong

We can use *rather/a bit/a little* before comparative forms:
The new house is **rather/a bit/a little smaller** than the old one.

- We use *quite as … (as …)* or *not quite as/so … (as …)* to make comparisons:
  His new book **isn't quite as interesting as** his first book.
  Kelly **isn't quite/as/so tall**.
- We use *very* with adjectives ending in *-ful* but not *-less*. (See 10e.)
  The information in this article is **very useful**. ✓
  The information in this article is **very useless**. ✗

173

10 QUITE, RATHER, ETC.; LINKING VERBS

Linking verbs

- A linking verb joins a subject to an adjective or clause. Here are some linking verbs:

appear	keep
be	look
become	seem
come	smell
feel	sound
get	stay
go	taste
grow	turn

- We can use different adjectives after linking verbs:
  They didn't want to **look suspicious**.
  I **feel sick**.
  He **seems happy**.
  This **tastes awful**!

- After some linking verbs, we can use *to be* + adjective:
  The house **seems to be empty**.
  The children **appeared to be** hungry.

- We can also use a *to*-infinitive after some linking verbs:
  She **seems to know** what she's doing.

- Here is a summary of the patterns after linking verbs:

Form	Example
linking verb + adjective	I **feel sick**. Her face **turned red**.
linking verb + *to be* + adjective	The fridge **seems to be empty**. He **appears to be French**.
linking verb + *to*-infinitive	They **seemed to know** her. She **appeared not to understand** what was going on.

PRACTICE

1 Correct the mistakes in the following sentences.

0 It was fairly good day, so we went for a walk.
It was a fairly good day, so we went for a walk.

1 Wembley Stadium is very enormous.
....

2 He's rather a noisy in class.
....

3 She's always been a quite hard-working.
....

4 I quite I like the theatre but I prefer the cinema.
....

5 Ed is rather much taller than his brother.
....

6 Yes, I quite to agree.
....

7 It was quite shock to get home and find the house burgled.
....

8 Well, I found the film bit boring.
....

9 The test seems it is quite easy.
....

2 Choose the correct answer.

0 The film was *quite* / *quite an* interesting but *fairly* / *a bit* too long.

1 We had *quite a* / *a quite* nice time at the party.

2 She's a *bit* / *very* careless.

3 I'm *quite* / *a bit* certain that you will pass the test if you work *a little* / *very* harder.

4 Don't look so worried – I promise you, I'm *very* / *a very* careful driver.

5 It came as *rather* / *rather an* unpleasant surprise to get a bill for 1,000 euros.

6 I was *a bit* / *very* pleased to get such a lovely present but *rather* / *quite a* disappointed that you couldn't come to the party.

7 This milk has gone *sour* / *to sour* – it smells!

8 If you water the plants, they will grow *healthy* / *to healthy* and *strong* / *a bit strong* in a month or so.

9 His hair has turned *grey* / *to grey*.

10 Dave appears *he understands* / *to understand* what really happened.

174

10 QUITE, RATHER, ETC.; LINKING VERBS

3 Choose the correct answer, A, B, C or D.

0 She can be .... bad-tempered in the mornings.
   A (quite) **B** a quite **C** quite a **D** quite the

1 In fact, she's .... unpleasant most of the time.
   A rather **B** a rather **C** rather an **D** rather the

2 That was .... good attempt but you still failed.
   A fairly **B** a fairly **C** fairly the **D** fairly your

3 Excuse her – she's usually .... shy with strangers.
   A a little **B** little bit **C** bit **D** a rather

4 The film was ....; my grandson screamed at one point.
   A quite fright **B** the quite fright **C** quite a fright **D** quite frightening

5 I'm .... at maths!
   A hopeless **B** very hopeless **C** quite a hopeless **D** a fairly hopeless

4 Choose the correct verb. Then use it in the correct form to complete the sentences.

0 Look at Jana; she _looks_ so pleased to have won the competition. (look, see)
1 Finding a cure for cancer still .... impossible. (stay, seem)
2 Avoiding illness is one thing; .... healthy is another. (sound, stay)
3 I .... quite exhausted after the race but I was happy I'd won. (feel, keep)
4 I believe him; he .... to be completely innocent of all charges. (look, appear)
5 She .... really worried when I phoned her this morning. (sound, turn)

5 Choose the correct answer.

Life in London

Someone once said that if you are tired of London, you are tired of life. Well, this is a bit of an exaggeration but London does (0)(*seem*)/ *look* to be an exciting multicultural city.

I arrived in London for the first time two years ago all the way from Tokyo to do a Master's degree in Civil Engineering. It was a bit of a culture shock. The city first (1) *appeared / sounded* to be grey and unwelcoming. Everybody (2) *seemed to be / appeared that they were* busy and for the first month, it (3) *kept / felt* pretty lonely. Meeting new people was (4) *quite / bit* difficult at first but many of the students at the university turned out to be (5) *rather / quite* friendlier than I had expected and I ended up moving in with some of them.

The flat I was staying in was actually (6) *much / bit* bigger than my flat in Tokyo. My new flatmates were from different countries and at first we found it (7) *a bit / quite a* difficult to relate to each other, especially to the British guy, who spoke (8) *quite a / a bit* quickly. We were (9) *fairly / a rather* shy about speaking at first. However, everyone was friendly and (10) *very / rather* more informal than back home; soon everyone (11) *turned / became* more relaxed and we got to know each other better. Living in London wasn't quite as difficult as it first (12) *appeared / grew* to be.

175

Vocabulary

10d Adjectives which are similar

ashamed, shameful, shy or embarrassed?

- *Ashamed* means 'feeling embarrassed and guilty because of something you have done'.
  (NB: *ashamed of*)
  *People who steal from the poor should be **ashamed of** themselves.*
- *Shameful* describes behaviour or actions that are so bad that someone should be ashamed:
  *The cruel way some people treat their pets is **shameful**.*
- *Shy* means 'nervous or embarrassed about meeting and speaking to other people, especially people you do not know'.
  (NB: *shy with*)
  *Jimmy is very **shy with** adults.*
- *Embarrassed* means 'feeling nervous and uncomfortable and worrying about what people think of you, especially in social situations'.
  (NB: *embarrassed about/at*)
  *You can imagine how **embarrassed** I felt when I realised I couldn't pay the bill.*

anxious, nervous, worried or bad-tempered?

- *Anxious* means 'feeling worried and nervous'. It can also mean 'feeling strongly that you want to do sth or want sth to happen'. (NB *anxious about/for*)
  *They were both **anxious about** their daughter's safety.*
  *We were all really **anxious for** news.*
- *Nervous* means 'worried or frightened about something, and unable to relax'.
  (NB: *nervous about*)
  *I was so **nervous about** the exam that I couldn't sleep.*
- *Worried* means 'unhappy because you keep thinking about a problem or about something bad that might happen'. (NB: *worried about*)
  *Where have you been? We were all very **worried about** you.*
- Someone who is *bad-tempered* becomes easily annoyed and talks in an angry way to people:
  *My brother is usually very **bad-tempered** in the mornings.*

afraid, scared or frightened?

Form	Meaning/Use	Example
afraid + *to*-infinitive	frightened because you think that you may get hurt or that sth bad may happen	She was **afraid to eat** it in case it was poisonous.
afraid of + noun/-*ing*		Most criminals are **afraid of being** caught.
scared + *to*-infinitive	frightened of sth or nervous about sth	She lay on the floor, too **scared to move**.
scared of + noun/-*ing*		I've always been **scared of dogs**.
frightened + *to*-infinitive	feeling afraid	Pete was too **frightened to speak**.
frightened of + noun/-*ing*		She was **frightened of walking** home alone in the dark.

Afraid, *scared* and *frightened* can also be followed by a *that* clause:
*I was **afraid** (that) **they would laugh** at me.*
*She was **scared** (that) **she was going to fail**.*
*The man was **frightened** (that) **the police would find** him.*

10 ADJECTIVES WHICH ARE SIMILAR

amusing or enjoyable?

- *Amusing* means 'funny and entertaining':
  We all thought it was a highly **amusing** film.
- *Enjoyable* means 'giving you pleasure':
  It was a very **enjoyable** experience.

sympathetic or likeable?

- *Sympathetic* means 'caring and feeling sorry about someone's problems'. (NB: *sympathetic to/towards*)
  I didn't feel at all **sympathetic towards** her. It was all her fault.
- *Likeable* means 'nice and easy to like':
  He's a selfish man and not at all **likeable**.

tiring or tiresome?

- *Tiring* means 'making you feel tired':
  Looking after children can be very **tiring**.
- *Tiresome* means 'making you feel annoyed or impatient':
  I find these so-called jokes extremely **tiresome**.

typical, usual or ordinary?

- *Typical* means 'having the usual features or qualities of a particular group or thing'. It can also mean 'happening or behaving in the way that you would expect'. (NB: *typical of*)
  It was a **typical** English summer: rain every second day!
  It was **typical of** him to be late.
- *Usual* means 'happening, done or existing most of the time or in most situations':
  I'll meet you at the **usual** time.
  I finished work later than **usual**.
- Ordinary means 'average, not different or special':
  It was just an **ordinary** house in an **ordinary** street.

PRACTICE

1 Complete the sentences. Use the words in the box, or an adjective formed from the words in the box.

> afraid   ~~amuse~~   bad temper   embarrass   enjoy   like   ordinary
> shame (x2)   shy   sympathy   tire   worry

0 You may laugh but I don't find anything *amusing* about finding a snake in your tent in the middle of the night!
1 Gardening may be hard work but it can also be very …………; I think it's a wonderful way to spend one's time.
2 I needed a lift home but I was too ………… to ask the other guests because they were complete strangers.
3 I was ………… of myself for having lied to my mother. I shouldn't have done it.
4 When I speak English, I sometimes feel a bit …………, especially when I make mistakes.
5 The violent way he treated his children was just …………!
6 'I'm not ………… about money,' he said. 'I've got plenty!'
7 She had just got up and was really ………… – she started shouting at us.
8 He says that he's ………… of losing his job if he doesn't finish the report on time.
9 If Phil weren't so arrogant, he'd be quite …………; very few people like him now.
10 We've all had a very ………… day. Let's go to bed.
11 I prefer reading stories about the rich and famous. Stories about ………… people are so boring!
12 He's dealt with similar issues in the past, so he was very ………… about my problem.

10 ADJECTIVES WHICH ARE SIMILAR

2 Choose the correct answer.

0 I have always been afraid *of* / *about* spiders.
1 If you were threatened, would you be too afraid *to scream* / *of screaming*?
2 We were all afraid *of* / *that* something terrible had happened.
3 Have you always been afraid of *fly* / *flying*?
4 Come on! What are you *afraid* / *afraid of*?
5 It was pitch dark and we were too scared to *go* / *going* anywhere.
6 Leave the light on, please – the baby is scared *of* / *to* the dark.
7 I won't go near the fruit trees because I'm frightened *by* / *of* bees.
8 The teacher was always late but we were too frightened *to* / *that we* complain.
9 She started climbing, even though she was frightened *to fall* / *that she would fall*.
10 You're a big boy now; you shouldn't be frightened *of walking* / *that you walk* home alone.

3 Complete the text. Use the words in the box.

> afraid   amusing   anxious   ashamed   embarrassed   ~~enjoyable~~   nervous
> ordinary   shy   sympathetic   tiresome   typical   usual

Culture shock

Penny, a friend of mine, has just got back from a trip to Japan. It was a very (0) *enjoyable* experience but there were occasions, she says, when the degree of formality shown by her hosts led to moments of cultural confusion. At times, she even felt (1).......... about the mistakes she made. For example, it is (2).......... for Europeans to call each other by their first name; however, this is not the (3).......... way of addressing people in Japan. Now, because Penny was (4).......... to show everyone how friendly she was, she called everyone by their first name. Most people could tell she was a foreigner and were (5).......... but others became quite angry and showed little sympathy. Penny is not at all (6).......... – she loves meeting new people. But after the first few misunderstandings, she was (7).......... to say anything in case she offended someone.

At first, Penny found bowing to people quite (8).......... – she is, after all, an actress. But after a while, having to bow to everyone you meet became rather (9).......... .

I myself am quite an experienced traveller but I would feel really (10).......... about putting my foot in it in Japan because there, even (11).......... people observe the most elaborate rules of social behaviour. Silence, for example, is nothing to be (12).......... of in Japanese culture, but in the West we get rather worried if there are even short periods of silence at social gatherings.

> 'It's not that I'm **afraid of** death – I just don't want to be there when it happens.' WOODY ALLEN

10e Suffixes (4)

Remember that we normally use suffixes to change a word to a different part of speech:
season (noun) + *-al* → *seasonal* (adjective)
danger (noun) + *-ous* → *dangerous* (adjective)

See also: 1e, 3e, 4e, 12e, 13e

-ful, -less

- The suffix *-ful* shows that a quality exists. It means 'full of something' or 'having the quality of something or causing something':
  She's very **careful** about what she eats.
- The suffix *-less* shows that a quality does not exist. It means 'without something' or 'not doing or using something':
  You shouldn't be so **careless** when you write.
- Below are some common pairs of adjectives that end in *-ful* or *-less*:

Adjective	Meaning	Example
careful	trying to avoid doing anything wrong	She's a **careful** driver.
careless	not paying or showing enough attention	It was a **careless** mistake.
harmful	causing or likely to cause harm	Pollution is **harmful** to our health.
harmless	unable or unlikely to cause harm	The dog is **harmless** – it won't bite.
hopeful	believing that what you hope for will happen	It's difficult but I'm still **hopeful**.
hopeless	without hope	It's **hopeless** trying to convince him.
painful	causing pain	Is your ankle still **painful**?
painless	causing no pain	It'll be a **painless** operation – don't worry.
thoughtful	kind and caring about other people	That's very **thoughtful** of you. Thank you!
thoughtless	unkind and not caring about other people	It was **thoughtless** of you to mention his illness.
useful	helping you to do, get or achieve sth	The tourist office gave us some very **useful** advice.
useless	not useful or effective in any way	Her advice was absolutely **useless**!

- We can use *very* with adjectives ending in *-ful* but not with adjectives ending in *-less*. We often use *completely*, *absolutely*, *utterly*, etc. instead:
  The injection was **very painful**.
  This information is **absolutely useless** to me.

In the following, only one form is possible: either *-ful* or *-less*, not both: *dreadful*, *forgetful*, *grateful*, *skilful*, *stressful*, *successful*, *cloudless*, *homeless*, *ruthless*.

10 SUFFIXES (4)

-able, -ible

- We add *-able* and *-ible* to verbs to form adjectives that show that something can be done. Here are some examples:

Adjective	Meaning	Example
drink + able	safe to drink	Is the water **drinkable** here?
wash + able	that can be washed	The shirt is machine **washable**.
rely + able	that you can rely on	She's a very **reliable** colleague.
access + ible	that can be accessed	The island is only **accessible** by boat.
sense + ible	reasonable	That's a very **sensible** suggestion.

- Some adjectives ending in *-able* and *-ible* have a first part that does not exist on its own:
  edible   possible   palpable   visible

-ive

- We can also form adjectives by adding *-ive* to verbs or nouns:

Adjective	Meaning	Example
act + ive	always busy doing things; involved	Try to keep **active** – take some exercise every day.
expense + ive	costing a lot of money	Who bought you that **expensive** watch?

- Again, some of these adjectives have a first part that does not exist on its own:
  pensive
- Some of these adjectives take *-itive* instead:
  sense → sensitive
- We often add the prefix *in-* to form the negative of these adjectives:
  inactive   inexpensive   insensitive

See also: 13e

-ous

- We add *-ous* to some nouns to form adjectives:

Adjective	Meaning	Example
fame + ous	well-known	She's a **famous** singer.
courage + ous	brave	That was a **courageous** decision.

- *Famous* means 'well-known'. *Infamous* means 'well-known for being bad or evil':
  She became **famous** after winning a gold medal in the Olympics.
  This is a photo of Al Capone, the **infamous** gangster.

See also: 13e

Other suffixes

Other suffixes we use to form adjectives include:

Noun + -ic	Noun + -y	Noun + -ish
apologetic	guilty	babyish
chaotic	healthy	childish
economic	hungry	foolish
enthusiastic	salty	girlish
heroic	scary	selfish
historic	speedy	sheepish
optimistic	thirsty	
pessimistic	wealthy	
realistic		
scientific		
sympathetic		
tragic		

Noun + -al	Noun + -ist
national	elitist
racial	sexist

-ant	-ent
arrogant	affluent
distant	dependent
hesitant	different
ignorant	efficient
important	violent

See also: 13e

SUFFIXES (4) — 10

PRACTICE

1 Complete the adjectives in the following sentences. Use suffixes.

0 Stop behaving like a six-year-old! Sometimes you're so child*ish*.
1 After the race, we were all really thirst..... .
2 If I won the lottery, I'd be very wealth..... .
3 Jack the Ripper was an infam..... serial killer.
4 You don't sound very enthusiast..... about the party; don't you want to come?
5 This film is not suit..... for children, I'm afraid.
6 Don't worry. The treatment is pain..... . You won't feel a thing.
7 It's a very interesting article about the harm..... effects of smoking.
8 His first book was very success..... . It sold thousands of copies.

2 Complete the sentences with adjectives. Use the underlined words to help you.

0 It was an experience we all <u>enjoyed</u>. It was an *enjoyable* experience.
1 We had a marvellous time. I'll <u>never forget</u> it. It was ....
2 She's <u>always forgetting</u> things. She's very ....
3 That water is <u>not good enough to drink</u>. It's not ....
4 I find her novels <u>interesting to read</u>. They're highly ....
5 Are you sure the website <u>can be accessed</u>? Is it ....?
6 This injection will <u>cause you a little pain</u>. It will be a little ....
7 We <u>haven't given up hope</u> of finding survivors. We're still ....
8 I <u>can understand</u> her reaction. Her reaction was ....
9 They <u>showed sympathy</u> for her. They were very .... towards her.
10 He <u>does not easily tolerate</u> other people's opinions. He's not very ....
11 She <u>showed such courage</u>, didn't she? She was ...., wasn't she?

3 Complete the article. Use words formed from the words in CAPITALS at the end of some of the lines.

Earthquake rocks eastern Turkey

Thousands of people have been left (0) *homeless* following an earthquake in eastern Turkey. The earthquake was nearly eight points on the Richter scale and was so (1) .... that it was felt in neighbouring countries. It caused (2) .... damage to homes and public buildings. The government said the situation is (3) .... and that they are doing their best to make things better. However, they said they were (4) .... that life could soon get back to normal.

Residents were warned that it could be (5) .... to return to their homes until they had been checked and people should be (6) .... when visiting their homes. 'In fact, it would be more (7) .... to avoid entering damaged buildings completely,' the spokesperson said. 'We are (8) .... that there will be no aftershocks but it is advisable to take precautions,' he added. There is a shortage of (9) .... water in areas struck by the quake.

'The damage will have serious (10) .... consequences for years to come,' said the mayor of one of the towns most affected by the quake.

HOME
POWER
EXTEND
DREAD
OPTIMIST
DANGER
CARE
SENSE
HOPE
DRINK
ECONOMY

---

*He's such a **careful** driver that he always looks both ways before hitting something.*

Exam practice 5

Part 1

For questions **1–12**, read the text below and decide which answer (**A**, **B**, **C** or **D**) best fits each gap. There is an example at the beginning (**0**).

TEEN FASHION

It is widely believed that boys are less interested in fashion (0).......... girls. While it is true that fashion for guys is not as widely followed (1).......... fashion for girls, it is becoming more and more important. Girls' fashion (2).......... to change more often, or at least it is more widely advertised. You can't help noticing when fashion gets (3).......... . One minute everyone is wearing one particular brand of trainers; six months later, something new is in and a perfectly good pair of trainers gets pushed to the back of the wardrobe.

At some schools, the abolition of uniforms has also had (4).......... an impact on what teenagers wear. In other schools, where school uniforms are (5).......... common, keeping up with teenage fashion is less (6).......... than in schools where kids can wear casual clothes. Nowadays, it costs (7).......... and more to stay in fashion and this can mean some pupils feel (8).......... if what they are wearing is not trendy enough. Some kids may even feel (9).......... if their parents don't have (10).......... to buy them the latest gear. The pressure from friends and the media to be trendy is so great (11).......... it is difficult to resist. For adults, it is easier to ignore the peer pressure but (12).......... a teenager – boy or girl – you need a lot of courage to say no to fashion.

0	**A** that	**B** as	**C** than *(circled)*	**D** from
1	**A** as	**B** than	**C** so	**D** that
2	**A** looks	**B** comes	**C** becomes	**D** seems
3	**A** serious	**B** a serious	**C** as serious	**D** most serious
4	**A** fairly	**B** quite	**C** very	**D** really
5	**A** as	**B** more	**C** most	**D** so
6	**A** profitable	**B** wealthy	**C** economic	**D** expensive
7	**A** even	**B** much	**C** more	**D** most
8	**A** shy	**B** shameful	**C** shameless	**D** embarrassed
9	**A** ashamed	**B** shameful	**C** shameless	**D** shy
10	**A** such money	**B** too much money	**C** enough money	**D** money enough
11	**A** as	**B** that	**C** than	**D** like
12	**A** as	**B** from	**C** with	**D** like

SCORE / 12

Part 2

For questions **13-24**, read the text below and think of the word which best fits each gap. Use only **one** word in each gap. There is an example at the beginning (**0**).

THE MYSTERY OF STONEHENGE

Stonehenge is one of England's (0) ....*most*.... famous landmarks. It is a group of large, tall stones that are arranged in circles on Salisbury Plain in the south of England. They are (13) .... big and heavy that their transportation over from Wales, 240 miles away, (14) .... to us today almost miraculous. Who could have carried them such (15) .... distance without the help of modern technology? The question is also why they used such huge stones; and why are there so (16) .... of them? What purpose did they serve? It must have been quite (17) .... accomplishment to build this mysterious monument. It has been estimated the construction of the site required (18) .... than thirty million hours of labour.

A lot of theories seem to (19) .... been put forward to explain the stones' existence. The stones seem (20) .... have been put there about 4,000 years ago for religious reasons, some people say. Today, this theory is less popular (21) .... it used to be. Most people think that Stonehenge was used (22) .... a huge astronomical instrument, to study the sun, moon and stars. However, scientists simply don't have (23) .... evidence to come to a final conclusion. Whatever its origins, Stonehenge remains one of (24) .... most fascinating monuments in the world.

SCORE _____ / 12

Part 3

For questions **25–34**, read the text below. Use the word given in capitals at the end of some of the lines to form a word that fits in the gap **in the same line**. There is an example at the beginning (**0**).

We all know now what a ⁽⁰⁾ *powerful* tool information technology is. It is more or less ⁽²⁵⁾.......... to live a full life in the twenty-first century without being ⁽²⁶⁾.......... with computers and how to make the most of them. They are incredibly ⁽²⁷⁾.......... in so many ways.	POWER IMPOSSIBILITY COMFORT USE
I used to have no idea about them – I was really ⁽²⁸⁾.......... at anything technical and I felt very ⁽²⁹⁾.......... whenever people asked me to do anything on the computer. When I first started using them, I made a lot of mistakes and would feel very ⁽³⁰⁾.......... when people referred to the latest ⁽³¹⁾.......... developments and I didn't know what they were talking about. But now I know enough not to feel ashamed or completely ⁽³²⁾.......... when my friends discuss the latest gadgets. I can get by but I am really amazed by how ⁽³³⁾.......... anything digital seems to be for young people. They grew up with computers and they are so ⁽³⁴⁾.......... . They can find their way around the computer so easily. It is very impressive.	HOPE ANXIETY EMBARRASS TECHNOLOGY IGNORE NATURE KNOWLEDGE

SCORE _____ / 10

Part 4

For questions **35–42**, complete the second sentence so that it has a similar meaning to the first sentence, using the word given. **Do not change the word given.** You must use between **two** and **five** words, including the word given. Here is an example (0).

Example:

0 So, do you regret what you did?
   SORRY
   So, ………are you sorry for……… what you did?

35 I think his wife is a journalist.
   MARRIED
   I think he's ………………………………… a journalist.

36 I don't like cooking very much.
   FOND
   I ………………………………… cooking.

37 I didn't expect you to behave like that.
   SURPRISED
   I ………………………………… your behaviour.

38 Ben is shorter than Keith.
   TALL
   Ben ………………………………… Keith.

39 I couldn't help laughing because the story was really funny.
   SUCH
   It was ………………………………… I couldn't help laughing.

40 He wasn't strong enough to carry that box.
   HEAVY
   The box was far ………………………………… carry.

41 If the plan fails, it will be your fault.
   RESPONSIBLE
   You will ………………………………… the failure of the plan.

42 She's often critical.
   TYPICAL
   It's ………………………………… to be critical.

SCORE / 16

TOTAL SCORE / 50

11

AGENDA

Grammar
- 11a Adverbs: use and form
- 11b Adverbs: word order
- 11c Adverbs: comparison

Vocabulary
- 11d Adverbs: different forms and meanings
- 11e Seeing and hearing

Entry test

1 Complete the sentences. Use an adverb formed from the adjectives in the box.

beautiful   day   happy   probable   quiet

1 Bessie plays the cello ………… .
2 Mark closed the door ………… so that he wouldn't wake the baby up.
3 The children were playing ………… on the beach.
4 I wonder why our friends haven't arrived. They've ………… been delayed by the traffic.
5 The museum is open ………… from nine to five.

Now look at 11a on pages 188-190. SCORE / 5

2 Put the words in the correct order.

6 opened / she / slowly / door / the
……………………………………………
7 laughing / always / he / class / is / in
……………………………………………
8 probably / she / French / doesn't / speak
……………………………………………
9 he / dangerously / drove / along / the / Sunday / on / motorway
……………………………………………
10 very / have / I / much / liked / music / always
……………………………………………

Now look at 11b on pages 191-193. SCORE / 5

ENTRY TEST 11

3 Choose the correct answer, A, B, C or D.

11 You must try and get to the lesson ....
  A earlier   B the earlier   C more earlier   D more early

12 She works .... than me.
  A more hard   B more hardly   C much harder   D much more hardly

13 I use the car .... often than I used to.
  A less   B least   C the more   D most

14 He speaks German .... than me.
  A weller   B more well   C better   D best

15 We all played badly but Kevin played ...., I think.
  A most badly   B the most badly   C the badliest   D the worst

Now look at 11c on pages 194–195.

SCORE ___ / 5

4 Choose the correct answer, A, B, C or D.

16 I don't .... what you mean at all. Can you explain?
  A realise   B see   C take   D make out

17 Could I have a .... at your newspaper for a minute?
  A look   B sight   C read   D borrow

18 Are you .... the radio or shall I switch it off?
  A hearing   B listening   C hearing at   D listening to

19 Have you heard .... Nick? He's had an accident.
  A for   B of   C around   D about

20 Will you .... after the cat for us while we're on holiday?
  A take   B watch   C look   D mind

Now look at 11d on pages 196–197.

SCORE ___ / 5

5 Choose the correct answer, A, B, C or D.

21 Her parents often complain because she comes home ....
  A late   B lately   C later   D latest

22 Read the letter .... – I want to know what Emma says.
  A loud   B loudly   C aloud   D more loud

23 His English is not very .... but his French is excellent.
  A high   B good   C well   D fluently

24 The dentist told him to open his mouth ....
  A wide   B widely   C deep   D deeply

25 They sat .... to each other.
  A close   B closely   C closed   D closest

Now look at 11e on pages 198–201.

SCORE ___ / 5

TOTAL SCORE ___ / 25

187

Grammar

11a Adverbs: use and form

Use

- We use adverbs to modify verbs, adjectives or clauses.
- Adverbs of manner describe how someone does something:
  She read the book **quickly**.
  They behaved **foolishly**.
  She played **beautifully**. ✓
  ~~She played **beautiful**.~~ ✗
  You must drive **carefully**. ✓
  ~~You must drive **careful**.~~ ✗
- Adverbs of place and time describe where or when something happens:
  I'll wait **here**. (adverb of place)
  Let's go **tomorrow**. (adverb of time)
- Adverbs of frequency describe how often something happens:
  We **usually** have dinner at eight.
- We use adverbs of degree to make adjectives stronger or weaker:
  It's **very** cold in winter.
- We can also use adverbs like *frankly, easily, by far*, etc. to modify superlatives:
  This is quite **frankly** the worst essay I've ever read.
  It was **easily** the best party I've ever been to.
- There are other types of adverb, for example linking adverbs like *also* and comment adverbs like *sadly*:
  I went with Tina and Eddie; Trevor came along **as well**.
  Sadly, the poor dog didn't make it.
- When a phrase is used as an adverb, we call it an adverbial phrase. For example:
  You're driving **too fast**.
  Let's go **tomorrow afternoon**.
  There's a huge truck **behind you**.

Form

- We form most adverbs (especially adverbs of manner) by adding *-ly* to an adjective:

Adjective	Adverb	Example
beautiful	beautifully	She plays the violin **beautifully**.
brilliant	brilliantly	He played **brilliantly** and won.
careful	carefully	I wish you would drive more **carefully**!
effective	effectively	You can communicate more **effectively** with email.
efficient	efficiently	The event had been very **efficiently** organised.
excited	excitedly	'We won!' she said **excitedly**.
hurried	hurriedly	They left the room **hurriedly**.
occasional	occasionally	I **occasionally** eat meat.
shy	shyly	She walked **shyly** into the room.
truthful	truthfully	Answer **truthfully**: did you do it?
undoubted	undoubtedly	**Undoubtedly**, there will be problems.
unexpected	unexpectedly	Peter turned up **unexpectedly**.
wholehearted	wholeheartedly	I **wholeheartedly** agree with you.

- For adjectives ending in *-le*, we drop the *-e* and only add *-y*:

Adjective	Adverb	Example
gentle	gently	They broke the news **gently**.
probable	probably	They are **probably** on their way now.
simple	simply	I **simply** don't believe you.
suitable	suitably	Bob wasn't **suitably** dressed.
terrible	terribly	Bessie played **terribly** that night.

- For adjectives ending in *-y*, we change the *-y* to *-i* before adding *-ly*:

Adjective	Adverb	Example
easy	easily	Our team is **easily** the best.
noisy	noisily	The kids were playing **noisily** in the garden.

- For adjectives ending in *-ic*, we add *-ally*:

Adjective	Adverb	Example
automatic	automatically	The machine will give you your money back **automatically**.
heroic	heroically	The soldiers fought **heroically**.
tragic	tragically	He died **tragically**.

- Some adverbs ending in *-ly* come from nouns:

Adjective	Adverb	Example
day	daily	Newspapers are delivered **daily**. (= every day)
fortnight	fortnightly	The magazine is published **fortnightly**. (= every two weeks)
hour	hourly	The database is updated **hourly**. (= every hour)
month	monthly	They meet **monthly** to discuss progress. (= every month)
week	weekly	The newspaper is published **weekly**. (= every week)
year	yearly	We pay the fees **yearly**. (= every year)

- Some words ending in *-ly* are adjectives, not adverbs:
a **friendly** police officer   a **silly** story
a **lonely** life   **lovely** weather   an **ugly** painting
- We cannot add *-ly* to these adjectives to form adverbs. Instead, we use phrases like in a … way/manner/fashion:
I've never met a police officer who behaves **in a friendly way**.
She spoke **in a** rather **silly manner**.
He lived his life **in a lonely fashion**.
- Some adverbs have the same form as adjectives. Examples include: *fast, hard, long, far, early, late*:
drive **fast** (adverb)   a **fast** driver (adjective)
work **hard** (adverb)   **hard** work (adjective)

See also: 11d

- The adverb for *public* is *publicly*:
He was **publicly** humiliated. ✓
He was **publically** humiliated. ✗
- The adverb for *true* is *truly*:
He was a **truly** great President.
- For adjectives ending in *-full*, we add *-y*:
I **fully** agree with you.
- The adverb for *good* is *well*:
Did you sleep **well**?
Did I do **well** in the test? ✓
Did I do **good** in the test? ✗

11 ADVERBS: USE AND FORM

PRACTICE

1 Complete the table. If an adverb cannot be formed from the adjective/noun, use an appropriate phrase.

Adjective/Noun	Adverb/Phrase	Adjective/Noun	Adverb/Phrase
suitable	suitably	lonely	
silly	in a silly way	tragic	
unlucky		year	
lovely		efficient	
possible		fast	
ugly		hard	
awful		public	
full		good	

2 Complete the sentences. Use adverbs formed from the words in brackets.

0 He treats his dog *terribly* (terrible).
1 The coffee machine switches off .... (automatic).
2 She touched him on the arm .... (gentle).
3 Heather turned up at the party .... (unexpected).
4 It's .... (probable) too late to catch the plane now.
5 The exam was .... (surprising) easy – everyone passed.
6 'I have a question,' she said, raising her hand .... (shy).
7 There was a .... (true) beautiful view from the bedroom.
8 He fought .... (heroic) against the disease.

3 Complete the sentences. Use adverbs formed from the words in the box.

> angry beautiful careful day early easy good month
> noise soft tragic

0 The orchestra played the symphony *beautifully*, I thought.
1 Val spoke so .... I could hardly hear her.
2 Hold the baby ...., please.
3 The children played .... in their room and kept their father awake.
4 The magazine is published ...., so we get twelve issues a year.
5 You could .... pass the test with a bit more work.
6 Come .... if you want to get a good seat.
7 I hope you do .... in your driving test.
8 Remember: you have to take the pills twice ....
9 The man looked at his son .... and said, 'Go to your room now!'
10 ...., her daughter died in a car accident.

190

11b Adverbs: word order

Group 1: initial, middle or end position

Most adverbs of manner (e.g. *slowly*) and some adverbs of time (e.g. *once*) and frequency (e.g. *occasionally*) can come at the beginning, in the middle (before the main verb) or at the end of a sentence. They modify verbs or clauses. The choice of position is a matter of emphasis.

Beginning of sentence	Middle of sentence	End of sentence
Slowly, she opened the door.	She **slowly** opened the door.	She opened the door **slowly**.
Once I had a motorbike.	I **once** had a motorbike.	I had a motorbike **once**.
Occasionally, he loses his temper.	He **occasionally** loses his temper.	He loses his temper **occasionally**.

Group 2: initial or end position

- Many adverbs of time (e.g. *yesterday*) and place (e.g. *outside*) usually come at the end of a sentence but they can also come at the beginning:

Beginning of sentence	End of sentence
Yesterday, I finished work early.	I finished work early **yesterday**.
Outside, it was raining.	It was raining **outside**.

- Adverbial phrases usually come at the end:
  There's a sports car **in the fast lane**.
  I'll be with you **in a moment**. ✓
  I'll be **in a moment** with you. ✗
- However, there are exceptions:
  In January, he expects to get a pay rise.
  He expects to get a pay rise **in January**.

Group 3: middle position

- Some adverbs of frequency (e.g. *always*), degree (e.g. *nearly*), as well as other adverbs like *definitely* and *probably* usually come in the middle of the sentence, before the main verb:
  I **always** get up early.
  I **never** drink milk.
  I've **nearly** finished.
  She **probably** thinks everything's all right.
  She **never** apologises. ✓
  Never she apologises. ✗

- Here are some more examples of adverbs in group 3:

Frequency	always, ever, frequently, hardly, never, normally, often, rarely, seldom, sometimes, usually
Degree	absolutely, extremely, fairly, hardly, nearly, quite, really
Other	also, certainly, definitely, even, just, merely, only, probably, suddenly

- Adverbs in group 3 go immediately after auxiliary verbs (*be, have, do*) and modal verbs (*can, may, should*, etc.):
  I've **never** drunk iced tea.
  You should **definitely** accept the offer.
  She'll **probably** come to the wedding.
  I've **nearly** finished.
- However, when the verb is negative, adverbs that express degree of certainty (e.g. *certainly, definitely, probably*, etc.) come before the auxiliary:
  He **probably** won't come to the party.
  She **certainly** can't put up with the situation.

Group 4: end position

- Adverbs of manner (e.g. *well, badly*) and adverbs of place and time (e.g. *here* and *now*) often come at the end of a sentence:
  He comes home **late**.
  She sings **well**.
  He played **badly**.

11 ADVERBS: WORD ORDER

- Adverbial phrases (e.g. *in the playground, at home, on Sunday morning*) often come at the end of the sentence (see, however, group 2 on page 191):
  I like music **very much**. ✓
  ~~I like **very much** music.~~ ✗
  She speaks English **very well**. ✓
  ~~She **very well** speaks English.~~ ✗
  He woke up with a headache **on Sunday morning**.
  They were standing **in the playground**.

- When there are two clauses in the sentence, the position of the adverb or adverbial phrase can change the meaning:
  He promised **immediately** that he would pay for the damage. (= an immediate promise)
  He promised that he would pay for the damage **immediately**. (= a promise that he would pay immediately)

- Here are some more examples of adverbs in group 4:

Manner	as well, badly, cheerfully, happily, mildly, politely, quickly, regularly, sweetly, tenderly
Place	in London, in the stadium, at the cinema, on the dance floor, by the television
Time	daily, late, monthly, once, at once, at six o'clock, on the hour, on Tuesday

- We often use more than one adverb or adverbial phrase in a sentence. When this is the case, the usual order is: manner → place → time:

	Manner	Place	Time
They played	badly	at Wembley	on Saturday.
She waited	patiently	in her room	all morning.

- However, single-word adverbs can come before adverbial phrases:
  I saw him **yesterday in the park**.
- And shorter phrases can come before longer ones:
  I'll see you **at eight outside the cinema**.

PRACTICE

1 Rewrite the sentences with the adverbs in the correct place. If a sentence is correct, put a tick (✓) on the line.

0 The payments are made monthly.
   ....✓.................

00 I went yesterday to the post office.
   I went to the post office yesterday.

1 I've become interested in skiing recently.
   ....

2 We play football after school often.
   ....

3 Very carefully he drives on the motorway.
   ....

4 I don't get up always early.
   ....

5 I've never visited the United States.
   ....

6 Outside he's waiting.
   ....

7 Only I like ice cream, not pudding.
   ....

8 I cooked and washed the dishes as well.
   ....

192

ADVERBS: WORD ORDER **11**

2 Rewrite the sentences. Put the adverbs in brackets in the correct place.

0   I like travelling by plane. (very much)
    I like travelling by plane very much.

1   You won't finish your homework if you don't hurry up. (in time)
    ....

2   I'll finish my project. (probably, on Friday)
    ....

3   Doesn't she play the piano? (well)
    ....

4   We arrived. (on Sunday, in London)
    ....

5   She won't be coming to work. (today, probably)
    ....

6   He performed. (superbly, at the National Theatre, on Saturday)
    ....

7   She visits her mother. (at the weekend, usually, in hospital)
    ....

8   I remember seeing him. (definitely, outside the shop)
    ....

9   Can you come? (at six o'clock, to my office)
    ....

10 We go camping. (for a few days, occasionally)
    ....

3 Choose the correct answer.

Hypochondria: It's all in your head

I have a friend who worries about his health a lot. He (0) *all the time talks about it / talks about it all the time*. He isn't interested in anything else – I'm (1) *really starting / starting really* to worry about him.

When he feels an ache, (2) *immediately he thinks / he immediately thinks* he has a serious illness. He worries so much that he (3) *relaxes hardly ever / hardly ever relaxes*. His fear of falling ill means (4) *often he misses / he often misses* work because at the first sign of a cold, he decides to stay at home till the symptoms have gone. When (5) *well he feels / he feels well*, he goes back to work but he finds it difficult to concentrate with all the people coughing and sneezing in the office. (6) *Once last year / Last once year*, he even went to work wearing (7) *over his nose and mouth a mask / a mask over his nose and mouth*. He looked really strange!

He is (8) *always looking up / looking up always* his symptoms on the Internet to find out if they mean he has a serious disease. He goes (9) *once a month to the doctor / to the doctor once a month* (at least!) and tells her he feels terrible. (10) *On Friday, he went / He went on Friday* to the doctor again; she examined him and listened (11) *very patiently to him / to him very patiently* before telling him there was nothing wrong with him. (12) *Hopefully, she will realise / She will realise hopefully* soon that there is something wrong with him and get him the help he does need!

'I **never** travel without my diary – one should **always** have something sensational to read in the train.' OSCAR WILDE

193

11c Adverbs: comparison

One-syllable adverbs

- One-syllable adverbs take *-er* in the comparative and (*the*) *-est* in the superlative:
  Bill ran **fast**. John ran **faster than** Bill. Gary ran **the fastest**.
  They work **hard**. The girls work **harder**. The boys work **the hardest**.

Adverb	Comparative	Superlative
early	earlier	the earliest
fast	faster	the fastest
hard	harder	the hardest
high	higher	the highest
late	later	the latest
long	longer	the longest
loud	louder	the loudest
low	lower	the lowest
near	nearer	the nearest
quick	quicker	the quickest
slow	slower	the slowest
soon	sooner	the soonest

- To form the comparative and superlative of *early*, we change *-y* to *-i* before adding *-er/-est*:
  She arrived **early**.
  She arrived **earlier than** expected.
  She arrived **the earliest** of them all.
  You must come **earlier**. ✓
  ~~You must come **more early**.~~ ✗

Adverbs with two or more syllables

- To form the comparative and superlative of most adverbs with two or more syllables, we use *more … than* and *the most …* .
  Can you work **more quietly**? ✓
  ~~Can you work **quietlier**?~~ ✗
  All the girls sing **beautifully**, but Sarah sings **the most beautifully**, I think.

- We can also use *less … than* and *the least …* with adverbs:
  She drives **less carefully** than her brother.
- We can also use *as* + adverb + *as* or *not as/so* + adverb + *as*:
  Jenny did**n't** play **as well as** Lisa.

He couldn't take his job **more seriously** if he tried.

Irregular adverbs

- Some adverbs have irregular comparative and superlative forms.
  Bessie plays the piano **well**.
  She plays the piano **better than** Ella.
  She plays **the best** of all the girls in the class.
  Terry did **badly** in the test. Tom did even **worse than** him.

Adverb	Comparative	Superlative
a lot	more	the most
badly	worse	the worst
far	farther/further	the farthest/furthest
little	less	the least
much	more	the most
well	better	the best

- We can use *farther/further* and *farthest/furthest* in the same way.
  We'd better not go any **farther/further** tonight.

For *far* used as an adjective, see **9a**

194

ADVERBS: COMPARISON 11

PRACTICE

1 Complete the sentences. Use the correct form of the adverbs in brackets. Add any other words necessary.

0 My wife drives *more carefully than* (carefully) I do.
1 She works …………… (efficiently) everyone else in the office.
2 I play chess …………… (badly) my son.
3 He got up …………… (early) me.
4 Of all the students in my class, Amanda works …………… (hard).
5 She doesn't drive …………… (dangerously) as her husband.
6 I play football …………… (often) before now that I'm unemployed.
7 She didn't do as …………… (well) her brother in the test.
8 The person who runs …………… (fast) will win first prize.
9 You ate …………… (much) anybody else at the party.
10 How much …………… (far) is it to the bus station?

2 Complete the sentences. Use the correct form of the adverbs in the box. Add any other words necessary.

> badly ~~carefully~~ close early fast fluently hard imaginatively
> long loudly often

0 You'll have an accident if you don't drive *more carefully*.
1 She should work …………… if she wants to pass her Maths test.
2 You should have got there …………… if you wanted to get a good seat.
3 Can you speak ……………, please? We can't hear you at the back.
4 I didn't play well but Harry played even …………… I did.
5 I took a taxi because if I had come by bus, it would have taken me much …………… .
6 'I'm fed up with staying in all the time!' 'Well, go out ……………, then.'
7 Of all my classmates, Rob writes …………… . His stories are always fascinating.
8 He didn't run …………… as Pete; he came second.
9 Of the three sisters, Irene speaks English …………… .
10 Come a little …………… so you can see better.

> *He who laughs last, laughs **longest**.*

Vocabulary

11d Adverbs: different forms and meanings

Adverbs with the same form as the adjective

We already know that some adverbs have the same form as the adjective:
We had an **early** breakfast. (adjective)   We left **early**. (adverb)

Adjectives that form two adverbs

- Some adjectives form two different adverbs: one that is the same as the adjective and one ending in *-ly*:

Adverb	Meaning	Example
deep	a long way into or below the surface of sth	The box had been hidden **deep** into the ground.
deeply	very; very much	We are all **deeply** grateful.
direct	without stopping or changing direction	We flew **direct** to Rome.
directly	with no other person/action/process between	You'll be **directly** responsible to your manager.
	immediately	We left **directly** after the meeting.
	exactly in a particular position or direction	She looked **directly** at us.
free	without paying	We got into the cinema **free**.
freely	without anyone stopping or limiting sth	He comes and goes **freely**.
hard	using a lot of effort, energy or attention	He always works **hard**.
	with a lot of force	She pushed the door **hard**.
hardly	almost not	No, he's not my friend. We **hardly** know each other.
high	at or to a level high above the ground	He can jump **high**.
highly	very	He's a **highly** successful businessman.
	to a high level or standard	It's a **highly** paid job.
	with admiration	I think **highly** of you.
last	after everything or everyone else	He came **last** in the race.
	most recently	When did you **last** see Eric?
lastly	finally	**Lastly**, I'd like to thank Mrs Jones.
late	after the usual or arranged time	Do you have to work **late** today?
lately	recently	Have you seen Natasha **lately**?
right	correctly	You guessed **right**.
rightly	justifiably	He was **rightly** upset.
wide	completely	Open your mouth **wide**.
widely	in many places or by many people	She has travelled **widely**.

ADVERBS: DIFFERENT FORMS AND MEANINGS 11

- Sometimes, the two adverbs formed from the same adjective have the same or a similar meaning:

Adverbs	Example
loud/loudly	Don't talk so **loud/loudly**.
quick/quickly	Get out of here, **quick**! They ran as **quickly** as they could.
rough/roughly	He plays **rough**. She grabbed his hand **roughly**. (both = not gently or carefully)
tight/tightly	Hold on **tight**! He held on **tightly**.
wrong/wrongly	You've done it all **wrong**! He even spelt his own name **wrongly**!

PRACTICE

1 Complete the sentences. Use adjectives or adverbs from pages 196–197.

0 If she tries ..**hard**.., she may succeed in breaking the world record.
1 No, we didn't make any stops – we drove .... to the hotel.
2 You don't need to buy a ticket; members travel ....
3 The name of the suspect is .... known in town – nearly everyone knows him.
4 It's a(n) .... time since I saw her – two years, I think.
5 Her injury prevented her from moving ....
6 I was so shocked I could .... speak.
7 .... now, Tommy; Hurry up; your school bus is here.
8 Sorry I'm late; have you been waiting ....?
9 When I .... saw Adam, he said he hadn't been feeling well.
10 The dentist asked her to open her mouth ....
11 ...., I'd like to thank my teacher Mr Fox.
12 My name is .... spelt on this form. It's *Allan*, not *Alan*.
13 Don't drive so ....! Slow down!
14 It hasn't rained much .... – the last time was two months ago.
15 He's a very .... runner. He's amazing!
16 Nadia is in her .... twenties – twenty-two, I think.

2 Complete the text. Use the adverbs in the box. There are four extra words.

> hard   hardly   high   highly   late
> ~~lately~~   long   quickly   right   rightly
> wide   widely

Catch that thief!

There have been a number of burglaries in our neighbourhood (0) **lately**.
We are not sure who is to blame but it is (1) .... believed that the burglaries are the work of one gang. The police are still investigating the matter and know very little for certain. The public, (2) .... or wrongly, blame the police for not acting more (3) .... and claim that police officers aren't working as (4) .... as they should. Most people do not think very (5) .... of the police and indeed so far they have only questioned one suspect. Whenever they are called in to investigate a burglary, it takes them so (6) .... to get to the scene of the crime that it is always too (7) .... to catch the culprits!

*Still waters run **deep**.*

197

11e Seeing and hearing

Seeing

Verb	Meaning	Example
see	notice or examine sth with your eyes	I can't **see** a thing without my glasses!
	understand	I **see** what you mean.
	watch a TV programme, performance, etc.	Two million people **saw** the game.
	find out	**See** if there's any cheese in the fridge.
look (at)	turn your eyes towards sth so that you can see it	**Look**! A snake! **Look at** me when I'm talking to you.
look after sb/sth	take care of sb/sth	Don't worry; I'll **look after** the kids tomorrow. Will you **look after** the baby while I'm out? ✓ Will you **look for** the baby while I'm out? ✗
look for sb/sth	try to find sb/sth	I'm **looking for** Steve – have you seen him? I'm **looking for** my keys. ✓ I'm looking my keys. ✗
look forward to sth	be excited and pleased about sth that is going to happen	I'm really **looking forward to** our holiday. We're **looking forward to** seeing you again.
look into sth	try to find out the truth about sth	The police are **looking into** the disappearance of the two children.
look through sth	look for sth among a pile of papers, in a drawer, etc.	'I can't find my keys.' 'Have you **looked through** your pockets?'
look up sth; look sth up	try to find information in a book, on a computer, etc.	He **looked up** the word in his dictionary.
have a look (at sth)	look at sth	Can you just **have** a quick **look at** the engine for me?
gaze (at sb/sth)	look at sb/sth for a long time, often without realising	She was **gazing at** the beautiful landscape.
gaze into sth		Patrick was **gazing into** the fire.
glance (at/up/down/etc.)	quickly look at sb or sth	He **glanced** nervously at his watch. She **glanced** round the room.
glance through sth	read sth very quickly	Can you **glance through** my essay and tell me what you think of it?
glimpse sb/sth	to see sb or sth for a moment without getting a complete view of them	I **glimpsed** her face in the crowd and then she was gone.
catch a glimpse of sb/sth		I only **caught a glimpse of** him as he drove off.
catch sight of sb/sth	to see sb/sth for a moment	I **caught sight of** Mary as she walked into the supermarket.

198

notice sb/sth	see, hear or feel sb/sth	Cathy **noticed** that Isabelle was restless. I was too busy to **notice** how hungry I was!
stare (at sb/sth)	look at sb/sth for a long time without moving your eyes	She **stared at** the page for several minutes; she wasn't sure what to write.
stare into space	look at nothing	He just sat there, **staring into space**.
watch (sb/sth)	look at sb/sth for a period of time, paying attention to what is happening	Harriet **watched** the man with interest as he walked in. I'm **watching** TV. ✓ I'm **seeing** TV. ✗
keep an eye on sb/sth	take care of sb/sth; look after sb/sth	Will you **keep an eye on** the kids while I pop out for a moment?

Hearing

Verb	Meaning	Example
hear sb/sth	know a sound is being made, using your ears	Did you **hear** that sound?
hear sb doing sth		I think I can **hear** someone knocking.
hear sb do sth		I didn't **hear** her go out.
hear about	be told or find out sth	Have you **heard about** the fire at the factory?
hear (that)		I **hear** (**that**) you've been selected to play in the team.
hear from sb	receive news or information from sb	Have you **heard from** Sarah lately?
hear of sb/sth	know that sb/sth exists	I've never **heard of** him before.
be hearing things	imagine you can hear sth when really there is no sound	I must **be hearing things** – I was sure someone called my name.
listen (to sb/sth)	pay attention to what sb is saying or to a sound that you can hear	**Listen** – there's a strange noise coming from the engine. I'm **listening to** the radio. ✓ I'm **listening** the radio. ✗ I'm **listening to** the news. ✓ I'm **hearing** the news. ✗
	consider what sb says and accept their advice	I told her not to do it but she wouldn't **listen**. I wish I'd **listened to** my friend.
listen hard	listen carefully	I **listened hard** but could hear nothing.
be all ears	be very keen to hear what sb is going to tell you	As soon as I mentioned money, Karen **was all ears**.
lend an ear	listen patiently to what sb says	I'm always here to **lend an ear** if you need to talk.

11 SEEING AND HEARING

PRACTICE

1 Complete the sentences. Use the correct form of a verb from pages 198–199.

0 I didn't ..*hear*.. you come in because I was ..*watching*.. TV.
1 Ann's really angry with me and I can .... why.
2 Joe didn't .... the phone because he was .... to music.
3 I've never .... of a composer called Piccolini.
4 I haven't .... my son in Australia for over a year.
5 She .... nervously behind her to see if anyone was following her.
6 I only .... a glimpse of Larry as he rushed past my office this morning.
7 The little girl was waving at him but he didn't seem to ....
8 I'm .... for my wallet – have you seen it anywhere?
9 .... carefully to what I've got to say because I'm not going to say it again.
10 I .... that you're going away on Saturday; where are you going this time?
11 I wish you'd stop .... at me like that. It's not polite, you know!
12 I don't have much time – I'll just .... through the report.

2 Complete the second sentence so that it has a similar meaning to the first sentence, using the word given. Use between two and five words. Do not change the word given.

0 Nobody told them about the accident.
   HEAR
   They did ..*not hear about*.. the accident.

1 The police are investigating the murder.
   LOOKING
   The police .... the murder.

2 My sister will take care of the children while we're out.
   AFTER
   My sister .... the children while we're out.

3 Are you excited about seeing your cousins after all this time?
   FORWARD
   Are you .... your cousins after all this time?

4 I haven't had any news from Alex for months.
   HEARD
   I haven't .... Alex for months.

5 I thought I heard a noise but it must have been just my imagination.
   THINGS
   I must have been .... when I thought I heard a noise.

6 She's always ready to listen when people have a problem.
   LEND
   She is always ready .... when people have a problem.

7 I thought I saw somebody hiding behind the tree.
   GLIMPSE
   I thought I .... of somebody hiding behind the tree.

8 Could you look after Tommy while I take a shower?
   EYE
   Could you .... Tommy while I take a shower?

9 I'm really very keen to hear what you have to say – go on!
   EARS
   I'm .... – go on!

10 He read the letter very quickly and threw it away.
   GLANCED
   He .... the letter and threw it away.

3 Choose the correct answer.

0 I can see really (well) / carefully with my new glasses.
1 Georgia looked *directly / badly* at Hans and said 'No!'
2 He *suddenly / fast* noticed the pet hamster had gone.
3 I *once / carefully* heard her say she revises in the bath!
4 Please listen *closely / suitably* to my instructions.
5 He was *barely / beautifully* watching as the child fell.

4 Read the story and choose the correct answer, A, B, C or D.

A CHANCE MEETING

This was my first visit to Los Angeles and I was really looking forward (0).......... it. I had heard a lot (1).......... L.A. being the city of the stars and I was hoping to (2).......... sight of somebody famous; I had my camera ready just in case. I sat at a pavement café and (3).......... the people going by in case I spotted any well-known faces.

It was all very impressive: there were huge skyscrapers and I spent a long time just (4).......... in amazement at the glossy buildings. At one moment, I was too busy staring (5).......... the massive US Bank Tower building to (6).......... where I was going, so I bumped into a woman on the pavement. I apologised to her. When she asked me if I was from England, I thought the voice sounded familiar; I was sure I had (7).......... it somewhere before.

Then I (8).......... another look at her and realised it was Stephanie Gibson, the singer. I was speechless! 'Yes, I am,' I replied. 'Really?' she said. 'Have you heard (9).......... a place called Crosby?' 'Yes, of course,' I said. 'That's near Scunthorpe, where I come from.' I thought I was hearing (10).......... but she went on: 'That's incredible! I've always wanted to meet someone from that part of the world. Hey, are you free right now for a quick coffee?' I just couldn't believe it!

0	**A** at	**B** at	(**C** to)	**D** for
1	**A** from	**B** of	**C** about	**D** in
2	**A** catch	**B** take	**C** make	**D** have
3	**A** looked	**B** noticed	**C** watched	**D** saw
4	**A** glancing	**B** glimpsing	**C** gazing	**D** seeing
5	**A** to	**B** in	**C** on	**D** at
6	**A** catch	**B** glance	**C** notice	**D** find
7	**A** heard	**B** listened	**C** listened to	**D** sounded
8	**A** made	**B** took	**C** did	**D** saw
9	**A** from	**B** of	**C** for	**D** on
10	**A** noises	**B** sounds	**C** words	**D** things

12

AGENDA

Grammar
- 12a Articles
- 12b Determiners
- 12c Countable and uncountable nouns

Vocabulary
- 12d Uncountable nouns ending in -s, plural nouns, collective nouns
- 12e Suffixes (5)

Entry test

1 Choose the correct answer.

1 She got a first class degree from *Oxford University* / *the Oxford University*.
2 Jones was found guilty and sentenced to five years in *prison* / *the prison*.
3 Can we meet *outside hospital* / *outside the hospital* at about six o'clock?
4 Mum, there's *a spider* / *the spider* crawling all over my arm!
5 She punched her attacker in *face* / *the face* and he ran off.

Now look at 12a on pages 204–207.

SCORE / 5

2 Choose the correct answer, A, B, C or D.

6 There are already .... people waiting outside to buy tickets.
   A some   **B** a lot   **C** lots   **D** a little

7 I would be glad to answer .... questions you may have.
   A some   **B** every   **C** any   **D** few

8 Could you please go and get .... chair from next door?
   A other   **B** another   **C** more   **D** a few

9 Unfortunately, there was .... we could do to help the old man.
   A few   **B** a few   **C** little   **D** a little

10 We haven't got .... money but we can buy our tickets.
   A many   **B** much   **C** several   **D** plenty

Now look at 12b on pages 208–211.

SCORE / 5

ENTRY TEST 12

3 **Choose the correct answer, A, B, C or D.**

11 If you want .... sensible advice, go to Jack.
   A a   B many   C a few   D some

12 I don't need all .... money.
   A this   B these   C them   D those

13 I forgot to take the spaghetti out of the water and .... went soft.
   A they   B all   C it   D these

14 She's excellent at languages but her Spanish .... better than her Italian.
   A is   B are   C it's   D they're

15 I need ....
   A a scissor   B a scissors   B a pair of scissor   D a pair of scissors

Now look at **12c** on pages 212–215.   SCORE   / 5

4 **Choose the correct answer.**

16 Physics *is / are* one of my favourite subjects.
17 Have you seen my shorts? I can't find *it / them* anywhere.
18 They have a lovely house on the *outskirt / outskirts* of the city.
19 I believe *congratulation is / congratulations are* in order.
20 You should have asked someone to give you *a direction / directions* to the police station.

Now look at **12d** on pages 216–218.   SCORE   / 5

5 **Complete the sentences. Use words formed from the words in CAPITALS at the end of the lines.**

21 She's just come out of a long period of ....; she's fine now.   **DEPRESS**
22 Although he's a rich businessman, he's not known for his ....   **GENEROUS**
23 The Prime Minister's speech got a lot of .... in the media.   **PUBLIC**
24 He finally agreed to take part in the show but with ....   **RELUCTANT**
25 There were three .... guards outside the bank.   **SECURE**

Now look at **12e** on pages 219–223.   SCORE   / 5

                                                         TOTAL SCORE   / 25

Grammar

12a Articles

Use of articles with different kinds of noun

Here is a summary of the way we use articles with different kinds of noun:

Article	Noun	Example
indefinite (*a/an*)	singular countable	She has **a bicycle** already. Take **an umbrella** with you.
definite (*the*)	singular countable	**The** red **bicycle** is mine.
	plural countable	**The bicycles** are in the shed.
	uncountable	**The salt** is in the cupboard.
no article	singular countable	Zoe is in **hospital**.
	plural countable	They use **bicycles** to get to work.
	uncountable	**Salt** is cheap.

Indefinite article (*a/an*)

Use	Example
to talk about sb/sth that has not been mentioned before; to talk about sb/sth for the first time	I've just seen **a** car coming up the drive. There's **a** spider in the bath.
to talk about one person, thing, etc., without saying which person, thing, etc. we mean	I'd like **an** orange. (= any orange, not a specific one) I want **a** new computer. (= any computer, not a specific one)
to refer to people and things in general	Is **a** spider **an** insect? (= all spiders) **A** teacher ought to be patient. (= all teachers)
to mean 'one', with some numbers and fractions	**a** hundred, **a** thousand, **a** third
to mean 'each' or 'per'	twice **a** week (= twice each week) I get fifty pounds **a** day. (= each day) He was driving at 110 miles **an** hour. (= per hour)
when we classify or define things or people (e.g. say what job sb does, what sth is used for, etc.)	He's **a** teacher. A dictionary is **a** book that explains the meanings of words.
with adjectives followed by nouns, in descriptions	He was **a** tall young man. It was **a** beautiful day.
before sb's name, when we don't know the person	There's **a** Mr Wilkins here to see you.
with some illnesses, especially ones that aren't serious	I've got **a** headache. She's got **a** cold.
in certain phrases, especially ones that express an amount or quantity	**a** few, **a** little, **a** lot, **a** great deal
after *what* or *such*, for emphasis	What **a** day it's been! He's such **a** fool!

Note that the choice of *a* or *an* depends on pronunciation, not on spelling: we use *a* before a consonant sound and *an* before a vowel sound. Compare:

*a **b**ook*	*a **c**omputer*	*a **p**rofessor*
*an **o**rchestra*	*an **e**mail*	*an **i**gloo*

but:

*a **e**uro*	*a **u**niversity*	*a **o**ne-year-old child*
*an **h**our*	*an **M**P*	

Definite article (*the*)

Use	Example
to talk about sb/sth you have mentioned before	*I've got a cat and a dog. **The** cat's name is Bob and **the** dog's name is Rosie.*
to talk about sb/sth specific	*We went to **the** café that's next to the post office.* *I want **the** red dress.* (= not any dress)
to talk about sth that is unique	*What time does **the** moon rise?* (= There is only one moon.) *London is **the** capital of Britain.* (= Britain only has one capital.)
to refer to people, animals or things in general	***The** white tiger is an endangered species.* (= all white tigers)
with inventions	*Alexander Graham Bell invented **the** telephone.*
with musical instruments	*She plays **the** piano.*
with superlatives	*Which is **the** tallest building in the world?*
with the names of certain countries	***the** United States, **the** United Kingdom, **the** Netherlands, **the** Lebanon, **the** Czech Republic*
with the names of groups of islands	***the** Philippines, **the** Maldives*
with the names of some mountain ranges	***the** Alps, **the** Pyrenees, **the** Himalayas*
with the names of oceans, seas, rivers, deserts and regions	***the** Pacific, **the** Atlantic, **the** Aegean Sea, **the** North Sea, **the** Thames, **the** Mississippi, **the** Sahara Desert, **the** Gobi Desert*
with the names of hotels, theatres, museums and newspapers	***the** Hilton, **the** Sheraton, **the** National Theatre, **the** Natural History Museum, **the** Times*
with some important buildings	***the** White House, **the** Houses of Parliament*
to refer to the media or types of entertainment	***the** cinema, **the** theatre, **the** radio, **the** press, **the** opera*
with surnames, when we are referring to a whole family	***the** Jones, **the** Mitchells*
with the names of groups	***the** Beatles, **the** Rolling Stones*
with adjectives used as nouns to refer to a group of people	***the** sick, **the** injured, **the** rich, **the** young*
with nationalities, to refer to a group of people	***the** Japanese, **the** Asians, **the** French*
in dates	***the** fourteenth of July, March **the** twenty-fifth*
in some phrases referring to our physical environment	***the** sea, **the** mountains, **the** countryside, **the** weather*
to refer to a place or person that people visit regularly	***the** doctor, **the** dentist, **the** hairdresser*
to refer to a part of sb's body	*She hit him on **the** ear.* (= his ear) *I punched him on **the** nose.* (= his nose)

12 ARTICLES

No article

Use	Example
with plural countable nouns, to talk about sb/sth in general	I buy magazines about computers. I like music. Dogs love bones.
with uncountable nouns, especially abstract nouns or nouns referring to substances	She hates dishonesty. Many people are afraid of death. Chocolate is bad for your teeth. Gold is expensive.
with adjectives that are not followed by nouns	Her husband is tall. (But: She's married to **a** tall man.) The film was excellent. (But: It was **an** excellent film.)
with the names of people	Sarah didn't come with us last night. Mr Edwards will be with you in a moment.
with the names of countries, states, cities, towns, etc.	France, New York, London, Texas, Devon
with the names of continents	Asia, Europe, Africa
with the names of mountains and lakes	Mount Everest, Mount Olympus, Lake Geneva, Lake Ontario
with the names of streets, roads, squares and parks	Oxford Street, Fifth Avenue, Brighton Road, Trafalgar Square, Hyde Park
with the names of shops, banks and restaurants	Harrod's, Barclays Bank, McDonald's
with the names of airports or stations	Gatwick airport, Charing Cross Station
with the names of universities	Cambridge University, York University (But: **The** University of York)
with the names of churches or cathedrals	St Martin's Church, St Paul's Cathedral
with the names of magazines	People magazine, Hello magazine
with languages	She speaks German.
with games, sports and school subjects	I love chess. How often do you play tennis? Geography has always been my favourite subject.
with meals	Have you had lunch yet? Dinner's ready.
with some diseases and illnesses	They haven't found a cure for cancer yet. She has diabetes.
with ways of travelling/means of transport	travel by car/bus/train; go on foot
with some buildings and institutions, when we are referring to their main function or basic purpose	He was sent to prison. She goes to school. Compare: He's in hospital. (= He's a patient there.) He went to **the** hospital to visit his friend. (= not as a patient) She's at school. (= as a pupil) My mum will be waiting for us outside **the** school. (= We are referring to the building, not its purpose.)
in some common phrases	at work, at home, in bed, watch TV, listen to music

> ARTICLES 12

PRACTICE

1 Complete the sentences. Use *a*, *the* or no article (–).

0 **The** audience clapped and cheered.
1 My friend says .... British are not very friendly but I disagree.
2 If we do not protect .... nature, our environment will get worse and worse.
3 I pick up .... kids from .... school and take them home when .... Mandy is at .... work.
4 Take these letters to .... post office, will you?
5 Are we going round to .... Wilsons for supper on Saturday?
6 Watch out! There's .... car right behind you!
7 What will you do if they cut .... electricity off?
8 She kissed him on .... cheek.
9 The government should tax .... rich more and .... poor less.
10 .... power doesn't interest him but .... money does.
11 We arrived at .... Heathrow and got .... taxi, which took us to .... Oxford Street.
12 We did about ten kilometres .... day on our cycling trip.

2 Articles have been removed from the following text. Rewrite it, including the missing articles.

London Bridge is falling down

Romans invaded Britain in 43AD and chasing ancient Britons along the Thames, they came to first place that was easy to cross. They built garrison there – and London was born. They also built bridge over river. Garrison became major trading post. Later, bridge suffered neglect and whole area was raided by Vikings.

In 886AD, Alfred the Great drove out raiders, bridge was repaired and city prospered again. Hundred years later, Vikings returned but King Ethelred sailed up Thames, attached ropes to London Bridge, headed downriver and pulled it down.

3 Complete the article. Use *a*, *the* or no article (–).

The Beatles

In 1957, (0) **a** young man called John Lennon from (1) .... Liverpool decided to form (2) .... pop group called *The Quarrymen*. In (3) .... same year, (4) .... Lennon invited (5) .... friend called Paul McCartney, then only fifteen, to join the group as (6) .... guitarist. McCartney, in turn, invited George Harrison (7) .... following February. Ringo Starr became the fourth band member.

(8) .... name of the band was changed to *The Beatles* and it became one of (9) .... most commercially successful and critically acclaimed acts in (10) .... history of (11) .... popular music. They built their reputation playing clubs in (12) .... Liverpool and (13) .... Hamburg in (14) .... Germany over a three-year period from 1960. They achieved (15) .... success in (16) .... United Kingdom with their first single, *Love Me Do*, and gained international popularity over the next couple of years, touring extensively until 1966. Then they spent (17) .... lot of time in the recording studio until their end in 1970.

Following (18) .... break-up of the band, each member found (19) .... success independently in musical careers, though Lennon himself was sadly murdered outside his home in (20) .... New York in 1980. He was shot by (21) .... man at the entrance of (22) .... building where he lived.

During The Beatles' studio years, they produced some of their finest music, including (23) .... album *Sgt. Pepper's Lonely Hearts Club Band* (1967), widely regarded as (24) .... masterpiece. The Beatles are the best-selling band in the history of (25) .... popular music. They have had more number one albums in (26) .... charts than any other musical act. They have sold more albums in (27) .... USA than any other artist. Their influence on popular culture is (28) .... unparalleled.

207

12b Determiners

- Determiners include *a*, *an* and *the* and other words that come before nouns. Here is a list of common determiners:

a lot/lots of	*enough*	*much*
all	*every*	*neither*
another	*(a) few*	*none (of)*
any	*(a) little*	*other*
both	*many*	*several*
each	*more*	*some*
either	*most*	

For articles, see 12a

- We use determiners in the following ways:

Determiner	Meaning/Use	Examples
all/all of	the whole of an amount, thing or type of thing; every one of a number of people or things	He had spent **all** (**of**) his life working in a factory. He spent it **all** bottling lemon juice.
	NB: We use *all of*, not *all* before pronouns (e.g. we say *all of them*, not *all them*).	There was a terrible storm but **all of us** managed to get back safely.
another	an additional person or thing (used with singular countable nouns)	We need **another** chair.
any	used with uncountable or plural nouns in negative sentences and questions, to refer to an amount or number of sth	I don't have **any** money. Do you have **any** money? I'm not sure if she has **any** brothers. ✓ I'm not sure if she has **some** brothers. ✗
	used with singular countable nouns to refer to one of a number of things or people, when it does not matter which one	We can go to **any** restaurant you like.
	as much as possible	I need **any** help I can get.
both/both of	used to refer to two people or things together	**Both** (**of**) her parents are doctors.
	used with *and* (*both … and …*) to say that sth is true of two people or things	He has lived in **both** Britain **and** France.
	NB: 1 We use *both of*, not *both* before pronouns (e.g. we say *both of them*, not *both them*). 2 *Both* is always followed by a plural verb.	'I don't know which book to buy.' 'Why don't you buy **both of them**?'
each/each of	every one of two or more things or people, considered separately	Jane had a blister on **each** foot. **Each of** the children was given a present.
	NB: *Each* is followed by a singular noun but *each of* is followed by a plural noun/pronoun and a singular verb.	**Each child was** given a present.

DETERMINERS 12

Determiner	Meaning/Use	Examples
either/either of	one or the other of two things or people	*Can **either of** you help me with the housework?*
	used in negative sentences, to show that sth is true about both of two things or people	*I've lived in New York and Chicago but I didn't like **either** city very much.*
	NB: 1 We use *either of*, not *either* before pronouns (e.g. we say *either of them*, not *either them*). 2 *Either* is followed by a singular noun and verb.	*'Do you want the big bag or the small bag?'* *'**Either of them** will do.'* ***Either** bag is fine.*
every	each one of a group of things or people	***Every** student has to fill in a questionnaire.*
	used to emphasise that you are talking about the whole of sth	*I enjoyed **every** minute of the film.*
	used to indicate that sth happens at regular intervals of time or distance	*Richard visits his mother **every** week.* *You should change the oil **every** 5,000 miles.*
a few/a few of	a small number of sth (used with plural countable nouns, to mean 'not many but enough')	*Yes, we have **a few** copies of the book available.* *I've read **a few of** her books.*
few/few of	a small number of sth (used with plural countable nouns, to mean 'not many and possibly not enough')	*Unfortunately, we have **few** copies of the book available.* ***Few of** the customers complained.*
a little/a little of	a small amount of sth (used with uncountable nouns to mean 'not much but enough')	*We've got **a little** sugar left.* *The city is regaining **a little of** its former glory.*
little	a small amount (used with uncountable nouns to mean 'not much and possibly not enough')	*Unfortunately, by then we had **little** money left.*
a lot of/lots of	a large number or amount (used with plural countable and uncountable nouns)	*There were **a lot of/lots of** people at the party.*
many/many of	a large number of sth (used with plural countable nouns)	***Many** people find this kind of movie boring.* ***Many of** our staff are part-time.* *How **many** books did you buy?*
much/much of	a large amount of sth (used with uncountable nouns, often in negative sentences and questions)	*There isn't **much** time – let's go!* *How **much** money did you spend?*
most/most of	nearly all (used with plural countable and uncountable nouns)	***Most** universities offer a wide range of courses.* ***Most of** the people there were strangers.*
	NB: We use *most of*, not *most* before pronouns.	***Most of them** offer a wide range of courses.*
more	a larger number or amount (used with plural countable and uncountable nouns)	*We need **more** chairs.* *We need **more** money.*
	NB: 1 We use *more of*, not *more* before pronouns. 2 With *more*, we often imply a comparison (without stating it)	*I'd like **more of** you to attend our weekly meetings.* *We sell **more of** these maps.* (= more than other kinds of maps)

12 DETERMINERS

Determiner	Meaning/Use	Examples
neither/neither of	not one or the other of two people or things (used with positive verbs)	**Neither** parent cares what happens to the child.
	NB: 1 We use *neither of*, not *neither* before pronouns. 2 *Neither* is followed by a singular verb and noun.	Both players have been warned but **neither of them seems** to be taking it seriously.
none of	not any amount of sth or not one of a group of people or things (used with plural countable and uncountable nouns, and followed by a positive verb)	**None of** my friends phone me any more. *All of us didn't want to go to bed.* ✗ **None** of us **wanted** to go to bed. ✓
other	used to refer to all the people or things in a group apart from the one you have already mentioned/that is already known about	She works harder than all the **other** children in the class.
	NB: We can use *others* or *the others* on its own, without a noun	**The others** are waiting in the office. **Others** want this job if you turn it down.
several/several of	more than a few but not a lot (used with plural countable nouns)	Milk will keep for **several** days in the fridge.
	NB: We use *several of*, not *several* before pronouns	**Several of us** think it's a bad idea.
some/some of	used with uncountable or plural nouns in affirmative sentences, to refer to an amount or number of sth	There are **some people** waiting outside. There is **some cheese** in the fridge.
	used with singular countable nouns to refer to one of a number of things or people, when it does not matter which one	She married **some** farmer in South Africa.
	used in requests and offers	Could I have **some** bread? Would you like **some** orange juice?
	used to refer to a fairly large number or amount of sth (slightly more formal)	It will be **some** time before the bridge is finished.
	NB: We use *some of*, not *some* before pronouns.	**Some of us** decided to stay at home.

- *Others* means 'other people'. *The others* means 'those not mentioned already':
  *Some people like horror films but **others** hate them.*
  *Two climbers went to the top and **the others** waited in the tent.*
- We do not usually use two determiners together:
  Either other plan is hopeless. ✗
  Either plan is hopeless. ✓
  Both plans are hopeless. ✓
- We always use an article before singular countable nouns:
  *I didn't buy him **a present**.* ✓
  I didn't buy him present. ✗

*Some people like watching horror films but **others** hate them.*

*Two climbers went to the top and **the others** waited in the tent.*

210

DETERMINERS 12

PRACTICE

1 Choose the correct answer.

0 *Neither /* ⟨*Neither of*⟩ *you need worry –
I'm not going to ask you for a loan.*
1 *None / Each* of the children will be met at the station, so they will be safe.
2 The price is sixty pounds a week, then ten pounds for *each / some* extra day.
3 *Any / Every* item has been carefully checked and they are all fine.
4 *Each / Every* of the children had the same weight at birth.
5 I have asked them both and *neither / both* of them knows the answer.
6 I have *all / every* CD the group has ever made.
7 Freda had to stop and rest after *every / many* hundred metres or so.
8 Sadly, there were *few / a few* people at the concert.
9 I'd like to ask *few / a few* questions if you don't mind.
10 Fortunately, I had *little / a little* time to spare.
11 She had very *few / little* money left – just *a few / a little* coins.
12 I had never seen so *much / many* stars in the sky.
13 Like *most / most of* people, I love chocolate!
14 The court case cost them *few / several* million dollars.
15 My mother has inherited *some / another* land in Australia.
16 Would you like *some / any* tea?
17 Can you pass me *other / another* mug?
18 We only spent *many / a few* days in Rome.
19 I can get to Edinburgh by plane or train but *either / neither* way it is very expensive.
20 There's *a few / a little* cake left – it's on the kitchen table.

2 Look at the results of the survey. Then complete the article. Use a determiner in each gap.

Survey: Is there life on other planets?

Number of people interviewed: *400*
Age: *18+*

Question	Yes	No
1 Is there life on other planets?	350	50
2 Has the Earth been visited by other species?	25	325
3 Have you seen a UFO?	3	397
4 Do you believe those who claim they've seen a UFO?	15	385
5 Do you have evidence of the existence of UFOs?	0	400
6 Do you believe we will get evidence in the future?	12	388

Do you believe in UFOs?

In our survey, we asked 400 people whether they believed there was life on (0) *other* planets. The answer (1) .... people gave us was that there must be (2) .... planets in the universe with (3) .... kind of life on them. They thought it was unlikely that (4) .... of the planets in the universe were deserted except for ours. On the other hand, very (5) .... people thought we had actually been visited by any (6) .... species. Hardly (7) .... of the people we interviewed claimed they had seen a UFO and only a (8) .... believed stories told by (9) .... people of meetings with aliens. (10) .... of those who said they had first-hand experience could offer (11) .... proof and sadly, it seemed there was very (12) .... chance that anyone would come up with such proof in the future. (13) .... of the people in the survey were children or teenagers – they were (14) .... adults.

211

12c Countable and uncountable nouns

Countable and uncountable nouns

- Countable nouns refer to things we can count. A countable noun has singular and plural forms:
  apple → **apples**   child → **children**
- Uncountable nouns refer to things we cannot count. An uncountable noun has no plural form and we do not use it with *a/an*:
  We need new **furniture**.
  Poverty can lead to **unhappiness** and **despair**.
- Here are some common errors:
  ~~The money **are** insufficient.~~ ✗
  The money **is** insufficient ✓
  ~~They have **many works** to do.~~ ✗
  They have **a lot of work** to do. ✓
  ~~The news **are** very hopeful.~~ ✗
  The news **is** very hopeful. ✓
  ~~She gave me **a** good advice.~~ ✗
  She gave me **some** good advice. ✓
  ~~For long **travels**, we use the train.~~ ✗
  For long **journeys**, we use the train. ✓
- Below is a summary of some common uses of countable and uncountable nouns with determiners:

	Example (countable)	Example (uncountable)
article + noun	a book, the book, books, the books	cheese, the cheese
some + noun	some books	some cheese
any + noun	any book, any books	any cheese
enough + noun	enough books	enough cheese
many + noun	many books	(not possible)
few/a few + noun	(a) few books	(not possible)
less + noun	(not possible)	less cheese
little/a little + noun	(not possible)	(a) little cheese
much + noun	(not possible)	much cheese
this/that + noun	this/that book	this/that cheese
these/those + noun	these/those books	(not possible)

- We can also say:
  This is **a** fine **cheese**. (= a fine variety or type)
  These **cheeses** are produced only in Italy. (= these types of cheese)
- We can say *one fish, two fish, one deer, two deer*. We can also say *all the fishes in the sea*. (= the different types of fish)

Plural forms

Here are some nouns with regular and irregular plural forms:

Singular	Plural
Regular	
computer	computer**s**
journey	journey**s**
address	address**es**
city	cit**ies**
leaf	lea**ves**
Irregular	
aircraft	aircraft
child	children
cod	cod
deer	deer
foot	feet
fish	fish
fruit	fruit
man	men
mouse	mice
rendezvous	rendezvous
series	series
species	species
sheep	sheep
tooth	teeth
woman	women

Common mistakes with uncountable nouns

- Some uncountable nouns are often countable in other languages and may cause special difficulty. Here are some of the most common ones:
  She gave me **advice** but I didn't listen.
  Could you help me to carry all this **baggage**?
  The **countryside** here is beautiful.
  Accidents cause a lot of **damage** – be careful.
  I don't feel comfortable with electronic **equipment**.
  This **evidence** is not very reliable.
  I like your **furniture** – where did you get it?
  Your **hair** looks great – how do you get it to look like that?
  She is in very good **health**.
  The teacher gives a lot of **homework** and expects it in on time.
  Where do you get your **information** from – is it reliable enough?
  Do you have much **knowledge** of economic theory?
  I don't need this **money** – take it back.
  The **news** says the weather is going to get better.
  I've got **permission** to go.
  You've made **progress** – keep trying.
  I had a lot of **work** to do in town and I've only just finished it. (Compare: *I had lots of **jobs** and I've only just finished them.*)

- The words *means*, *series* and *species* look like plural nouns but they are countable and have singular forms:
  They found that the only **means** to cross the river was to swim.
  Which is your favourite **series** on TV?
  One **species** is destroyed in forest fires every day.

- **Spaghetti** looks like a plural noun but it is uncountable:
  The **spaghetti** is ready.

Common uncountable nouns

- Here is a list of uncountable nouns. Some of them are sometimes used as countable nouns, when we refer to a particular variety or example:

absence	equipment	love
advice	evil	luck
age	evidence	luggage
agriculture	existence	machinery
anger	experience	money
atmosphere	failure	music
baggage	faith	nature
beauty	fear	news
behaviour	flesh	nonsense
bread	food	paper
childhood	freedom	peace
comfort	fun	permission
concern	furniture	poverty
confidence	ground	pride
countryside	growth	progress
courage	hair	reality
damage	hate	research
death	happiness	rubbish
democracy	health	seaside
depression	help	spaghetti
design	homework	traffic
duty	ice	training
earth	information	transport
education	intelligence	travel
electricity	justice	weather
energy	knowledge	work
environment	life	worth

12 COUNTABLE AND UNCOUNTABLE NOUNS

- To count uncountable nouns, or to refer to a specific amount of something, we can use phrases like *a piece of*, *a bit of*, *a slice of*, etc. Here are some examples:

a bar of chocolate	a drop of water	a litre of water	a slice of cake
a bit of cheese	a glass of orange juice	a lump of sugar	a spoonful of salt
a blob of paint	a gram of sugar	a piece of furniture	a spot of blood
a bottle of cola	a handful of rice	a pile of rubbish	a touch of glamour
a can of lemonade	a jar of jam	a pool of blood	a tube of toothpaste
a carton of milk	a kilo of rice	a portion of chicken	
a cup of coffee	a loaf of bread	a sheet of paper	

- Some nouns can be both countable and uncountable. Here are examples:

Noun	Example (countable)	Example (uncountable)
chicken	He sat there and ate **a** whole **chicken**.	I'll have **some chicken** and chips, please.
coffee	I'd love **a coffee** now. (= a cup)	Is there **any coffee** left?
experience	Failing an exam was **a** new **experience** for me.	Have you had any previous **experience**?
fruit	A kumquat is **an** exotic **fruit**.	You should eat **fruit** every day.
hair	The cat has left white **hairs** all over the sofa.	Get your **hair** cut – it's getting too long.
juice	I'd like **an** orange **juice**, please. (= a glass)	There's **some** apple **juice** in the fridge.
noise	I heard **a noise** outside the window.	Stop making so **much noise**!

- Sometimes the countable and uncountable forms can have completely different meanings:

Noun	Example (countable)	Example (uncountable)
iron	Is the **iron** hot enough?	Spinach is full of **iron**.
paper	Dad's reading his **paper**. (= newspaper)	You'll need **some paper** to write on.
wood	There's a **wood** near our house.	His sculpture was made of **wood**.
work	the complete **works** of Shakespeare	I've got a bit of **work** to do.

PRACTICE

1 **Complete the crossword.**

Across

4 Smoking can seriously damage your ………!
5 Peaches have furry red and yellow skin and sweet yellow ……… .
8 I have to move all my ……… to my new house by the weekend.
9 I still stand by my claim that ……… make better drivers than men.
12 They swallowed their ……… and apologised.
13 With all the ……… in the world, I'm still not likely to pass this test!
14 The Giant Panda is an endangered ……… .

214

COUNTABLE AND UNCOUNTABLE NOUNS **12**

Down

1 By the time he got back, his .... had grown past his shoulders.
2 No wonder she looks so tired; she's got twelve .... to look after!
3 Have you heard from your parents? What's their latest .... ?
6 I find listening to .... very relaxing.
7 She didn't have much .... of American history, so she couldn't answer the questions.
10 It's a fascinating story about the eternal struggle between good and ....
11 I've got a great deal of .... left to do.

2 Choose the correct answer.

0 I need some *advice* / *advices* on buying a house – I've never bought one before.
1 This type of bear has been declared an endangered *specy* / *species*.
2 I saw some *deer* / *deers* grazing in the field and took a picture.
3 I heard *strange* / *a strange* noise next door.
4 *Equipment* / *Equipments* which is used by dentists should be kept clean.
5 Could you get me *a paper* / *some paper* from the newsagent's, please?
6 Students cannot leave class without *permission* / *permissions*.
7 I saw *an advertisement* / *some advertisement* for the car in a newspaper.
8 You'll find all the *tool* / *tools* you need in the garden shed.
9 *Hamlet* is one of Shakespeare's finest *work* / *works*.
10 There *isn't enough room* / *aren't enough rooms* for all those bags in my car.

3 Complete the sentences. Use the correct form of the words in the box.

| carton | cup | glass | gram |
| litre | piece (x2) | slice | tube |

0 I'll need a **carton** of milk for the cake.
1 I've already had three .... of coffee today.
2 You'll need three .... of paint for the garden fence.
3 Let me give you a .... of advice.
4 Could I have a .... of water, please?
5 Can you get me a .... of toothpaste from the supermarket?
6 Now pour the mixture into a large bowl and add 250 .... of sugar.
7 She wrote something on a .... of paper and gave it to Alex.
8 Would you like another .... of cake?

4 Read the text and choose the correct answer.

MEDITERRANEAN DIET

If you want (0) *a* / *some* good advice on what to eat in order to enjoy (1) *good health* / *a good health*, why not try a Mediterranean diet? Those who live in the Mediterranean have among the highest life expectancies in the world, so they are in a good position to give us (2) *information* / *informations* about a healthy diet. The Med diet dictates that you eat (3) *much* / *plenty of* vegetables and use (4) *olive oil* / *an olive oil* regularly in cooking and in salads. Other characteristics of this particular diet are dairy products (mainly (5) *cheese* / *a cheese* and yoghurt), some (6) *fish* / *fishes* and chicken (but not too (7) *much* / *many*), up to four eggs a week, only (8) *a few* / *a little* red meat and (9) *a few* / *a little* glasses of wine a week. But how typical is this diet of what people actually eat in these countries? Many begin the day with coffee, though in some countries a lot of orange (10) *juice is* / *juices are* also consumed in the morning. Some will have a (11) *pile* / *piece* of cheese and a (12) *slice* / *tube* of bread. Pies are popular breakfast snacks in Greece and they are usually made with (13) *cheese* / *cheeses*. However, in order to maintain (14) *healthy diet* / *a healthy diet*, it is advisable not to eat more than a couple of cheese pies a week.

215

Vocabulary

12d Uncountable nouns ending in -s, plural nouns, collective nouns

Uncountable nouns ending in -s

- Some nouns end in -s but are uncountable and take a singular verb:
  Physics is very difficult. **Maths is** a compulsory subject at school.
- Here are some more examples:

aerobics	classics	genetics	mathematics	mumps
athletics	economics	linguistics	measles	physics

  ~~Mathematics are~~ ~~my favourite subject.~~ ✗ **Mathematics is** my favourite subject. ✓
  ~~Measles are~~ ~~an infectious disease.~~ ✗ **Measles is** an infectious disease. ✓

- Some nouns can be both uncountable and plural but with a difference in meaning:
  Politics is a dirty business (= activities involved in gaining and using power in public life)
  His **politics are** fairly conservative. (= his political beliefs)

Plural nouns

- Some nouns are always plural and take a plural verb:
  All my **belongings are** in that bag. His **clothes were** old and dirty.
  I believe **congratulations are** in order!
- Here are some common plural nouns:

Noun	Example
belongings	He packed his few **belongings** in a suitcase and left.
clothes	All my **clothes** are in that wardrobe.
congratulations	**Congratulations** on your wedding.
contents	He emptied the **contents** of his pocket.
earnings	Average **earnings** for office workers are rising.
outskirts	The **outskirts** of the city are a very nice place to live.
premises	The police escorted him off the **premises**.
remains	They've just discovered the **remains** of an ancient castle.
surroundings	Working in pleasant **surroundings** is important.

- Some nouns for things with two parts (often clothes, tools or equipment) also end in -s and are always plural. They include:

binoculars	goods	overalls	scales	sunglasses	trunks
braces	handcuffs	pants	scissors	spectacles	underpants
dungarees	headquarters	pliers	shorts	tights	
glasses	jeans	pyjamas	stairs	trousers	

  His **glasses are** new. The **scissors are** in the drawer.
  The **shorts** she was wearing **were** too big. My **trousers are** dirty.

- To count these nouns, we use *a pair of*:
  a pair of scissors *a pair of* glasses
  a pair of jeans *a pair of* tights
- When we use *a pair of* with these nouns, the verb that follows is singular:
  This pair of jeans is new.
  These jeans are new.
- Some nouns can have a different meaning when they are in the plural. Compare:
  *I would like to speak to someone in **authority**.* (uncountable noun)
  *The British **authorities** are investigating the issue.* (plural noun)
- Here are some more examples:

Singular/Plural	Plural
The house was in a terrible **condition**.	The **conditions** in the prison were terrible.
He's a member of the Environmental Research **Foundation**.	The **foundations** of the building were laid ten years ago.
Time is our most valuable **resource**.	We do not have the **resources** to deal with the problem.
She faints at the **sight** of blood.	Let's go and see the **sights**.
'URL' is the technical **term** for what is often called a 'web address'.	Have you read the **terms** of the agreement?
Air **travel** is becoming cheaper.	His **travels** provided good material for a book.

Collective nouns

- Collective nouns refer to a group of people or things (e.g. *army, committee, team*). We can think of them as either a single unit or as members of a group. They can be followed by a singular verb or a plural verb:
  *The **team is** the best in the country.* (= the group as a whole)
  *The **team are** confident of victory.* (= each member of the group)
  *The **Council is** building a new road.* (= the group as a whole)
  *The **Council are** voting on the issue.* (= each member of the group)
- Here is a list of common collective nouns:

army	crew	group	staff
audience	data	jury	team
the BBC	the European Union	media	the United Nations
community	family	herd	
class	gang	press	
committee	government	public	

- These nouns take only a plural verb:
  Cattle are kept for their meat.
  *The **police have** been called in.*

217

12 UNCOUNTABLE NOUNS ENDING IN -S, PLURAL NOUNS, COLLECTIVE NOUNS

Practice

1 **Choose the correct answer.**

0 You're very lucky; travelling around the world, staying in nice hotels, with all *expense /* (*expenses*) paid!
1 The mass *media / medias* have enormous power nowadays.
2 In the summer, you can't go round wearing *a trouser / trousers* all the time. You'll need a nice *short / pair of shorts*.
3 Can you pass me *this / those* scissors, please?
4 The *jury / juries* have weighed all the evidence and have found the accused guilty.
5 The *audience / audiences* have requested that no *refreshment is / refreshments are* brought into the auditorium.
6 They stole my few *belonging / belongings*.
7 When she returned, she wrote a book about her *travel / travels* in South Africa.
8 We're running out of food and water – we'll have to ask for more *supply / supplies*.
9 They laid the *foundation / foundations* of the building months ago but they haven't started building yet.
10 *Have / Has* maths always been your favourite subject?

2 **Complete the sentences. Use the correct form of a verb or a pronoun in each gap.**

0 Physics ...*is*... an interesting subject but I've never been very good at ...*it*....
1 Athletics .... less popular before the Olympics made .... fashionable.
2 Politics .... by no means the only area where women are doing better.
3 Classics .... what I wanted to study but my parents persuaded me that economics .... more useful.
4 If you need more information, remember: our staff .... always here to help.
5 The goods .... being packed now; .... will be delivered first thing tomorrow morning.
6 I can't find my pyjamas anywhere! I left .... on my bed this morning!
7 The police .... co-operating with the authorities in other countries in order to gather more evidence.
8 The government .... planning new taxes.
9 The company's headquarters .... in London, I think.
10 I've always thought that aerobics .... really boring.
11 .... mumps an infectious disease?
12 The pliers .... over there – on the kitchen table.

12e Suffixes (5)

Remember that we normally use suffixes to change a word to a different part of speech.

See also: 1e, 3e, 4e, 10e, 13e

-ion

- We add *-ion*, *-tion*, etc. to a verb to form a noun:
  invent + -ion → invention   decorate + -ion → decoration
- Here are some nouns with the suffix *-ion*. Note the changes in spelling:

Verb ending	Suffix	Examples
-ss	+ -ion	confess → confession, depress → depression, impress → impression
-se	+ -ion	confuse → confusion, immerse → immersion, revise → revision
-nt	+ -ion	invent → invention
-ate	+ -ion	decorate → decoration, educate → education, excavate → excavation
-de	+ -sion	collide → collision, conclude → conclusion, decide → decision, explode → explosion, exclude → exclusion
-it	+ -sion	admit → admission, omit → omission, permit → permission (but: limit → limitation, visit → visitation)
-ere	+ -sion	adhere → adhesion, cohere → cohesion
-ert	+ -sion	divert → diversion, invert → inversion
-nd	+ -sion	expand → expansion, extend → extension
-ce	+ -tion	deduce → deduction, produce → production, reduce → reduction
-se, -ite, -ote	+ -ation	accuse → accusation, invite → invitation, quote → quotation
-ge, -ve, -ire	+ -ation	allege → allegation, starve → starvation, admire → admiration
-t	+ -ation	adapt → adaptation
-er	+ -ation	alter → alteration
-rm	+ -ation	form → formation
-py	+ -ation	occupy → occupation
-ue	+ -ation	value → valuation
-ify	+ -ication	classify → classification, identify → identification, qualify → qualification
-ish	+ -ition	abolish → abolition, demolish → demolition
-ose	+ -ition	impose → imposition, oppose → opposition
-eat	+ -ition	repeat → repetition
-dd, -nd	+ -ition	add → addition, rend → rendition

12 SUFFIXES (5)

- Some nouns ending in *-ion* do not have a first part that can exist on its own:
  incursion   jubilation   nutrition   tradition
- Some nouns ending in *-ion* are formed from adjectives:
  precise → precision   profuse → profusion

-ity

- We add *-ity* to an adjective to form a noun:
  active + -ity → activity   invisible + -ity → invisibility
- Here are some nouns with the suffix *-ity*. Note the changes in spelling:

Adjective ending	Suffix	Examples
-e	+ -ity	active → activity, mobile → mobility, secure → security, severe → severity
-ive	+ -ity	creative → creativity, productive → productivity, sensitive → sensitivity (but: authoritative → authority)
-id	+ -ity	humid → humidity, stupid → stupidity, valid → validity
-nal	+ -ity	eternal → eternity, national → nationality
-al, -an, -ar	+ -ity	equal → equality, human → humanity, similar → similarity
-ary	+ -ity	necessary → necessity
-ic	+ -ity	public → publicity
-or	+ -ity	major → majority, minor → minority
-ous	+ -osity	curious → curiosity, generous → generosity (but: hilarious → hilarity, prosperous → prosperity)
-ble	+ -bility	acceptable → acceptability, credible → credibility, flexible → flexibility, invisible → invisibility, possible → possibility, reliable → reliability, sensible → sensibility (but: hospitable → hospitality)

- Some nouns ending in *-ity* do not have a first part that can exist on its own:
  affinity   calamity   heredity   vicinity
- Compare *sensitivity* and *sensibility*: we use *sensitivity* to refer to the ability to understand other people's feelings and problems. We use *sensibility* to refer to the ability to understand feelings, especially those expressed in literature or art:
  *To teach young children, you need lots of **sensitivity** and imagination.*
  *An art critic is a person of **sensibility** and perception.*

*To teach, you need **sensitivity** and **imagination**.*

SUFFIXES (5) 12

Other suffixes

Here are some more adjective and noun suffixes:

Noun suffix	Examples
-ure	close → closure, pleasant → pleasure, press → pressure
-ence	consequent → consequence, correspond → correspondence, exist → existence, patient → patience, refer → reference
-ance	appear → appearance, guide → guidance, insure → insurance, perform → performance, reluctant → reluctance
-y	brave → bravery, cruel → cruelty, discover → discovery, honest → honesty, jealous → jealousy, loyal → loyalty, miserable → misery, sympathetic → sympathy
-cy	fluent → fluency, frequent → frequency, efficient → efficiency, private → privacy, tend → tendency

Adjective suffix	Examples
-cal	geography → geographical, history → historical, music → musical, philosophy → philosophical, psychology → psychological

PRACTICE

1 **Complete the table.**

Noun	Verb	Noun	Verb
discussion	*discuss*	expansion	....
decision	....	opposition	....
abolition	....	graduation	....
addition	....	identification	....
accusation	....	decoration	....
inversion	....	occupation	....
demolition	....	collision	....
repetition	....	permission	....
complication	....	qualification	....
confession	....	starvation	....
adhesion	....	admiration	....
conclusion	....	classification	....
extension	....	explosion	....

12 SUFFIXES (5)

2 Complete the sentences. Use words formed from the words in CAPITALS at the end of the lines.

0	The poor dog had died of *starvation*.	STARVE
1	Her .... is what I admire most about her.	LOYAL
2	There is a .... of a new earthquake in the region.	POSSIBLE
3	She went through a long period of .... when she lost her job.	DEPRESS
4	The .... of the bomb was heard several kilometres away.	EXPLODE
5	What made you choose law as a ....?	PROFESS
6	My first .... of her was favourable.	IMPRESS
7	Scientists have made important .... in this field.	DISCOVER
8	That must have been a tough .... to make.	DECIDE
9	The .... of people in this city live in flats.	MAJOR
10	The insurance plan can offer your family financial	SECURE
11	We have great .... for him as an artist.	ADMIRE
12	Her car was in .... with a truck.	COLLIDE

3 Complete the second sentence so that it has a similar meaning to the first sentence, using the word given. Use between two and five words. Do not change the word given.

0 Good teaching makes children more curious.
ENCOURAGES
Good teaching *encourages curiosity* in children.

1 I am very pleased to introduce our next speaker.
GREAT
It gives me .... to introduce our next speaker.

2 They corresponded for twenty years.
LASTED
Their .... twenty years.

3 Do we have any proof that life exists on other planets?
PROVE
Can we .... of life on other planets?

4 She didn't refer to the matter in the meeting.
NO
She made .... to the matter in the meeting.

5 The Curies are famous for discovering radium.
THEIR
The Curies are famous .... of radium.

6 The twins are not at all similar.
ANY
There isn't .... between the twins.

7 I am fully responsible for the accident.
FULL
I accept .... for the accident.

8 Earthquakes have become more frequent recently.
INCREASED
The .... recently.

9 I'm not sure whether the new system is efficient.
OF
I'm not sure about .... the new system.

10 They were still discussing the project when I asked him.
UNDER
The project was still .... when I asked him.

222

SUFFIXES (5) 12

4 Complete the article. Use words formed from the words in CAPITALS at the end of the lines.

How to learn vocabulary

Students are under enormous (0) **pressure** to learn huge amounts of vocabulary but they are rarely given (1) .... as to how to go about it. They have a (2) .... to try and learn long lists by heart but this is hardly the most (3) .... approach to the problem. The golden rule is to do lots of (4) .... at regular intervals. Secondly, students should concentrate on words with the highest (5) ...., particularly everyday words which also improve the students' (6) .... They should also take every (7) .... to use the words in communication – there is considerable (8) .... evidence that learners who like using the foreign language improve their oral (9) .... and their overall (10) .... of the language much more rapidly than students who are (11) .... to practise the language in real-life situations.

PRESS
GUIDE
TEND
EFFICIENCY
REVISE
FREQUENT
FLUENT
OPPORTUNE
PSYCHOLOGY
PERFORM
ACQUIRE
RELUCTANCE

Exam practice 6

Part 1

For questions **1–12**, read the text below and decide which answer (**A**, **B**, **C** or **D**) best fits each gap. There is an example at the beginning (**0**).

COMFORT FOOD

(0).......... 'comfort food' refers to food which we eat in order to feel a little (1).......... when we are feeling down – we (2).......... eat comfort food at moments of psychological stress. In some cases, comfort food has to do with feelings of nostalgia – (3).......... of us has different memories of what our mother or grandmother used to make when we were young. Comfort food can be (4).......... comforting and healthy as long as it makes us feel better afterwards. So, although comfort foods are not necessarily always good for our health (5).........., they may be of some benefit if they help to cheer us up.

(6).......... individual has their own idea of what comfort food is. In one piece of research, it was shown that a (7).......... of males in the USA preferred things like steak, casseroles and soup while the majority of women preferred chocolate and ice cream. And it is well known that teenagers choose (8).......... when they want to relax.

Comfort food, then, must take (9).......... the responsibility for the obesity in modern society. People do not eat (10).......... fresh fruit; experts say we should eat a (11).......... fruit every day – an apple, an orange – whatever. And last but not least, most people usually eat too fast – they are always in a hurry to get the meal over as quickly (12).......... they can. Instead of fast food, we should be thinking more of 'slow food'.

0	A	Term	B	A term	C	The term (circled)	D	Each term
1	A	good	B	well	C	better	D	more well
2	A	quickly	B	usually	C	already	D	rarely
3	A	every	B	another	C	each	D	all
4	A	both	B	either	C	and	D	enough
5	A	direct	B	as direct	C	directly	D	most directly
6	A	All	B	Several	C	Every	D	Other
7	A	many	B	much	C	deal	D	lot
8	A	fast food	B	a fast food	C	the fast food	D	the fast foods
9	A	most	B	every	C	some	D	some of
10	A	plenty	B	enough	C	most	D	a lot
11	A	few	B	piece	C	little	D	more
12	A	than	B	like	C	that	D	as

SCORE / 12

224

Part 2

For questions **13–24**, read the text below and think of the word which best fits each gap. Use only **one** word in each gap. There is an example at the beginning (**0**).

OUT OF WORK

She was having (0) ......**a**...... slow, leisurely breakfast. There was no rush. She didn't have anything to do that day – she was 'free'. She was going to stay in and go through all the papers, looking (13) .... work. If that didn't come up with anything, she would try (14) .... Internet.

She finished her coffee and poured herself (15) .... cup – it was her third that morning. She buttered another (16) .... of toast. The show she had been in had finished a couple of weeks before. It had been a great success. It had been seen by a (17) .... of people and the reviews had also been positive. Most importantly, she had made (18) .... money from it to keep her going for a month or so. But now the money (19) .... running out. It had been said that money was the root of all evil but she thought that not having enough of it was not doing her (20) .... good, either. She had to find a way to make more money. She was hoping to find (21) .... job in the theatre but there were very (22) .... jobs on offer. These were hard times and the competition was fierce. She had found ads for two jobs which she could do but (23) .... of them were in Liverpool and she didn't fancy that because most (24) .... her friends lived in London or nearby. She put the paper down and turned on her laptop.

SCORE / 12

Part 3

For questions **25–34**, read the text below. Use the word given in capitals at the end of some of the lines to form a word that fits in the gap **in the same line**. There is an example at the beginning (**0**).

There was a time when all you needed to get a job were the right **(0)** *qualifications*. But nowadays, apart from looking carefully at your **(25)**.......... form and CV, employers are more and more interested in finding out whether you have the right personal qualities. So it is also important to have good **(26)**.......... from any previous employers or teachers. It is also vital that you make the right **(27)**.......... at the interview. More and more employers are looking for what is often called 'emotional **(28)**..........'. This means you are someone who is good at listening and putting yourself in someone else's position; It means you are able to find **(29)**.......... to problems and to work well with other people in a spirit of **(30)**.......... and understanding of other people's feelings. It also includes the **(31)**.......... to understand other people's motives and to make the most of them. All in all, you not only need to be **(32)**.......... in the job but also to be aware of other people's feelings and needs. Your success in whatever **(33)**.......... you choose will depend on your practical skills as well as your **(34)**.......... as a person.

QUALIFY
APPLY

REFER
IMPRESS

INTELLIGENT

SOLVE
CO-OPERATE
ABLE

EFFICIENCY

OCCUPY
SENSITIVE

SCORE ___ / 10

Part 4

For questions **35–42**, complete the second sentence so that it has a similar meaning to the first sentence, using the word given. **Do not change the word given.** You must use between **two** and **five** words, including the word given. Here is an example (0).

Example:

0 He is the most dangerous driver I know.
   DRIVES
   Nobody I know .... *drives as dangerously* .... as he does.

35 They didn't waste any time leaving the building.
   QUICKLY
   They left the building .... they could.

36 They played quite badly in the final match.
   VERY
   They didn't .... in the final match.

37 I can't wait for the summer holidays.
   FORWARD
   I'm really .... the summer holidays.

38 I don't go to the doctor as I often as I used to.
   LESS
   I go to the doctor .... I used to.

39 They are still investigating the disappearance of his daughter.
   LOOKING
   They are still .... the disappearance of his daughter.

40 Don't worry, I'll look after the kids while you're out.
   EYE
   Don't worry, I'll .... the kids while you're out.

41 Tina lives in Brighton and so does Amanda.
   BOTH
   Tina .... in Brighton.

42 I am very pleased to announce the winners of our competition.
   GREAT
   It gives .... to announce the winners of our competition.

SCORE / 16

TOTAL SCORE / 50

13

AGENDA

Grammar
- 13a Relative clauses
- 13b Participles
- 13c Linking words and phrases: contrast

Vocabulary
- 13d Phrasal verbs with *get*
- 13e Suffixes (6)

Entry test

1 Choose the correct answer.

1 The woman *who lives / who she lives* next door is a university professor.
2 This is the town *when / where* I grew up.
3 That's the man *that his / whose* house was burnt down.
4 The company *which / where* he works has gone bankrupt.
5 Jill, who works as a nurse, *has / she has* just written her first book.

Now look at 13a on pages 230–233.

SCORE ___ / 5

2 Choose the correct answer, A, B, C or D.

6 I saw a woman .... in the corner on her own, so I went over to see if she was OK.
   A stand   B to stand   C standing   D who she was standing

7 She was lying in the middle of the road, ... for help.
   A cry   B crying   C as crying   D be crying

8 He just sits around all day, ... nothing.
   A does   B to do   C be doing   D doing

9 .... that I wouldn't pass the exam, I didn't take it.
   A Knew   B Have known   C To know   D Knowing

10 .... our meal, we had a cup of coffee.
   A Finished   B Have finished   C Having finished   D We have finished

Now look at 13b on pages 234–235.

SCORE ___ / 5

ENTRY TEST 13

3 Choose the correct answer, A, B, C or D.

11 .... the house is old, it's still in very good condition.
   A Although   B Even   C Despite   D No matter

12 She liked her job in spite of .... salary wasn't very good.
   A her   B in fact her   C the fact her   D the fact that her

13 Despite ...., she wouldn't take her coat off.
   A it was hot   B that it was hot   C the heat   D of the heat

14 I was hoping to deal with this matter quickly. ...., it is more difficult than I thought.
   A No matter   B Despite   C Although   D However

15 I'm going to get this qualification, ... long it takes.
   A no matter   B however   C nevertheless   D while

Now look at **13c** on pages 236–237.   SCORE ____ / 5

4 Choose the correct answer, A, B, C or D.

16 If we're going to share the same office, we'd better learn to get ....
   A by   B around   C along   D off

17 Did you get your money .... when the concert was cancelled?
   A over   B back   C away   D out

18 I have a meeting till eleven but I should be able to get .... before then.
   A away   B in   C off   D up

19 I got .... the Arts Faculty at the University of London to study history.
   A through   B off   C into   D from

20 She still hasn't got .... the shock, it seems.
   A through   B off   C back   D over

Now look at **13d** on pages 238–239.   SCORE ____ / 5

5 Complete the sentences. Use words formed from the words in CAPITALS at the end of the lines.

21 When did you decide to become a .... footballer?   PROFESSION
22 The audience cheered and clapped in ....   APPROVE
23 I have little faith in the .... justice system.   CRIME
24 All his colleagues were .... of his success.   ENVY
25 The two men .... to kill her unless she did as they asked.   THREAT

Now look at **13e** on pages 240–243.   SCORE ____ / 5

TOTAL SCORE ____ / 25

229

Grammar

13a Relative clauses

Relative clauses give more information about the person, thing, place, etc. that we are talking about. They are introduced by a relative pronoun or adverb (*who*, *which*, *whose*, *where*, etc.). There are two types of relative clause: defining relative clauses and non-defining relative clauses.

Defining relative clauses

- Defining relative clauses identify which person, thing, place, etc. we mean exactly. They are also called identifying relative clauses. We cannot leave the relative clause out of the sentence because without it, the sentence would sound incomplete.
  *This is the car **that I saw here yesterday**.*
- The table below shows how relative pronouns are used in defining relative clauses:

	Subject	**Object**	**Possession**
People	who/that	who/whom/that	whose
	She's the woman **who/that lives next door**.	She's the woman (**who/whom/that**) I saw on TV last night.	She's the woman **whose car was stolen last night**.
Things/Animals	which/that	which/that	whose
	I don't want a car **which/that breaks down all the time**.	This is the house (**which/that**) we bought.	That's the shop **whose windows were smashed**.
	That's the kind of dog **which/that makes a good pet**.	It's the kind of dog (**which/that**) I'd like to have.	That's the dog **whose owner was arrested**.

- We do not use commas in defining relative clauses.
- We can leave out the relative pronoun if it is the object of the clause:
  *It's the kind of job (**which/that**) I'd like to have.*
- When the verb has a preposition, we usually put the preposition at the end of the relative clause:
  *Miss Berry was the person (who/that) I sent the letter **to**.*
  *Is this the book (which/that) you were looking **for**?*
- In formal English, we can put the preposition before the relative pronouns *whom* or *which* (but not before *who* or *that*):
  *Miss Berry was the person **to whom** I sent the letter.* (formal) ✓
  *Is this the book **for which** you were looking?* (formal and uncommon) ✓
  ~~*Miss Berry was the person **to who** I sent the letter.*~~ ✗
  ~~*Is this the book **for that** you were looking?*~~ ✗
- *Whom* is rather formal. We usually use *who* instead, except when we say *to/for/with/*etc. *whom*:
  *Is she the person **to whom** you gave the letter?*
  ~~*He's the person **whom** I saw with her.*~~ ✗
  *He's the person **who** I saw with her.* ✓

230

Non-defining relative clauses

- Non-defining relative clauses give additional information about the person, thing, place, etc. we are talking about. They are also called non-identifying relative clauses. A sentence would still make sense if we left out the non-defining relative clause.
  *The summer here, **which I don't like**, lasts for months.*
  The summer here lasts for months.
- The table below shows how relative pronouns are used in non-defining relative clauses:

	Subject	Object	Possession
People	who	who/whom	whose
	*His wife, **who is French**, speaks three languages.*	*His wife, **who/whom I met in Paris**, is French.*	*His wife, **whose car was stolen**, called the police.*
Things/Animals	which	which	whose
	*The book, **which was published in 2011**, is brilliant.*	*The book, **which I read last week**, is brilliant.*	*The book, **whose title I can't remember**, has already sold thousands of copies.*
	*The dog, **which looked very friendly**, was huge.*	*The dog, **which I hadn't seen until then**, was huge.*	*The dog, **whose name was Spot**, was huge.*

- We cannot use the relative pronoun *that* in non-defining relative clauses.
- We cannot leave out the relative pronoun in non-defining relative clauses.
- We use commas to separate the non-defining relative clause from the main clause. Note the possible difference in meaning between defining (without commas) and non-defining relative clauses (with commas):
  *The young man **who lives next door** has a dog.* (= The relative clause *(who lives next door)* explains who I'm talking about. Without it, the listener won't know who I'm referring to.)
  *The young man, **who lives next door**, has a dog.* (= The listener knows who 'the young man' is. The relative clause *(who lives next door)* is extra information.)

Relative adverbs

- We use the relative adverbs *when*, *where* and *why* in relative clauses, to refer to time, place and reason. We can use *when* and *where* in both defining and non-defining relative clauses. *Why* is only used in defining relative clauses.

Adverb	Defining	Non-defining
when	*That was the year **when I graduated**.*	*I met Fred in 2010, **when I moved to York**.*
where	*That's the spot **where the statue will be built**.*	*Lyon, **where my dad grew up**, is a big city.*
why	*Did he tell you the reason **why you were fired**?*	–

- In defining relative clauses, we can use *that* instead of *when* and *why* (but not *where*):
  *That was the year **when/that** my parents got married.*
  *That's the reason **why/that** I didn't want her to know!*
- In defining relative clauses, we can use a preposition and *which* instead of a relative adverb:
  *That's the factory **where** they make chemicals.*
  *That's the factory **in which** they make chemicals.*
  *That's the factory **(which)** they make chemicals **in**.*

13 RELATIVE CLAUSES

Coordinating relative clauses

- In coordinating relative clauses, *which* refers to the whole main clause.
  *She lied to him, **which made him furious**.* (= *which* refers to *She had lied to him*.)
- Coordinating relative clauses always come after the main clause, and are separated from it with a comma.
  *I decided to join them, **which was a bad idea**.*

whatever, whichever, etc.

We use *whatever whichever*, *whoever*, *wherever* and *whenever* to talk about a person, thing, place, etc., when it does not matter who, what, which, etc. *Whichever* usually comes before a noun; *whatever*, *whoever*, *wherever* and *whenever* usually come before a clause:

Things/Actions	whichever	Buy **whichever** book you want. (= any book you want)
	whatever	**Whatever** she can do to help, she will. (= anything she can do)
People	whoever	Invite **whoever** you like. (= anyone)
Places	wherever	I'll go **wherever** I like. (= to any place)
Time	whenever	Come **whenever** you like. (= any time)

PRACTICE

1 Join the sentences. Use non-defining relative clauses. Use the second sentence in the relative clause.

0 Mrs Cooper is always very patient. She teaches French.
   Mrs. Cooper, who teaches French, is always very patient.

1 The new director is very popular. He gets on well with everyone.
   ....

2 London was amazing. We spent our holidays there.
   ....

3 The film was called *Finding Grace*. I enjoyed it very much.
   ....

4 Our cat is called William. We've had him for five years.
   ....

5 2008 was the happiest year of my life. I met my wife then.
   ....

6 The castle was built in the sixteenth century. It's the oldest building in our town.
   ....

7 Tim speaks Spanish. His wife is from Peru.
   ....

8 My sister is a vet. She lives in Canada.
   ....

232

RELATIVE CLAUSES 13

2 Rewrite the sentences. Put the preposition at the end. Omit the relative pronoun if it is not necessary.

0 Computer programming is something about which I know little.
   Computer programming is something I know little about.

1 It was a mistake for which they have already apologised.
   ....

2 Maths is a subject in which she has little interest.
   ....

3 It was Mr Edwards to whom they sold the house.
   ....

4 It was the Queen to whom the Prime Minister sent the letter.
   ....

5 It was the bank from which he had borrowed money.
   ....

6 That was the year in which I was born.
   ....

7 March 25th is the day on which the country celebrates its independence.
   ....

8 That's the hospital in which the twins were born.
   ....

9 That's the island on which we spent our honeymoon.
   ....

10 These are the reasons for which I chose to marry him.
   ....

3 Rewrite sentences 7–10 from Exercise 2 using *when*, *where* or *why*.

6 *That was the year when I was born.*
7 ....
8 ....
9 ....
10 ....

4 Complete the text. Use relative pronouns or adverbs.

Van Gogh:
the sadness will last forever

Van Gogh was a Dutch painter (0) *whose* work has had a huge influence on 20th century art but (1) .... was not appreciated during his lifetime. His paintings, (2) .... are known for their vivid colours, have a very distinctive style. (3) .... beholds one of them can't help but be moved. And today, his works are priceless – (4) .... they come up for auction, they sell for millions of pounds. (5) .... he painted – self portraits, landscapes, portraits or sunflowers – is worth a lot of money today.

In his early adulthood, Van Gogh travelled between The Hague and Paris, after (6) .... he taught in England. In 1885, (7) .... he was thirty-two, he painted his first major work, *The Potato Eaters*, (8) .... was quite a dark work. In his next works, he began to use the vivid colours for (9) .... he became famous.

In 1886, he moved to Paris, (10) .... he discovered the French Impressionists. The reason (11) .... they were called this was after a painting by Claude Monet (12) .... was called *Impression – Sunrise*. Van Gogh's brother, Theo, (13) .... was a great influence on Van Gogh, had a large collection of Impressionist paintings.

On 27 July 1890, aged thirty-seven, Van Gogh shot himself; he died two days later. His brother Theo, (14) .... was at his side at the end, said his brother's last words were: *the sadness will last forever*.

> *People **who live in glass houses** shouldn't throw stones.*

233

13b Participles

Present participles

We use present participles (the *-ing* form of a verb):

- to replace a relative clause:
  Anyone **who arrives late** will not be admitted.
  → Anyone **arriving late** will not be admitted.

- to replace *and* + a coordinate clause. The two actions in the sentence may happen at the same time or at different times. Compare:
  She stood there **and waited** for him to turn up.
  → She stood there, **waiting** for him to turn up.
  (= actions happening at the same time)
  Laughing and shouting, the children ran out of the room. (= actions happening at the same time)
  He **turned off the light and** went to bed.
  → **Turning off the light**, he went to bed.
  (= actions happening one after the other)
  Closing the door behind her, she got into the car and drove off. (= actions happening one after the other)

- to replace a clause beginning with a linker of reason:
  She didn't go to the party **because she knew** John wouldn't be there.
  → **Knowing** that John wouldn't be there, she didn't go to the party.

- to replace a clause beginning with a linker of result:
  He **was exhausted, so** he went straight to bed.
  → **Being** exhausted, he went straight to bed.

- to replace a time clause beginning with *when, after, before, as soon as, while*, etc.:
  When he realised he had left the lights on, he asked the taxi driver to turn back.
  → **Realising** he had left the lights on, he asked the taxi driver to turn back.

- as adjectives:
  a **burning** house (= a house that is on fire)
  falling leaves (= leaves that fall)

Past participles

We use past participles to replace passive verb forms. We use them:

- to replace a passive relative clause:
  She lives in a house **that was built** in the nineteenth century.
  → She lives in a house **built** in the nineteenth century.

- to replace a clause beginning with linkers of reason, result or contrast:
  The cinema **is located** in the city centre, **so** it's very popular.
  → **Located** in the city centre, the cinema is very popular.
  Although it was released twenty years ago, the song is still very popular.
  → **Although released** twenty years ago, the song is still very popular.

- to replace clauses of condition:
  If I were given the opportunity, I would move back to Canada.
  → **Given** the opportunity, I would move back to Canada.

- We can also use past participles as adjectives:
  a **broken** vase   a **haunted** house

Perfect participles

We use perfect participles (*having* + past participle):

- to replace *and* + coordinate clause, when we want to emphasise that one action happened before another:
  I **had finished** my work and was getting ready for bed.
  Having finished my work, I was getting ready for bed.

- to replace a linker of reason/result + present perfect/past perfect:
  He's broken his leg, **so** he can't play tomorrow.
  Having broken his leg, he can't play tomorrow.
  I was furious **because I had found out** he'd lied to me.
  Having found out he'd lied to me, I was furious.

PARTICIPLES 13

PRACTICE

1 Rewrite the sentences. Use participle clauses.

0 She was doing the high jump and she twisted her ankle.
She twisted her ankle doing the high jump.

1 Bill was listening to the lecture and he fell asleep.
....

2 I wanted to finish my work, so I decided to stay in.
....

3 He was well-qualified for the job, so he got it.
....

4 When I realised how rude I'd been, I apologised.
....

5 He left early because he wanted to catch the first bus.
....

2 Join the sentences. Begin each sentence with a perfect participle.

0 Anne handed in her script. She had answered all the questions.
Having answered all the questions, Anne handed in her script.

1 He sent her an email. He had tried phoning her several times.
....

2 I had received an invitation. I felt I had to go to the party.
....

3 He couldn't get in. He had lost his key.
....

4 She had picked up her luggage. She went to look for a taxi.
....

> *Happiness is **being** busy with the unimportant.*

3 Complete the story. Use the present or past participle forms of the verbs in brackets.

Eve

She sat at the window (0) *watching* (watch) the evening getting darker. She gazed at the snow (1) .... (fall) gently on the rooftops. She felt tired. The street was quiet. Few people were around, for it was bitterly cold. (2) .... (exhaust) after a long day's work in the store, she was happy to sit there, (3) .... (think) of the past. In the distance, she could hear children (4) .... (shout) and (5) .... (laugh) as they chased each other. At the end of the road, there was an empty patch of ground (6) .... (cover) with weeds. They used to play hide and seek there. A strange, bad-tempered man who lived nearby disapproved. He would turn up suddenly, (7) .... (follow) by a dog and (8) .... (hold) a long stick. (9) .... (terrify), they would run away when they saw him (10) .... (come). He would chase them off the field, (11) .... (shout) words she didn't understand. Now she could hear the children (12) .... (play) the same games. Memories.

The houses were old; theirs was a terraced house (13) .... (build) a long time ago. The house next door was even older and some people said it was (14) .... (haunt). (15) .... (pass by) at night, she would sometimes hear noises. She shivered. She heard footsteps (16) .... (walk) along the concrete pavement and (17) .... (crunch) on the path leading to the (18) .... (desert) house. (19) .... (puzzle) and somewhat (20) .... (scare), she drew the curtains to get a better look. Who could it be?

13c Linking words and phrases: contrast

- To link two clauses that express contrasting ideas, we often use *but*:
  *Jack works very hard **but** he doesn't have a lot of money.*
- We can express contrast using other conjunctions such as:
  Although/Though/Even though *Jack works very hard, he doesn't have a lot of money.*
  In spite of/Despite *working very hard, Jack doesn't have a lot of money.*
  *Jack works very hard, **yet** he doesn't have a lot of money.*
  *Jack works very hard. **Nevertheless**, he doesn't have a lot of money.*
  *Jack works very hard. **However**, he doesn't have a lot of money.*
  Whereas *Jack works very hard, he doesn't have a lot of money.*
  While *Jack works very hard, he doesn't have a lot of money.*
  On the one hand, *Jack works very hard. **On the other** (**hand**), he doesn't have a lot of money.*
- Note the structures that some of these linking words and phrases are followed by:

Word/Phrase	Followed by	Example
although/though/even though	+ clause + comma	***Even though*** *she was invited, she didn't go.*
in spite of/despite	+ noun + comma	***In spite of her success,*** *she's very modest.*
	+ -ing + comma	***In spite of being*** *successful, she's very modest.*
	+ the fact that + clause + comma	***In spite of the fact that*** *she's successful, she's very modest.*
Nevertheless/However	+ comma + clause	*I was offended. **However/Nevertheless**, I didn't say anything.*
Whereas/While	+ clause + comma	***Whereas/While*** *Kevin was for the idea, the others weren't.*

- We can reverse the order of the two clauses. Note the change in punctuation: when the contrast clause comes first, we use a comma. When it comes second, we don't use a comma.
  In spite of the cold, *we went to the beach.*
  *We went to the beach **in spite of the cold**.*
  Although it was cold, *we went to the beach.*
  *We went to the beach **although it was cold**.*
- *Even though* is often more emphatic than *although* or *though*. We use it to emphasise the contrast:
  *I can still remember that day, **even though** it was a long time ago.*
- *However* and *nevertheless* can be used in the same way. *Nevertheless* is considered slightly more formal:
  *What you said was true. **However/Nevertheless**, it was a little unkind.*
- We use *whereas* to say that although something is true of one thing, it is not true of another:
  *Why are some cancers curable **whereas** others are not?*

13 LINKING WORDS AND PHRASES: CONTRAST

PRACTICE

1 Match 1–6 with a–g to make sentences.

0 Even though she set off early, **d**
1 I like holidays in the mountains
2 Despite public protests,
3 In spite of high prices,
4 She works in a hospital
5 The economic situation has been quite difficult.
6 Even though I don't really like going to football matches,

a whereas my wife loves the seaside.
b while her husband is a taxi driver.
c it'll be better than staying at home.
d she still arrived late.
e consumer goods are selling well.
f However, it is getting better now.
g the government decided to build a road through the wood.

2 Choose the correct answer.

0 *(Even though)* / *Nevertheless* she joined the company only a year ago, she has already been promoted twice.
1 Fast food is cheap *however* / *whereas* food in a proper restaurant is more expensive.
2 We went out *even though* / *despite* the rain.
3 *Yet* / *Although* he was only twelve, he won first prize in the competition.
4 They loved each other, *yet* / *in spite* they decided to part.
5 The children are very clever. *While* / *However*, they can be very noisy at times.
6 In spite *of making* / *that she made* a lot of mistakes, she still passed the test.

3 Complete the article. Use one word in each gap.

Retail therapy

Retail therapy makes us feel better. In spite of the ⁽⁰⁾ **fact** that we have hit hard times, people still find money to go shopping. Even ⁽¹⁾………. they can't afford to spend too much, they keep up the habit.

In some cases, they don't buy anything at all, ⁽²⁾………. they still get pleasure from window shopping. The main point of this 'retail therapy' is to cheer ourselves up. In ⁽³⁾………. of struggling to make ends meet, people still find ways of practising this 'hobby'. ⁽⁴⁾………. though it's popular, it's a really strange kind of habit. On the one ⁽⁵⁾………. , people are worried about the contents of their wallet and on the ⁽⁶⁾………. , they waste money on things which they can do without. And ⁽⁷⁾………. the fact that we are going through a global economic crisis, prices are still going up.

⁽⁸⁾………. retail therapy may seem to be a harmless hobby, it can become an addiction, and is particularly serious in young people. ⁽⁹⁾………. , the addiction itself is not treated as seriously as other addictions. ⁽¹⁰⁾………. people can get professional or medical help for many other addictions, serial shoppers are simply encouraged to get … more retail therapy.

'*Although* I disagree with what you say, I will defend to the death your right to say it.' VOLTAIRE

237

Vocabulary

13d Phrasal verbs with *get*

Here are some common phrasal verbs with *get*:

Phrasal verb	Meaning/Use	Example
get across sth; get sth across	succeed in communicating sth to sb	I couldn't **get** my **message across** to them.
get around	go or travel to different places	In my job, I **get around** quite a lot.
get around to	do sth that you have been intending to do for some time	I hope to **get around to** dealing with your request later today.
get away	leave; escape	The three men **got away** in a stolen car.
get away with sth	not be caught or punished for sth you have done wrong.	I don't know how they manage to **get away with** treating their employees like that.
get back	return	We **got back** home in time for dinner.
get back sth; get sth back	obtain sth again, after having lost it or given it to sb	Did you **get back** the money you lent her?
get back to sb	talk to or phone sb later	I'm a bit busy at the moment. Can I **get back to** you?
get by	have enough money to buy the things you need but no more	She can just about **get by** on her pension. *I get on with the little I have.* ✗ *I get by with the little I have.* ✓
get sb down	make sb feel unhappy and tired	All the criticism is **getting her down**.
get down sth; get sth down	write sth	The reporters were trying to **get down** everything he said.
get in	enter a place	The door was locked, so we couldn't **get in**.
get in(to)	be allowed to be a student at a university, college, etc.	He **got into** Harvard to study law.
get off	finish work and leave the place where you work	Mark usually **gets off** at six.
get on	make progress; deal with a job or situation	He's new but he's **getting on** fine.
get on (with) sb	have a friendly relationship with sb	How does Gina **get on with** her colleagues?
get on (with) sth	continue doing sth	**Get on with** your work!
get over sth	become well again after an illness	She's still trying to **get over** that cold.
	begin to feel better after an unpleasant or upsetting experience	Parents never really **get over** the death of a child.
get round sth	find a solution to a problem	We'll have to **get round** the problem somehow.
get through (to sb)	succeed in reaching sb by telephone	At last, I managed to **get through to** one of the managers!
get together	meet with sb in order to spend time with each other	Let's **get together** for dinner next week, shall we?

PHRASAL VERBS WITH GET 13

PRACTICE

1 Complete the sentences. Use the correct particles.

0 Gill managed to get ..*away*.. from the man and call the police.
1 Just because he's been working here a long time, he thinks he can get ………. with being late every day!
2 I never lend books because I never get them ………. .
3 With four kids to feed, Jenny just about gets ………. on her salary.
4 She worked hard and managed to get ………. Cambridge University.
5 I tried your number several times but I couldn't get ………. .
6 Although they sometimes shout at each other, they actually get ………. well.
7 All these problems are really getting me ………. .
8 It took me a long time to get ………. my friend's death.
9 We must get ………. for a drink sometime.
10 What time do you usually get ………. work?

2 Complete the second sentence so that it has a similar meaning to the first sentence, using the word given. Use between two and five words. Do not change the word given.

0 It's a difficult problem but we'll find a solution somehow.
   GET
   It's a difficult problem but we'll *get round* it somehow.
1 They have a friendly relationship with their neighbours.
   GET
   They …………… their neighbours.
2 I've been phoning all day but I still haven't managed to speak to her.
   GET
   I've been phoning all day but I haven't been able …………… to her.
3 Please just continue with what you're doing until I return.
   GET
   Please just …………… what you're doing until I return.
4 It's important to make young people understand that smoking isn't cool.
   GET
   It's important to …………… to young people that smoking isn't cool.
5 I find stories about death depressing.
   GETS
   It …………… to hear stories about death.

3 Complete the text. Use the correct particles.

It had been months since Ron had seen Julia. He thought he would never get (0) ..*over*.. her. He missed her and he was really depressed. The whole situation was getting him (1) ………. and it seemed that nothing would cheer him up.

He tried to get (2) ………. with his studies but he found it difficult to concentrate. His friends asked him what was up but he couldn't explain; he found it difficult to get (3) ………. to them just how special Julia had been. He occasionally met new people and although he got (4) ………. well with them, they didn't compare to Julia.

He had now spent all his money and he was broke. He had lent Julia some money and now it looked like he wasn't going to get it (5) ………. . He barely had enough money to get (6) ………. and although he wanted to find a summer job, he just couldn't get (7) ………. to writing his CV. He really needed a break – to get (8) ………. from it all.

He texted Julia but got no reply. He still believed that if they could get (9) ………. and discuss things, everything would be just fine again.

> *If you can't **get away** for a holiday, stay home and tip every second person you meet.*

239

13e Suffixes (6)

- Remember that we normally use suffixes to change a word to a different part of speech.

See also: 1e, 3e, 4e, 10e and 12e

- Here are some more suffixes that we use to change nouns into other parts of speech. Note the changes in spelling:

Noun	+ Suffix	Adjective
accident	+ -al	accidental
Bible	+ -al	biblical
clinic	+ -al	clinical
crime	+ -al	criminal
critic	+ -al	critical
culture	+ -al	cultural
habit	+ -al	habitual
music	+ -al	musical
nation	+ -al	national
origin	+ -al	original
option	+ -al	optional
profession	+ -al	professional
race	+ -al	racial
season	+ -al	seasonal
economy	+ -ical	economical

(NB: to nouns ending in -y, we add -ical:
history → historical, surgery → surgical;
But: industry → industrial)

- Some adjectives ending in -al do not have a first part that can exist on its own:
 abnormal   diagonal

- Some words ending in -al are nouns. They are formed from verbs:
 approve → approval
 propose → proposal
 survive → survival

Noun	+ Suffix	Adjective
addict	+ -ive	addictive
effect	+ -ive	effective
expense	+ -ive	expensive

- Some adjectives ending in -ive are formed from verbs:
 act → active
 create → creative

Noun	+ Suffix	Adjective
bigamy	+ -ous	bigamous
courage	+ -ous	courageous
danger	+ -ous	dangerous
envy	+ -ous	envious
fame	+ -ous	famous
fury	+ -ous	furious
glory	+ -ous	glorious
jealousy	+ -ous	jealous
humour	+ -ous	humorous
mystery	+ -ous	mysterious
space	+ -ous	spacious

- Some adjectives ending in -ous do not have a first part that can exist on its own:
 anxious   curious   enormous   generous
 obvious   precious   serious

Noun	+ Suffix	Noun
arson	+ -ist	arsonist
bigamy	+ -ist	bigamist
novel	+ -ist	novelist
piano	+ -ist	pianist
race	+ -ist	racist
science	+ -ist	scientist
terror	+ -ist	terrorist

SUFFIXES (6) 13

- We can also add the suffix *-ism* to some of the nouns in the last table on page 240, to form other nouns. Nouns ending in *-ism* usually indicate a belief or principle:
  race → racism
  terror → terrorism
- We can also add the suffix *-ist* to nouns to form adjectives:
  sex → a sexist attitude

Noun	+ Suffix	Noun
duke	+ -dom	dukedom
king	+ -dom	kingdom
star	+ -dom	stardom

- Some nouns ending in *-dom* are formed from verbs or adjectives:
  bore → boredom
  free → freedom

We can use the suffix *-en* to form verbs:

Noun	Adjective	Verb
breadth	broad	broad**en**
depth	deep	deep**en**
threat	threatening	threat**en**
width	wide	wid**en**

US spelling

- The ending *-our* used in British English is usually spelt *-or* in American English:

British English	American English
favour	favor
labour	labor
neighbour	neighbor
behaviour	behavior

- Both *-ise* (*realise*, *criticise*) and *-ize* (*realize*, *criticize*) are acceptable in British English but American English only uses *-ize*.

Practice

1 Complete the sentences. Use the correct form of the adjectives, nouns and verbs from pages 240–241.

0 The hijacker **threatened** to shoot the hostages if he was not allowed to go free.
1 She didn't have her parents' .... but she got married anyway.
2 You're always very .... of my work – you never praise me!
3 We can't buy that car. It's far too ....
4 All his colleagues were so .... of his success.
5 Journalists claim that .... of expression is essential if they are to report the truth.
6 Jane Austen is a famous English ....
7 I'm absolutely .... with you for taking my car without asking!
8 No, I'm not a(n) .... photographer – it's just a hobby.
9 These nuts are ....! I just can't stop eating them!
10 Her husband, a psychiatrist, works for the .... Institute of Mental Health.
11 The computer course is .... – you don't have to do it but you can if you want to.
12 A person who commits the crime of deliberately setting fire to something is called a(n) ....
13 Working abroad helped me .... my horizons – I learnt so many things.
14 .... still haven't managed to find a cure for cancer.
15 They really need to .... that road – it's much too narrow!

241

13 SUFFIXES (6)

2 Complete the sentences. Use words formed from the words in brackets.

0 I'd rather buy a smaller car – it's more **economical** (economy) to run.
1 Her success made everyone else really .... (envy).
2 These athletes are our .... (nation) heroes!
3 This book will .... (broad) your knowledge of English.
4 He committed a .... (crime) offence and was arrested.
5 Unfortunately, the treatment was not at all .... (effect).
6 The film is a .... (humour) look at life in the Internet Age.
7 I think Anton Rubinstein was one of the greatest .... (piano) of all time.
8 The course is an opportunity for students to .... (deep) their understanding of similar environmental issues.
9 Everyone should be allowed .... (free) of choice, I think.
10 He made a .... (propose), which the committee accepted.
11 Dogs often chew on things out of sheer .... (bore).
12 That wasn't a very .... (origin) idea!

3 Complete the crossword.

Across
2 Great Britain and Northern Ireland are also known as the United ....
4 The adjectival form of *bigamy*.
6 Harry was .... to finish his studies and finally get a job.
8 .... are still working on a cure for AIDS.

Down
1 An adjectival form of *pity*.
3 Adam gets .... every time another man looks at his wife.
5 Someone who plays the cello is called a(n) ....
6 Margery is eighty-eight but she's still very ....; she walks everywhere.
7 A person travelling in a canoe is called a(n) ....

242

SUFFIXES (6) 13

4 Complete the article. Use words formed from the words in CAPITALS at the end of some of the lines.

Science or Art?

As a student, my dream was to go to university and study to become a (0) **scientist**. The fact that I became a musician was quite (1) .... — SCIENCE / ACCIDENT

It all started when my parents bought me a second-hand piano when I was twelve years old. It was old and not very (2) .... I must admit I had no idea how to play it and I was absolutely (3) .... at my dad for not getting me that bike I wanted! The piano wasn't even my favourite instrument. I much preferred the guitar, like most teenagers. — EXPENSE / FURY

My (4) .... ability was discovered by my first teacher, who was very encouraging. She had been a (5) .... musician and I must say she was a very inspiring and (6) .... teacher. She was a very talented (7) .... and in her youth, she had played in many (8) .... orchestras. She was very patient and cheerful, even when she was (9) .... of my mistakes. When the time came for me to decide on what to do at university, my parents gave me complete (10) .... to choose what I wanted. In the end, I followed the footsteps of my great teacher. — MUSIC / PROFESSION / ORIGIN / PIANO / FAME / CRITIC / FREE

243

14

AGENDA

Grammar
- 14a Prepositions of time, place and movement
- 14b Prepositions after verbs and nouns
- 14c *it* and *there*

Vocabulary
- 14d Prepositional phrases
- 14e Phrasal verbs with *put*

Entry test

1 Choose the correct answer.

1 I'm busy now – I'll be with you *at / in* a few minutes.
2 They'll be going *in / to* Paris for a few days at Easter.
3 We'd been waiting ages *at / in* the bus stop before the bus arrived.
4 I read about the fire *in / to* Sunday News.
5 We arrived *at / in* France after a long day.

Now look at 14a on pages 246–249.   SCORE / 5

2 Choose the correct answer, A, B, C or D.

6 Her parents don't approve .... her friends.
   A about   **B** of   **C** on   **D** to

7 I'll never forgive him .... lying to me.
   A about   **B** of   **C** on   **D** for

8 They still haven't managed to find a solution .... the problem.
   A for   **B** to   **C** at   **D** from

9 What's your opinion .... his latest film?
   A for   **B** about   **C** to   **D** of

10 They blamed him .... the accident.
   A for   **B** about   **C** with   **D** to

Now look at 14b on pages 250–251.   SCORE / 5

ENTRY TEST 14

3 **Complete the sentences. Use *it* or *there*.**

11 Apparently, ...it... is cheaper to go by train.
12 ...There... are much cheaper flights at the weekend.
13 ...It... seems that no one really knows where he is.
14 ...There... was a loud crash as the car hit the lamp post.
15 ...There... must be something we can do to help her.

Now look at **14c** on pages 252–253.

SCORE / 5

4 **Choose the correct answer, A, B, C or D.**

16 Can you please be quiet for a bit – I'm .... the phone.
   A to   B in   C on   D at
17 .... behalf of everyone here, I would like to thank you for your help.
   A At   B In   C For   D On
18 .... the way, did you remember to tell Tina about the party?
   A On   B By   C To   D From
19 A number of species are .... danger of extinction.
   A in   B on   C at   D to
20 It was my fault we lost the game – .... some extent, anyway.
   A in   B at   C from   D to

Now look at **14d** on pages 254–256.

SCORE / 5

5 **Complete the sentences. Use the particles in the box.**

off   on   out   through   up

21 I will not put ...up... with your rudeness any longer!
22 If you just hang on, I'll put you ...through... to the marketing department.
23 Would you like some tea? Shall I put the kettle ...on...?
24 She's still busy, so she's put the meeting ...off... for an hour.
25 The army had to be called in to help put ...out... the forest fire.

Now look at **14e** on pages 257–258.

SCORE / 5

TOTAL SCORE / 25

245

Grammar

14a Prepositions of time, place and movement

Prepositions of time

Preposition	Use	Examples
at	with clock times and points of time in the day	**at** nine o'clock, **at** 6.35 **at** midnight, **at** noon, **at** dawn, **at** lunchtime, **at** night
	with holiday periods	**at** Christmas, **at** Easter, **at** Ramadan
	in some phrases	**at** the weekend/**at** weekends, **at** the moment, **at** present, **at** the time, **at** the beginning, **at** the end, **at** last, **at** times
in	with the main parts of the day	**in** the morning, **in** the afternoon, **in** the evening
	with years, months, seasons and centuries	**in** 2011, **in** March, **in** (the) winter, **in** the twentieth century
	for things that will happen at the end of the period mentioned	**in** an hour, **in** a couple of minutes, **in** a week, **in** a moment
on	with dates and specific days	**on** 8th August, **on** Tuesday, **on** Fridays, **on** weekdays, **on** New Year's Day, **on** Christmas Day, **on** Wednesday morning, **on** a fine day, **on** the day of arrival
by	means 'before or not later than the point in time mentioned'	We must finish **by** Monday.
until	means 'up to the point in time mentioned'	I'll be at the library **until** noon.
during	means 'from the beginning to the end of a period in time' or 'at some point in a period in time'	He worked as a waiter **during** the summer. (= all through the summer) She fell asleep **during** the lecture. (= at some point in the lecture)

PREPOSITIONS OF TIME, PLACE AND MOVEMENT 14

Prepositions of place

Preposition	Use	Examples
at	shows an exact position or particular place where sb/sth is or where sth is happening	There was a huge queue **at** the bus stop.
	in some phrases	**at** the top/bottom, **at** the corner, **at** the crossroads, **at** home, **at** school, **at** work, **at** Brenda's, **at** the wedding/funeral, **at** the end of the road, **at** 18 Hill Street, **at** the door
in	at a point within an area or a space; into sth (e.g. a container)	No running is allowed **in** the building. I'm **in** the living room. The photos are **in** that box over there. We arrived **in** the US on Wednesday. (But: We arrived **at** the station at six.)
	in some phrases	**in** an armchair, **in** bed, **in** the centre, **in** the country, **in** the world, **in** hospital, **in** prison, **in** the centre of town, **in** the north/south, **in** the middle, **in** the sky, **in** town, **in** London/Europe, **in** Hill Street (but **at** 18 Hill Street)
on	touching or forming part of a surface	The laptop's **on** my desk. There was a portrait of her **on** the wall.
	in some phrases	**on** the beach, **on** an island, **on** the coast, **on** board, **on** a cruise, **on** an excursion, **on** a trip, **on** a tour, **on** Earth, **on** a stool, **on** a farm, **on** a mountain, **on** the radio, **on** TV, **on** page 3, **on** the pavement, **on** a screen, **on** top of sth, **on** the corner, **on** the left/right, **on** the second floor
under	at a lower level than sth or covered by sth	The dog hid **under** the bed. She was holding a purse **under** her arm.
over	above or higher than sth, without touching it	You can hang that painting **over** the sofa.
above	in a higher position than sth else	They live in the apartment **above** ours.
near	only a short distance from sb or sth	Do you live **near** here?
next to	close to sb or sth, with nothing in between	She sat **next to** her husband.
beside	next to or very close to the side of sb or sth	Come and sit **beside** me.
by	beside or near sth	She stood **by** the window.
in front of	further forward than sb or sth	He sits **in front of** me at school.
behind	at or towards the back of sb or sth	She hid **behind** the door.
between	in or through the space that separates two things, people or places	He sat **between** Nick and Amanda.
among	in or through the middle of a group of people or things	We saw a small hut **among** the trees.
opposite	facing sb or sth	There's an Internet café **opposite** the library.

14 PREPOSITIONS OF TIME, PLACE AND MOVEMENT

Prepositions of movement

We generally use prepositions of movement with verbs that indicate movement, such as *come, go, walk, run, move, throw,* etc.

Preposition	Use	Examples
into	towards the inside or inner part of sth	She came **into** the room. I saw him going **into** the shop. Get back **into** bed.
onto	moving to a position on a surface, area or object	He walked **onto** the stage.
out of	away from the inside of sth	Get **out of** my room! He walked **out of** the office.
to	towards/in the direction of sb/sth	I returned **to** England last month. I'm going **to** Room 3 for a seminar.
from	starting at a particular place or position	What time did he come home **from** school?
towards	moving, looking, facing, etc. in the direction of sb/sth	He noticed two policemen coming **towards** him. All the windows face **towards** the river.
up	towards a higher place or position	Let's walk **up** the hill.
down	towards a lower place or position	She fell **down** the stairs.
over	from one side of sth to the other side of it	The man jumped **over** the fence.
along	from one place on sth such as a line, road or edge towards the other end of it	They were driving **along** Willow Road.
across	from one side of sth to the other	He swam **across** the river.
through	into one side or end of an entrance, passage, hole, etc. and out of the other side or end	The burglars must have got in **through** the window.
past	up to and beyond a person or place, without stopping	She walked right **past** me.
off	down or away from a place	I fell **off** my bike. The boy jumped **off** his bed.

We arrived in Loutro on the island of Crete and found a small hotel at the end of the bay.

PREPOSITIONS OF TIME, PLACE AND MOVEMENT 14

Practice

1 Choose the correct answer.

0 **In** / On the morning, we went at / **to** the shops and then had lunch **in** / off the café.

1 You have mud at / **on** your shoes! Wipe them at / **on** the mat before you come **into** / along the house.

2 They walked **into** / from the restaurant and sat down at / **on** a corner table.

3 I found this photo between / **among** the books in / **on** my desk.

4 She got off / **out of** the shop and **into** / across a red car that was parked **in front of** / below our house.

5 It says **in** / on the paper that they're getting married in / **at** the spring in / **on** a small church in / **on** the island of Santorini in Greece.

6 We'll be here **until** / by Friday. Then, **at** / in eight o'clock in / **on** Saturday morning, we're flying in / **to** London.

7 In / **On** Tuesday morning, I'm going in / **to** town to put some money **into** / onto my bank account.

8 The robbers jumped above / **over** the fence, climbed **up** / off a ladder and got **into** / across the room **through** / past the window.

9 I'd never been **to** / at the United States before, so when we arrived at / **in** JFK airport I felt really excited.

10 She stood up and walked **to** / at the window. She saw a woman sitting at / **on** a bench in / **under** a tree, reading a book.

2 Complete the time phrases. Use *at*, *in* or *on*.

0 ...at... present
1 ...at... 6.30 p.m.
2 ...in... the afternoon
3 ...on... Wednesday afternoon
4 ...in... an hour
5 ...at... weekends
6 ...on... weekdays
7 ...on... a cold day
8 ...in... a week
9 ...at... the beginning
10 ...in... a moment
11 ...at... the moment
12 ...in... 2012
13 ...on... her birthday
14 ...at... midnight
15 ...on... 25th March
16 ...on... a winter's night

4 Read the text and choose the correct answer.

Travel blog: Icaria

Last year, (0) **in** / on July, I had the opportunity to go (1) **to** / into Greece with my friends. We spent two weeks (2) in / **on** the island of Icaria, (3) **in** / on a small fishing village (4) **at** / to the end of a long dirt road. We arrived (5) **at** / on the village (6) **at** / on around midday. We walked (7) **along** / through the main road and (8) **into** / over the main square. The whole place was asleep! (9) At / **In** the afternoon, a lot of people have a siesta. There was no one around, so we went down (10) at / **to** the bay and had a swim. And then we lay (11) at / **on** the beach for a couple of hours. It was lovely. Afterwards, we went for a walk to the Temple of Artemis, built (12) **in** / at the second century with stone brought (13) past / **from** the beach on the neighbouring island of Fourni. It was a great first day, on one of the most beautiful Greek islands. I recommend it.

'Truth lies **at** the bottom of a well.' DEMOCRITUS

14b Prepositions after verbs and nouns

Verb + preposition

Here are some common verbs that are often used with particular prepositions:

about	with	to	for	of
care	agree	apologise	admire	accuse
dream	collide	belong	apologise	approve
forget	compare	go	care	consist
hear	cope	lead	forgive	die
know	deal	listen	pay	dream
laugh	provide (sb)	refer	punish	remind
quarrel	quarrel	shout	wait	smell
worry	sympathise	speak	work	taste

at	in	from	on
aim	arrive	come	bet
arrive	believe	differ	congratulate
laugh	include	discourage	count
look	involve	protect	decide
shout	persist	recover	insist
smile	result	save	rely
stare	succeed	suffer	spend

connect with, connect to

- *Connect to* means 'join two or more things together':
  First, **connect** the speakers **to** the CD player.
- *Connect with* means 'realise that a fact, event or person is related to something':
  The police did not **connect** her **with** the crime.
- Note that with the noun (*connection*) we often use *between*:
  There is a proven **connection between** smoking and cancer.

hear of, hear about, hear from:

- *Hear of* means 'know that someone or something exists because they have been mentioned to you before':
  I've never **heard of** him in my life.
- *Hear about* means 'be told or find out a piece of information':
  Have you **heard about** the fire?

- *Hear from* means 'receive news or information from someone':
  Have you **heard from** Sarah lately?

pay for, pay by, pay in

- We pay *for* something that we buy:
  She **paid** £200 **for** the tickets.
- *Pay by* means 'pay using':
  Can I **pay by** credit card?
- We pay *in* a particular currency:
  Can I **pay in** euros?

shout at, shout to, shout for, shout in

- We shout *at* somebody because we are angry with them:
  I wish you'd stop **shouting at** the children!
- We shout *to* somebody so that they can hear us:
  'I'm here!' she **shouted to** Mark.
- *Shout for something* means 'shout in order to get something':
  He rushed out of the house, **shouting for** help.
- *Shout in* + noun means 'shout because of':
  Nikki **shouted in** pain.

Noun + preposition

Here are some common nouns that are often used with particular prepositions:

with	of	to	from	about
agreement	advantage	invitation	departure	agreement
connection	approval	objection	extract	argument
contract	description	reply	protection	complaint
interview	disadvantage	solution	recovery	debate
relationship	experience	thanks	release	information
trouble	lack	threat	resignation	warning

between	in	for	on
choice	belief	excuse	advice
comparison	decrease	opportunity	attack
connection	delay	reason	congratulations
difference	expert	reputation	effect
fight	failure	respect	expert
relationship	increase	responsibility	influence

PRACTICE

1 Complete the table. Find the preposition that is used with each group of verbs and nouns.

Verbs	Preposition
0 object, refer, manage, explain, compare, invite, talk	to
1 forgive, blame, charge, care, apply, arrest, search	for
2 tell, boast, care, complain, argue, hear	about
3 smile, throw, glance	at
4 concentrate, depend, rely	on
5 charge, communicate, connect, argue, interfere	with

Nouns	Preposition
6 damage, invitation, solution, email, alternative	to
7 demand, need, advertisement, payment	for
8 knowledge, experience, opinion, taste, drawing	of

2 Complete the sentences. Use the correct prepositions.

0 Why are you staring **at** me like that?
1 It's hard to see the difference **between** the centre and the liberal party.
2 He's an expert **in** electronic music.
3 The twins differ **from** each other in many ways.
4 The government have known **about** the scandal for months.
5 She's been suffering **from** headaches since the accident.
6 She gave the police a detailed description **of** the man.
7 Congratulations **on** your wedding!
8 Grandma's still recovering **from** her heart attack.
9 I never received an invitation **to** her house-warming party.
10 I haven't heard **from** Dan for months.
11 While the teacher was writing on the board, the kids were shouting **at** each other.
12 I don't see any connection **between** the book and the film at all.
13 Her parents didn't approve **of** her moving to Canada.
14 Have you ever heard **of** a painter called Tiepolo?
15 I need more information **about** the product.

3 Complete the article. Use the correct prepositions.

Internet: for and against

Recently, there has been a huge increase (0) **in** the number of people using the Internet. At the same time, there has also been much debate about the influence of the Internet (1) **on** our lives. The World Wide Web has connected people across cities and continents but in other ways it has adversely affected relationships (2) **between** people. It has indeed succeeded (3) **in** making contact between people quick and easy but it is important to also remind ourselves (4) **of** the dangers, especially in the area of security and privacy. We need to find a solution (5) **to** this problem. Nowadays, we hear a lot (6) **about** cybercrime and hackers, and everyone agrees we must deal (7) **with** these kind of threats (8) **to** Internet users, which discourage many people (9) **from** using the net at all. And, of course, parents also worry a lot (10) **about** children being exposed to material that isn't suitable for their age group.

However, the advantages (11) **of** using the Internet are also numerous. For example, online shopping has made buying and paying (12) **for** goods so much easier.

*'I like **talking to** a brick wall; it's the only thing in the world that never contradicts me.'* OSCAR WILDE

251

14c *it* and *there*

it

Here is a summary of some common uses of *it*:

Use	Examples
to talk about the weather	*It's* been sunny all week. *It* snowed heavily last winter.
to talk about time	*It's* six o'clock. *It's* two months since I last saw Alex.
before *take* + time reference, to talk about a period of time	*It's* going to take five hours to get there.
to talk about distance	*It's* only 500 metres from here to the school.

it as a preparatory subject

- We can use *it* as a preparatory subject, when the real subject comes later in a sentence. We often use *it* in the following structures:
  - *it* + *be* + adjective/noun + *to*-infinitive:
    It's **useful to know** how to use a computer.
    It's **easy to buy** what you want in a big city.
    It **was a surprise to see** him there.
  - *it* + *be* + adjective/noun + (*that*) clause:
    It **was amazing that** no one was hurt.
    It's **a pity that** he didn't get the job.
  - *it* + *be* + adjective/noun + *-ing* form:
    It's **no use trying** to change her mind.
- We often use *it* with *be* to emphasise that we are talking about one particular person, thing, place, etc. and not any other:
  It was Jim who stole the money.
  It was Milan they went to, not Madrid.

there

- We use *there* + *be* to say that something exists or happens:
  If you're not busy, **there's** something I'd like to ask you.
  There's some milk in the fridge.
  There are some very good films on this week.
  There's been an accident at the crossroads.
  There's going to be trouble.

- We can use *there* with all tenses of *be*, as well as with modal verbs:
  There was no money in her wallet.
  There will be someone waiting for you at the airport when you arrive.
  There must be a solution to the problem.
  There may be life on other planets.

- We often use *there* with the verbs *seem*, *appear*, *happen* and *tend* before *be*:
  There seems to be a bit of a problem.
  There appears to be a traffic jam further up the road.
  There happens to be a lot about me that you don't know!

- We can also use a *to*-infinitive or a gerund after *there*:
  I don't want **there to be** any trouble.
  What's the chance of **there being** an election this year?

- *There* is also often used in the following structure:
  there is sure/likely/bound/certain to be …:
  If there's discussion, **there is bound to be** disagreement.
  There is sure to be trouble when he finds out about this!

- In spoken and informal English, *there* and the auxiliary are usually contracted:
  there is → there's   there will be → there'll be
  there has been → there's been

14 IT AND THERE

PRACTICE

1 Choose the correct answer.

0 *It* / *There* takes me one hour to get home from work.
1 *It's* / *There's* a pity you didn't come to the party; we had a lovely time.
2 He put on his coat because *it* / *there* was getting cold.
3 What's the chance of *it* / *there* being another earthquake in the area?
4 *It* / *There* has to be some mistake – I've never seen him before in my life!
5 *It's* / *There's* been some time since I wrote to you as I've been very busy.
6 *It* / *There* was a strange-looking man standing outside the shop.
7 Is *it* / *there* life after death? I wonder.
8 *It* / *There* has to be some kind of explanation for such strange behaviour.
9 *It* / *There* was a very pleasant surprise to see Marianne and Keith at the party.
10 *It's* / *There's* three kilometres to the beach from my place.
11 *It's* / *There's* no doubt she'll win the contest.
12 *It* / *There* seems that they won't have the report ready on time.
13 *It* / *There* appeared to be a lack of communication between them.
14 *It's* / *There's* a Mr Roberts here to see you.
15 *It* / *There* took them eight years to build this bridge.

2 Complete the article. Use *it* or *there*.

Is there life on other planets?

Many scientists believe (0) **it** is possible that (1) .... is life elsewhere in the universe, but actually finding it is the difficult part.

First of all, we don't know exactly what form of life (2) .... might be on planets outside our solar system, so (3) .... is difficult to know how to search for it. Second, the universe is a big place and (4) .... takes space vehicles and even radio signals too long to reach the kind of distances where other life forms might exist.

(5) .... is easier to find out about conditions on Mars, the planet in our solar system where (6) .... is a possibility of finding signs of life. (7) .... is now known that conditions on Mars are similar to the conditions in Antarctica, except that (8) .... is a lack of oxygen! So we can guess what forms of life might be able to survive there, and (9) .... are projects under way to send machines to Mars to look for these kinds of life. Any life that we find might be very different from life on Earth.

Of course, (10) .... is possible that there is another dimension in our universe that we don't know about. Remember, (11) .... are billions of galaxies and we inhabit just one of them! (12) .... would be small-minded to believe that we are the only planet with life in this universe.

253

Vocabulary

14d Prepositional phrases

- We often use prepositions in fixed phrases, where little variation is possible. Some prepositions go with groups of similar words:
  at: at breakfast, at lunch, at dinner, at supper
  for: for example, for instance
  on: on the phone, on my mobile

- Sometimes we use more than one preposition in phrases:
  out of date   **out of** fashion

- Words with related meanings often go with different prepositions:
  in cash   **by** credit card
  on earth   **in** the world
  by accident   **on** purpose
  at the bottom   **in** the bottom left-hand corner
  by car   **on** foot
  on holiday   **at** work
  in a loud voice   **at** the top of my voice

- Below are some common prepositional phrases

at	by	for	in	on	out of
at all times	**by** accident	**for** a change	**in** (the) future	**on** a diet	**out of** breath
at arm's length	**by** airmail	**for** a visit	**in** a loud voice	**on** account of	**out of** control
at breakfast	**by** bus/train	**for** a walk	**in** a sense	**on** arrival	**out of** danger
at dawn	**by** chance	**for** a while	**in** addition (to)	**on** average	**out of** date
at daybreak	**by** cheque	**for** ages	**in** answer (to)	**on** behalf of	**out of** doors
at fault	**by** coincidence	**for** better or	**in** cash	**on** board	**out of** earshot
at first	**by** email	worse	**in** charge	**on** business	**out of** fashion
at first sight	**by** far	**for** breakfast	**in** conclusion	**on** condition	**out of** favour
at home	**by** fax/phone	**for** ever	**in** control	that	**out of** luck
at last	**by** hand	**for** example	**in** danger	**on** duty	**out of** money
at least	**by** heart	**for** fear of	**in** detail	**on** fire	**out of** my own
at once	**by** means of	**for** fun	**in** effect	**on** foot	pocket
at present	**by** mistake	**for** good	**in** favour of	**on** holiday	**out of** order
at sea	**by** myself	**for** granted	**in** general	**on** leave	**out of** practice
at the beginning	**by** nature	**for** life	**in** haste	**on** my own	**out of** print
at the bottom	**by** no means	**for** luck	**in** my opinion	**on** no account	**out of** season
at the end	**by** sea/land/air	**for** my sake	**in** other words	**on** purpose	**out of** sight
at the latest	**by** sight	**for** nothing	**in** pairs	**on** second	**out of** the way
at the moment	**by** the arm	**for** now	**in** private	thoughts	**out of** time
at the same time	**by** the rules	**for** pleasure	**in** the news	**on** the left/right	**out of** touch
at times	**by** the way	**for** sale	**in** the West	**on** the other	**out of** tune
at work	day **by** day	**for** short	**in** time	hand	**out of** use
		for the moment		**on** the phone	**out of** work
				on the whole	
				on time	

254

PREPOSITIONAL PHRASES   14

to	up	from
to date	*up* and down	*from* … to …
to my advantage	*up* and running	*from* bad to worse
to my amazement	*up* north	*from* experience
to my surprise	*up*-to-date	*from* morning to night
to some degree	*up* to now	*from* my point of view
to some extent	(be) *up* to something	*from* now on
to the full	*up* to you	*from* place to place
to the point	*up* until/till	*from* time to time

at the beginning or in the beginning?

- *At the beginning* is usually followed by *of* + noun:
  We're leaving for France **at the beginning** of the month.
- *In the beginning* is not usually followed by a noun (or *of*):
  In the beginning, I really enjoyed my job; now I don't.

at the end or in the end?

- *At the end* (*of*) refers to the final part of a period of time, event, activity, story, etc.:
  He's leaving **at the end** of October.
- *In the end* means 'after a period of time or after everything has been done':
  We waited and waited. **In the end**, we decided to go back home.

on time or in time?

- *On time* means 'at the planned time':
  Was your train **on time**?
- *In time* means 'early enough for something/to do something':
  If we hurry, we'll be there **in time** for lunch.
- *In time* can also mean 'after a period of time, when a situation has changed':
  In time, things will get better.

by bus or on the bus?

- *By bus* refers to the way you travel, to using a bus as a means of transport:
  I usually go to work **by bus**.
- *On the bus* refers to where you are while travelling:
  There were a lot of people **on the bus**.

made of or made from?

- We use *made of* when something keeps its nature, character or attributes after the process of making.
- We use *made from* when something changes during the process of making. Compare:
  The shirt is **made of** cotton. (Cotton is still cotton after the shirt is made.)
  The box is **made of** plastic. (Plastic is still plastic after the box is made.)
  Wine is **made from** grapes. (Grapes are not grapes any more after wine is made.)
  Bread is **made from** flour, water and yeast. (The ingredients change form during the process of making.)

*Joe almost gave up but **in the end**, he reached the top of the mountain.*

14 PREPOSITIONAL PHRASES

PRACTICE

1 Choose the correct answer.

0 In /(From) my point of view, there's little advantage in buying shares now.
1 His health is going from / in bad for / to worse.
2 Your report was excellent: brief and on / to the point. Well done!
3 She accepted the award in /(on) behalf of her husband.
4 Would you please be quiet? I'm at /(on) the phone!
5 You don't think he would have broken the window on / from purpose, do you?
6 He's the officer at / in charge of the investigation.
7 When Romeo met Juliet, it was love at / on first sight.
8 Why don't you send him the file in / by email?
9 After the accident, she was rushed to hospital; she is out of / off danger now.
10 We'll never make it in / on time for the meeting!

2 Complete the sentences. Use the correct prepositions.

0 The report, which will be ready **at** the beginning of next week, will be sent to you **by** email.
1 I agree with you .... some extent but .... general, I would have put things differently.
2 .... the beginning, I really liked the book. Now I don't because .... the end, the hero gets killed – and I hate books with sad endings!
3 He's been **out of** work for over six months; he can't afford to go **on** holiday.
4 I thought the chair was made .... wood; .... my surprise, Jo told me it was all plastic.
5 He was standing **in** the middle of the room, trying to learn that poem **by** heart.

6 **In** my opinion, he's the best football player **in** the world today.
7 **For** dessert, we had a lovely cake made **from** almonds, chocolate and strawberries.
8 Please make sure you arrive **on** time from now **on**.
9 Shall we go **by** bus or **on** foot?
10 'Is Kate **at** work?' 'No, she's **on** leave until 16th April, I think.'

3 Complete the article. Use the correct prepositions.

The way we listen

New technology is always (0) **in** the news. Developments are taking place so quickly that new devices quickly go (1) **out** of date. When the cassette tape first appeared, it made records look very clumsy. To use a record player, you had to listen to music (2) **at** home but cassette recorders were portable and allowed you to listen to music (3) **at** all times and wherever you chose: you could listen (4) **at** work, in the park or on a picnic. Then came the Walkman. The Walkman was (5) **at** first a huge success, allowing you to listen to music (6) **on** your own, while you were out taking the dog (7) **out** for a walk, for example. Next came the CD along with the CD Walkman, and the sound quality was excellent.

But even that went quickly (8) **out** of fashion with the appearance of MP3 and MP4 files, which can do everything CDs can and much more. So in a short space of time, we have gone (9) **from** using records to MPEG files. (10) **In** time, CD sales will disappear completely – (11) **at** the moment, most people only buy CDs when they want to get someone a nice present for their birthday or for Christmas. Before you know it, MP3 and MP4 files will be (12) **out** of favour as well. What is next?

256

14e Phrasal verbs with *put*

Here are some common phrasal verbs with *put*:

Phrasal verb	Meaning/Use	Example
put across sth; *put sth across*	explain your ideas, beliefs, etc. in a way that people can understand	The union representative was able to **put** her argument **across** effectively.
put over sth; *put sth over*	explain your ideas, beliefs, etc. in a way that people can understand	The union representative was able to **put** her argument **over** effectively.
put away sth; *put sth away*	put sth in the place where it is usually kept	Let me just **put** these books **away**.
put back sth; *put sth back*	postpone; arrange for an event to start at a later time or date	They've **put back** the meeting to next Thursday.
put down sth; *put sth down*	write sth, especially a name or number, on a piece of paper or on a list	I'll **put** your name **down** on the list.
	criticise sb	She **puts** me **down** all the time.
put forward sth; *put sth forward*	suggest a plan, proposal, etc. for other people to consider or discuss	Professor Kaplan has **put forward** a theory.
put off sth; *put sth off*	delay doing sth or arrange to do sth at a later time or date, esp. because of a problem	The match has been **put off** till next week.
put on sth; *put sth on*	put a piece of clothing on your body	**Put** your coat **on** before you go outside.
	switch on a light or piece of equipment	It's freezing! **Put** the heater **on**.
put out sth; *put sth out*	make a flame or fire stop burning	**Put** that cigarette **out** immediately.
put sb through (to) sb	connect sb to sb else on the phone	Hold on; I'll try to **put** you **through** to Mrs Wakeman.
put up sth; *put sth up*	build sth	They're **putting up** some new office blocks.
	increase the cost or value of sth	Our landlord's **put** the rent **up**.
put up sb; *put sb up*	let sb stay in your house and give them meals	We can **put** you **up** for tonight.
put up with sb/sth	accept an unpleasant situation or person without complaining	How do you **put up with** all this noise?

257

14 PHRASAL VERBS WITH PUT

PRACTICE

1 Complete the sentences. Use phrasal verbs with *put*.

0 She's an excellent speaker; she really knows how to ..**put**.. a message ..**across**.. .
1 I will not ..**put up with**.. your bad temper any longer! I've had enough!
2 All the hotels are full; can you ..**put**.. me ..**up**.. for the night?
3 He opened the door and ..**put on**.. the light.
4 The government has decided to ..**put up**.. income tax again!
5 The building caught fire but the firemen soon ..**put**.. it ..**out**.. .
6 'Could I speak to the manager?' 'Certainly. I'll ..**put**.. you ..**through**..
7 What are your toys still doing on the floor? Please ..**put**.. them ..**away**.. .
8 It was raining, so they had to ..**put**.. the trip ..**back**.. to next week.

2 Complete the second sentence so that it has a similar meaning to the first sentence, using the verb *put*. Use between two and five words.

0 A good teacher should be able to explain things clearly.
   PUT
   A good teacher should be able to ..**put things across**.. clearly.

1 It would be very useful if you could propose something in writing.
   PUT
   It would be very useful if you could ..**put forward**.. a proposal in writing.

2 If you keep delaying going to the doctor, it will only make things worse.
   PUT
   The longer you ..**put off**.. to the doctor, the worse it will be.

3 Don't forget to wear a hat.
   PUT
   Don't forget ..**to put on**.. a hat.

4 They're planning to build a cinema complex near the park.
   PUT
   They're planning to ..**put up**.. a cinema complex near the park.

5 The price of electrical goods has increased again.
   PUT
   They've ..**put up**.. the price of electrical goods again.

6 The receptionist tried to connect me but the line was engaged.
   PUT
   The receptionist tried to ..**put me through**.. but the line was engaged.

7 I won't accept being treated like a child any more!
   PUT
   I won't ..**put up with**.. being treated like a child any more!

8 Why do you have to make me look stupid in front of my friends like that?
   PUT
   Why do you have to ..**put me down**.. in front of my friends like that?

9 The fire service extinguished the fire.
   PUT
   The fire service ..**put out**.. the fire.

10 He asked me if I could let him stay in my house for a few days.
   PUT
   He asked me if I could ..**put him up**.. for a few days.

> 'This is the sort of English **up with** which I will not **put**.' Winston Churchill, on coming across the grammar rule which says we should not end a sentence with a preposition.

Exam practice 7

Part 1

For questions **1–12**, read the text below and decide which answer (**A**, **B**, **C** or **D**) best fits each gap. There is an example at the beginning (**0**).

ON YOUR BIKE!

If you're getting fed up ⁽⁰⁾.......... time looking for parking space, my advice to you is to consider the bicycle as an alternative means of transport. Cycling is probably the cheapest and healthiest way of getting about in our congested city centres. ⁽¹⁾.......... it is convenient and environmentally desirable, it can be an unattractive choice ⁽²⁾.......... a cold wintry morning. It is much easier ⁽³⁾.......... on a nice warm bus or jump into your car, ⁽⁴⁾.......... the sight of cyclists as they weave their way in and ⁽⁵⁾.......... the traffic may fill you with envy as you sit ⁽⁶⁾.......... in yet another traffic jam. In spite of the ⁽⁷⁾.......... that worsening pollution is getting many people ⁽⁸⁾.......... , causing more and more health problems, and ⁽⁹⁾.......... it is fashionable to express one's approval ⁽¹⁰⁾.......... the environmentally safe bicycle, ⁽¹¹⁾.......... hard to deny the danger cyclists face in sharing the road with cars. ⁽¹²⁾.......... cycling is not as risky as it looks at first sight, there are more and more accidents involving cyclists.

0	A	waste	B	to waste	C	(with wasting)	D	wasted
1	A	Despite	B	In spite	C	Even as	D	Although
2	A	in	B	on	C	at	D	of
3	A	travel	B	to travel	C	to travelling	D	that you travel
4	A	though	B	even	C	despite	D	in spite
5	A	off	B	of	C	out of	D	about
6	A	wait	B	to wait	C	waiting	D	to waiting
7	A	truth	B	event	C	reality	D	fact
8	A	round	B	over	C	down	D	off
9	A	while	B	even as	C	despite	D	in spite of
10	A	of	B	to	C	about	D	for
11	A	it's	B	there's	C	there seems	D	there appears
12	A	However	B	Nevertheless	C	Yet	D	Even though

SCORE / 12

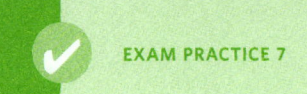

Part 2

For questions **13–24**, read the text below and think of the word which best fits each gap. Use only **one** word in each gap. There is an example at the beginning (**0**).

OUT OF WORK

The best time to visit Switzerland is (0) ...in... the summer – (13) .... effect, this means sometime between June and September. It is a great place to relax and (14) .... away from it all and if you are interested in winter sports, a trip to Switzerland during the winter months will satisfy even the most demanding. As far as the weather is concerned, (15) .... is a good chance of snow at least till June, especially (16) .... high altitudes and, in some places, all year round. (17) .... can get quite hot in the summer (18) .... the rest of the year, you should be prepared for cold weather.

The biggest expense while (19) .... Switzerland is likely to be long-distance transport, accommodation and eating out, none of (20) .... are cheap. Switzerland is a notoriously expensive tourist destination, so unless you choose to get around (21) .... car, you will be using Swiss public transport, (22) .... may pinch your pocket, and even staying in a modest hotel will not be cheap. In (23) .... of the cost, which is synonymous with quality, Switzerland has something to offer everyone. And don't forget to pick up some cheese and chocolates (24) .... the end of your stay!

SCORE / 12

Part 3

For questions **25–34**, read the text below. Use the word given in capitals at the end of some of the lines to form a word that fits in the gap **in the same line**. There is an example at the beginning (**0**).

Travel has been made much easier by modern means of transport and for the ⁽⁰⁾ **majority** of people, flying to a holiday destination is reasonably ⁽²⁵⁾.......... . Even flying across the globe is not as ⁽²⁶⁾.......... as it used to be. Thus, even in times of crisis, the international ⁽²⁷⁾.......... industry continues to be profitable. Moreover, people still travel to other countries for ⁽²⁸⁾.......... reasons, in spite of the growth of the Internet and ⁽²⁹⁾.......... online communication.

In theory, all this ⁽³⁰⁾.......... travel should be making us more knowledgeable and tolerant of other cultures. But how true is the saying that travel ⁽³¹⁾.......... the mind? Does getting to know how other people live widen our ⁽³²⁾.......... horizons or does it confirm us in our narrow beliefs about others? What effect does it have on us to experience the ⁽³³⁾.......... of other nations first hand? Does it make us more positive towards other cultures or just more ⁽³⁴⁾.......... ?

MAJOR
ECONOMY
EXPENSE
TOUR

PROFESSION
EFFECT
GLOBE

BROAD
CULTURE

BEHAVE
CRITIC

SCORE _____ / 10

EXAM PRACTICE 7

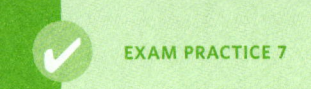

Part 4

For questions **35-42**, complete the second sentence so that it has a similar meaning to the first sentence, using the word given. **Do not change the word given.** You must use between **two** and **five** words, including the word given. Here is an example (0).

Example:

0   One day, you'll recover from the shock of losing her.
    GET
    One day, you'll ....*get over*................ the shock of losing her.

35 I overslept but I still managed to catch the train.
    SPITE
    In .... that I overslept, I still managed to catch the train.

36 I won't tolerate this sort of behaviour any longer.
    PUT
    I won't .... this sort of behaviour any longer.

37 I don't know a word of French but I still had a good time in Paris.
    EVEN
    I had a good time in Paris, ... can't speak French.

38 That's the woman who had her car stolen last week.
    WHOSE
    That's .... was stolen last week.

39 I don't know – I'll find out and speak to you later.
    BACK
    I don't know – I'll find out and .... you.

40 I grew up in that village.
    WHERE
    That's .... grew up.

41 You don't think he meant to do it, do you?
    PURPOSE
    You don't think he ...., do you?

42 You may have done the right thing after all.
    POSSIBLE
    It .... did the right thing after all.

SCORE / 16

TOTAL SCORE / 50

Word store (topic-related)

These exercises, each organised into groups related to topics, will help you to build your store of very useful words and phrases.

Living conditions

1 Complete the words in the text.

> We live in a ⁽⁰⁾ d**etached** house in the old part of the ⁽¹⁾ c............... It has three ⁽²⁾ f............... and a basement, which I use as a study. It's got a small front ⁽³⁾ g............... and a lovely view over the bay. Many people dream of buying a ⁽⁴⁾ c............... in the country where they can escape to at weekends. Others even hope to own a ⁽⁵⁾ v............... in a beautiful location on the coast. Most people here, however, live in ⁽⁶⁾ f............... There are a lot of students living here in rented ⁽⁷⁾ r............... and bedsits.

2 Complete the sentences. Use the words below.

> armchair   bulb   chest   corkscrew   cupboard   cushions   ~~drawer~~   dressing
> fireplace   iron   lamp   light switch   plug   sofa   stools   wardrobe

0 The scissors are in my desk ..**drawer**...
1 My bedroom doesn't have a(n) ...., so I don't have anywhere to hang my clothes.
2 When she gets home, she sits in a comfortable .... in front of the fire.
3 The three children were all sitting on the ...., watching television.
4 I think we've got some sugar in the .... in the kitchen.
5 The .... is on the wall just as you go into the room. Just press it.
6 Make sure your hands are dry when you put the .... into the socket, otherwise you might get an electric shock.
7 There were several couples in the pub sitting on .... at the bar, drinking.
8 I can't open this bottle of wine because I don't have a(n) ....
9 He had never used a(n) .... before, so he scorched his new shirt.
10 She sat at the .... table, looking at herself in the mirror.
11 I keep my socks and underwear in a(n) .... of drawers in my bedroom.
12 It's too dark to read in here; why don't you get a reading ....?
13 The .... on the landing has gone and I can't see a thing – can you put a new one in?
14 There were not enough chairs, so some people had to sit on .... on the floor.
15 On cold winter days, we used to sit round the .... to keep warm.

263

WORD STORE

3 Read the text in Exercise 1 again. Find words with the following meanings.

0 a bedroom which is also used as a living room ....bedsit............
1 a large house in the country ....
2 a small house in the country ....
3 a house not joined to any other ....
4 a set of rooms below ground level ....
5 a room used for work or reading ....

4 Complete the table. Write the words in the box in the correct column. You must write one word in two columns.

attic   basement   bedsit   block of flats   bungalow   cellar   corkscrew
cottage   detached house   ground floor   hall   ironing board   landing
loft   power point   remote control   semi-detached house   study   table mat
tea towel   terraced house   villa   washing-up liquid

Types of home	Parts of a house	Things we find in a house
	attic	

5 Complete the sentences. Use the words below. Sometimes more than one answer is possible.

clock   dishwasher   door handle   electricity   light   MP4 player
paint   power supply   radio   tap   the staircase   the stairs   TV
washing machine   water supply

0 It's dark in here – turn the ....light........... on.
1 The .... has come off.
2 She fell down ....
3 The .... broke down yesterday.
4 My .... was cut off.
5 The batteries in my .... have run out. I must get some new ones.
6 We have to put the .... back one hour tonight.

264

WORD STORE

Social relationships

1 Complete the words in the text.

A nuclear family consists of only a (0) hu**sband**, (1) w............... and children. In my country, an extended (2) f............... is more common. It consists not only of (3) p............... and children but also of (4) g..............., aunts, uncles and (5) c............... My (6) g............... lives with us and loves looking after her grandchildren. My mum's brother, my (7) U............... George, is a widower and has lived with us since (8) A............... Helen died. He is also my godfather.

2 Look at the family tree and the clues and complete the crossword. What is the secret word?

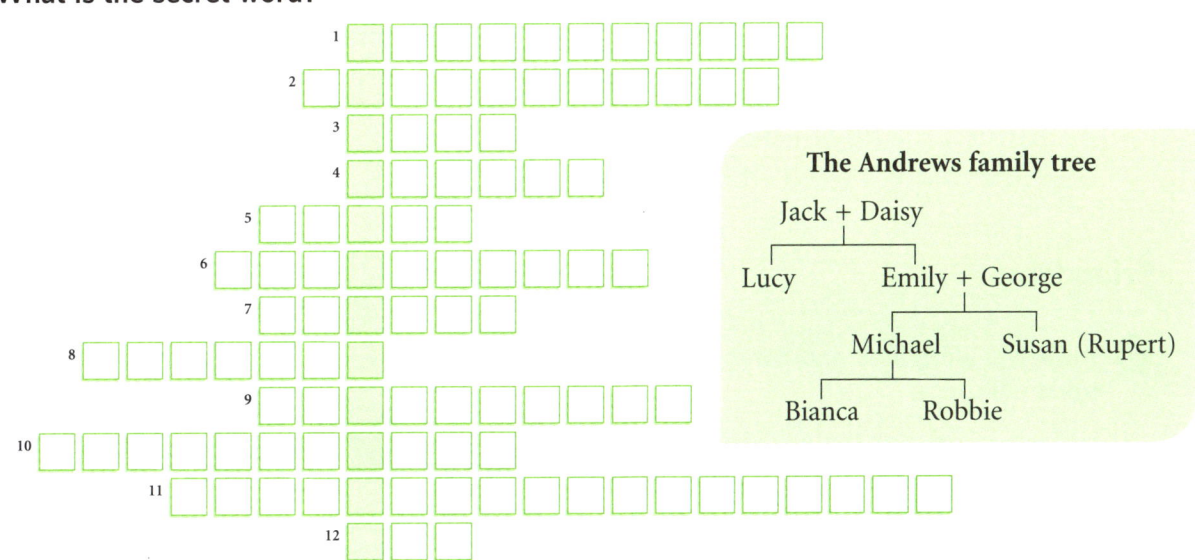

The Andrews family tree

Jack + Daisy
├── Lucy
└── Emily + George
    ├── Michael
    │   ├── Bianca
    │   └── Robbie
    └── Susan (Rupert)

1 Susan's parents, Emily and George, are Australian. Jack is her ....
2 Jack emigrated to Australia and married Daisy. Daisy is Susan's ....
3 They had another daughter, Lucy – so Emily has a sister. Lucy is Susan's ....
4 When Susan's brother Michael got married, he had two children, Bianca and Robbie. Now Susan has a niece and a ....
5 Susan's dad died a few years ago and her mum became a ....
6 Emily remarried and her new husband, Bill, is a lawyer. Bill is Susan's ....
7 Susan's engaged. Her .... is called Rupert. He's twenty-two and he's a computer programmer.
8 Rupert's mum died when he was at university and so Rupert's dad is a ....
9 Rupert's dad is getting married to Maria soon, and Maria will be Rupert's ....
10 When Susan and Rupert get married, Rupert's dad will be Susan's ....
11 Bianca is Jack and Daisy's ....
12 Robbie is Michael's ....

The secret word is ....

WORD STORE

3 Complete the text. Use the correct form of the words below.

> anniversary best engage fall get go honeymoon in
> know marriage meet ~~stranger~~ to to wedding

Love at first sight

Last August, Tony and Julie were complete (0) *strangers*. They hadn't even heard of each other. They first (1) .... at Michael's twenty-first birthday party and they took (2) .... each other immediately. As they got to (3) .... each other, they realised they had many things (4) .... common. After the party, they began to (5) .... out together. Before long, they had (6) .... in love. They decided to get (7) .... and then, if all went well, (8) .... married a year later. Julie said she didn't believe (9) .... was a good idea before they had both found good jobs. In the end, the (10) .... took place in August, on the first (11) .... of their meeting at Michael's party. Their (12) .... man was Michael, who had invited them (13) .... his party a year before. For their (14) ...., they went on a two-week cruise of the Aegean islands.

Friendship

1 Study the word web and complete the sentences. Sometimes more than one answer is possible.

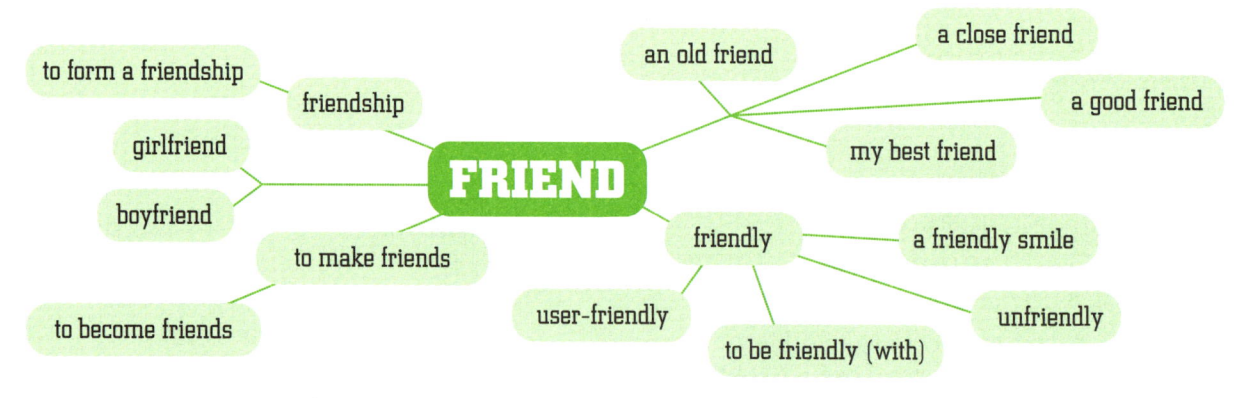

- to form a friendship
- friendship
- girlfriend
- boyfriend
- to make friends
- to become friends

FRIEND

- an old friend
- a close friend
- a good friend
- my best friend
- friendly
- a friendly smile
- user-friendly
- to be friendly (with)
- unfriendly

0 She's cheerful and ..*friendly*.. the whole time.
1 The new student in the class is upset because we've been .... towards him.
2 Our .... developed quickly over the weeks that followed.
3 She's not a very .... friend – she's just an acquaintance.
4 The two boys .... friends very quickly.
5 I've just bought a new computer but the manual is not very .... – I can't understand a word it says.

266

WORD STORE

2 First read the text and underline four phrasal verbs. Then complete the sentences. Use the particles below. You will use some of them more than once. Some of the phrasal verbs in the sentences appear in the text.

down   off   out   up

Stuck-Up

Kelly's a really difficult person to <u>get on with</u> – she's already <u>fallen out with</u> her best friend. The way she <u>looks down on</u> everyone else really <u>puts people off</u> her – many people think she's a bit of a snob but I think it's just the way she's been brought up. You see, she was an only child in a very well-off family, so she's probably been spoilt.

0   I don't get ….*on*…. very well with my boss because he thinks I don't work hard enough.
1   She fell ………….. with her boyfriend but after a while they made up again.
2   He looks ………….. to his father and always listens carefully to his advice.
3   Just because she's got more money than her neighbours, she looks ………….. on them.
4   She's very popular with colleagues because she's always ready to help them ………….. if they have problems.
5   She was born in France but didn't grow ………….. there – she was brought ………….. by her grandparents in Spain.
6   She used to go ………….. with a boy called Jack but they've broken ………….. for good now – what put him ………….. her was her arrogance.

Occupations

1 Complete the words in the text.

And a good job, too!

There is a lot of (0) u*nemployment* nowadays, so it is getting more and more difficult to get the kind of (1) j………….. you really want. Then you have to decide what is more important to you – how much you (2) e………….. or job satisfaction? Do you want to work with your hands (called (3) m………….. work) or do you prefer to work in an office (called (4) c………….. work)? Do you prefer to work indoors or (5) o…………..?

Whatever you decide, when you are thinking about a career or applying for a job, you will find the following vocabulary useful:

- apply for a job
- make a lot of money
- belong to a union
- dismiss someone from a job
- make an application
- have a large income
- join a union
- employ someone
- earn a good wage
- retire from work
- hand in one's resignation
- give someone a job

WORD STORE

2 Complete the phrases. Use the words below.

> career   experience   interview   job   ~~management~~   offer   pension
> promotion   qualifications   reference   sack   salary   trainee   wage

0 go into **management**
1 choose a(n) .... in computers
2 go for a(n) ....
3 get a(n) .... as a waiter
4 get the ....
5 earn a decent weekly ....
6 get an annual .... increase
7 get a(n) .... at sixty-five
8 win ....
9 get a good .... from your tutor
10 have the right .... for the job
11 have two years' relevant ....
12 accept a(n) .... of a job
13 take a young person on as a(n) ....

3 Number the steps in Joe Bloggs' career in the correct order.

a He was promoted to assistant to the sales manager. ☐
b He took up gardening as a hobby. ☐
c He looked for a job. ☐
d He was appointed managing director. ☐
e He made an application. ☐
f He was offered the job. ☐
g He was out of work. ☐
h He retired. ☐
i He went for an interview. ☐
j He worked as a clerk. ☐
k He got the job of sales manager. ☐
l He gave in his resignation. **l**

4 Study the word web and complete the sentences. Use one word in each gap.

- work as a journalist/architect
- work in a hotel/hairdresser's/restaurant
- work for a computer company
- work at McDonald's/that bookshop/the George Hotel

WORK

- hard   heavy   boring   manual   seasonal
- be out of work / come home from work / take time off work
- find   look for   get   start
- full-time / part-time
- well paid   badly paid

0 Why don't you go out and look **for** work instead of sitting around all day doing nothing?
1 Jane works .... a software developer for Microsoft.
2 My dad worked .... a factory all his life.
3 His wife works .... the local council.
4 I'll tell you about the problem when you come home .... work.
5 Arthur has been out .... work ever since they closed the mine.
6 Her boss gave her time .... work to go and see the doctor.

WORD STORE

5 Study the table. Then replace the underlined words in the sentences with the correct form of a phrasal verb from the table.

Verb	Meaning	Example
carry out sth; carry sth out	do sth that needs to be done	Those repairs must be **carried out**.
deal with sb	do business with sb, or take an action to do with work	In my job, I have to **deal with** a lot of different people.
deal with sth	take the correct action to complete a piece of work or solve a problem	The problem is being **dealt with**.
get on	be successful in one's career	If you want to **get on** in your career, you'll have to work hard.
take on work; take work on	agree to do a job	You've **taken on** too much **work** – slow down a bit.
take on sb; take sb on	employ sb	We're **taking** ten waiters **on** this summer.
take over	move into or continue doing a job previously done by sb else	Who will **take over** now that Smith has resigned?
take up sth; take sth up	start working at a new job	She **took up** her first teaching post in 1970.

0 The new manager will <u>begin</u> his duties in September.　　take up
1 After looking at his qualifications, they decided to <u>offer him the job</u>.　　..............
2 He's <u>doing</u> far too much and will make himself ill.　　..............
3 You'll have to make some sacrifices if you want to <u>be successful</u> in the business.　　..............
4 Who do you think is going to <u>be the new director</u> when Santana retires?　　..............
5 Will you <u>handle</u> any complaints while I'm away?　　..............
6 She <u>did</u> all the tasks successfully.　　..............

Education

1 Complete the words in the text.

Education differs from country to country. In Britain, school consists of pre-school, ⁽⁰⁾ **primary** school and ⁽¹⁾ s.............. school. ⁽²⁾ M.............. for different subjects are given in figures out of 10, 20 or 100. ⁽³⁾ G.............. are usually expressed in letters – A, B, C, etc. A certificate is given for success in a particular ⁽⁴⁾ a.............. of study (for example, the Cambridge First Certificate). A diploma is awarded by colleges and a ⁽⁵⁾ d.............. by universities.

WORD STORE

2 Study the table. Then complete the phrases with the words in the box.

| classes | diploma | exercise | grade | grades | heart | ~~management~~ |
| place | private | revise | year |

Verb	Expressions
do	do (= study for) a degree in (0) **management**; do (= complete) an exam/a(n) (1).........; do (= carry out) an experiment; do (= carry out) research into traffic pollution; do (= study) maths/history
gain	gain a good degree/education; gain experience
get	get a good education; get information/advice; get a(n) (2).......... at university; get into university; get a grant; get good/bad marks/(3)..........; get a good report; get a degree/certificate/(4)..........
go	go to university/college/evening (5)..........
have	have good knowledge of marketing strategies; have (6).......... lessons
make	make progress; make a mistake; make the (7)..........
study	study mathematics/notes/a diagram; study for a test/an exam/a degree
take	take a course/an exam; take notes (while listening or reading); take a break from studying; take a(n) (8).......... off to travel
teach	teach a lesson/a class; teach English/media studies; teach at a school/college/university
Other	attend classes/a private language school/university carry out research into environmental effects of tourism cheat in an exam copy from someone else give a lecture/a talk/a demonstration learn a poem by (9)..........; memorise the facts pay attention (in class) prepare/(10).......... for an exam sit for/sit an exam

3 Choose the correct answer.

0 She *got* / *took* a good report from her teachers.
1 They said she had *done* / *made* progress in all subjects.
2 She had *done* / *made* very few mistakes in her tests.
3 She is well-behaved and *pays* / *gives* attention in class.
4 She never *cheats* / *steals* in exams.
5 She always *takes* / *does* notes when the teacher talks.
6 She likes physics and enjoys *doing* / *making* experiments.
7 She hates being disturbed when she is *revising* / *reading* for an exam.
8 She feels a bit nervous when she has to *sit* / *revise* an exam.
9 She wants to *get* / *go* into university.
10 When she *gets* / *takes* her degree, she wants to go abroad.

4 Cross out the wrong answer in each pair. If neither is possible, cross out both.

People in education

(0) A / ~~The~~ professor is not (1) a / the teacher in (2) a / the secondary school, but has (3) a / the highest academic position in (4) a / the university. (5) A / The lecturer is (6) a / the university teacher. Lecturers – and professors – give (7) a / the lectures. Students in Britain usually have (8) a / the tutor who gives them (9) a / the advice and teaches students in small groups. You graduate from university with (10) a / the degree. If you do (11) a / the postgraduate work, you will have (12) a / the supervisor to help and advise you.

5 Match the nouns (1–7) with their definitions (a–h).

0 someone with the highest academic position in a university — e
1 someone in charge of a school
2 someone who is still at university, studying for their first degree
3 someone who has successfully completed their first degree at university
4 someone responsible for courses in a private school
5 someone in the same class as you at school
6 someone who teaches at a college or university
7 someone responsible for teaching a small group of students

a head teacher
b lecturer
c graduate
d undergraduate
e professor
f tutor
g director of studies
h classmate

6 Read the text and choose the correct answer.

A (0) **nursery** / secondary school is for children aged two to five. A (1) primary / secondary school includes infant school and lasts from the age of five to eleven. In Britain, at the age of nine, some children go to (2) middle / comprehensive school before going to (3) primary / secondary school. Bright pupils sometimes go to (4) infant / grammar school after taking an examination but most children go to a mixed ability (5) comprehensive / infant school. A (6) public / state school in England is private and parents pay for their children to attend. A (7) public / state school is free.

7 Number the story in the correct order.

a Her research is in international law.
b When she was at playschool, Maria played and had fun. — 1
c After finishing her BA, she took a year off.
d In her infant school, she began learning how to read and write.
e She got into grammar school and did well in all subjects.
f When she was at junior school, she loved history.
g She got a place at university to do law.
h She graduated with a first-class degree.
i She decided to do postgraduate work.
j In the sixth form, she studied A-levels to get into university.

WORD STORE

The arts

1 Complete the words in the text.

Robert Pattinson is one of the most popular film ⁽⁰⁾ **actors** today, especially with teenagers. He ⁽¹⁾ p………. the part of Edward Cullen, a vampire, in the *Twilight* series. But he began his acting ⁽²⁾ c………. as an amateur, not in films but on the ⁽³⁾ s………. He played various small ⁽⁴⁾ r………. in the theatre, in classic ⁽⁵⁾ p………. such as *Macbeth* and *Our Town*. Pattinson is also a talented ⁽⁶⁾ m………. – he plays the guitar and piano. He also appears as the singer of two songs on the *Twilight* ⁽⁷⁾ s……….

2 Complete the table. Write the words in the box in the correct column. Some words go in more than one column.

act audience auditorium biography brush canvas cast CD chapter character comedy concert costume drama edition encore exhibition first night horror illustration landscape lighting love story magazine matinee microphone musical musician novel opera orchestra performance picture play plot poetry pop premiere programme rehearsal role scene scenery science fiction screen screenplay script sculpture set short story singer soundtrack stage subtitles thriller tragedy trailer volume watercolour western

Literature	Music	Theatre	Cinema	Art
		act		

3 Complete the sentences. Use words from Exercise 2.

0 There was a huge marble **sculpture** of Venus outside the museum.
1 The director got very angry when the actor failed to turn up to the …………..
2 The ………….. for this film was written by a famous novelist.
3 The ………….. applauded at the end of the performance.
4 The whole ………….. performed brilliantly.
5 The first ………….. of a book is often worth more if it is signed by the author.
6 The ………….. of the film includes some great songs.
7 All the performers were dressed in period …………..
8 I went to a rock ………….. on Saturday.
9 According to the ………….., Act 3 starts at 8.30.
10 Children's books appeal to children if they have attractive …………..

272

4 Complete the words in the text. They are all connected with the theatre.

The most difficult role

They say *Hamlet* is the most difficult ⁽⁰⁾ r**o**l**e** for an actor to play and one of the most difficult ⁽¹⁾ p............. to direct. Laurence Olivier gave one of the best ⁽²⁾ p............. of his career as Hamlet. There are always several performances of *Hamlet* being ⁽³⁾ p............. on all over the world at any one time. The irony is that although we know more about Hamlet than almost any other ⁽⁴⁾ c............. in literature, we hardly know anything about the ⁽⁵⁾ a............. of the play, William Shakespeare.

5 List the words and phrases that can be used with each verb below.

Example: put on a play, a performance, …

act in	direct	produce	see
appear in	get	publish	set
broadcast	give	put on	watch
compose	play	review	write

a performance, a difficult part, a show, Hamlet, a review, a horror movie, a play, a film, a symphony, a video, a production, the leading role, a new edition, a new book, the scene, a CD, the story, a piece of music, a recital, a concert

6 Complete the sentences. Use words from Exercise 5.

0 I don't like ..horror.. movies; I prefer comedies.
1 The story is .... in nineteenth-century France.
2 The play got really fantastic .... from the critics.
3 Brad Pitt has already .... in several award-winning films.
4 Who plays the .... of the monster in the film?
5 His Othello was one of the worst .... of his career. It was awful.
6 The play was first .... on television.
7 The film was directed by Spielberg and .... by Paramount Pictures.
8 Who .... the music for the film?
9 Her first novel was .... by Penguin books.
10 Let's stay in and .... a film on TV tonight.

WORD STORE

7 Study the table. Then answer the questions that follow using a phrasal verb or phrase from the list.

Verb/Phrase	Meaning	Example
come up (in the exam)	appear as a question in an exam; be set in the exam	I wonder what's going to **come up** in the exam on Monday.
get in; get into sth	enter a school, university	You have to pass a lot of exams to **get into** university.
get through (sth)	pass (an exam)	I'm afraid you didn't **get through** your exam.
give in sth; give sth in	give homework, an essay, etc. to a teacher	You should **have given** in this work last week.
look up sth; look sth up	try to find information in a book, on a computer, etc.	If you don't know what it means, **look it up** in the dictionary.
pay attention (to sth/sb)	listen to what sb is saying	You should **pay attention** to the teacher in class.
put up your hand	raise your hand	Please **put up your hand** if you want to speak.
send down sb; send sb down	tell sb to leave a college or university because of bad behaviour	She was **sent down** because she cheated in the test.
stay up	go to bed late	I used to **stay up** all night revising for my exams.
take up sth; take sth up	become interested in and start doing a new activity	She's going to **take up** the guitar.

1 What would you do if you wanted to ask your teacher a question without shouting out?
2 What do you do if you have an exam the next day and you need to revise?
3 What would you do if you wanted to learn another foreign language?
4 What would you say to explain what happened to a student who cheated?
5 What do you do in class if you listen carefully to your teacher?
6 What does your teacher say to you when you pass an exam?
7 What would you do if you wanted to find out what *serendipity* means?
8 What would you have to do if you wanted to study to be a doctor?
9 What do you say to tell your friend you hope a question will be set in the exam?
10 What would your teacher say if you were late with an essay?

WORD STORE

Sports

1 Study the word web and complete the sentences. Use one word in each gap.

Word web around SPORT:
- starter referee umpire
- spectator
- fit unfit
- equipment
- game
- sportsman sportswoman athlete competitor opponent
- the Olympics
- event
- hall centre stadium track field pitch
- be fond of be keen on be good at compete in a sport/for your country
- indoor outdoor motor winter summer water athletics

0 He's going to ..**compete**.. in the London marathon.
1 I enjoy watching football but I've never been very good ………… it.
2 At our local sports centre, you can play a wide variety of ………… sports.
3 I'm not too keen ………… sports such as boxing.
4 The ………… you need for skiing, like boots and a ski suit, can be quite expensive.
5 Simon beat his ………… in the second round.
6 Are you fond ………… sports like tennis?
7 Which do you prefer – summer or ………… sports?
8 Is swimming a(n) ………… or indoor sport in your country?
9 Personally, I think the ………… should have awarded a penalty.
10 Athletes have to be extremely ………… if they want to compete successfully.

2 Study the word web and complete the sentences. Use one word in each gap.

Word web around BALL:
- beach ball golf ball football tennis ball
- basketball volleyball football softball
- play for a team/your country beat a team/player/side kick off score a goal/point win a game/set/match/competition/Cup take a shot at goal play a game of
- pitch court field course
- throw touch kick hit shoot bounce pass catch head punch volley lob smash
- bat club racquet stick
- team side
- match game set
- player defender striker goalkeeper

0 How about a(n) ..**game**.. of table tennis?
1 Ronaldo took a shot ………… goal but the goalkeeper caught the ball.
2 A good basketball player must be able to ………… the ball to other players.
3 Brazil ………… Germany 2–1.
4 In table tennis, you must let the ball ………… on the table before you hit it.
5 My brother plays ………… the local team.
6 How many times has Germany ………… the World Cup?
7 If he gets this game, he'll win the set and could win the …………

WORD STORE

3 Complete the table. Write the words in the box in the correct column. Some words go in more than one column.

> athletics basketball bat boots bowls boxing canoeing captain club coach
> course court defender diving field fishing football goalkeeper golf ground
> hockey judge manager motor racing net oar pitch player pool racquet referee
> ring rod skiing skis snooker squash stadium stick striker swimming team
> tennis track trunks umpire volleyball whistle

Places	Sport/Activities	People	Equipment
	athletics		

4 Complete the sentences. Use words from Exercise 3.

0 There are nine players in a baseball ....**team**....
1 In hockey, players hit and control the ball with a(n) ....
2 You can't row without one or two ....
3 The person who selects the players for a game is the ....
4 In table tennis you hit the ball with a round ....
5 The official who makes sure players follow the rules in games like tennis, squash and basketball is the ....
6 London's most famous venue for international matches is Wembley ....
7 When there is a foul during a football match, the referee blows his ....
8 The football player who tries to score goals is called a(n) ....
9 We play squash and tennis on an indoor ....
10 Marathon runners make one circuit of the .... before leaving the stadium.

276

Hobbies

1 Complete the words in the text.

In your own time

Most of us have a(n) ⁽⁰⁾ h.o.b.b.y. that we do in our spare time. Some of us do things like surf the ⁽¹⁾ N............., or make things like model planes. Others play cards or board ⁽²⁾ g............. like backgammon, while others like to ⁽³⁾ c............. things such as stamps and antiques. I ⁽⁴⁾ s............. a lot of my summer holidays snorkelling in the sea. My brother goes away almost every weekend either walking or ⁽⁵⁾ c............. in the mountains. His favourite hobby is taking ⁽⁶⁾ p............. of rare flowers. My aunt, who is eighty, has a magnificent ⁽⁷⁾ c............. of traditional music, and still goes to ⁽⁸⁾ d............. classes. So, there is much more to life than watching television!

2 Write what hobbies/activities the equipment below can be used in.

Equipment	Hobby
wax	making candles, batik printing
camera	
boots	
mountain bike	
tweezers	
hoe	
brush	
rope	
glue	
needle	
palette	

WORD STORE

3 Complete the sentences. Use the correct form of the verbs in the box.

do   go   have   make   take

0 When we were little, we used to ......go..... fishing with my grandad at weekends.
1 She .... excellent photographs of people in markets.
2 Shall we .... mountain climbing this weekend?
3 If you've nothing to do, let's .... a game of cards.
4 You should .... some exercise; come to the gym with me.
5 He .... model planes using matches and thin paper.
6 Jenny has been .... guitar lessons for several years.
7 She .... a lot of sewing in her spare time.
8 Would you describe .... shopping as a hobby?
9 Lola's helping the children .... animals out of cake dough.
10 Chess is a great game to play but it .... too much time.
11 I don't seem to .... enough time for all my hobbies!
12 We're .... swimming later on – do you want to come?

4 Complete the sentences. Use words formed from the words in CAPITALS at the end of the lines.

0	Dave's hobbies include reading and ..photography..	PHOTOGRAPH
1	Funland is an .... park in London.	AMUSE
2	My friends think men who knit are hilariously	FUN
3	Visiting the theme park was a really .... experience.	ENJOY
4	It was .... to lie on the beach doing absolutely nothing.	PLEASE
5	We could hear loud .... coming from the flat downstairs.	LAUGH
6	The .... asked us to smile at the camera.	PHOTOGRAPH
7	He kept the children amused with his .... stories.	HUMOUR
8	Thank you very much for a .... evening.	DELIGHT
9	I don't find jokes about sick people at all	AMUSE
10	So, what are your favourite free-time .... ?	ACT
11	It's so .... to sit by the sea and watch dolphins playing.	PEACE
12	My idea of perfect .... is a shopping trip to Paris.	HAPPY

Travel and tourism

1 Study the tables. Then complete the sentences on page 280.

Accommodation	Journey	Transport
Stay in a/an:		**Travel/Go:**
bed & breakfast (b. & b.) cabin camp cottage guesthouse hotel inn motel self-catering flat youth hostel	a car/bus/train journey crossing drive flight tour trip day trip business trip round trip package holiday voyage scheduled/charter flight	by air/sea/rail by car/taxi/bus/coach by bike/train by boat/ferry/ship by plane by public transport on foot
	ramble trek walk	

People	Places	Objects	Actions
guest holiday-maker sightseer tourist traveller visitor	bus stop bus station train station taxi rank	backpack baggage bags holdall luggage suitcase trolley	plan an itinerary book a holiday/flight/ticket (to) buy a ticket reserve a seat/room
courier guide host(ess) steward(ess) customs officer coach driver porter receptionist ticket officer travel agent	airport arrivals departures departure lounge gate terminal		travel to depart from drive/fly/sail (to) set off set out arrive at/in get in at (time) land at/in check in check out (of)
	harbour port	boarding card cheques credit card foreign currency passport (a return/one-way) ticket traveller's cheques visa	
	abroad overseas		do some/go sightseeing go on an excursion/a trip (to) pay the bill/pay (for) run out of petrol/money miss the bus/train/plane

279

WORD STORE

0 And then we ran out of petrol and had to walk the rest of the way.
1 I usually go to the airport .... train.
2 Our .... was delayed and we spent two hours in the .... at the airport.
3 If we don't hurry, we'll .... the bus and we'll have to go .... foot.
4 Please have your boarding card, ticket and .... ready for inspection.
5 At the hotel, the .... gave us our room numbers and a .... took our bags to our rooms.
6 Next day we paid the .... and .... of the hotel.
7 We boarded the .... to the island but then the .... was rough and everyone was sick.
8 I'd like to .... a package .... to Spain.

2 Complete the words in the text.

When planning a (0) h**oliday**, you must first decide where you are going. Next, you need to decide where you're going to (1) s.............. and how you're going to travel – (2) b.............. plane, car, train or boat. You may need to visit a travel (3) a.............. who will organise your tickets. If you are flying abroad, it's best to (4) b.............. in advance to make sure you get the (5) f.............. you want and a good (6) h.............. Don't forget to arrange to have some foreign (7) c.............. and to have enough (8) t.............. cheques.

3 Complete the second sentence so that it has a similar meaning to the first sentence, using the word given. Use between two and five words. Do not change the word given.

0 I think the excursions were the best thing about language school.
   GOING
   What I liked most about language school was going on excursions.
1 I'd like to see the sights before we find somewhere to stay.
   SIGHTSEEING
   I'd like .... before we find somewhere to stay.
2 If you want a good room, you should book in advance.
   RESERVATION
   If you want a good room, you should .... in advance.
3 I usually go to work by bus but yesterday I went by train.
   TAKE
   I usually .... but yesterday I went by train.
4 Make sure you have enough petrol if you're driving in the mountains.
   RUN
   Make sure you .... of petrol if you're driving in the mountains.
5 You have to pay for and leave your hotel room by noon tomorrow.
   CHECK
   You have to .... your room by noon tomorrow.

Shopping

1 Study the table. Then complete the sentences. Use one word in each gap.

People	Places	Objects	Actions
(regular) customer client	baker's bookshop boutique bureau de change butcher's chemist's	bank card cash cheque book credit card debit card store card	borrow (sth) from sb lend (sth) to/lend sb sth
(shop/sales) assistant manager (member of) staff			afford buy sth can/can't afford sth cut prices
baker butcher chemist fishmonger florist greengrocer jeweller newsagent optician shopkeeper stall holder trader	department store DIY store drycleaner's fishmonger's florist's greengrocer's jeweller's newsagent's off-licence (charity/local/second- hand) shop kiosk (street) market supermarket toyshop	bargain (mail order) catalogue carrier bag designer label goods faulty goods product price rate of exchange receipt sales tax (VAT)	exchange sth (for sth else) get a discount go shopping order sth pay (in) cash/by cheque pay a deposit pay for sth (at a reduced price) take sth back try sth on
		cash desk checkout 'pay here' shop window till	see to sb serve (a customer) gift-wrap sth
	the high street (in) the sales shopping centre shopping mall		

0 If the skirt is too small, you can take it ....**back**.... and get a larger size.
1 I'm sorry but you can't pay .... these with a credit card. Have you got a debit ....?
2 I can't .... to buy a new computer – I'll have to borrow some money .... my parents.
3 Can I .... a discount if I pay in ....?
4 I don't usually .... shopping in the high street; I enjoy finding .... in the market.
5 Excuse me, can I try these trousers .... before I buy them?
6 Is meat cheaper in the .... or from your local ....?
7 Will you .... me some cash so that I can .... for the parking?
8 You'll get the best exchange .... at that .... de change over there.
9 Do you prefer cheap goods or those with a(n) .... label?
10 How much does it cost to have this clock gift-..............?

281

WORD STORE

2 Match the definitions with a word or phrase from the table on page 281.

0 a shop where you can buy flowers and plants ....florist's..........
1 someone who serves customers in a shop ....
2 the main shopping street in a town ....
3 the place where you can buy paint, screws, etc. ....
4 a shop where you can buy medicines ....
5 the bag you get in a supermarket to hold your shopping ....
6 a shop that sells fruit and vegetables ....
7 the place where you can exchange foreign currency ....
8 a large shop on several floors selling a wide variety of goods ....
9 a small building in the street selling newspapers, sweets, etc. ....
10 the place where you pay for things in a supermarket ....

3 Complete the table. Write the words in the box in the correct column.

aspirin   aubergine   banana   bean   boots   bubble bath   carrot   chocolate
cigarettes   comic   courgette   crisps   denim jacket   drill   evening gown   gum
hairbrush   hammer   high heels   jewellery   lawnmower   lettuce   magazine
medicines   melon   mushroom   nail   nappies   newspaper   paint   peach   pencil
perfume   plum   saw   screwdriver   shampoo   shirt   shoes   stamp   stationery
sunglasses   suntan lotion   toilet paper   tool kit   toothpaste   torch   trousers
underwear   wrench

Newsagent's	Chemist's	Boutique	Greengrocer's	DIY store
	aspirin			

4 Complete these phrases with a word from the box.

bar   bottle   box   bunch   can   carton   jar   packet
sachet   tin   tub   tube

0 a ...carton... of milk or orange juice
1 a .... of cola or beer
2 a .... of soap or milk chocolate
3 a .... of yoghurt or margarine
4 a .... of chocolates or tissues
5 a .... of toothpaste or glue
6 a .... of mineral water or wine
7 a .... of beans or paint
8 a .... of biscuits or cigarettes
9 a .... of flowers or grapes
10 a free .... of shampoo or moisturiser
11 a .... of pickles or jam

282

WORD STORE

Food and restaurants

1 Complete the words in the text.

> A vegetarian is someone who eats only (0) v.<u>egetables</u>, bread, fruit, eggs, etc. and doesn't eat (1) m............... However, some do eat (2) f..............., which I find strange. Others eat chicken but not (3) r............... meat. A vegan doesn't eat meat, fish or any (4) d............... products such as eggs, milk and (5) c............... They do eat fruit and (6) n............... A (7) g............... knows a lot about food and enjoys good food and (8) w............... A (9) c............... is someone who prepares and cooks food in a hotel or (10) r...............

2 Complete the table. Write the words in the box in the correct column.

> <s>apple</s> aubergine bacon basil beef cabbage cauliflower chicken chives chop coconut cod coriander courgette cucumber fig grape haddock joint lamb lettuce liver lobster mackerel mango mussel mutton nectarine octopus oregano parsley plaice plum pork prawn rosemary salami salmon sardine satsuma sausage shrimp spinach squid strawberry thyme trout watermelon

Vegetables	Fish	Herbs	Seafood	Fruit	Meat
				apple	

283

WORD STORE

3 Match 1–12 with a–m to make compound nouns.

0 hot — g
1 roast
2 shepherd's
3 chop
4 spring
5 fish and
6 spaghetti
7 lamb
8 fortune
9 toad-in-the-
10 bacon and
11 Yorkshire
12 sweet and

a cookie
b beef
c eggs
d rolls
e chops
f hole
g dog
h pudding
i chips
j sour pork
k pie
l Bolognese
m suey

4 Match the dishes (1–8) with the definitions (a–i).

0 hot dog — f
1 custard
2 moussaka
3 stew
4 paella
5 Christmas pudding
6 apple crumble
7 hummus
8 haggis

a a Spanish dish made with rice, meat, fish and vegetables
b a sweet yellow sauce that is made with milk, sugar, eggs and flour
c a Scottish dish that looks like a large round sausage
d a soft mixture of chickpeas, oil and garlic
e meat and vegetables cooked slowly in liquid
f a cooked sausage served in a long bread roll
g a sweet dish that contains a lot of dried fruit
h a Greek dish made from meat, cheese and aubergines
i a sweet dish of fruit covered with a dry mixture of flour, butter and sugar and baked

5 Choose the correct answer.

0 It's best to *fry* / *grill* an omelette in a deep pan.
1 Potatoes are delicious if you *roast* / *bake* them in their jackets.
2 *Steamed* / *Fried* vegetables are very healthy.
3 *Barbecued* / *Roasted* meat tastes better if you cook it slowly in the oven.
4 Put the trout under the *barbecue* / *grill* for ten minutes.
5 *Melt* / *Boil* the butter and then add in the sugar and milk.
6 Put some oil in the pan and *roast* / *sauté* the onions for five minutes.
7 I love the smell of *baked* / *barbecued* lamb chops from next-door's garden.
8 *Roast* / *Boil* the cabbage for twelve minutes.

WORD STORE

6 Complete the words in the text.

Have you been to 'Bar None'? We went yesterday and it was great. I'm glad we had (0) b.ooked. because the restaurant was full. I asked the (1) w............. to bring us a wine (2) l............. so that we could decide what to drink. For my (3) s............., I chose garlic mushrooms and for my main (4) c............., I ordered a casserole with pork (5) c............., sage and white wine. For (6) d............., I had crème caramel with ice cream. I asked our waiter to bring the (7) b............. and I had to pay cash because they wouldn't take (8) c............. cards. I left the waiter quite a large (9) t............. as I was very pleased with the (10) s..............

7 Choose the odd one out.

0 water cola (bread) wine juice
1 meal food cuisine feast corkscrew
2 wine starter main course appetiser dessert
3 boil fry bake bowl grill
4 slice boil chop grate peel
5 salty savoury pan sweet bitter
6 dish meal bowl plate cup
7 courgette mushroom bean plum broccoli
8 bill tip receipt menu cheque

8 Complete the sentences. Use one word in each gap.

0 She served a wonderful meal ......to...... more than thirty guests.
1 If the goods are faulty, take them .... to the shop.
2 Try to cut down .... cakes if you want to lose weight.
3 We've run .... of sugar; can you get some from the supermarket?
4 Serve the steak .... potatoes and peas.
5 I didn't feel like cooking, so we phoned .... a pizza.
6 She took the pie out of the oven and sprinkled the top .... cheese.
7 If you clear the table, I'll wash ....
8 You can leave the table when you have eaten .... all your food.
9 There's no food in the fridge – let's go .... to your mum's house.
10 I'm taking my girlfriend .... to dinner this evening.

WORD STORE

Weather

1 Study the table. Then choose the correct answer.

Kind	Description		Verbs and expressions	
blizzard	**good**	**bad**	pour (with rain)	bright and sunny
breeze			pour down	cold and damp/misty
cloud	bright	chilly	bucket down	bright and frosty
dew	dry	changeable	be drenched/soaked	fine and dry
downpour	fine	cloudy		hot and sticky/humid
drizzle	hot	cold	a gentle/light/strong	hot and stuffy
fog	mild	damp	breeze	sunny and warm
frost	scorching	dark	a bit chilly	warm and dry
gale	sunny	dull	black/dark/grey clouds	wet and overcast/windy
heat wave	warm	foggy	be bitterly/freezing cold	
hurricane		freezing	a lovely day	
lightning		frosty	thick fog	
mist		grey	strong gales	
rain		humid	be boiling hot	
shower		icy	a light/thin mist	
sleet		misty	heavy/light rain/shower	
slush		overcast	a blue/grey sky	
smog		showery	a thick smog	
snow		stormy	a cold/hot spell	
snowfall		stuffy	a terrible storm/	
snowflakes		unsettled	thunderstorm	
snowstorm		wet	a break in the weather	
sun		windy	good/lovely weather	
sunshine			awful/bad/terrible	
storm			weather	
thunder/			a strong wind	
thunderstorm				
wind				

0 The *breeze /* ⟨*fog*⟩ was so thick we couldn't see further than a metre.
1 Hopefully, it will be *dry / frosty* for the match this afternoon.
2 It will be rather hot and *humid / chilly* tomorrow.
3 It's been such *scorching / unsettled* weather – one day dry and the next wet and cold.
4 It was *pouring / drenching* with rain when we went out.
5 It was a terrible *smog / storm* – our fence was blown down.
6 The weather forecast for Friday is for dry sunny *spells / breezes*.
7 After such a cold night, the grass was covered with *gale / frost*.
8 It was *boiling / bucketing* hot during the day and we could hardly move until evening.
9 It was a beautiful spring morning. A light *gale / breeze* was blowing.
10 You're *drenched / scorched*! Come on in and sit by the fire.

286

WORD STORE

2 Match the definitions with words from the table on page 286. Use one word in each gap.

0 a short period of heavy rain — *downpour*
1 describes weather that often changes — ....
2 describes weather when the air feels hot and wet — ....
3 small drops of water that form on the ground at night — ....
4 dark and cloudy — ....
5 a very strong wind — ....
6 dirty air that looks like a mixture of smoke and fog — ....
7 describes extremely hot weather — ....
8 cloudy air near the ground that is difficult to see through — ....
9 describes very cold weather — ....
10 rain in very small, light drops — ....
11 When it rains heavily, we can say, 'It's .... down.' — ....

3 Complete the words in the text.

The British are well known for always chatting about their weather. This is because the weather in Britain is so **(0)** c*hangeable* – you never know what it will be **(1)** l.............. A popular greeting is '**(2)** L.............. weather for the time of year' or, if the weather is bad, 'Isn't this weather **(3)** a..............?' If it's raining, they might say 'Great weather for ducks!' You will often hear people add '**(4)** w.............. permitting' when they say they plan to play golf, garden or put out the washing. Most postcards from a holiday in Greece or Spain begin: 'It's **(5)** b.............. hot here,' even when local people think it's just a normal **(6)** b.............. and sunny day. There are many expressions in English which show the importance of the weather in people's lives. For example, feeling **(7)** 'u.............. the weather' means feeling slightly ill. If you 'make **(8)** h.............. weather of a job', it means you make it seem more difficult than it really is, and if you 'keep a weather eye on something', you give it your full attention – as the British do with their weather!

Surprisingly warm for this time of year, isn't it?

4 Complete the phrases. Use the words in the box. You can use some of the words more than once. Sometimes more than one answer is possible.

| bitterly | boiling | dark | dry | freezing | heavy | hot | lovely |
| mild | strong | thick |

0 *boiling* hot
1 a .... warm day
2 a .... climate
3 .... cold
4 .... clouds
5 a .... spell
6 .... rain
7 .... wind
8 .... fog
9 .... weather

287

WORD STORE

5 Replace the underlined words with the correct ones.

0 It was a bitterly <u>warm</u> day in the middle of winter. .....cold.....
1 The rain was pouring <u>over</u>, so we had to cancel the picnic. ....
2 Take a coat – it could be a <u>piece</u> chilly later on. ....
3 It was <u>boiling</u> cold this morning and the roads were icy. ....
4 <u>Pretty</u> weather for the time of year, isn't it? ....
5 Driving conditions were bad due to the thick <u>breeze</u>. ....
6 Sailors were warned that <u>great</u> gales were expected during the night. ....
7 The poor woman was struck by <u>thunder</u> and killed. ....
8 Look at those huge dark <u>mists</u>; it looks like it's going to rain. ....
9 It was a <u>freezing</u> hot morning, so we decided to go for a swim. ....
10 'It's snowing!' he said, wiping the <u>snowfall</u> that had landed on his nose. ....

6 Choose the correct answer.

A

Greece enjoys a Mediterranean ⁽⁰⁾ *weather /* (climate) most of the year, with warm to hot days and ⁽¹⁾ *mild / changeable* nights. However, in the middle of summer, it can be ⁽²⁾ *lightly / unbearably* hot and stuffy, and winter can be ⁽³⁾ *chilly / humid*. December and January can be very cold and in February it is often rainy. April can be ⁽⁴⁾ *changeable / smokey*, with sunny days interrupted by windy ⁽⁵⁾ *showery / bucketing* weather.

B

Most of Spain is always warm from April to October, though it can occasionally be cold and ⁽⁶⁾ *rainy / scorching* in the north, especially in the mountains. The south is ⁽⁷⁾ *amazingly / bitterly* mild throughout the year — it hardly has a winter.

C

Britain has a very changeable climate. Although long periods of ⁽⁸⁾ *fine / overcast* weather occur each year, it is not easy to ⁽⁹⁾ *forecast / cast* the weather accurately, while you can get ⁽¹⁰⁾ *soaked / bucketed* during any season! The north of the country is much colder and ⁽¹¹⁾ *bright / windy* in winter, often with quite heavy ⁽¹²⁾ *snowflakes / snowfalls*. The southwest has milder weather.

WORD STORE

7 Match the situations (1-10) with the expressions (a-k). You can use a dictionary to help you.

0 Because bad luck isn't repeated in the same place, I parked where my car had been stolen. ☐ j
1 Don't spend all your money now – you might need some later. ☐
2 No one trusted her after she was caught stealing from the toyshop. ☐
3 I'm not feeling too good today. I think I'll stay in bed and rest. ☐
4 I think a lot of fuss is being made over something very unimportant. ☐
5 The report was far too detailed – we needed only the basic information. ☐
6 I never receive complaints but now I have had ten in a row! ☐
7 He's out playing tennis whatever the weather. ☐
8 I can't think clearly about what happened just before the accident. ☐
9 This good luck is too good to last – something is bound to go wrong. ☐
10 When I was in hospital, I lost a lot of weight – something good came out of it! ☐

a Every cloud has a silver lining.
b the calm before the storm
c be under a cloud
d it never rains but it pours
e be in a fog
f come rain come shine
g make heavy weather of something
h save something for a rainy day
i be a storm in a teacup
j Lightning never strikes twice.
k feel under the weather

Our environment and the natural world

1 Look at this picture. Write down the words for the parts numbered 1-10.

0 t<u>rees</u>
1 c.
2 s.
3 b.
4 h.
5 l.
6 w.
7 w.
8 r.
9 m.
10 r.

289

WORD STORE

2 Write pairs of words. Use one word from A and one word from B for each pair. Then say which is the bigger of the two.

| A | beach bush gulf mountain pond river road rock sea town wood |
| B | bay city coast forest hill lake lane ocean pebble stream tree |

0 beach – coast .... coast ....
1 ....
2 ....
3 ....
4 ....
5 ....
6 ....
7 ....
8 ....
9 ....
10 ....

3 Match the definitions with words from Exercise 2.

0 water that moves across the land and is narrower than a river — stream
1 a large area of water surrounded by land
2 a small area with trees
3 a large mass of salt water between continents
4 a length of sand and small stones at the edge of the sea
5 a particular part of the land that is higher
6 a narrow route through the countryside for animals and people on foot
7 a large area of an ocean where the coast is curved
8 a wide stretch of land covered with trees
9 a tall plant with long branches and a trunk
10 a small area of water, for example in a garden
11 a small smooth stone on a beach
12 a large area with homes, shops and streets
13 a low plant with many branches
14 the edge of land where it joins sea water
15 a part of the land that is much higher than the land around it
16 an area of salt water near land
17 a prepared route through the countryside or towns for vehicles
18 an area of the sea inside a curved part of the coast
19 a place with many streets, offices, factories, shops and homes
20 a large piece of stone

4 Complete the text. Use the words in the box.

> atmosphere   coal   energy   environmental   exhaust   fuel
> greenhouse   recycling   resources   waves   weather

Save it!

In recent years, the number of (0) *environmental* problems has increased dangerously. One of the most serious problems is changes to the (1) ...., which has led to the (2) '.............. effect'; this is making most climates warmer. It is already affecting several areas of the world with unusual (3) ...., causing droughts or heavy storms. Cutting down on (4) .... fumes from vehicles would help solve the problem. Natural (5) .... such as oil and (6) .... are not endless, so using other forms of (7) .... such as wind, sun, water and even sea (8) .... would help preserve our planet. Very soon we will be able to drive cars in cities and towns that run on electricity – a much cleaner (9) .... than petrol. And we can also help to conserve finite resources by (10) .... things made of glass, aluminium, plastic and paper.

5 Complete the sentences. Use words formed from the words in CAPITALS at the end of the lines.

0 The article talks about *renewable* sources of energy such as solar power. **RENEW**
1 What can we do to reduce the .... of the atmosphere? **POLLUTE**
2 The change in the climate has produced .... floods. **DISASTER**
3 Many rare species are threatened with .... **EXTINCT**
4 Many of the gases produced by factories are .... to our health. **HARM**
5 Exhaust fumes have .... effects on the environment. **DAMAGE**
6 Many countries must try and control the growth of the .... **POPULATE**
7 Protecting the environment is essential to our .... **SURVIVE**
8 The .... of the environment is everyone's responsibility. **PROTECT**
9 While some countries get richer, the .... in others gets worse. **POOR**
10 Millions of people in the world are threatened with .... **STARVE**

6 Complete the phrases. Use the words in the box. You can use some of the words more than once. Sometimes more than one answer is possible.

> changes   disaster   effect   energy   fuels   fumes   gases   jams   layer
> pollution   rain   rain forest   resources   transport   warming   waste products

0 environmental *effect, changes, disaster, pollution, resources*
1 acid ....
2 tropical ....
3 exhaust ....
4 global ....
5 ozone ....
6 nuclear ....
7 public ....
8 traffic ....
9 natural ....
10 air ....
11 sea ....
12 solar ....
13 finite ....
14 greenhouse ....
15 clean ....
16 recycled ....
17 noise ....
18 renewable ....

291

WORD STORE

7 Complete the second sentence so that it has a similar meaning to the first sentence, using the word given to make a phrasal verb.

0 Never leave the tap running when you're not using it.
TURN
Always *turn off the tap* when you're not using it.

1 We can't be sure the weather is going to be sunny on Saturday.
COUNT
We can't .... being sunny on Saturday.

2 They should ban nuclear energy completely.
AWAY
They should .... nuclear energy completely.

3 If cloudy weather depresses you, go and live in Spain.
DOWN
If cloudy weather ...., go and live in Spain.

4 We may not have any water left in a few years.
RUN
We may .... water in a few years.

5 We must stop the Council from demolishing that old building.
PULL
We mustn't let the Council .... that old building.

6 Our cities would be cleaner if cars used electricity instead of petrol.
RAN
Our cities would be cleaner if cars .... electricity instead of petrol.

7 There are dozens of things you can do to reduce the energy you waste.
CUT
There are dozens of things you can do to .... the energy you waste.

8 The committee have suggested a plan for reducing greenhouse emissions.
FORWARD
The committee have .... a plan for reducing greenhouse emissions.

The media

1 Complete the text.

Media revolution

It is clear that the digital revolution is not just another addition to our technical repertoire, like the old (0) *cassette* recorder, the video or CD (1) p............. Digital technology is a completely new way of interacting with other users. Computers have become an essential part of our work and leisure. Mobile (2) p............. mean people can contact us wherever we are, at any time of the day or night. In schools, the (3) i............. whiteboard makes lessons more exciting. Letters have nearly become extinct and have been replaced by (4) e............. Journalists still write for newspapers and (5) m............. but now they also have their own (6) b............. on the Net, where they can express their opinions. Most teenagers now have their own personal (7) c............. and spend hours every day sitting in front of a (8) s............., adding things on their Facebook page or sending short Tweet messages to friends.

WORD STORE

2 Match the definitions with the words in the box.

> article   celebrity   circulation   commercial   correspondent
> documentary   editor   headline   journalist   periodical   press

0 a piece of writing about a particular subject in a newspaper or magazine ... *article*
1 a reporter whose job it is to report news from a particular area ....
2 the number of copies a newspaper or magazine sells each day, week, month, etc. ....
3 an advertisement on television or radio ....
4 a film that gives facts and information about a subject ....
5 a famous person ....
6 a magazine, especially one about a technical subject ....
7 someone who writes news reports for a newspaper or magazine ....
8 the title of a newspaper report, printed in large letters ....
9 newspapers and magazines, and the people who work for them ....
10 the person who decides what goes in a newspaper or magazine ....

3 Match the definitions with the words in the box.

> CD-ROM   hard disk   key   keyboard   laptop   modem
> mouse   mouse mat   scanner   screen   speakers

0 a machine that can copy pictures or printed documents so that they can be stored on a computer ... *scanner*
1 a small object that you move with your hand to operate a computer ....
2 the flat part of a computer on which you see pictures or information ....
3 a board with buttons which you press to put information into a computer ....
4 a flat object inside a computer that is used for storing information ....
5 the parts of a computer where the sound comes out ....
6 the flat piece of rubber or plastic which you move a mouse on ....
7 a round disk on which large quantities of information can be stored ....
8 a type of small computer you can carry with you ....
9 a button with a letter or symbol which you press to operate a computer ....
10 equipment which allows information to be sent from one computer to another using a telephone line ....

WORD STORE

4 Choose a word from A and a word from B to make compound nouns. Make as many pairs as possible.

Example: action replay.

A
action cable celebrity
chat children's
commercial current
digital educational game
light live nature news
press radio soap sports
television video

B
affairs break broadcast
channel commentator
conference entertainment
guest listener opera
programme recorder
replay report show
station television viewer

5 Choose a word from A and a word from B to make compound nouns. Make as many pairs as possible.

Example: answering machine.

A
answering
cordless email fax
long mobile
phone play
wrong

B
address
back book
distance machine
message number
phone

6 Complete the sentences with words from Exercises 4 and 5.

0 The first episode of that soap …opera… aired in 2009.
1 It must have cost you a lot to make that long-………… phone call to Australia.
2 He's not at home but we can call him on his ………… phone.
3 I want to send a message to Hanneke in Leiden. Do you have her email …………?
4 The Prime Minister will hold a news ………… in the morning.
5 I tried to phone the school but a policeman answered – it was the ………… number.
6 He won the money on a popular ………… show on television.
7 I phoned Jane but she was out, so I left a message on her ………… machine.
8 She's a famous TV chat ………… host.
9 *Good Morning Scotland* is my favourite radio ………… .
10 They showed an action ………… of the first goal.

294

7 Read the text and choose the correct answer, A, B, C or D.

The medium is the message

One of the two greatest inventions of the last millennium was the printing (0).......... in the 15th century. This changed the way people obtained (1).......... but also they way they saw the world. There is a difference in how we see things in (2).......... and, for example, on an electronic (3).......... . Watching TV has a hypnotic effect that goes beyond what (4).......... happens to be on. And today there are so many TV (5).......... to choose from that TV can be really addictive, just as (6).......... the Internet can be.

This brings us to the second greatest invention of the millennium: the computer. Marshall McLuhan said that the new (7).......... change us and the world. We see this principle at work in every kind of (8).......... When films started to talk, we started to talk like them. When computers started to link up on the Internet, we too started connecting and interacting (9).......... people all around the world, through social (10).......... sites and groups of 'friends' – or strangers.

0	A machine	B (press)	C computer	D paper
1	A details	B information	C dates	D content
2	A print	B press	C printer	D printed
3	A wall	B scene	C film	D screen
4	A station	B programme	C sight	D view
5	A channels	B canals	C sites	D presenters
6	A moving	B choosing	C surfing	D viewing
7	A media	B mediums	C messages	D modems
8	A technology	B technique	C equipment	D tool
9	A to	B with	C at	D in
10	A building	B connecting	C networking	D corresponding

WORD STORE

8 Complete the sentences. Use the correct form of the phrasal verbs in the box.

> back up   bring out   call back   get through   hang up   key in
> put down   shut down   ~~skim through~~   switch off   switch over

0 I've only managed to **skim through** the first few chapters.
1 If you don't recognise the caller's voice and you are worried, …………… .
2 You must …………… your password to enter the site.
3 It's boring – let's …………… to another channel.
4 Always …………… your work or you may lose it.
5 Don't forget to …………… the light before you come to bed.
6 They've just …………… her novel in paperback.
7 I tried many times but I couldn't …………… Her line is busy.
8 The book was much too exciting to ……………, so I missed lunch.
9 Jim phoned while you were in the shower. I told him you'd …………… later.
10 Remember to save all your work before you …………… the computer.

Science and technology

1 Complete the table.

Verb	Noun	Person
(0) **invent**	invention	(1) ……………
produce	(2) …………… / production	producer
observe	(3) ……………	observer
design	design	(4) ……………
develop	(5) ……………	developer
discover	(6) ……………	discoverer
explore	(7) ……………	explorer
research	research	(8) ……………
program	program	(9) ……………
(10) ……………	engine	engineer
build	(11) ……………	builder
conserve	(12) ……………	(13) ……………
create	(14) ……………	(15) ……………
specialise	specialisation	(16) ……………
supervise	(17) ……………	(18) ……………
(19) ……………	instruction	instructor
sponsor	sponsorship	(20) ……………

2 Complete the sentences. Use words from Exercise 1.

0 They're going to ...design... a new computer program that will help with the task.
1 The same civil .... who built the roads is now building the new bridge.
2 They called in a(n) .... to knock down the wall between the two rooms.
3 Scientists have been carrying out .... to find a cure for the disease.
4 The company which .... the drug has had to pay a lot of money to the victims.
5 The .... of space began with the launch of the Soviet satellite 'Sputnik 1'.
6 Penicillin was one of the most important .... of the twentieth century.
7 Walt Disney, the .... of Mickey Mouse, died a very rich man.
8 You'll need to go to university if you want to become a computer ....
9 A property .... buys land and builds offices or homes on it.
10 The theory is based on a detailed .... of many patients.
11 Mark is a web .... He can help us with our new business website.
12 Money is not an issue, as the project is being .... by various companies, as well as the government.
13 The computer has been .... to identify geometric shapes and forms.

3 What do we call someone who works in the following areas?

0	building	..builder..	8	managing	....	16	medicine	....
1	plumbing	....	9	selling	....	17	surgery	....
2	electricity	....	10	photography	....	18	science	....
3	carpentry	....	11	psychology	....	19	biology	....
4	decorating	....	12	manufacturing	....	20	chemistry	....
5	architecture	....	13	research	....	21	physics	....
6	hairdressing	....	14	archaeology	....	22	history	....
7	teaching	....	15	astronomy	....	23	law	....

4 Who helps with the following problems?

0 They're accusing me of theft! ...lawyer...
1 I wish that tap would stop dripping! ....
2 I feel depressed – no one likes me. ....
3 Don't you think a few private lessons would help him to pass? ....
4 I need extra sockets in the living room. ....
5 The paint is peeling off all the windows outside. ....
6 Your hair looks a mess. It's far too long. ....
7 I feel awful and I have a rash on my chest. ....
8 We'll need help with the design to get best use of the light. ....
9 We've found a coin in the garden and it looks very old. ....
10 I'm going into hospital to have the lump removed. ....

WORD STORE

5 Complete the sentences. Use the correct form of the verbs in the box.
You can use some verbs more than once.

> design   develop   discover   invent   pioneer   study

0 The physicians Marie Curie and her husband Pierre *discovered* the element radium and won the Nobel Prize for physics.
1 After years of ...., Freud .... a theory of the mind which has changed for ever the way we view ourselves.
2 Brunel .... the Clifton Suspension Bridge.
3 Marco Polo made journeys through Asia and wrote a book describing what he had ....
4 I wonder who .... the very first computer?
5 Einstein .... the theory of relativity which replaced Newton's theories of gravity.
6 Frank Lloyd Wright .... the Imperial Hotel in Tokyo and the Guggenheim Museum in New York.
7 Florence Nightingale .... effective nursing care and improvements in public health.
8 In 1930 Clyde Tombaugh .... Pluto after many years .... the night sky.

Health

1 Complete the words in the text.

A picture of health

People nowadays are more health-conscious than they used to be. We jog to keep (0) f*it* or take other forms of regular (1) e............ . Thousands of us go to a (2) g............ on a regular basis. Many more (3) d............ to lose weight. Fortunately, (4) s............ has been banned on most flights and in most public places because everyone agrees it does (5) h............ to our health. However, there are killer (6) d............ like AIDS and cancer which still seem to be incurable. And malaria is the biggest cause of (7) d............ in the Third World. Heart (8) a............ remain the most common cause of death in Europe. The importance of health is reflected in everyday expressions such as 'to drink to someone's health' or saying 'Your good health!' as we drink a glass of wine.

WORD STORE

2 Study the table. Then match the definitions with the words from the table.

Nouns		Verbs/Phrases	Adjectives	
ache bruise disease fever illness injury lump mental illness nausea nervous breakdown pain rash stomach bug spots temperature wound	bandage check-up cure (medical) examination medicine ointment operation pill plaster prescription recovery surgery symptom treatment X-ray	be (critically/seriously) ill be under the weather break sth catch sth die (from sth) get better go/come down with sth have (a disease) infect sb recover (from a disease/operation) sprain sth suffer (from sth) vomit	bruised cut depressed fine fit frail healthy hot hurt ill injured insane nauseous sick sane strong unfit unhealthy unwell weak well wounded	curable fatal harmful incurable infectious inoperable minor numb painful poisonous slight sore swollen terminal
backache earache headache stomachache toothache	clinic hospital operating theatre out-patients surgery ward	be bad/good for you be in agony be in good shape be in a bad way be in poor health be out of condition have something wrong with you		
	epidemic outbreak	bandage sth cure sb ease the pain examine sb inject (sb with) sth nurse sb operate (on sb) prescribe sth plaster sth treat sb (for sth) vaccinate sb (against sth) X-ray sb/a part of your body		

0 permanently and seriously mentally ill   *insane*
1 to use a needle to put medicine into someone's body   ....
2 a soft substance you rub on your skin as a treatment   ....
3 a large room in a hospital where people who need medical treatment stay   ....
4 a pain in your head   ....
5 a doctor writes on it what medicine a sick person needs   ....
6 many cases of an infectious disease occurring at the same time   ....
7 that causes a person to die   ....
8 an illness of the mind   ....
9 to make someone who is ill well again   ....
10 thin and weak because you are old or very ill   ....

WORD STORE

3 Complete the sentences. Use the words in the box. You can use the table on page 299 to help you. You can use some of the words more than once.

> against   for   from   in   on   out   with

0 She's been suffering ...**from**... headaches since the accident.
1 Children should be vaccinated .... measles and rubella.
2 Paul won't be in work today – he's gone down .... flu.
3 Pollution in cities is causing more and more children to be treated .... asthma.
4 You're so .... of condition! Don't you think swimming every morning will help?
5 Too many people die .... lung cancer due to smoking.
6 If you have a fever, there is definitely something wrong .... you.
7 I spent the weekend in a health farm and feel .... really good shape now.
8 She's still recovering .... the stomach bug she picked up on holiday.
9 It's best that we operate .... you and remove the lump.
10 I've injected your mother .... a painkiller so that she can sleep.

4 Complete the sentences. Use the words in the box.

> aching   die   fainted   had   hurt   lie down   painless   suffered   symptoms

0 I'm feeling ill – I think I'd better go and ..**lie down**..
1 I felt so dizzy that I nearly ....
2 I had to have an internal examination but it was quite ....
3 They gave me an injection and it really ....
4 The .... are a high temperature and a rash.
5 He .... a heart attack and had to be rushed to hospital.
6 The doctor prescribed some drops for my earache but it's still ....
7 He .... from an incurable illness for many years.
8 I hope I .... in my bed of old age.

5 Finish the sentences. Use as many words and phrases from the box as possible.

> a broken wrist   a cold   a consultant   a headache   a sore throat   a surgeon   a virus
> an arm   an aspirin   an earache   an infection   an injection   an operation   cancer
> depressed   dizzy   fatal   fit   flu   her temperature   her to hospital   his tooth out
> hot   ill   in agony   in great pain   in plaster   incurable   inoperable   into hospital
> jogging   measles   mumps   nauseous   numb   painful   sick   some rest   sore
> stitches   this medicine   your ankle   your blood pressure   your doctor   your wrist

0 I feel ..**ill/fit**..
1 I feel …
2 You must have …
3 I've got …
4 Be careful you don't catch …
5 You need to see …
6 I'm afraid it's …
7 He'll take …
8 You've sprained …
9 She's …
10 It feels …

300

6 Match 1–10 with a–k to make sentences.

0 They're going to operate — e
1 If you've got a bad headache,
2 You have a heart problem and
3 He sprained his ankle and
4 She went out in the pouring rain and caught
5 She's not at work because she's gone down
6 He works out in the gym because
7 She went on a diet and
8 He had spots all over his face because
9 After aerobics last week
10 Not all cancers are

a with flu.
b incurable.
c lost weight.
d was in great pain for days.
e on his knee.
f need an operation.
g he had measles.
h a cold.
i he wants to feel fit.
j take an aspirin.
k my feet felt really sore.

7 Complete the parts of the body.

0 thumb (you have one on each hand)
1 l............. (two parts of your mouth)
2 e............. (you hear with these)
3 g............. (your teeth grow in them)
4 e............. (the middle part of your arm)
5 s............. (the bottom surface of your foot)
6 h............. (the curved back part of your foot)
7 k............. (the joint in the middle of your leg)
8 c............. (the part below your mouth)
9 s............. (the part below your chest)
10 n............. (it joins your head to your shoulders)
11 w............. (you put your watch round it)
12 c............. (the soft round part of your face below each of your eyes)
13 e............. (the piece of skin that covers your eye when it's closed)
14 n............. (the holes at the end of your nose)
15 s............. (the front part of your lower leg)
16 f............. (the part of your face above your eyes)
17 t............. (the front part of your neck)

WORD STORE

8 Complete the second sentence so that it has a similar meaning to the first sentence, using the word given. Use between two and five words. Do not change the word given.

0 I had to have a tooth extracted last week.
   OUT
   I had my *tooth taken out* last week.

1 Has he recovered from his illness yet?
   OVER
   Has he .... his illness yet?

2 She took care of him while he was ill.
   AFTER
   She .... while he was ill.

3 I've gained a lot of weight since Christmas.
   ON
   I've .... a lot of weight since Christmas.

4 The effect of the drug will stop soon.
   OFF
   The effect of the drug .... soon.

5 He fainted but regained consciousness after a few minutes.
   ROUND
   He fainted but .... after a few minutes.

6 She caught flu and had to have time off work.
   DOWN
   She .... flu and had to have time off work.

7 She had a lovely baby girl in March.
   BIRTH
   She .... a lovely baby girl in March.

8 Michelle often has terrible headaches.
   FROM
   Michelle often .... terrible headaches.

Crime

1 Complete the words in the text.

It's a crime

Thieves have been around for centuries, probably for as long as humans, but armed (0) *robbery* is a more recent phenomenon. Unfortunately, women have always been the (1) v.............. of rape and domestic (2) v.............. . (3) F.............. has been around ever since printing has been used to make money or produce documents. Rich people or their children are sometimes (4) k.............. and are not set free until a ransom has been paid. The twentieth century saw the appearance of organised (5) c.............. – hijacking, drug-smuggling or drug-trafficking, for example. Statistics show an alarming (6) r.............. in the rate of violent crimes and crimes to do with the (7) i.............. sale of arms across the world. Perhaps the most recent crime of all is (8) h.............. into computers to access information that helps competitors in industry. This increase in international crime makes one wonder whether it is still true to say 'Crime doesn't pay'.

WORD STORE

2 Complete the table.

Verb (phrase)	Noun	Person
(0) accuse	(1)	accused
start a fire deliberately	arson	(2) ....
blackmail	(3)	blackmailer
burgle	(4)	burglar
commit a crime	crime	(5) ....
hack into a computer	hacking	(6) ....
hijack	(7)	hijacker
imprison	prison/imprisonment	(8) ....
kidnap	kidnapping	(9) ....
kill	(10)	killer
mug	(11)	mugger
commit an offence	offence	(12) ....
pickpockets	(13)	pickpocket
rob	(14)	(15) ....
shoplift	(16)	shoplifter
stalk	stalking	(17) ....
steal	(18)	thief
(19)	suspicion	(20) ....

3 Which crimes are being described in the following situations?
Use words from the box.

> blackmail   ~~burglary~~   domestic violence   fraud   hijacking   kidnapping   looting
> mugging   murder   robbery   shoplifting   theft   vandalism

0 People broke into our house and stole our video camera.   burglary
1 Youths attacked her in the street and ran off with her handbag.   ....
2 The pilot was forced to take the plane to Tashkent.   ....
3 She killed him by poisoning his coffee.   ....
4 Why do middle-class women steal food from supermarkets?   ....
5 Having made no profit that year, he set fire to his own factory.   ....
6 Crowds of protestors broke shop windows and stole goods.   ....
7 He threatened to tell the newspapers unless he got a thousand pounds.   ....
8 Someone has stolen my purse from my desk.   ....
9 The clerk handed over the money when they threatened to shoot him.   ....
10 They were accused of deliberately smashing the phone box.   ....
11 The boy would be harmed unless his parents paid the money.   ....
12 The woman was often seen with bruises on her face.   ....

303

WORD STORE

4 Complete the sentences. Use the correct form of the verbs and phrases in the box.

> accuse   appear   break   call in   commit   confess   deny   face   look into
> pay a fine   plead   put   return a verdict   ~~sentence~~   serve   take up

0 The accused was found guilty and **sentenced** to five years in prison.
1 I'm .... in court tomorrow and the prosecution will be opposing bail.
2 The owners were .... of setting fire to their own premises.
3 He was made to .... of 200 euros for parking in the wrong place.
4 She was arrested and .... on trial for murdering her husband.
5 The best lawyer in the country .... her case and won.
6 Police are still .... the disappearance of the two children.
7 The FBI has been .... to investigate the crime.
8 You will be .... a number of serious charges when you go before the judge.
9 You have .... a minor offence, so I will be lenient with my sentence.
10 The jury .... of not guilty.
11 If you .... guilty, the judge will probably reduce the sentence.
12 The man .... to the murder and was arrested.
13 Jones was found guilty. He is going to .... a twenty-five-month sentence for theft.
14 Of course he deserves to be punished – he .... the law, didn't he?
15 She .... all charges and insisted on her innocence.

5 Complete the text. Use words formed from the words in CAPITALS at the end of some of the lines.

An innocent man

Last night, Joe Bloggs was arrested on (0) **suspicion** of robbery. The   SUSPECT
police had no (1) .... that he had committed the crime and Joe   PROVE
denied the (2) .... saying he had a good alibi. When he was   CHARGE
put on (3) ...., the police called several witnesses to the stand   TRY
but Joe's lawyer, Simon Richards, defended his client well and tried
to prove that Joe had not done anything (4) .... However,   LEGAL
the jury found Joe (5) .... and he was sentenced to six months   GUILT
in prison. Joe was not a (6) .... He had never committed a   CRIME
crime before and this was a very heavy (7) .... Most people   PUNISH
were convinced of Joe's (8) .... and Richards appealed against   INNOCENT
the verdict.

304

Answer key

Unit 1

Entry test
1 am staying   2 flows   3 is becoming
4 are thinking   5 depends
6 originated   7 has already won
8 discussed   9 have been trying
10 haven't found
11 C   12 B   13 D   14 D   15 B
16 B   17 A   18 A   19 C   20 B
21 D   22 C   23 A   24 B   25 C

Practice 1a   p. 15

1
1 'm sleeping   2 'm only working
3 aren't listening   4 talks   5 see, goes out, meets   6 make   7 feel
8 appears   9 're just hearing
10 do you think

2
1 is waiting   2 don't travel   3 am considering   4 ends   5 feel/am feeling
6 are having   7 Do you see   8 are relying on   9 wish   10 do you think

3
1 never use, am driving   2 get, never seem   3 prefers, always argues
4 always forgets, starts   5 are always moaning, never help   6 is always criticising, doesn't have   7 goes out, always depends   8 never shop, are always   9 always smell, pass   10 is always borrowing, never pays

4
1 am staying   2 costs   3 am having
4 looks   5 depends   6 love
7 make   8 tastes   9 is going
10 Are you still studying

5
1 This week, the government is holding a conference on nuclear energy.
2 Water consists of hydrogen and oxygen.
3 Things are getting more and more expensive all the time. It really makes me angry!
4 I've got nowhere to live, so I'm staying with a friend for now.
5 Does this car belong to you, sir?
6 You are always moaning! Stop it!
7 In the novel, the story takes place in Florence.

Practice 1b   p. 19

1
1 discovered   2 wrote   3 read
4 wanted   5 started   6 have been
7 have seen   8 has become   9 allowed
10 has done   11 has polluted   12 made

2
1 originally studied, graduated   2 have now completed   3 have been trying
4 have worked   5 was   6 have applied
7 have not managed   8 applied
9 started, have not obtained   10 have not applied   11 hoped   12 have been waiting, have not received

3
1 has made   2 has had   3 has done
4 has brought   5 have been writing
6 had to   7 got   8 took   9 have sent
10 received   11 has been teaching
12 have been sitting   13 haven't finished

Practice 1c   p. 21

1
1 had been climbing, reached
2 reached, had beaten   3 was flying, made   4 discovered, had believed
5 made, was sitting

2
1 had been raining   2 had spent
3 was having   4 had been trying
5 was snowing, had been snowing, had covered   6 were running, were screaming, had knocked, had drawn
7 had set off, was waiting, had been waiting   8 had broken into, had dropped, were climbing

3
1 had achieved   2 had already designed
3 had made   4 was studying   5 had been using   6 had taken   7 had flooded
8 had been asking   9 was working
10 had planned

Practice 1d   p. 24

1
1 for   2 During   3 During   4 While
5 during   6 For   7 Since   8 before
9 already   10 still   11 yet   12 ago

2
1 since   2 from   3 until   4 already
5 before   6 for   7 still   8 During
9 yet   10 while   11 since   12 since
13 ago   14 already   15 during

3
1 ago   2 during   3 before   4 for
5 from   6 already   7 yet   8 still
9 yet   10 ago

4
1 The design of the building is similar to others that have already been built/ been built already.
2 I'm sorry, your dry cleaning isn't ready yet.
3 Lucy asked me to email the office in Vienna but I've already done it/done it already.
4 Do you still need my help?
5 I still haven't told Sam about the accident.
6 It's still raining, so there's no point in going to the beach yet.
7 Has your uncle arrived yet?
8 I've already waited a whole hour/ waited a whole hour already and he hasn't come yet.

Practice 1e   p. 27

1
1 photographer   2 guitarist
3 dishwasher   4 ability   5 friendship
6 exploration   7 arrangement   8 actor
9 building   10 importance
11 childhood   12 excitement
13 happiness   14 trainee   15 division
16 performance   17 tin opener
18 refugee   19 kindness   20 greatness

2
1 employment   2 Equality
3 politicians   4 occupations
5 employers   6 qualifications
7 treatment   8 promotion
9 achievements   10 improvement

Unit 2

Entry test
1 'll   2 miss   3 'll   4 Shall I go
5 're going to   6 C   7 D   8 D   9 A
10 C   11 B   12 C   13 B   14 C   15 D
16 A   17 C   18 C   19 D   20 B
21 over   22 im   23 un   24 dis
25 under

305

ANSWER KEY

Practice 2a — p. 31

1
1 f 2 g 3 h 4 a 5 b 6 i 7 d
8 e 9 o 10 l 11 j 12 k 13 c
14 m

2
1 Shall 2 'll be 3 will 4 Shall we
5 'm seeing 6 'll be 7 shall I
8 won't 9 will 10 Will 11 won't
forget 12 won't be

Practice 2b — p. 33

1
1 is going to crash 2 am not coming/
am not going to come 3 will make
4 starts 5 will mind 6 are going
to cry 7 closes 8 will go 9 leaves
10 are having/are going to have

2
1 Shall 2 be 3 going 4 will 5 Is
6 will

3
1 will help 2 will be 3 is going to be
4 will come 5 isn't going to be 6 will
need 7 will test 8 will definitely regret
9 will bring 10 will be

Practice 2c — p. 35

1
1 a will be, b will have been 2 a was
going to finish, b will finish 3 a will be
sunbathing, b will sunbathe 4 a will be
sleeping, b will have slept 5 a were
flying, b will be flying 6 a will be
driving, b will drive

2
1 will be 2 will be working 3 will
have completed 4 will be 5 will have
finished 6 will have spent 7 will be
jumping 8 Will you be going 9 will
have arrived 10 will see

Practice 2d — p. 37

1
1 get on 2 set off 3 fall behind
4 kept, up 5 get back 6 take up
7 give up 8 hold on 9 carries on
10 grow up

2
1 was brought up 2 carry on
3 fallen behind with 4 going to get
5 stayed up 6 have put off
7 was held up 8 called off

Practice 2e — p. 38

1
1 independent 2 impolite 3 undo
4 co-driver 5 disapprove 6 misbehave
7 illogical 8 unzip 9 misinform
10 disagree 11 overeat 12 prehistoric
13 transatlantic 14 postgraduate
15 immoral 16 mishear
17 misinterpret 18 international
19 oversleep 20 irrelevant
21 disbelieve 22 overcrowded
23 misunderstand 24 prenatal/postnatal
25 illegal

2
Across: 1 IL 2 TRANS 5 UNDER
7 PRO 8 IN 10 OVER 11 ANTI
13 MIS
Down: 1 INTER 3 SUPER 4 CO
5 UN 6 DIS 8 IR 9 POST 12 IM

3
1 unsuccessful 2 mistook
3 impossible 4 misunderstood
5 dislike 6 disappeared
7 unfortunately 8 overcharged
9 misread 10 international

Exam practice 1

Part 1
1 C 2 A 3 B 4 A 5 D 6 B 7 A
8 D 9 A 10 C 11 B 12 B

Part 2
13 since 14 were 15 is 16 have
17 yet 18 will 19 going 20 is
21 are 22 do 23 is 24 be

Part 3
25 visitors 26 invention 27 friendship
28 hackers 29 weaknesses
30 information 31 users
32 excitement 33 Teachers
34 education

Part 4
35 haven't seen Helen since
36 to call off 37 while I was watching
38 had never seen 39 since he was
40 is working as 41 have been
cooking for 42 have you known

Unit 3

Entry test
1 had to 2 should 3 will 4 needn't
5 couldn't
6 D 7 B 8 C 9 A 10 B
11 D 12 C 13 D 14 C 15 C
16 D 17 C 18 C 19 D 20 B
21 B 22 C 23 D 24 B 25 A

Practice 3a — p. 48

1
1 had to 2 don't have to 3 have got
4 have to 5 don't need to 6 weren't
allowed to 7 needn't 8 didn't need
9 could 10 Did you have to

2
1 wasn't able to 2 she could run
3 was able to get 4 didn't have to
5 weren't allowed to stay 6 needn't
have taken 7 had to wear 8 have
(got) to find

Practice 3b — p. 51

1
1 can't 2 may 3 will 4 must
5 can't 6 might 7 may 8 could
9 should 10 could

2
1 d 2 c 3 b 4 h 5 a 6 g 7 f
8 e 9 h 10 b

3
1 That'll 2 must 3 could 4 should
5 can't 6 must 7 could 8 Would

Practice 3c — p. 53

1
1 because 2 Since 3 Because
4 in order not to 5 due to 6 as a
result of 7 in order to 8 so that
9 so 10 so that

2
1 in order to 2 so 3 As a result
4 Owing 5 Since 6 because of
7 so as 8 so as not 9 so 10 thanks

3
1 to 2 because 3 due 4 To
5 As/Since/Because 6 so 7 order
8 so 9 because 10 as 11 result
12 to

Practice 3d — p. 57

1
1 have any experience 2 take part
3 bring, to an end 4 Take a seat
5 have a shower 6 take place
7 have fun 8 have lunch 9 have time
10 bring charges

2
1 have 2 have 3 take 4 have
5 take/bring 6 have 7 take 8 take
9 bring 10 take 11 brings

ANSWER KEY

3
1 up 2 off 3 back 4 after 5 on
6 up 7 on 8 off 9 in 10 out

Practice 3e — p. 58

1

divide	*division*
intend	intention
investigate	investigation
omit	omission
organise	organisation
preserve	preservation
prevent	prevention
produce	production
repeat	repetition
satisfy	satisfaction
solve	solution
react	reaction
tempt	temptation

2
1 attraction 2 recognition 3 hesitation
4 explanation 5 promotion
6 cancellations

3
1 calculations, the bill comes
2 give their daughter the education
3 take part in the competition
4 a thorough investigation
5 given an invitation 6 celebrations are

4
1 communication 2 pollution
3 destruction 4 starvation
5 exhaustion 6 foundations
7 protection 8 competition
9 creation 10 Cooperation

Unit 4

Entry test
1 did you pay 2 have 3 didn't you
4 How long 5 Whose
6 C 7 D 8 B 9 D 10 D
11 B 12 A 13 D 14 A 15 B
16 D 17 C 18 C 19 D 20 A
21 D 22 D 23 C 24 A 25 C

Practice 4a — p. 63

1
1 Where did you grow up?
2 What did you like doing at school?
3 What were you like as a child?
4 When did you decide to become an actor?
5 How did your parents react?
6 What did they say when you told them?
7 How old were you when you left home?
8 What was your first job in the theatre?
9 What kind of directors do you like working with?
10 How many films have you made?

2
1 Where do you live?
2 Who did you give the book to?
3 Who lent you the money?
4 When did you get married?
5 Which dress do you like?
6 Which pullover would you like?
7 What kind of pullovers do you like?
8 Who phoned Harry?
9 Who did Heather phone?
10 What did she say?
11 How often do you go to the cinema?
12 How long does the journey take/is the journey?
13 How do you (usually) get to work?
14 Where does he keep the key?
15 How much milk is there (left)?

Practice 4b — p. 65

1
1 doesn't he 2 is there 3 isn't it, shall we 4 haven't you, do you
5 were you, would I 6 do you
7 couldn't you 8 wouldn't you
9 didn't she, should she 10 don't they
11 aren't I 12 will you 13 did it
14 has he 15 have they

2
Suggested answers
1 amazing book, isn't it 2 plenty of time, haven't we 3 some tea, shall we
4 on the list, aren't I 5 go for a walk, shall we 6 leaves from Platform 2, doesn't it 7 me the salt, will you
8 been eating cake, haven't you 9 will you 10 leaving tomorrow morning, aren't we

Practice 4c — p. 67

1
1 I have 2 he doesn't 3 I would/so
4 I'm not 5 you do 6 I think
7 I hadn't 8 not/he can't

2
1 Can't you? 2 Do they? 3 Would you? 4 Won't you? 5 Has she?
6 Won't it? 7 Does he? 8 Doesn't she?

3
1 Haven't 2 can 3 Shouldn't 4 Do
5 Would 6 could 7 Don't 8 won't
9 Should 10 hasn't

4
1 g 2 e 3 h 4 i 5 k 6 a 7 c
8 b 9 j 10 d

Practice 4d — p. 70

1
do: a job, badly, French, good, harm, housework, maths, research, some work, something for a living, the dishes, the washing-up, well, your hair, your homework
make: a cup of coffee, a decision, a difference, a living, a mistake, a phone call, a profit, a suggestion, an appointment, an offer, fun of somebody, money, noise, the bed

2
1 d 2 k 3 a 4 f 5 h 6 j 7 b
8 g 9 c 10 e

3
1 do 2 make 3 do 4 make 5 do
6 made 7 doing 8 make 9 Do
10 do 11 made 12 do 13 make
14 did 15 make 16 done
17 making/made 18 do

4
1 making 2 do 3 do 4 do 5 do
6 do 7 make 8 do 9 doing
10 make

5
1 making 2 make 3 do 4 do
5 make 6 do 7 made 8 do
9 made 10 up 11 without 12 make

Practice 4e — p. 74

1

Verb/Adjective	Noun
inherit	*inheritance*
convenient	convenience
clumsy	clumsiness
obey	obedience
invest	investment
develop	development
kind	kindness
effective	effectiveness
fair	fairness
prefer	preference
innocent	innocence

Verb/Adjective	Noun
improve	improvement
willing	willingness
retire	retirement
silent	silence
disappoint	disappointment
excite	excitement
polite	politeness
argue	argument
punish	punishment
selfish	selfishness
grow	growth

307

ANSWER KEY

2
1 Absence 2 happiness 3 confidence
4 Ignorance 5 Kindness 6 Patience
7 Silence

3
1 U 2 C 3 U 4 U 5 C 6 U
7 C 8 C 9 U 10 C 11 U

4
1 intelligent 2 careless 3 patient
4 deep 5 arrogant 6 ugly 7 wide
8 empty 9 confident 10 millionth

5

Verb/Adjective	Noun
great	*greatness*
disturb	disturbance
correspond	correspondence
emerge	emergence
sleep	sleepiness
resist	resistance

Verb/Adjective	Noun
insure	insurance
annoy	annoyance
empty	emptiness
defend	defence
commit	commitment
fulfil	fulfilment

6
1 growth 2 thirtieth
3 self-confidence 4 management
5 patience 6 strengths
7 open-mindedness 8 weaknesses
9 reluctance 10 advertisements

Exam practice 2

Part 1
1 B 2 C 3 B 4 C 5 B 6 A 7 B
8 C 9 D 10 A 11 B 12 C

Part 2
13 well 14 do 15 make 16 my
17 result 18 have 19 with 20 able
21 must/should/could 22 to
23 have/need 24 order

Part 3
25 qualifications 26 invitation
27 competition 28 employment
29 conservation 30 construction
31 organisation 32 strengths
33 commitment 34 thirtieth

Part 4
35 is taking care of 36 might not have heard 37 concentrate because of
38 in order to 39 ought to have had
40 owing to the 41 as a result
42 was allowed to take

Unit 5

Entry test
1 don't 2 can 3 unless 4 had
5 were
6 D 7 C 8 C 9 D 10 A
11 B 12 C 13 D 14 D 15 D
16 B 17 B 18 B 19 C 20 B
21 decode 22 semi-final 23 ex-wife
24 monolingual 25 multicoloured

Practice 5a p. 83

1
1 am not 2 was/were 3 would join
4 will be 5 stop 6 don't give
7 starts 8 should make 9 Take
10 would go

2
1 If I'm not busy, I'll pick you up. If I wasn't/weren't busy, I'd pick you up.
2 If you fall, you'll break your leg. If you fell, you'd break your leg.
3 If we don't leave now, we'll be late. If we didn't leave now, we'd be late.
4 If you get the job, we'll have a party. If you got the job, we'd have a party.
5 If the questions are easy, everyone will pass the test. If the questions were easy, everyone would pass the test.

3
1 as long as you promise 2 I could help 3 provided (that) we win
4 unless you have/you've got/you've bought 5 in case we decide

Practice 5b p. 84

1
1 had come, would have visited
2 had known, wouldn't have got
3 hadn't destroyed, wouldn't need
4 hadn't left, might have met
5 hadn't spent, wouldn't be
6 could have become, was/were/had been
7 had tried, would have got
8 wouldn't have got, had missed
9 had met, would be
10 hadn't seen, would have been

2
1 I had had enough money, I would have taken a taxi
2 I had been interested in the film, I would have gone to the cinema
3 we had taken the wrong turning, we wouldn't have arrived late
4 wouldn't have committed suicide if he hadn't thought Juliet was dead
5 wouldn't have been punished if he hadn't lied
6 would have gone to the wedding if I had been invited
7 I hadn't been afraid of the dark, I would have gone downstairs
8 you had trained hard enough, you would have won
9 he had apologised, she would have forgiven him
10 she had had a car, she wouldn't have had to take a taxi

3
1 been 2 would 3 have 4 would
5 have 6 would 7 is 8 if 9 would
10 would 11 unless

Practice 5c p. 87

1
1 had 2 was/were 3 hadn't spent
4 wouldn't watch 5 wouldn't do
6 hadn't spoken 7 weren't building/hadn't built 8 could come
9 could go 10 hadn't told
11 hadn't lost 12 would turn up

2
1 he would drive more carefully, he had let someone else drive
2 I hadn't been so rude to her, I hadn't lost my temper
3 they played/would play fewer computer games, they watched/would watch less TV
4 we/people recycled/would recycle more paper, we/people respected/would respect the environment
5 I had revised for it, I had worked harder
6 I'd got to the bus stop five minutes earlier, I hadn't forgotten to set the alarm
7 they used/would use their bikes instead, they used/would use their cars less often

3
Suggested answers
1 I wish/If only he would turn the tap off.
2 I wish/If only Jamie would calm down.
3 I wish/If only people would stop hunting animals for sport.
4 I wish/If only the people next door would turn their TV down.
5 I wish/If only he/she/my friend would stop complaining (about everything all the time).
6 I wish/If only my team would win/had won.
7 I wish/If only people would recycle more.
8 I wish/If only it rained/would rain more.

ANSWER KEY

4

Suggested answers
1 she would dance/she was/were dancing with me   2 she wasn't/weren't leaving
3 she had married/was marrying me
4 I had saved the goal   5 you would be more careful/drive more carefully
6 I'd brought my swimming trunks
7 I had studied/worked harder

Practice 5d — p. 91

1
1 wanted   2 hope   3 wish   4 hoping
5 expecting   6 waiting for   7 expect
8 looking forward to   9 loved   10 like
11 like   12 wait   13 to see   14 to see

2
1 listening   2 of   3 look   4 playing
5 wait   6 on   7 to   8 to   9 for
10 could

Practice 5e — p. 92

1
Suggested answers
1 semi-final: one of two sports games whose winners then compete against each other to decide who wins the whole competition
2 ex-partner: former partner
3 substandard: not as good as the average, and not acceptable
4 multi-national: having or involving people from several countries
5 subsection: a part of a section
6 minibus: a small bus
7 decaffeinated: without caffeine
8 defrost: get or make sth warmer until it is not frozen or until the ice melts
9 multicoloured: with lots of colours
10 deregulate: to remove rules and controls from sth
11 subzero: below zero
12 ex-wife: former wife
13 denationalise: to sell a business or industry so that it is no longer owned by the state
14 microorganism: a very small living thing/organism
15 derail: (of a train) go off the tracks
16 miniskirt: a short skirt
17 subsoil: the layer of soil that is under the surface level
18 microchip: a very small chip
19 decode: discover the meaning of a message written in a code
20 semicircle: half a circle

2
1 A   2 B   3 D   4 A   5 B   6 B
7 C   8 D   9 B   10 B

3
1 semi-final   2 multi-national
3 sub-zero   4 ex-husband
5 Macroeconomics   6 debug
7 microchip   8 decode

Unit 6

Entry test
1 A   2 A   3 C   4 D   5 B
6 B   7 A   8 D   9 C   10 D
11 C   12 C   13 C   14 A   15 D
16 B   17 A   18 C   19 D   20 A
21 more time   22 the time   23 a waste
24 had an   25 Take your

Practice 6a — p. 97

1
1 When   2 until   3 before   4 By the time   5 as soon as   6 Supposing
7 Whether   8 When   9 As soon as
10 provided

2
1 come   2 are   3 finish/have finished
4 get   5 tell   6 plays   7 promise
8 bring it back   9 get   10 finishes/has finished

3
1 not   2 If   3 occurs/happens
4 soon
5 Provided/Providing   6 until   7 in
8 as

Practice 6b — p. 99

1
1 take   2 due   3 are not to   4 point
5 of giving up   6 No matter
7 However   8 to be   9 Whoever
10 are

2
1 announcing   2 bursting   3 to arrive/arriving   4 to perform   5 to expire
6 to leave   7 tries   8 see   9 hire
10 hide   11 runs   12 move

3
1 on   2 is   3 due/going   4 Wherever
5 is   6 to   7 of   8 to   9 Whatever
10 what

Practice 6c — p. 102

1
1 f   2 c   3 k   4 e   5 i   6 a   7 m
8 d   9 l   10 h   11 b   12 j

2
1 C   2 A   3 C   4 B   5 A   6 B
7 C   8 C   9 C   10 C

3
1 visited, to spend   2 fixed, painted
3 to go, stay   4 helped, do   5 told, keep   6 to take, didn't stop

4
1 (high/about) time you bought a
2 would prefer it   3 rather you didn't spend   4 would sooner study   5 prefer you to sleep/prefer it if you slept   6 high time you told   7 for me to pick up
8 would rather you didn't   9 time you had   10 rather than go/going

Practice 6d — p. 105

1
1 by   2 later   3 then   4 after
5 till   6 later   7 by   8 till   9 After
10 in

2
1 in   2 later   3 Then   4 Afterwards/Then   5 after   6 by   7 until/till
8 as far

3
1 to   2 later   3 until/till   4 after
5 until/till   6 After   7 to   8 After
9 then   10 that   11 then   12 until/till

Practice 6e — p. 107

1
1 m   2 l   3 a   4 j   5 e   6 b   7 g
8 d   9 i   10 h   11 c   12 f

2
1 pass   2 day   3 spend   4 taking
5 take   6 wasting   7 takes   8 spent
9 have   10 on   11 in   12 have

3
1 spend (more)   2 on time   3 takes time   4 time to   5 is time for
6 have a good time   7 waste of time
8 waste your time   9 have (enough) time to   10 in time

Exam practice 3

Part 1
1 C   2 A   3 A   4 B   5 A   6 A
7 D   8 C   9 A   10 B   11 B   12 D

ANSWER KEY

Part 2
13 about/high 14 of 15 would
16 would/did 17 if 18 look 19 to
20 stand/bear 21 had 22 listening
23 would 24 than

Part 3
25 neighbourhood 26 competition
27 championship 28 personality
29 achievements 30 greatness
31 poverty 32 affluence
33 organisation 34 inspiration

Part 4
35 until he has 36 in case we have to
37 looking forward to seeing 38 as soon as Penny arrives 39 would rather read 40 unless we have 41 as long as 42 arrived/been on time

Unit 7

Entry test
1 is being treated 2 was 3 had been
4 be 5 isn't
6 A 7 C 8 B 9 C 10 D
11 B 12 A 13 B 14 B 15 D
16 A 17 C 18 D 19 C 20 C
21 dish 22 heating 23 human
24 break 25 attack

Practice 7a — p. 115

1
1 is broadcast 2 is being interviewed
3 was closed down 4 will/is going to be installed 5 will have been elected
6 has already been paid 7 had been burgled 8 was being evacuated 9 will/are going to be introduced 10 are sold

2
1 A new school is being built in West Street.
2 He has just been arrested on suspicion of murder.
3 Her new book will be published next month.
4 The new motorway will have been completed by Christmas.
5 The hotel rooms have just been cleaned.
6 Her bike was stolen last night.
7 The machine is going to be repaired tomorrow.
8 Her car was being serviced when I called her.
9 The project had been finished by Friday.
10 He may be invited to the wedding.

3
1 is known 2 is inserted 3 has just been published 4 were reported 5 has been recorded 6 have been lost 7 will be lost 8 are not taken 9 may be avoided 10 have already been installed
11 has been reported 12 are skimmed

Practice 7b — p. 118

1
1 by 2 by 3 with 4 by 5 with
6 by 7 with 8 with

2
1 A bottle of milk was given to each of the children.
Each of the children was given a bottle of milk.
2 £50 will be paid to the workers.
The workers will be paid £50.
3 The job may be offered to her.
She may be offered the job.
4 French is taught to the students.
The students are taught French.
5 The sights were shown to us.
We were shown the sights.
6 A story is being told to the children.
The children are being told a story.
7 A lot of money was given to them.
They were given a lot of money.
8 An email has just been sent to me.
I've just been sent an email.

3
1 is said to be 2 was thought to be
3 was given/paid to the architect
4 believed to have 5 was considered to be 6 is/was supposed to be 7 was agreed that 8 students were shown
9 was taught everything I know
10 photos were taken with

Practice 7c — p. 121

1
1 have your eyes tested 2 had it made 3 have it serviced 4 have central heating installed 5 have just had it redecorated 6 am having it repaired
7 have it dry-cleaned 8 have it cut down 9 have that cavity filled
10 had a swimming pool built

2
1 have 2 stolen/taken 3 got
4 got/were 5 repaired/fixed
6 have/get 7 it 8 painted 9 to
10 have/get 11 get/be

Practice 7d — p. 123

1
1 a 2 h 3 c 4 f 5 b 6 g 7 i
8 e

2
1 cold 2 the car 3 going 4 it
5 the kids 6 those wet clothes
7 to the end 8 the joke

3
1 receive 2 obtain 3 make 4 obtain
5 buy 6 become 7 make 8 receive
9 receive 10 receive 11 understand
12 receive 13 understand

Practice 7e — p. 125

1
Countable: *heart attack*, *high school*, letterbox, news bulletin, parking meter, personal computer, police station, post office, remote control, sleeping bag, swimming pool, washing machine
Uncountable: *air conditioning*, *human nature*, old age, pocket money, show business, social work, soda water, toilet paper, washing powder, washing-up liquid, water skiing, writing paper

2
noun + noun: 1 a 2 g 3 c 4 i 5 b
6 f 7 d 8 h
adjective + noun: 1 i 2 a 3 g 4 b
5 e 6 h 7 f 8 d
gapped sentences: 1 zebra crossing
2 central heating 3 pocket money
4 high school 5 common sense
6 remote control 7 dry cleaner's
8 burglar alarm 9 credit card
10 social worker

3
Across: 1 DRY 2 SUN 7 HEATING
8 INVERTED 9 MAKE 10 GUM
11 SENSE
Down: 1 DRIVING 2 STUDIES
3 JUNK 4 FRIES 5 PARK 6 STOP
7 HUMAN

4
1 setback 2 hold-up 3 getaway
4 checkout 5 breakout 6 breakup
7 takeaway 8 take-off 9 printout
10 check-in

5
1 common 2 sunglasses 3 heels
4 make-up 5 mobile 6 text
7 skateboards 8 roller 9 junk
10 hot 11 tomato 12 stomach
13 licence 14 traffic 15 fast

Unit 8

Entry test
1 suggested 2 explained 3 begged
4 not to go 5 had been
6 B 7 D 8 B 9 A 10 C
11 C 12 D 13 B 14 B 15 C
16 C 17 A 18 D 19 C 20 B
21 amusing 22 disappointed
23 annoying 24 boring 25 charming

310

ANSWER KEY

Practice 8a — p. 132

1
1 (that) he hadn't been anywhere near the scene of the crime
2 (that) that/the spot was the best place for a picnic
3 (that) they were leaving the following day/the day after
4 to answer the phone
5 (that) she had given me the money the previous week/the week before
6 to put my hands up
7 not to work so hard
8 to lend him the money

2
1 h 2 a 3 k 4 b 5 g 6 c 7 j
8 e 9 d 10 f

3
1 He announced (that) he was going to retire soon.
2 She asked the waiter to bring them the wine list.
3 He boasted that their team would easily beat ours.
4 She begged him to give her another chance.
5 He claimed that he was innocent.
6 She explained that she had been late because she had missed her bus.
7 He suggested playing/that we should play/that we played a game.
8 She reminded him to phone Alex.
9 He warned us that the water was deep.
10 She advised the student to be more careful in the future.

4
1 said 2 told 3 not 4 was 5 asked
6 had 7 could 8 that 9 would
10 had 11 following 12 was

Practice 8b — p. 135

1
1 I had 2 I was 3 I had 4 whether
5 the journey had taken 6 I liked
7 had told 8 I thought 9 inquired
10 I could

2
1 if/whether he was still living in London
2 whether I worked in the central branch or in the provinces
3 whether he was going to give her the money or not
4 if/whether he had brought the book back
5 if/whether it was snowing in Manchester
6 if/whether I was married
7 if/whether he had been eating properly
8 if/whether I would like to join them the following day/the day after
9 if/whether she spoke French
10 if/whether he had finished

3
1 The man asked us how far the stadium was. 2 She asked who had bought the Picasso painting. 3 Mrs Fox asked what they had been doing.
4 Jo asked Ben how long he had lived there. 5 I asked Pam how often she visited her cousins. 6 She asked me why I was laughing. 7 I asked them how long they had been waiting.
8 Harry asked what she had said.
9 She asked her friend what she should do. 10 I asked them where they were going to stay.

4
1 had 2 wanted 3 asked/inquired
4 was 5 knew 6 could 7 where
8 if/whether 9 going

Practice 8c — p. 139

1
1 to drive 2 postponing 3 their arrival
4 to see 5 to buy 6 seeing 7 stay
8 seeing 9 tidy 10 to upset

2
1 painting 2 missing 3 painting
4 painting 5 to allow 6 to send
7 going/to go 8 turning up

3
1 to inform you that 2 would rather work 3 didn't let us enter
4 suggested starting/that we should start/that we started 5 succeeded in getting 6 appears to be locked
7 looking forward to going 8 insisted on paying

Practice 8d — p. 142

1
1 told, tell 2 telling, convince/persuade 3 give, talk 4 say/said, tell 5 say/said, say 6 told, talking
7 told, said 8 gave, turned down
9 deny, tell 10 convince/persuade, tell

2
1 say 2 rejected 3 turned down
4 denied 5 told 6 talk 7 persuade
8 to sign 9 convinced 10 to accept
11 that there are 12 give 13 give
14 said

Practice 8e — p. 143

1
1 amusing 2 interesting 3 annoyed
4 flattering 5 boring 6 interested
7 embarrassed 8 moving 9 surprised
10 bored 11 annoying 12 irritated

2
1 depressed 2 interested 3 annoying
4 surprised 5 frightening 6 relaxing
7 bored 8 confused 9 embarrassing
10 disgusting

3
Students' own answers

4
Students' own answers

5
Across: 2 INTERESTED 5 HEATED
6 AMUSED 8 SURPRISED
9 FREEZING 10 AGEING
11 REWARDING 12 TERRIFIED
Down: 1 CAPTIVATING
3 TRUSTING 4 TOUCHED
7 HUMILIATED 10 ARMED

Exam practice 4

Part 1
1 C 2 B 3 D 4 B 5 C 6 B
7 A 8 D 9 D 10 C 11 B 12 D

Part 2
13 to 14 if/whether 15 to 16 said/replied/answered 17 about 18 you
19 not 20 stealing/taking 21 him
22 asked 23 had 24 let

Part 3
25 inspiring 26 encouraging 27 bored
28 interested 29 exhausted
30 reading 31 fascinating 32 terrified
33 swimming 34 amazing

Part 4
35 are known as 36 was directed by
37 cannot be denied that 38 had/got her car repaired by 39 to get my car serviced 40 won't let us bring
41 is supposed to be 42 is going to be pulled

Unit 9

Entry test

1 more 2 loveliest 3 worst 4 lot
5 slightly less
6 D 7 B 8 C 9 B 10 C
11 black leather 12 new Japanese
13 lovely red 14 posh German sports
15 a beautiful old
16 D 17 B 18 C 19 C 20 D
21 B 22 C 23 D 24 A 25 B

311

ANSWER KEY

Practice 9a — p. 154

1
1 the most intelligent   2 the hottest
3 more careful   4 better   5 the happiest   6 more comfortable than
7 older/elder   8 further   9 worse
10 simpler   11 the luckiest
12 friendlier than   13 more suitable
14 the oldest

2
1 gentler than/more gentle than
2 more modest   3 louder   4 nicer
5 richer   6 better   7 higher than
8 longer   9 cheaper   10 the most violent   11 safer   12 worse   13 more pleasant   14 happier   15 more relaxed
16 the most beautiful   17 the best

Practice 9b — p. 156

1
1 C   2 B   3 D   4 C   5 D

2
1 ashamed of   2 interested in   3 absent from   4 typical of   5 amused by
6 excited about   7 involved in
8 shocked by   9 good at   10 famous for   11 crowded with   12 proud of
13 engaged to   14 right about
15 different from

Practice 9c — p. 157

1
1 a big wooden spoon   2 ✓
3 a delicious big birthday cake
4 a small round plastic button
5 a large old frying pan   6 ✓
7 a beautiful pink silk blouse
8 a large round ball   9 ✓
10 an ugly old wooden desk

Practice 9d — p. 162

1
1 high   2 slim   3 last   4 natural
5 strong   6 great   7 big   8 skinny
9 latest   10 taller   11 thinner   12 little
13 foreign   14 short   15 strange

2
1 thin   2 last   3 latest   4 natural
5 weak   6 great   7 large   8 greatest
9 foreign   10 physical

3
1 bomb   2 house   3 temperature
4 man   5 occasion   6 excuse   7 cloth
8 gossip   9 year   10 money   11 plants
12 food   13 clothes

4
Across: 6 STRONG   7 PHYSICAL
8 LATEST   11 TALL   13 LAST
15 FOREIGN   16 LARGEST   18 SLIM
19 NATURAL   20 WEAK
Down: 1 POWERFUL   2 LITTLE
3 SHORT   4 BIG   5 STRANGE
9 THIN   10 SMALL   12 HIGHEST
14 SKINNY   17 GREAT

Practice 9e — p. 164

1
1 i   2 o   3 a   4 k   5 g   6 b   7 m
8 c   9 j   10 d   11 l   12 f   13 n
14 h

2
Physical appearance: *dark-haired*, well-dressed, long-legged, good-looking, green-eyed
Personality: absent-minded, easy-going, hard-working, kind-hearted, self-confident
Other: second-hand, newly-married, best-selling, brand-new, air-conditioned

3
1 newly-married   2 well-dressed
3 good-looking   4 second-hand
5 best-selling   6 absent-minded
7 self-confident   8 hard-working
9 easy-going   10 air-conditioned

4
1 distance   2 off   3 up   4 class
5 made   6 tempered   7 up   8 known
9 headed   10 sighted   11 badly
12 fashioned

Unit 10

Entry test
1 as   2 so   3 as   4 as   5 and
6 B   7 A   8 A   9 B   10 C
11 C   12 D   13 D   14 B   15 D
16 D   17 C   18 D   19 A   20 B
21 careless   22 suitable   23 painless
24 sensitive   25 forgetful

Practice 10a — p. 169

1
1 the same day as   2 the same time as
3 as/so heavy as   4 hair colour/colour hair as   5 his mum, like his dad
6 as/so tall as   7 the same school/college as   8 geography as Bob (was)
9 good at maths as Tony (was)   10 at English as   11 (just) as good at history as   12 as a coal miner   13 much money as Tony (does)   14 as/so successful as Tony (has)

Practice 10b — p. 171

1
1 b   2 g   3 c   4 a   5 d   6 f

2
1 such   2 such   3 such a   4 so
5 so
6 so   7 so   8 such a   9 so   10 so

3
1 enough   2 enough   3 too   4 very
5 too   6 enough   7 enough   8 very
9 very   10 very

4
1 too heavy for me to   2 not tall enough to reach   3 so sad that
4 speaks English so well   5 isn't old enough to   6 weren't high enough
7 were so many people   8 was so strong (that)   9 too hot (for me) to
10 have enough money to buy

Practice 10c — p. 174

1
1 Wembley Stadium is (absolutely) enormous.
2 He's rather noisy in class.
3 She's always been quite hard-working.
4 I quite like the theatre but I prefer the cinema.
5 Ed is much taller than his brother.
6 Yes, I quite agree.
7 It was quite a shock to get home and find the house burgled.
8 Well, I found the film a bit boring.
9 The test seems (to be) quite easy.

2
1 quite a   2 bit   3 quite, a little
4 a very   5 rather an   6 very, rather
7 sour   8 healthy, strong   9 grey
10 to understand

3
1 A   2 B   3 A   4 C   5 A

4
1 seems   2 staying   3 felt
4 appears   5 sounded

5
1 appeared   2 seemed to be   3 felt
4 quite   5 rather   6 much   7 a bit
8 a bit   9 fairly   10 rather
11 became   12 appeared

312

ANSWER KEY

Practice 10d p. 177

1
1 enjoyable 2 shy 3 ashamed
4 embarrassed 5 shameful
6 worried 7 bad-tempered 8 afraid
9 likeable 10 tiring 11 ordinary
12 sympathetic

2
1 to scream 2 that 3 flying
4 afraid of 5 go 6 of 7 of 8 to
9 that she would fall 10 of walking

3
1 embarrassed 2 typical 3 usual
4 anxious 5 sympathetic 6 shy
7 afraid 8 amusing 9 tiresome
10 nervous 11 ordinary 12 ashamed

Practice 10e p. 181

1
1 thirsty 2 wealthy 3 infamous
4 enthusiastic 5 suitable 6 painless
7 harmful 8 successful

2
1 unforgettable 2 forgetful
3 drinkable 4 readable 5 accessible
6 painful 7 hopeful
8 understandable 9 sympathetic
10 tolerant 11 courageous

3
1 powerful 2 extensive 3 dreadful
4 optimistic 5 dangerous 6 careful
7 sensible 8 hopeful 9 drinkable
10 economic

Exam practice 5

Part 1
1 A 2 D 3 A 4 B 5 B 6 D
7 C 8 D 9 A 10 C 11 B 12 A

Part 2
13 so 14 seems/appears 15 a
16 many 17 an 18 more 19 have
20 to 21 than 22 as 23 enough
24 the

Part 3
25 impossible 26 comfortable
27 useful 28 hopeless 29 anxious
30 embarrassed 31 technological
32 ignorant 33 natural
34 knowledgeable

Part 4
35 married to 36 am not (very) fond of
37 was surprised at/by 38 isn't as tall
as 39 such a funny story (that) 40 too
heavy for him to 41 be responsible for
42 typical of her

Unit 11

Entry test
1 beautifully 2 quietly 3 happily
4 probably 5 daily
6 She opened the door slowly./She
slowly opened the door./Slowly, she
opened the door.
7 He is always laughing in class.
8 She probably doesn't speak French.
9 He drove dangerously along the
motorway on Sunday.
10 I have always liked music very much.
11 A 12 C 13 A 14 C 15 D
16 B 17 A 18 D 19 D 20 C
21 A 22 C 23 B 24 A 25 A

Practice 11a p. 190

1

Adjective/Noun	Adverb/Phrase
suitable	suitably
silly	in a silly way
unlucky	unluckily
lovely	in a lovely way/manner/fashion
possible	possibly
ugly	in an ugly way/manner/fashion
awful	awfully
full	fully

Adjective/Noun	Adverb/Phrase
lonely	in a lonely way/manner/fashion
tragic	tragically
year	yearly
efficient	efficiently
fast	fast
hard	hard
public	publicly
good	well

2
1 automatically 2 gently
3 unexpectedly 4 probably
5 surprisingly 6 shyly 7 truly
8 heroically

3
1 softly 2 carefully 3 noisily
4 monthly 5 easily 6 early 7 well
8 daily 9 angrily 10 Tragically

Practice 11b p. 192

1
1 ✓ 2 We often play football after
school./After school, we often play
football.
3 He drives very carefully on the
motorway. 4 I don't always get up
early. 5 ✓ 6 He's waiting outside.
7 I only like ice cream/I like ice cream
only, not pudding. 8 ✓

2
1 You won't finish your homework in
time if you don't hurry up.
2 I'll probably finish my project on
Friday.
3 Doesn't she play the piano well?
4 We arrived in London on Sunday./On
Sunday, we arrived in London.
5 She probably won't be coming to
work today.
6 He performed superbly at the
National Theatre on Saturday.
7 She usually visits her mother in
hospital at the weekend.
8 I definitely remember seeing him
outside the shop.
9 Can you come to my office at six
o'clock?
10 We occasionally go camping for a
few days.

3
1 really starting 2 he immediately thinks
3 hardly ever relaxes 4 he often misses
5 he feels well 6 Once last year
7 a mask over his nose and mouth
8 always looking up 9 to the doctor
once a month 10 On Friday, he went
11 to him very patiently 12 Hopefully,
she will realise

Practice 11c p. 195

1
1 more efficiently than 2 worse than
3 earlier than 4 the hardest 5 as/so
dangerously 6 more often than
7 well as 8 the fastest 9 more than
10 farther/further

2
1 harder 2 earlier 3 more loudly
4 worse than 5 longer 6 more often
7 the most imaginatively 8 as/so fast
9 the most fluently 10 closer

Practice 11d p. 197

1
1 directly 2 free 3 widely 4 long
5 freely 6 hardly 7 Quick 8 long
9 last 10 wide 11 Lastly 12 wrongly
13 fast 14 lately 15 fast 16 early

2
1 widely 2 rightly 3 quickly 4 hard
5 highly 6 long 7 late

313

ANSWER KEY

Practice 11e — p. 200

1
1 see 2 hear, listening 3 heard
4 seen 5 looked 6 caught
7 notice 8 looking 9 Listen
10 hear/heard 11 staring/looking
12 glance

2
1 are looking into 2 will look after
3 looking forward to seeing 4 heard from 5 hearing things 6 to lend an ear 7 caught a glimpse 8 keep an eye on 9 all ears 10 glanced through

3
1 directly 2 suddenly 3 once
4 closely 5 barely

4
1 C 2 A 3 C 4 C 5 D 6 C
7 A 8 B 9 B 10 D

Unit 12

Entry test
1 Oxford University 2 prison
3 outside the hospital 4 a spider
5 the face
6 A 7 C 8 B 9 C 10 B
11 D 12 A 13 C 14 A 15 D
16 is 17 them 18 outskirts
19 congratulations are 20 directions
21 depression 22 generosity
23 publicity 24 reluctance 25 security

Practice 12a — p. 207

1
1 the 2 - 3 the, -, -, - 4 the
5 the 6 a 7 the 8 the 9 the, the
10 -, - 11 -, a, - 12 a

2
The Romans invaded Britain in 43AD and chasing the ancient Britons along the Thames, they came to the first place that was easy to cross. They built a garrison there – and London was born. They also built a bridge over the river. The garrison became a major trading post. Later, the bridge suffered neglect and the whole area was raided by the Vikings.
In 886AD, Alfred the Great drove out the raiders, the bridge was repaired and the city prospered again. A hundred years later, the Vikings returned but King Ethelred sailed up the Thames, attached ropes to London Bridge, headed downriver and pulled it down.

3
1 - 2 a 3 the 4 - 5 a 6 a
7 the 8 The 9 the 10 the 11 -
12 - 13 - 14 - 15 - 16 the
17 a 18 the 19 - 20 - 21 a
22 the 23 the 24 a 25 - 26 the
27 the 28 -

Practice 12b — p. 211

1
1 Each 2 each 3 Every 4 Each
5 neither 6 every 7 every 8 few
9 a few 10 a little 11 little, a few
12 many 13 most 14 several
15 some 16 some 17 another
18 a few 19 either 20 a little

2
1 most 2 other/some 3 some
4 all 5 few 6 other 7 any 8 few
9 some/several/other 10 None
11 any 12 little 13 None 14 all

Practice 12c — p. 214

1
Across: 4 HEALTH 5 FLESH
8 FURNITURE 9 WOMEN
12 PRIDE 13 LUCK 14 SPECIES
Down: 1 HAIR 2 CHILDREN
3 NEWS 6 MUSIC 7 KNOWLEDGE
10 EVIL 11 WORK

2
1 species 2 deer 3 a strange
4 Equipment 5 a paper 6 permission
7 an advertisement 8 tools 9 works
10 isn't enough room

3
1 cups 2 litres 3 piece 4 glass
5 tube 6 grams 7 piece 8 slice

4
1 good health 2 information
3 plenty of 4 olive oil 5 cheese
6 fish 7 much 8 a little 9 a few
10 juice is 11 piece 12 slice
13 cheese 14 a healthy diet

Practice 12d — p. 218

1
1 media 2 trousers, pair of shorts
3 those 4 jury 5 audience, refreshments are 6 belongings
7 travels 8 supplies 9 foundations
10 Has

2
1 was, it 2 is 3 is/was, is/was
4 is/are 5 are, they 6 them 7 are
8 is/are 9 are 10 is 11 Is 12 are

Practice 12e — p. 221

1

Noun	Verb
discussion	*discuss*
decision	decide
abolition	abolish
addition	add
accusation	accuse
inversion	invert
demolition	demolish
repetition	repeat
complication	complicate
confession	confess
adhesion	adhere
conclusion	conclude
extension	extend

Noun	Verb
expansion	expand
opposition	oppose
graduation	graduate
identification	identify
decoration	decorate
occupation	occupy
collision	collide
permission	permit
qualification	qualify
starvation	starve
admiration	admire
classification	classify
explosion	explode

2
1 loyalty 2 possibility 3 depression
4 explosion 5 profession
6 impression 7 discoveries
8 decision 9 majority 10 security
11 admiration 12 collision

3
1 great pleasure 2 correspondence lasted (for) 3 prove the existence
4 no reference 5 for the/their discovery 6 any similarity 7 full responsibility 8 frequency of earthquakes has increased 9 the efficiency of 10 under discussion

4
1 guidance 2 tendency 3 efficient
4 revision 5 frequency 6 fluency
7 opportunity 8 psychological
9 performance 10 acquisition
11 reluctant

ANSWER KEY

Exam practice 6
Part 1
1 C 2 B 3 C 4 A 5 C 6 C
7 D 8 A 9 D 10 B 11 C 12 D
Part 2
13 for 14 the 15 another 16 slice
17 lot 18 enough 19 was 20 much/any 21 a 22 few 23 both 24 of
Part 3
25 application 26 references
27 impression 28 intelligence
29 solutions 30 co-operation
31 ability 32 efficient 33 occupation
34 sensitivity
Part 4
35 as quickly as 36 play very well
37 looking forward to 38 less often than
39 looking into 40 keep an eye on
41 and Amanda both live 42 me great pleasure

Unit 13

Entry test
1 who lives 2 where 3 whose
4 where 5 has 6 C 7 B 8 D
9 D 10 C 11 A 12 D 13 C 14 D
15 B 16 C 17 B 18 A 19 C
20 D 21 professional 22 approval
23 criminal 24 envious 25 threatened

Practice 13a — p. 232
1
1 The new director, who gets on well with everyone, is very popular. 2 London, where we spent our holidays, was amazing. 3 The film, which I enjoyed very much, was called *Finding Grace*.
4 Our cat, which we've had for five years, is called William. 5 2008, when I met my wife, was the happiest year of my life.
6 The castle, which is the oldest building in our town, was built in the sixteenth century. 7 Tim, whose wife is from Peru, speaks Spanish. 8 My sister, who lives in Canada, is a vet.

2
1 It was a mistake they have already apologised for.
2 Maths is a subject she has little interest in.
3 It was Mr Edwards they sold the house to.
4 It was the Queen the Prime Minister sent the letter to.
5 It was the bank he had borrowed money from.
6 That was the year I was born in.
7 March 25th is the day the country celebrates its independence on.
8 That's the hospital the twins were born in.
9 That's the island we spent our honeymoon on.
10 These are the reasons I chose to marry him for.

3
7 March 25th is the day when the country celebrates its independence.
8 That's the hospital where the twins were born.
9 That's the island where we spent our honeymoon.
10 These are the reasons why I chose to marry him.

4
1 who 2 which 3 Whoever
4 whenever/wherever 5 Whatever
6 which 7 when 8 which 9 which
10 where 11 why 12 which 13 who
14 who

Practice 13b — p. 235
1
1 Bill fell asleep listening to the lecture.
2 Wanting to finish my work, I decided to stay in. 3 Being well-qualified for the job, she got it. 4 Realising how rude I'd been, I apologised. 5 Wanting to catch the first bus, he left early.

2
1 Having tried phoning her several times, he sent her an email.
2 Having received an invitation, I felt I had to go to the party.
3 Having lost his key, he couldn't get in.
4 Having picked up her luggage, she went to look for a taxi.

3
1 falling 2 Exhausted 3 thinking
4 shouting 5 laughing 6 covered
7 followed 8 holding 9 Terrified
10 coming 11 shouting 12 playing
13 built 14 haunted 15 Passing by
16 walking 17 crunching
18 deserted 19 Puzzled 20 scared

Practice 13c — p. 237
1
1 a 2 g 3 e 4 b 5 f 6 c

2
1 whereas 2 despite 3 Although
4 yet 5 However 6 of making

3
1 though 2 yet/but 3 spite
4 Even 5 hand 6 other 7 despite
8 Although/Though/While
9 However/Nevertheless
10 While/Whereas/Although/Though

Practice 13d — p. 239
1
1 away 2 back 3 by 4 into
5 through 6 on 7 down 8 over
9 together 10 off

2
1 get on (well) with 2 to get through
3 get on with 4 get across
5 gets me down

3
1 down 2 on 3 across 4 on
5 back 6 by 7 around/round
8 away 9 together

Practice 13e — p. 241
1
1 approval 2 critical 3 expensive
4 envious 5 freedom 6 novelist
7 furious 8 professional 9 addictive
10 National 11 optional 12 arsonist
13 broaden 14 Scientists 15 widen

2
1 envious 2 national 3 broaden
4 criminal 5 effective 6 humorous
7 pianists 8 deepen 9 freedom
10 proposal 11 boredom 12 original

3
Across: 2 KINGDOM 4 BIGAMOUS
6 ANXIOUS 8 SCIENTISTS
Down: 1 PITEOUS 3 JEALOUS
5 CELLIST 6 ACTIVE 7 CANOEIST

4
1 accidental 2 expensive 3 furious
4 musical 5 professional 6 original
7 pianist 8 famous 9 critical
10 freedom

Unit 14

Entry test
1 in 2 to 3 at 4 in 5 in
6 B 7 D 8 B 9 D 10 A
11 it 12 There 13 It 14 There
15 There
16 C 17 D 18 B 19 A 20 D
21 up 22 through 23 on
24 off 25 out

315

ANSWER KEY

Practice 14a — p. 249

1
1 on, on, into   2 into, at   3 among, on   4 out of, into, in front of   5 in, in, in, on   6 until, at, on, to   7 On, to, into   8 over, up, into, through   9 to, at   10 to, on, under

2
1 at   2 in   3 on   4 in   5 at   6 on   7 on   8 in   9 at   10 in   11 at   12 in   13 on   14 at   15 on   16 on

3
1 at   2 on   3 in   4 at   5 in   6 in   7 on   8 in   9 at   10 at   11 on   12 at   13 in   14 in   15 at   16 at   17 on   18 in

4
1 to   2 on   3 in   4 at   5 at   6 at   7 along   8 into   9 In   10 to   11 on   12 in   13 from

Practice 14b — p. 251

1
1 for   2 about   3 at   4 on   5 with   6 to   7 for   8 of

2
1 between   2 in/on   3 from   4 about   5 from   6 of   7 on   8 from   9 to   10 from   11 at   12 between   13 of   14 of   15 about

3
1 on   2 between   3 in   4 of   5 to   6 about   7 with   8 to   9 from   10 about   11 of   12 for

Practice 14c — p. 253

1
1 It's   2 it   3 there   4 There   5 It's   6 There   7 there   8 There   9 It   10 It's   11 There's   12 It   13 There   14 There's   15 It

2
1 there   2 there   3 it   4 it   5 It   6 there   7 It   8 there   9 there   10 it   11 there   12 It

Practice 14d — p. 256

1
1 from, to   2 to   3 on   4 on   5 on   6 in   7 at   8 by   9 out of   10 in

2
1 to, in   2 In, in   3 out of, on   4 of, to   5 in, by   6 In, in   7 For, from   8 on, on   9 by, on   10 at, on

3
1 out   2 at   3 at   4 at   5 at   6 on   7 for   8 out   9 from   10 In   11 at   12 out

Practice 14e — p. 258

1
1 put up with   2 put, up   3 put on   4 put up   5 put, out   6 put, through   7 put, away   8 put, back

2
1 put forward   2 put off   3 to put on   4 put up   5 put up   6 put me through   7 put up with   8 put me down   9 put out   10 put him up

Exam practice 7

Part 1
1 D   2 B   3 B   4 A   5 C   6 C   7 D   8 C   9 A   10 A   11 A   12 D

Part 2
13 in   14 get   15 there   16 at   17 It   18 but   19 in   20 which   21 by   22 which   23 spite   24 at

Part 3
25 economical   26 expensive   27 tourist   28 professional   29 effective   30 global   31 broadens   32 cultural   33 behaviour   34 critical

Part 4
35 spite of the fact   36 put up with   37 even though I   38 the woman whose car   39 get back to   40 the village where I   41 did it on purpose   42 is possible that you

Word store — p. 263

Living conditions

1
1 city   2 floors   3 garden   4 cottage   5 villa   6 flats   7 rooms

2
1 wardrobe   2 armchair   3 sofa   4 cupboard   5 light switch   6 plug   7 stools   8 corkscrew   9 iron   10 dressing   11 chest   12 lamp   13 bulb   14 cushions   15 fireplace

3
1 villa   2 cottage   3 detached (house)   4 basement   5 study

4
Types of home: bedsit, block of flats, bungalow, cottage, detached house, loft, semi-detached house, terraced house, villa
Parts of a house: *attic*, basement, cellar, ground floor, hall, landing, loft, study
Things we find in a house: corkscrew, ironing board, power point, remote control, table mat, tea towel, washing-up liquid

5
1 paint/door handle/tap   2 the stairs/the staircase   3 TV/dishwasher/washing machine/radio   4 electricity/water supply/power supply   5 clock/MP4 player/radio   6 clock

Social relationships

1
1 wife   2 family   3 parents   4 grandparents   5 cousins   6 grandmother   7 Uncle   8 Aunt

2
1 GRANDFATHER   2 GRANDMOTHER   3 AUNT   4 NEPHEW   5 WIDOW   6 STEPFATHER   7 FIANCÉ   8 WIDOWER   9 STEPMOTHER   10 FATHER-IN-LAW   11 GREATGRANDDAUGHTER   12 SON
The secret word is 'GRANDPARENTS'.

3
1 met   2 to   3 know   4 in   5 go   6 fallen   7 engaged   8 get   9 marriage   10 wedding   11 anniversary   12 best   13 to   14 honeymoon

Friendship

1
1 unfriendly   2 friendship   3 close   4 became/made   5 user-friendly

2
Phrasal verbs in text: *get on with*, fallen out with, looks down on, puts (people) off, brought up
1 out   2 up   3 down   4 out   5 up, up   6 out, up, off

Occupations

1
1 job   2 earn   3 manual   4 clerical   5 outdoors

2
1 career   2 interview   3 job   4 sack   5 wage   6 salary   7 pension   8 promotion   9 reference   10 qualifications   11 experience   12 offer   13 trainee

ANSWER KEY

3
1 l 2 g 3 c 4 e 5 i 6 f 7 j
8 a 9 k 10 d 11 h 12 b

4
1 as 2 in 3 for 4 from 5 of
6 off

5
1 take him on 2 taken on 3 get on
4 take over 5 deal with 6 carried out

Education

1
1 secondary 2 Marks 3 Grades
4 area 5 degree

2
1 exercise 2 place 3 grades
4 diploma 5 classes 6 private
7 grade 8 year 9 heart 10 revise

3
1 made 2 made 3 pays 4 cheats
5 takes 6 doing 7 revising 8 sit
9 get 10 gets

4
1 a / the 2 a / the 3 a / the
4 a / the 5 A / The 6 a / the
7 a / the 8 a / the 9 a / the
10 a / the 11 a / the 12 a / the

5
1 a 2 d 3 c 4 g 5 h 6 b 7 f

6
1 primary 2 middle 3 secondary
4 grammar 5 comprehensive
6 public 7 state

7
1 b 2 d 3 f 4 e 5 j 6 g 7 h
8 c 9 i 10 a

The arts

1
1 played/plays 2 career 3 stage
4 roles 5 plays 6 musician
7 soundtrack

2
Literature: biography, chapter, character, edition, horror, illustration, love story, magazine, novel, picture, plot, poetry, science fiction, short story, thriller
Music: audience, CD, concert, encore, microphone, musical, musician, opera, orchestra, performance, pop, rehearsal, singer, stage, volume, western
Theatre: act, audience, auditorium, biography, cast, character, comedy, costume, drama, first night, horror, lighting, love story, matinee, microphone, musical, performance, play, plot, premiere, programme, rehearsal, role, scene, scenery, science fiction, script, set, stage, thriller, tragedy
Cinema: audience, biography, cast, character, comedy, costume, drama, horror, lighting, love story, matinee, musical, performance, plot, premiere, role, scene, science fiction, screen, screenplay, script, set, soundtrack, subtitles, thriller, trailer, western
Art: brush, canvas, exhibition, illustration, landscape, picture, sculpture, watercolour

3
1 rehearsal 2 script/screenplay
3 audience 4 cast 5 edition
6 soundtrack 7 costume(s)
8 concert 9 programme
10 illustrations/pictures

4
1 plays 2 performances 3 put
4 character 5 author

5
act in: a film, Hamlet, a horror movie, a play, a production, a show, a video
appear in: a concert, a film, Hamlet, a horror movie, a play, a production, a recital, a show, a video, the scene
broadcast: a concert, Hamlet, a performance, a piece of music, a play, a production, a recital, a show, a symphony, a video
compose: a piece of music, a symphony
direct: a film, Hamlet, a horror movie, a play, a production, a show
get: a CD, a difficult part, the leading role, a new book, a new edition, a video
give: a concert, a performance, a recital, a show
play: a CD, Hamlet, a piece of music, the leading role, a video
produce: a CD, a concert, a film, Hamlet, a horror movie, a play, a show
publish: Hamlet, a new book, a new edition, a review, the story
put on: a concert, Hamlet, a play, a production, a show
review: a CD, a concert, a film, Hamlet, a horror movie, a new book, a new edition, a performance, a piece of music, a play, a production, a recital, a show, a video
see: a film, Hamlet, a horror movie, a play, a performance, a show
set: the scene
watch: a film, a horror movie, a play, a performance, a show, a video
write: a new book, a piece of music, a play, a review, a symphony, the story

6
1 set 2 reviews 3 appeared/acted
4 role/part 5 performances
6 broadcast 7 produced 8 composed/wrote 9 published 10 watch

7
Students' own answers

Sports

1
1 at 2 indoor 3 on 4 equipment
5 opponent 6 of 7 winter
8 outdoor 9 referee/umpire 10 fit

2
1 at 2 pass/throw 3 beat 4 bounce
5 for 6 won 7 game/match

3
Places: course, court, field, ground, pitch, pool, ring, stadium, track
Sport/Activities: athletics, basketball, bowls, boxing, canoeing, diving, fishing, football, golf, hockey, motor racing, pool, skiing, snooker, squash, swimming, tennis, volleyball
People: captain, coach, defender, goalkeeper, judge, manager, player, referee, striker, team, umpire
Equipment: basketball, bat, boots, bowls, club, football, net, oar, racquet, rod, skis, stick, trunks, volleyball, whistle

4
1 stick 2 oars 3 manager/captain/coach 4 bat 5 umpire 6 Stadium
7 whistle 8 striker 9 court
10 track

Hobbies

1
1 Net 2 games 3 collect 4 spend
5 climbing 6 photos/pictures
7 collection 8 dance/drama

2
Suggested answers
camera: photography, boots: walking/climbing/hiking/gardening, mountain bike: cycling, tweezers: stamp collecting, hoe: gardening, brush: painting, rope: climbing/abseiling, glue: stamp collecting/collage/making models (e.g. model planes), needle: sewing/knitting, palette: painting

3
1 takes 2 go 3 have 4 take/do
5 makes 6 taking 7 does 8 going
9 (to) make 10 takes 11 have
12 going

4
1 amusement 2 funny 3 enjoyable
4 pleasant 5 laughter
6 photographer 7 humorous
8 delightful 9 amusing
10 activities 11 peaceful
12 happiness

ANSWER KEY

Travel and tourism

1

1 by 2 flight, departure lounge
3 miss, on 4 passport 5 receptionist, porter 6 bill, checked out 7 boat/ferry/ship, crossing 8 book, holiday

2

1 stay 2 by 3 agent 4 book 5 flight
6 hotel 7 currency 8 travellers'

3

1 to go/to do some sightseeing
2 make a reservation 3 take the bus to work 4 don't run out 5 check out of

Shopping

1

1 for, card 2 afford, from 3 get, cash
4 go, bargains 5 on 6 supermarket, butcher('s) 7 lend, pay 8 rate, bureau 9 designer 10 wrapped

2

1 shop/sales assistant 2 the high street 3 DIY store 4 chemist's
5 carrier bag 6 greengrocer's
7 bureau de change 8 department store 9 kiosk 10 checkout

3

Newsagent's: chocolate, cigarettes, comic, crisps, gum, magazine, newspaper, pencil, stamp, stationery
Chemist's: *aspirin*, bubble bath, hairbrush, medicines, nappies, perfume, shampoo, suntan lotion, toilet paper, toothpaste
Boutique: boots, denim jacket, evening gown, high heels, jewellery, shirt, shoes, sunglasses, trousers, underwear
Greengrocer's: aubergine, banana, bean, carrot, courgette, lettuce, melon, mushroom, peach, plum
DIY store: drill, hammer, lawnmower, nail, paint, saw, screwdriver, tool kit, torch, wrench

4

1 can 2 bar 3 tub 4 box 5 tube
6 bottle 7 tin 8 packet 9 bunch
10 sachet 11 jar

Food and restaurants

1

1 meat 2 fish 3 red 4 dairy
5 cheese 6 nuts 7 gourmet
8 wine 9 chef 10 restaurant

2

Vegetables: aubergine, cabbage, cauliflower, courgette, cucumber, lettuce, spinach
Fish: cod, haddock, mackerel, plaice, salmon, sardine, trout
Herbs: basil, chives, coriander, oregano, parsley, rosemary, thyme
Seafood: lobster, mussel, octopus, prawn, shrimp, squid
Fruit: *apple*, coconut, fig, grape, mango, nectarine, plum, satsuma, strawberry, watermelon
Meat: bacon, beef, chicken, chop, joint, lamb, liver, mutton, pork, salami, sausage

3

1 b 2 k 3 m 4 d 5 i 6 l 7 e
8 a 9 f 10 c 11 h 12 j

4

1 b 2 h 3 e 4 a 5 g 6 i 7 d
8 c

5

1 bake 2 Steamed 3 Roasted 4 grill
5 Melt 6 sauté 7 barbecued 8 Boil

6

1 waiter 2 list 3 starter 4 course
5 chops 6 dessert 7 bill 8 credit
9 tip 10 service

7

1 corkscrew 2 wine 3 bowl 4 boil
5 pan 6 meal 7 plum 8 menu

8

1 back 2 on 3 out 4 with 5 for
6 with 7 up 8 up 9 over/round
10 out

Weather

1

1 dry 2 humid 3 unsettled
4 pouring 5 storm 6 spells 7 frost
8 boiling 9 breeze 10 drenched

2

1 unsettled/changeable 2 humid
3 dew 4 overcast 5 gale 6 smog
7 boiling/scorching 8 fog 9 freezing
10 drizzle 11 pouring/bucketing

3

1 like 2 Lovely 3 awful 4 weather
5 boiling 6 bright 7 under 8 heavy

4

1 lovely 2 mild/dry/hot 3 bitterly/freezing 4 dark 5 dry/hot 6 heavy
7 strong 8 thick 9 lovely/mild/dry/hot

5

1 down 2 bit 3 bitterly/freezing
4 Lovely 5 fog/smog 6 strong
7 lightning 8 clouds 9 boiling
10 snowflake

6

1 mild 2 unbearably 3 chilly
4 changeable 5 showery 6 rainy
7 amazingly 8 fine 9 forecast
10 soaked 11 windy 12 snowfalls

7

1 h 2 c 3 k 4 i 5 g 6 d 7 f
8 e 9 b 10 a

Our environment and the natural world

1

1 cliff 2 sea 3 beach 4 hill
5 lake 6 waterfall 7 wave 8 river
9 mountain 10 rocks

2

1 bush – tree, tree 2 gulf – bay, gulf
3 mountain – hill, mountain 4 pond – lake, lake 5 river – stream, river
6 road – lane, road 7 rock – pebble, rock 8 sea – ocean, ocean 9 town – city, city 10 wood – forest, forest

3

1 lake 2 wood 3 ocean 4 beach
5 hill 6 lane 7 gulf 8 forest
9 tree 10 pond 11 pebble 12 town
13 bush 14 coast 15 mountain
16 sea 17 road 18 bay 19 city
20 rock

4

1 atmosphere 2 greenhouse
3 weather 4 exhaust 5 resources
6 coal 7 energy 8 waves 9 fuel
10 recycling

5

1 pollution 2 disastrous 3 extinction
4 harmful 5 damaging 6 population
7 survival 8 protection 9 poverty
10 starvation

6

1 acid rain 2 tropical rain forest
3 exhaust fumes 4 global warming/disaster/changes/resources 5 ozone layer 6 nuclear energy/waste products 7 public transport 8 traffic jams 9 natural resources/gases/disaster 10 air pollution 11 sea pollution 12 solar energy 13 finite resources 14 greenhouse effect
15 clean fuels 16 recycled fuels/resources 17 noise pollution
18 renewable energy/resources

7

1 count on the weather 2 do away with 3 gets you down 4 run out of
5 pull down 6 ran on 7 cut down on 8 put forward

The media

1

1 player 2 phones 3 interactive
4 email(s) 5 magazines 6 blogs
7 computers 8 screen

318

ANSWER KEY

2
1 correspondent 2 circulation
3 commercial 4 documentary
5 celebrity 6 periodical 7 journalist
8 headline 9 press 10 editor

3
1 mouse 2 screen 3 keyboard
4 hard disk 5 speakers 6 mouse mat
7 CD-ROM 8 laptop 9 key
10 modem

4
cable channel/television, celebrity guest, chat show, children's programme/channel/show, commercial break, current affairs, digital television, educational programme, game show, light entertainment, live television/programme/show/entertainment, nature programme/channel, news channel/conference/broadcast, press report/conference, radio broadcast/commentator/listener/programme/show/station, soap opera, sports channel/commentator/programme, television channel/commentator/viewer/programme/show/broadcast/station, video recorder

5
cordless phone, email message/address, fax message/machine/number, long distance, mobile phone, phone message/number/book, play back, wrong number

6
1 distance 2 mobile 3 address
4 conference 5 wrong 6 game
7 answering 8 show 9 programme
10 replay

7
1 B 2 A 3 D 4 B 5 A 6 C
7 A 8 A 9 B 10 C

8
1 hang up 2 key in 3 switch over
4 back up 5 switch off 6 brought out 7 get through 8 put down
9 call back 10 shut down

Science and technology

1
1 inventor 2 product 3 observation
4 designer 5 development
6 discovery 7 exploration
8 researcher 9 programmer
10 engineer 11 building
12 conservation 13 conservationist
14 creation 15 creator 16 specialist
17 supervision 18 supervisor
19 instruct 20 sponsor

2
1 engineer 2 builder 3 research
4 produced 5 exploration
6 discoveries 7 creator
8 programmer 9 developer
10 observation 11 designer
12 sponsored 13 programmed

3
1 plumber 2 electrician 3 carpenter
4 decorator 5 architect
6 hairdresser 7 teacher 8 manager
9 seller 10 photographer
11 psychologist 12 manufacturer
13 researcher 14 archaeologist
15 astronomer 16 doctor/medic 17 surgeon 18 scientist
19 biologist 20 chemist 21 physicist
22 historian 23 lawyer

4
1 plumber 2 psychologist
3 teacher/tutor 4 electrician
5 painter/decorator 6 hairdresser
7 doctor 8 architect/designer
9 archaeologist 10 surgeon

5
1 study/studying, developed
2 designed 3 discovered
4 invented 5 developed 6 designed
7 pioneered 8 discovered, studying

Health

1
1 exercise 2 gym 3 died
4 smoking 5 harm 6 diseases
7 death 8 attacks

2
1 inject 2 ointment 3 ward
4 headache 5 prescription
6 epidemic 7 fatal/terminal
8 mental illness/nervous breakdown
9 cure 10 frail

3
1 against 2 with 3 for 4 out 5 from
6 with 7 in 8 from 9 on 10 with

4
1 fainted 2 painless 3 hurt
4 symptoms 5 had 6 aching
7 suffered 8 diet

5
1 1 I feel depressed/dizzy/fit/hot/ill/nauseous/sick. 2 You must have a broken wrist/a cold/a virus/an infection/an injection/an operation/cancer/flu/measles/mumps/stitches. 3 I've got a broken wrist/a cold/a headache/a sore throat/a virus/an earache/an infection/cancer/flu/measles/mumps. 4 Be careful you don't catch a cold/a virus/an infection/flu/measles. 5 You need to see a consultant/a surgeon/your doctor. 6 I'm afraid it's a broken wrist/a cold/a virus/an infection/cancer/fatal/flu/incurable/inoperable/measles/mumps/numb/painful/sore. 7 He'll take an aspirin/her temperature/her to hospital/his tooth out/this medicine/your blood pressure. 8 You've sprained your ankle/your wrist. 9 She's a consultant/a surgeon/depressed/dizzy/fit/ill/in agony/in great pain/jogging/nauseous/numb/sick/your doctor.
10 It feels hot/numb/painful/sore.

6
1 j 2 f 3 d 4 h 5 a 6 i 7 c
8 g 9 k 10 b

7
1 lips 2 ears 3 gums 4 elbow
5 sole 6 heel 7 knee 8 chin
9 stomach 10 neck 11 wrist
12 cheek 13 eyelid 14 nostrils
15 shin 16 forehead 17 throat

8
1 got over 2 looked after him 3 put on 4 will wear off 5 (he) came round 6 went down with 7 gave birth to 8 suffers from

Crime

1
1 victims 2 violence 3 Forgery
4 kidnapped 5 crime 6 rise
7 illegal 8 hacking

2
1 accusation 2 arsonist 3 blackmail
4 burglary 5 criminal 6 hacker
7 hijacking 8 prisoner 9 kidnapper
10 killing 11 mugging 12 offender
13 pickpocketing 14 robbery
15 robber 16 shoplifting 17 stalker
18 theft 19 suspect 20 suspect

3
1 mugging 2 hijacking 3 murder
4 shoplifting 5 fraud 6 looting
7 blackmail 8 theft 9 robbery
10 vandalism 11 kidnapping
12 domestic violence

4
1 appearing 2 accused 3 pay a fine
4 put 5 took up 6 looking into
7 called in 8 facing 9 committed
10 returned a verdict 11 plead
12 confessed 13 serve 14 broke
15 denied

5
1 proof 2 charges 3 trial 4 illegal
5 guilty 6 criminal 7 punishment
8 innocence